W9-ADU-037

Cambridge Companions to Culture

The Cambridge Companion to
Modern German Culture

One of the most intriguing questions of our time is how some of the masterpieces of modernity originated in a country in which personal liberty and democracy were slow to emerge. This *Companion* provides an authoritative account of modern German culture since the onset of industrialisation, the rise of mass society and the nation state. Newly researched and written by experts in their respective fields, individual chapters trace developments in German culture – including national identity, class, Jews in German society, minorities and women, the functions of folk and mass culture, poetry, drama, theatre, dance, music, art, architecture, cinema and mass media – from the nineteenth century to the present. Guidance is given for further reading and there is a chronology. In its totality the *Companion* shows how the political and social processes that shaped modern Germany are intertwined with cultural genres and their agendas of creative expression.

EVA KOLINSKY is Professor of Modern German Studies and Director of the Centre for the Study of German Culture and Society at Keele University. Her books include *Parties, Opposition and Society in West Germany* (1984), *Women in West Germany* (1989), and *Women in Contemporary Germany* (1993); and she has edited several volumes including *Opposition in Western Europe* (1987), *The Federal Republic of Germany: End of an Era* (1991) and *Between Hope and Fear: Everyday Life in Post-Unification East Germany* (1995).

WILFRIED VAN DER WILL is Professor of Modern German Studies at the University of Birmingham. His publications include *The German Novel and the Affluent Society* (with R. Hinton Thomas, 1968), *Arbeiterkulturbewegung in der Weimarer Republik* (with R. A. Burns, 1982), *Protest and Democracy* (with R. A. Burns, 1988) and *The Nazification of Art* (with Brandon Taylor, 1990).

The Cambridge Companion to
Modern German Culture

edited by
EVA KOLINSKY
and
WILFRIED VAN DER WILL

CAMBRIDGE
UNIVERSITY PRESS

PUBLISHED BY THE PRESS SYNDICATE OF THE UNIVERSITY OF CAMBRIDGE
The Pitt Building, Trumpington Street, Cambridge CB2, 1RP, United Kingdom

CAMBRIDGE UNIVERSITY PRESS
The Edinburgh Building, Cambridge CB2 2RU, UK   http://www.cup.cam.ac.uk
40 West 20th Street, New York, NY 10011–4211, USA   http://www.cup.org
10 Stamford Road, Oakleigh, Melbourne 3166, Australia

First published 1998

Printed in the United Kingdom at the University Press, Cambridge

Typeset in 9/13 pt Lexicon (*The Enschedé Font Foundry*), in QuarkXPress®   [SE]

A catalogue record for this book is available from the British Library

Library of Congress Cataloguing in Publication data
The Cambridge companion to modern German culture / edited by Eva Kolinsky
and Wilfried van der Will.
        p.   cm.
Includes bibliographical references and index.
ISBN 0 521 56032 2 (hardback)
ISBN 0 521 56870 6 (paperback)
1. Germany – Intellectual life.
2. Germany – Civilization.
3. Germany – Ethnic relations.
4. Arts, Modern – Germany.
I. Kolinsky, Eva.   II. Will, Wilfried van der, 1935– .
DD204.C36   1998   943 – dc21   98–35241 CIP

ISBN 0 521 56032 2 hardback
ISBN 0 521 56870 6 paperback

Contents

Illustrations

Contributors

HANS-GEORG BETZ is Professor of European Studies at Kok University, Istanbul.

IAIN BOYD WHYTE is Professor of Architecture at the University of Edinburgh.

ANDREW BOWIE is Professor of European Philosophy at Anglia Polytechnic University, Cambridge.

MARTIN BRADY is a Lecturer in Film Studies at the University of Westminster.

JOHN BREUILLY is Professor of Modern History at the University of Birmingham.

HOLGER BRIEL is a Lecturer in German Studies at the University of Surrey.

CAROLYN HÖFIG received her doctorate in modern European history from the University of California at Santa Cruz.

HELEN HUGHES is a Lecturer in German Studies at the University of Surrey.

MICHAEL HUXLEY is Deputy Head of the Performing Arts at de Montfort University, Leicester.

EVA KOLINSKY is Professor of Modern German Studies and Director of the Centre for the Study of German Culture and Society at Keele University.

KAREN LEEDER is Lecturer in German and Fellow at New College, Oxford.

ERIK LEVI is Senior Lecturer in Music at Royal Holloway and Bedford New College, University of London.

ANDREI MARKOVITS is Professor in the Department of Politics at the University of California at Santa Cruz and Senior Associate at the Center for European Studies, Harvard University.

BETH NOVECK, BA, MA Harvard University, has completed her studies at the Yale Law School and is practising in New York City.

MICHAEL PATTERSON is Professor of Performing Arts at de Montfort University, Leicester.

PETER PULZER is Professor Emeritus at All Souls College, Oxford and a Fellow of the German Studies Institute, University of Birmingham.

IRIT ROGOFF is Professor of Visual Arts at Goldsmith College, University of London.

MARTIN SWALES is Professor of German at University College London.

WILFRIED VAN DER WILL is Professor of Modern German Studies at the University of Birmingham.

Abbreviations

ADF *Allgemeiner Deutscher Frauenverein* (General Association of German Women)

ADMV *Allgemeiner Deutscher Musikverein* (General German Music Association)

AEG *Allgemeine Elektrizitäts-Gesellschaft* (General Electricity Company)

AG *Aktiengesellschaft* (Joint Stock Company)

ARD *Arbeitsgemeinschaft der öffentlich-rechtlichen Rundfunkanstalten der Bundersrepublik Deutschland* (Cooperative of the Public Service Broadcasting Institutions of the Federal Republic of Germany)

BDF *Bund Deutscher Frauenverbände* (Federation of German Women's Associations)

BDM *Bund Deutscher Mädel* (Federation of German Girls; Nazi organisation for German girls)

BPRS *Band Politisch–Revolutionärer Schriftsteller* (Union of Revolutionary Writers)

BVP *Bayrische Volkspartei* (Bavarian People's Party)

CDU *Christlich-Demokratische Union* (Christian Democratic Union)

CIAM *Congrès Internationaux d'Architecture Moderne* (International Congress of Modern Architecture)

D-Day Day of the Normandy landings by the armies of the Western Allies, 6 June 1944

DDP *Deutsche Demokratische Partei* (German Democratic Party)

DEFA *Deutsche Film Aktiengesellschaft* (German Film Production Company)

DNVP *Deutschnationale Volkspartei* (German National People's Party)

DP Displaced Person

DRP *Deutsche Reichspartei* (German Reich Party)

DVP *Deutsche Volkspartei* (German People's Party)

FDP *Freie Demokratische Partei* (Free Democratic Party)

FRG Federal Republic of Germany

GDP Gross Domestic Product
GDR German Democratic Republic
Gestapo *Geheime Staatspolizei* (Secret State Police in Nazi Germany)
ISCM International Society for Contemporary Music
KPD *Kommunistische Partei Deutschlands* (Communist Party of Germany)
LDPD *Liberal-Demokratische Partei Deutschlands* (Liberal Democratic Party of Germany)
NPD *Nationaldemokratische Partei Deutschlands* (National Democratic Party of Germany)
NSDAP *Nationalsozialistische Deutsche Arbeiterpartei* (National Socialist German Workers' Party)
NWDR *Nordwestdeutscher Rundfunk* (Northwest German Radio)
Ossi Derogatory term for a person whose attitudes and behaviour reflect having been brought up in East Germany
PDS *Partei des Demokratischen Sozialismus* (Party of Democratic Socialism)
PhD *Philosophiae Doctor* (Doctor of Philosophy)
POW Prisoner of War
RTL Luxemburg-based private television consortium
SA *Sturmabteilung* (Hitler's Storm Troopers)
SAT-1 First private German satellite television station
SED *Socialistische Einheitspartei Deutschlands* (Socialist Unity Party)
SPD *Sozialdemokratische Partei Deutschlands* (German Social Democratic Party)
SS *Schutzstaffel* (literally: 'Pretorian Platoon'; National Socialist elite formation)
Stasi *Staatssicherheit* (State Security, organised as a Ministry in the GDR)
Ufa *Universum-Film AG* (Universal Picture Shareholding Company)
USPD *Unabhängige Sozialdemokratische Partei Deutschlands* (Independent Social Democratic Party of Germany)
VDS *Verband Deutscher Studenten* (Association of German Students)
VE Day Victory in Europe Day (8 May 1945)
WDR *Westdeutscher Rundfunk* (West German Radio)
Wessi Derogatory term for a person whose attitudes and behaviour reflect having been brought up in West Germany
ZDF *Zweites Deutsches Fernsehen* (Second German Television, national public service broadcasting station based in Mainz)

Chronology

1789 French Revolution

1817 18–19 October: *Wartburg Fest* when German students called for liberalisation and national unity

1832 27–30 March: *Hambacher Fest*, largest public demonstration in support of democratic change and national unity prior to 1848 Revolution

1848 Revolution: attempt by German middle class to introduce constitutional democracy and national unification

1848–1849: Paulskirche Parliament: assembly to prepare constitutional monarchy and national unification; the title of German Emperor was offered to the King of Prussia in 1849. When he refused to accept it from a parliament, the revolution collapsed

1871–1918: Imperial Germany, first unified 'nation state' in Europe

1871 18 January: Official foundation of the second German Reich (Imperial Germany) in the Hall of Mirrors in Versailles, after the defeat of France in the 1870–1871 war

1871–1890: Otto von Bismarck in office as Chancellor of the Reich (Bismarck era)

1878 *Kulturkampf*: anti-Catholic campaign, orchestrated by Bismarck

1878–1890: *Sozialistengesetze*: anti-Socialist laws to block the development of the Social Democratic Party as a political force in Germany

1878 *Schutzzölle*: tariffs levied on imports of grain in order to protect East Elbian grain producers

1880 *Sozialversicherung*: introduction of a social security system, with provisions for old age pensions and sickness pay, laying the foundations of the modern welfare state

1896 Kyffhäuser memorial in the Harz mountains, remembering Barbarossa (Frederick II) and the dominance of Germany under him.

1913 *Völkerschlachtdenkmal*: memorial near Leipzig commemorating the centenary of Prussia's victory over Napoleon as the onset of national unification

1914–1918: First World War. The term 'Great War' is not used in Germany

1914 1 August: Outbreak of the First World War

1916 Control of war economy and politics by General Paul von Hindenburg, establishing a de facto military government. 'Law to Support the Fatherland' – *Vaterländisches Hilfsdienstgesetz* – places labour market and labour recruitment on a war footing

1917 Peace note by the German Reichstag, envisaging for the first time a peace without annexations

1917 onwards: Various strikes due to anti-war sentiments and extensive food shortages

1918 28 October: Introduction of parliamentary democracy with Prince Max von Baden as head of government. Retention of monarchy (Wilhelm II)

1918 11 November: Unconditional surrender of the German High Command and end of the war

1918 November: Revolutionary movement in Germany, establishment of Workers' and Soldiers' Councils in various German cities

1918 9 November: Proclamation of a Republic by Philipp Scheidemann from the Balcony of the Reichstag in Berlin. End of monarchy in Germany

1918 20 December: Provisional government by Council of People's Representatives, consisting of SPD and USPD

1919–1933: Weimar Republic

1919 20 January: Election to the *Nationalversammlung*, i.e. an elected assembly to prepare a new (democratic) constitution. First election in which all men and women aged 20 and over had full voting rights

1919 January: Failed communist uprising in Berlin led by a group called *Spartakus*

1919 January–March: Soviet republic in Bavaria and other left-wing/communist protests defeated with the help of para-military combat units known as *Freikorps* which later formed a core of right-extremist and National Socialist support

1919–1924: Friedrich Ebert (SPD), First President of the Weimar Republic

1925 (re-elected 1932): Paul von Hindenberg (DNVP), Second President of the Weimar Republic

1923 Escalation of post-war inflation to hyper-inflation and a complete collapse of the German currency

1924 Currency reform and stabilisation of the *Reichsmark*

1927 Introduction of unemployment insurance

1929 World economic crisis, onset of mass unemployment in Germany which rose to approx. 6 million by 1933

1930–1933 (30 January): Government without parliamentary majority and based on article 48 of the Weimar Constitution which permitted non-parliamentary government

1933–1945: National Socialism ('Third Reich')

1933 30 January: Adolf Hitler appointed Chancellor

1933 February: Burning of the Reichstag in Berlin, leading to 'Law for the Protection of People and State' which marks the end of Weimar democracy and parliamentary government

1933 18 March: Elections under Nazi control, resulting in a 40% vote for the NSDAP

1933 March: Enabling Act abolishing parliamentary democracy and instituting Nazi control of the political process in Germany

1933 1 April: Boycott of Jewish business; first nationally coordinated anti-Jewish campaign under the auspices of the SA

1933 April: Concentration camps established. Arrest and incarceration of 30,000 political opponents of the Nazi regime

1933 1 May: Occupation of trade union and SPD buildings, preceding a formal ban of trade unions and political parties other than the NSDAP

1933 10 May: Burning of the Books by Association of German Students (VDS)

1934 30 June: Night of the Long Knives: murder of the head of the SA, Ernst Röhm, and clamp-down on SA in order to curb radicalisation and win the confidence of the German army and its established elite

1934 2 August: Death of Paul von Hindenburg, President of the Reich. Hitler makes himself President of the Reich in addition to Chancellor and gives himself the title 'Führer'

1935 Nuremberg 'race' laws declaring Jews second-class citizens and banning marriages and sexual contacts between Germans and Jews

1935 Introduction of conscription for German males above the age of 18

1938 March, *Anschluss* i.e. incorporation of Austria into Nazi Germany

1938 9–10 November: Destruction of synagogues and ransacking of Jewish homes, a pogrom called *Reichskristallnacht* by the Nazis

1939 1 September: Nazi occupation of Poland. Outbreak of the Second World War

1942 20 January: Wannsee conference to implement the so-called 'Final Solution', i.e. the murder of Jews in Nazi-occupied Europe and

Germany in death camps (Auschwitz, Chelmo, Majdanek, Sobibor, Treblinka). The Holocaust claimed 6 million Jewish victims

1945 30 April: Hitler commits suicide in the Berlin Bunker

1945 8 May: Unconditional surrender of German High Command; end of Second World War

1945–1990: Post-war era: division and unification of Germany

1945–1949: Military government and division into four zones of occupation (American, British, French, Soviet)

from June 1945: Licensing of political parties

1946–1948: Elections at regional level in all Länder. Beginnings of parliamentary democracy in western zones of occupation and of socialist one-party dominance in Soviet Zone

1947 1 January: Creation of Bi-zone from American and British zones

1948 20 June: Currency reform and introduction of the Deutschmark in the Western Zones of occupation and in West Berlin; Soviet blockade of access to Berlin; supply of Berlin by air

1948 June: Introduction of the Ostmark in the Soviet zone of occupation

1948 Parliamentary Council of representatives from the Land parliaments. Drafting of the Basic Law, the provisional constitution for a west German state incorporating the three western zones of occupation

1949 23 May: Ratification of the Basic Law by a majority of the Land parliaments (all except Bavaria); creation of the Federal Republic of Germany

1949 7 October: Proclamation of the GDR by the 'People's Council' in Berlin

1949–1963: Konrad Adenauer, CDU, first Chancellor of the Federal Republic of Germany

1949–1971: Walter Ulbricht First Secretary of the SED and head of the GDR government

1952 Legislation in West Germany for restitution payments to Jewish Holocaust survivors and the families of Holocaust victims

1953 17 June: Uprising of building construction workers in Berlin and other East German cities, quelled with the aid of Soviet military. Wave of arrests in East Germany; in West Germany, 17 June declared Day of German Unity and national holiday

1957 Reform of West German pension legislation; pension payments from then on index-linked.

1961 13 August: Berlin Wall erected by GDR government to separate western sectors of Berlin from East with secure (guarded) border to quell defections of East Germans

1963–1966: Ludwig Erhard (CDU), first West German Minister of Economic Affairs and father of the 'economic miracle', became the second federal

Chancellor. Forced to resign in 1966 during the first post-war recession

1966–1969: Chancellor Kurt-Georg Kiesinger (CDU), heading a Grand Coalition government of CDU/CSU and SPD

1969   *Machtwechsel*. The SPD 'wins' the elections and is able to clinch a narrow majority for an SPD/FDP coalition government. Beginning of SPD/FDP period of coalitions until 1982

1969–1974: Willy Brandt (SPD) is federal Chancellor and masterminds Ostpolitik

1971–1989: Erich Honecker succeeds Walter Ulbricht as First Secretary of the SED and head of the GDR government

1972   Basic Treaty (Grundlagenvertrag) with the German Democratic Republic. Its key concept is that Germany consists of two states and one nation (*Zwei Staaten, eine Nation*)

1974–1982: Helmut Schmidt (SPD) federal Chancellor

1982   October to date: chancellorship of Helmut Kohl after FDP sided with the CDU in a 'constructive vote of no-confidence', i.e. voting a chancellor out of office by securing a parliamentary majority for a successor. Since 1982, CDU/CSU and FDP coalition government at national level

1989   Exodus of East Germans via Hungary and other routes to the West; mass demonstrations against East German socialist system leads to resignation of Erich Honecker

1989   9 October and until early 1990: Monday demonstrations in Leipzig. Early slogan 'we are *the* people' changes to 'we are *one* people'. Demands for a better GDR change to demands for abolition of GDR and unification

1989   9 November: Opening of the Berlin Wall, free movement between west and east Berlin. End of sealed GDR borders

1989, October–1990, March: Attempts by SED to reform itself and retain government position under Erich Krenz (formerly deputy leader of the SED) and Hans Modrow (formerly Mayor of Dresden). Coalition government, including member groups of the Round Table (citizens' movements)

1990   18 March: First free elections in GDR resulting in all-party coalition government headed by Lothar de Maizière (CDU)

1990   1 July: Currency union and introduction of Deutschmark in the GDR

1990   3 October: Re-constituted East German Länder formally apply to join the Federal Republic under article 23 of the Basic Law. Official date of German unification

1990   14 October: Elections in the five new Länder, Brandenburg,

Mecklenburg-West Pomerania, Saxony, Saxony-Anhalt and
Thuringia

1990   2 December: First all-German elections (won by CDU/CSU and FDP
coalition) and first elections in unified Berlin complete the political
unification of Germany

Map 1 Germany and Austria around 1871

Map 2 Germany after the Second World War

SWEDEN

BALTIC SEA

Warsaw

POLAND

Prague

HOSLOVAKIA

Vienna

TRIA

SCALE

0   100   200km

International borders

Germany's border in 1937

Furthest advance of US/British troops in the east
(to 7 May 1945)

Demarcation line between US/British and Soviet troops
(8 May – 30 June 1945)

Area from which US/British troops withdrew
after 30 June 1945

Borders of zones of occupation

Oder-Neisse line and demarcation line in East Prussia

Areas under Soviet administration after Potsdam Agreement

Areas under Polish administration after Potsdam Agreement

Berlin under four-power administration

The Federal Republic of Germany

NORTH SEA

BALTIC SEA

SCHLESWIG-HOLSTEIN

MECKLENBURG-POMERANIA

BREMEN

HAMBURG

LOWER SAXONY

BRANDENBURG

BERLIN

Hanover

SAXONY-ANHALT

NORTH RHINE-WESTPHALIA

SAXONY

Cologne

THURINGIA

HESSE

RHINELAND-PALATINATE

BAVARIA

SAARLAND

BADEN-WÜRTTEMBERG

Munich

SCALE

0   100   200   300   400 km

Map 3 Germany after unification in 1990

EVA KOLINSKY *and*
WILFRIED VAN DER WILL

In search of German culture:
an introduction

The divided culture

On 10 May 1933, the Association of German Students staged the burning of more than twenty thousand books in the square in front of Berlin's opera house. Like all National Socialist acts of allegedly spontaneous public violence, the burning of the books was carefully orchestrated. As they flung works of named writers such as Heinrich Mann, Erich Kästner, Sigmund Freud, Karl Marx, Erich Maria Remarque, Kurt Tucholsky and Carl von Ossietzky into the flames, and before they let everyone join in the destruction, nine specially selected 'callers' pronounced what they expected from a culture they would regard as German. Their declamations sounded like a litany of anti-modernism: 'Against decadence and moral decay! For decency and propriety in family and state!' 'Against anti-German views and political treason, for devotion to people and state!'

The cultural cleansing by the student ideologues of 1933 highlights more sharply than any other event in the history of German culture the rifts that have divided it. These manifested themselves well before the First World War in a division between cultural traditionalism and modernism. The year 1896, for instance, saw the erection of the Kyffhäuser memorial commemorating Frederick II, also known as Barbarossa, a medieval emperor and the subject of a myth of resurrection and national unification. In 1913, the *Völkerschlachtdenkmal*, a monumental structure near Leipzig, celebrated the victory over the French one hundred years earlier as the onset of German national unification. These pre-war years were also a high point of *Heimatkunst*, an essentially anti-modern glorification of pre-industrial rural life, traditional values and strong physiques. Yet, the same years saw the publication of Thomas Mann's *Buddenbrooks*, Theodor Fontane's *Effi Briest* and Georg Heym's poem '*Der Krieg*' (*The War*), while the journal *Der Sturm* and the group of painters known as *Der Blaue Reiter* were torchbearers of a 'cultural revolution' against conventionalism and protagonists of modernity. Both types of culture were in search of values and experiences that would transform or enhance the present, but they sought these in opposite directions, the former romanticising allegedly purer lifestyles while the latter demonised or deconstructed contemporary social and personal environments. These developments and contradictions of German culture, its social and political context and its manifestations in genres and works, are the subject matter of this *Companion*.

German meanings of culture

When the Latin word *cultura* entered the German language – via French – in the seventeenth century, it retained little of its original reference to tilling the soil but applied mainly to intellectual creativity and artistic endeavour. In English, 'culture' does not normally distinguish sharply between spiritual and technological manifestations. In German, *Kultur* came to signify intellectual, spiritual or artistic areas of creative activity that contributed to the self-enhancement of an individual, a group or the whole nation by remaining aloof from the common purposes of social, political, economic or technical life. In English, 'culture' and 'civilisation' have been perceived as complementary aspects of social organisation and development. In German, *Kultur* and *Zivilisation* were typically separated by contrastive meanings: while *Kultur* denoted manifestations of spiritual creativity, *Zivilisation* denoted manifestations of political and social organisation which were deemed to be of a lower order.

This juxtaposition of spiritual and political manifestations of human activity is at the heart of German culture. It is the juxtaposition of *Geist* and *Macht*, the realm of intellectual or spiritual endeavour and the realm of power and political control. This is not to say that *Geist* corresponds to culture and *Macht* to *Zivilisation*. Rather, in Germany the interplay between culture and its context, between *Geist* and *Macht*, writer and society, thinker and polity has been marred by the unresolved question of whether culture or the state should dominate. If freedom of expression is a prerequisite of culture, how could it flourish in a country like Germany where civil rights and democratic structures had yet to take root long after it had become a modern industrial power? Or was German culture hemmed in by the unresolved dichotomy between *Geist* and *Macht* and driven into an inner sanctum of reflection and creativity that made its voice distinctive but detached from the fray of social and political life? The foundations of German culture as a national culture predate the emergence of modern Germany. Here, industrial change failed to overthrow feudal structures of government and the social dominance of the aristocracy; citizens remained subjects and hence their emancipation remained an unmet promise; fears of social modernisation intensified as the 'feudal industrial' construct proved unable to curtail social, political and intellectual diversity. In such a country, culture was torn between *Geist* as the critique of *Macht* or as its glorification.

Culture and State: an historical perspective

When *Kultur* acquired its place in the German language, the Reformation had carved out a new scope for literary, artistic and musical creativity in religious services. Affluent trading cities such as Hamburg, Leipzig, Lübeck or Frankfurt sponsored their own church organists, composers or theatre companies and, above all, Germany's more than four hundred separate states tried to emulate the French model of cultural eminence and began to sustain as part of their absolutist reign musicians, orchestras and theatres. They also commissioned paintings or included writers among their courtiers. One of the legacies of this patchwork of small states is that each former principality, dukedom or kingdom in Germany still has a theatre, an orchestra and a strong commitment to the sponsorship of culture today.

The tradition of public sponsorship of culture by rulers or governments created opportunities and constraints. Johann Sebastian Bach's time in Leipzig entailed a constant battle with the city fathers for resources, while Joseph Haydn or Johann Wolfgang Goethe found their noble employers and protectors less intrusive. Wolfgang Amadeus Mozart could not bear the thought of spending a lifetime in the services of the Archbishop of Salzburg, but failed in his attempt to secure a court appointment. Instead he opted for the high-risk life of earning an income as a composer (and teacher). At the time of Mozart and Beethoven most lucrative commissions continued to emanate from the aristocracy and even Richard Wagner still depended on a royal patron half a century later. In the course of the nineteenth century, patronage by the nobility gave way to a civic culture of salaried posts in the numerous opera houses, orchestras, and a growing number of conservatoires and other cultural institutions.

Public sponsorship and the legacies of *Kleinstaaterei* left their imprint on culture. German princes set up or expanded universities in order to produce their own class of loyal civil servants. State support of higher education was intended to generate views favourable to the state but universities soon created their own cultural agenda. Schiller, Hegel, August Wilhelm Schlegel, Schelling, Fichte and many other protagonists of German literature and philosophy made their living as university professors. Indeed, universities soon became strongholds of political liberalism and cultural debate. When liberal German students and academics staged the *Wartburg Fest* in 1817 and called for democracy and a nation state, they were silenced by police and muzzled by repression.

During the first half of the nineteenth century a quest for liberty, equality, democracy and also for nationhood inspired German culture. The *salons*, informal meetings of writers, journalists, politicians, professional people and artists in the drawing rooms of educated middle-class women such as Dorothea Schlegel and Rahel Varnhagen, created a new public sphere of communication and debate. This era of German culture linked creative with political freedom and regarded artists, writers and thinkers as torchbearers of democracy. It came to an end in 1848 when Germany's bourgeois revolution failed and with it the bid of the German middle class for political and social equality. German liberalism had been based on middle-class demands for free trade and a constitutional framework to protect their economic and social space in society. After 1848, liberalism in Germany ceased to be concerned with democratic government but focused instead on the second theme that had always been present: the theme of nationalism. Rather than demanding political processes and parliaments to achieve equality, middle-class Germany settled for a presumed equality as Germans. As members of the German nation and in a firm alliance of interest with the aristocracy, the middle class claimed a centrality in the German state which was not borne out by political rights or social status. Education and culture emerged as key areas where superiority could be attained without the privileges of noble birth. In the manifestations of culture, freedom, equality or personal distinctiveness tended to be located in the inner sanctum of the individual. Society was portrayed as an arbitrary, external and frequently hostile world.

The two cultures of the German nation state

The German nation state, which was founded in 1871 under Prussian dominance, built its constitution on this mechanism of exclusion and inclusion by instituting a parliament without power, political parties without access to governmental responsibility and elections whose outcome did not determine the composition of government. Matters of state remained in the hands of the aristocracy, although Germany had become an industrial power and its nobility a mere minority in a growing and increasingly mobile population.

Nationalism was a protective shield against political exclusion. It was also a means to conjure up a sense of security that neither the economy nor the class structure actually afforded. Industrial expansion created its own history of boom and bust. It also created a rapidly expanding urban working class. Compared to agricultural labourers, the industrial working class enjoyed improved wages and constituted the fastest growing segment of the population in the last quarter of the nineteenth century. While the German middle class experienced its own situation as economically precarious, it perceived the emergence of the working class as a threat. Indeed, from 1878 to 1890 anti-Socialist legislation obstructed working-class organisations and criminalised their protagonists. In everyday middle-class culture, working people were deemed to be social enemies bent on undermining the authority of the state. When the Emperor, Wilhelm II, referred to socialists as 'louts without a fatherland' (*vaterlandslose Gesellen*) he expressed a widely shared sentiment.

German nationalism was middle-class nationalism with a sharp edge of social exclusion of those deemed not to belong. Such exclusion hit the working class but it also hit Jews and non-German minorities with different degrees of ferocity. The closing decade of the nineteenth century saw a rise of political anti-Semitism. In the eyes of the aristocracy, the military and middle-class Germany, anti-Semitism became an implicit assumption and formed part of an ideological notion of belonging to the German nation. The outbreak of the First World War temporarily glossed over the social rifts in the famous *Burgfrieden*, a truce among the social and political factions in order to fend off a greater common danger. Again, the German Emperor coined the phrase to catch the mood: 'I know no parties, I only know Germans.' (*Ich kenne Keine Parteien mehr, ich kenne nur noch Deutsche*)

The divisions of German society were replicated in German culture.

Nationalism, anti-Semitism and racism went hand in hand with an idealisation of the Middle Ages, the Renaissance and the presumption of an integrated daily life in pre-industrial times. Against the background of a developing mass society, the educated middle class looked to culture as a set of values that uplifted their lives and enhanced their nationalist orientation. A certain canon of books emerged which embodied these values and, significantly, these books became preferred presents to children at times when guidance for life seemed called for. For example Gustav Freytag's *Soll und Haben* (Debit and Credit), Langbehn's *Rembrandt als Erzieher* (Rembrandt the Educator) and Gobineau's *The Renaissance* were presented at teenage birthdays and confirmations or awarded as school prizes. All of them expounded the superiority of Germans, portrayed Jews and other minorities in negative terms and condemned modern times as decay. Karl May's stories of cowboys and Indians shaped the minds of young boys with a heroic view of combat and tribal living well into the 1950s, while girls learned how to grow into mothers and homemakers from books like *Heidi* or *Nesthäkchen* (Baby of the Family) until the National Socialists discovered to their acute embarrassment that their authoresses were Jewish.

It was the other culture, however, which put Germany on the map of modernity, the culture which did not allow itself to applaud the state. This culture was critical, incisive, ruthless, revealing and innovative. Explicitly or by implication, it set out to transcend and transform a social and political system which curtailed freedom and imposed conformity. The modern voice of confrontation, shock, interior monologue, disharmony and stark observation emerged before the First World War and triumphed in the 1920s. In its defence of the individual and of personal freedom, it highlighted the dehumanising and coercive forces in the modern world without retreating into the past to question modernity. The heir to the democratic fervour of early German liberalism, this strand of German culture carried the debate about personal rights and civil society that had been stifled in Imperial Germany. It was a culture of journals such as *Simplizissimus*, *Deutsche Rundschau* or *Neue Rundschau*, of impressionist and expressionist writing, music and art. The minutiae of political positions were less relevant than the intellectual scrutiny applied to the conventions of the day. This modern German culture instated the individual as the core in a world that had elevated the unspoken law of social conformity and prescribed behaviour above individual diversity, eccentricity or self-realisation.

Modern and anti-modern cultures in the Weimar Republic

When the defeat of Germany brought the First World War to an end in 1918, the German liberal tradition of 1848 reasserted itself in the democratic constitution that was drawn up in Weimar and gave Germany's first republic its name. The venue had been chosen to shield the constitutional assembly from clashes in Berlin between revolutionary forces and military detachments. Weimar, of course, was also the town of Goethe and Schiller and suggested a close link between the new polity and the best of the German cultural tradition.

In the troubled times of defeat, the forces of liberal democracy were initially in the ascendancy but failed to unite the nation internally. Large sections of society on the far Right and the far Left remained detached from the republican democratic venture. The Communists wanted a Soviet-style revolution while the established elites in the army, the economy, the judiciary and in education rejected parliamentary government and, above all, wanted a restoration of German national and political power. Notably, the middle classes found themselves threatened by social demotion through the war and hyper-inflation in its aftermath. On the whole, they never accepted the Weimar Republic but looked to more authoritarian solutions. This ultimately led to a collapse of the political centre and the rise of National Socialism.

Weimar German culture was equally divided, and encompassed the immense tensions between modernism and anti-modernism, liberalism and anti-liberalism, individualism and corporatism, *Gesellschaft* and *Gemeinschaft* and pushed them to their extremes. It was a culture not of consensus but of camps and combats, even of actual and latent civil war. The strident anti-modernism of the Right and the ardent modernism commonly associated with 'Weimar culture' largely concurred in a disdain for Germany's first democracy, though for different reasons. For the standard-bearers of German nationalism there was too much democracy and participation, while for the protagonists of social and political modernisation, democracy did not go far enough and was undermined by anti-democrats.

Before 1914, a re-birth of the German nation had been expected from a return to a lost past. Weimar Germany's anti-democrats, the conservative revolutionaries, located this re-birth in the future as the end-product of a revolution. They rejected the cultural legacies of humanism and the Enlightenment in favour of glorifying war as a positive experience based on enthusiasm, heroism and a sense of community. This critique of civil-isation and democracy inspired the paramilitary activism and political murders of the *Freikorps* as well as the conservative philosophy and thought in Oswald Spengler's *The Decline of the West* (1918–22), Ludwig Klages' *The Spirit as the Enemy of the Soul* (1929–32), Arthur Moeller van den Bruck's *The Third Reich* (1923) and Hans Zehrer's journal *Die Tat* (Action, from 1930) or Wilhelm Stapel's *Deutsches Volkstum* (from 1917). The Jünger brothers were leading voices of this anti-democratic culture. Ernst Jünger's *Storm of Steel* (1920) became one of the most widely read narratives to celebrate the war while the younger Friedrich Georg stated his case quite bluntly:

> Nationalism has something intoxicating, a wild and blood-based pride, a heroic and powerful sense of life ... It does not want tolerance because life knows no tolerance. It is fanatical, since everything blood-based is fanatical and unjust.[1]

While Jünger's barbaric vision was of a 'community of the blood', the forces supporting Weimar democracy sought, on the contrary, to legiti-mate it as a civil society. For all its elusive political consensus the Weimar Republic removed barriers to social and cultural modernisation. Rights of social participation and personal mobility which translated into cul-tural momentum were constitutionally enshrined for the first time in German history. Especially those groups whose emancipation or equal treatment had never been secure – political and social dissenters, Jews, women – now discovered and used the newly won freedom of expression. Not surprisingly, many advocates of modern culture originated from these groups and put their stamp on the new era. Largely restricted to the big cities, with Berlin the uncontested metropolis of modernity, these developments virtually bypassed small-town Germany. The urbanised, modern life-styles, fashions, shopping facilities, transport systems, cabarets and entertainment industries left behind and often alienated the non-urbanised Germany where about half the population still lived. In the cities, the old Germany of pre-war times had been blown away by images of modern life, by the transformation of employment and daily routines, by technology and the dominance of the machine over man in an era of rapid rationalisation, economic competitiveness and the blur-ring of traditional social roles.

These shocks of modernity found expression in a vibrant avant-garde culture. It was inspired by the new technologies of broadcasting, photo-graphy, printing, recording, steel and glass construction and stage management of theatre and dance to explore new boundaries of form and reflect in its works the exhilarating and the destructive impact of this new world on the individual. As will be shown in detail in this *Companion*, writers like Heinrich and Thomas Mann, Alfred Döblin, Franz Kafka, Hermann Broch and Joseph Roth, to name but a few, produced modern German literature that was also modern world literature. Some lived within the German nation state, others beyond its borders, but all wrote in German for a German-language readership and perceived their place as belonging to German culture. The political divisions of the German-speaking areas after 1918 did not blunt the cultural momentum. The Austro-Hungarian Empire was dismembered and separated German speakers in Czechoslovakia and the Alto Adige from Austria, while leaving Bismarckian Germany without Alsace-Lorraine substantially intact. In many ways the unfamiliar complexities of identity in the re-cast states mirrored those in modern society generally where competing values, interests, pressures of achievement and risks of failure exposed the individual to a precarious lack of orientation. Between the cultures of consumerism and traditionalism, of competing political ideologies and personal isolation, choices were often random and ill-fated. A core experience of the twenties in Germany, this search of the individual for orientation in a confusingly dissonant social environment emerged as the key theme of modern German culture.

Devastations of culture: the Nazi years

After 1933, the backward-looking strand that had glorified pre-industrial country life, pre-modern values or aggressive manliness was hailed as truly German. Yet Nazism also cultivated an ethos of industrial efficiency and a fascination with technology and mass communication as symbols of modernity and power. In any event, culture was expected to propagate or at least complement Nazi ideology. Subjected to the purposes of the state, culture was stripped of the all-important commitment to freedom of expression and the rights of the individual. *Macht* had eclipsed *Geist*. Writers and thinkers like Gottfried Benn, Arnolt Bronnen, Martin Heidegger, Hanns Johst and Carl Schmitt had rallied in support of National Socialism of their own volition, although some turned against it at a later stage. Arthur Dinter's anti-Semitic novel of 1917 *Die Sünde wider das Blut* (The Sin against the Blood) became a Nazi best-seller, as were the works of Gustav Frenssen, the Jünger brothers, Erwin Guido Kolbenheyer and

Agnes Miegel. Of course, the Nazis produced their own breed of cultural ideologues. Albert Speer, for instance, translated National Socialist concepts of power and leadership into grandiose buildings while Gerhard Schumann wrote widely read poems to enforce the political aims of the regime, including that of conditioning Germans for war. Referring to the literary products of the Nazi era, Thomas Mann wrote in 1945:

> It may be superstition, but I regard books which could as much as be printed between 1933 and 1945 in German as less than worthless and not good to pick up and touch. They reek of blood and disgrace. They should all be pulped.[2]

The culture of *Geist* and artistic modernity was dispersed abroad as artists, authors and intellectuals were hounded out of the country. Initially, most had remained close to the German borders and continued to perceive Germans and the German cultural tradition as a frame of reference for their work. Writers wrote in German in émigré periodicals, journalists tried to smuggle articles into Germany, intellectuals targeted as their readership those better Germans they knew to exist within the Nazi state. Few expected National Socialism to last for more than a handful of years. None believed that their first exile in France, Austria, Czechoslovakia, Holland or Denmark would become but a precarious staging post and their lives again be subject to danger as the German armies and persecutors advanced across Europe.

In exile, many of the 8,000 intellectuals who had been stripped of their citizenship by 1939 were unable to establish themselves professionally in their new countries of sojourn, and fell silent or even committed suicide. Others remained productive, unmasking the Nazi regime and its brown-shirted opportunists. Some found a new cultural context. Their work became less German in focus and contributed significantly to modern cultural development generally. For example, German architects in exile inspired American architecture and design; university professors recast the intellectual life in their new country and writers such as Bert Brecht, Thomas and Heinrich Mann or Anna Seghers produced lasting works of world literature. Others still excelled in popular culture: Felix Salten, the author of *Bambi* (1923), wrote successful film scripts while Max Reinhardt and Kurt Weill each continued their impact on the theatre and twentieth-century music.

Recasting culture after its destruction by National Socialism could not mean turning back to Weimar or beyond. Theodor W. Adorno, Max Horkheimer and Erich Fromm constructed a direct link between the

SS murderers, authoritarian patterns of socialisation in the German middle-class family and the use of violence. The educated SS officer in the concentration camp, in particular, and Nazi Germany in general proved that nurturing the cultural heritage provided no safeguard against the exercise of brutality. On the contrary, the foregrounding of the classical tradition in music, even inside the concentration camps, could function as a deceptive veil. After the demise of the Hitler regime, an intense search for answers set in as to why things could have gone so wrong in Germany and how a repetition might be prevented. No single formula emerged other than a keen sense that culture must not be directed by the state and that *Geist* must be jealous of its own independence and never again allow itself to be dominated by *Macht*.

Post-war agendas

When the first post-war congress of writers was held in 1947, it pledged to 'keep awake the moral awareness of the damage and the suffering inflicted by the Hitler regime on the peoples of the world' and overcome the cultural devastation that had been wrought:

> The impact of barbarism on intellectual life inflicted a destruction on Germany which is unprecedented in our history. More than ever, the situation requires the utmost effort and most sacred obligation towards the word, the most rigorous search for truth, the constant awareness of our responsibility and educational task that are the essence of the written word.[3]

History had already divided Germany and recast the context for cultural renewal. Occupation and the establishment of American, British, Soviet and French military governments in their zones of influence were intended to ensure that Germany would never again rise to economic prominence in Europe or unleash a war on the world. Within months, however, the anti-Nazi alliance of the war years fell apart as the Cold War split East from West. The creation in 1949 of two German states on either side of the Iron Curtain, one socialist, the other capitalist, one a so-called people's democracy (*Volksdemokratie*), dominated by a single party, the other a parliamentary democracy along Western lines, implanted the bipolar divisions of the world into post-war Germany and German culture.

In the East, culture was challenged to relate to the political and social agenda of the day. Freedom of expression alone was deemed insufficient in linking culture to the socialist transformation. Writing in 1947, the

East German poet Stephan Hermlin argued that too many writers had sheltered from fascism by avoiding reference to the present in their work and focusing instead on nature, emotions or distant subjects. By writing on 'all-too-comfortable themes' they effectively opted for retreat when that was no longer justified:

> What is at stake today is the refusal to treat the all-too-comfortable themes. The real freedom of the young writer can only consist in a responsible, voluntary choice of the most difficult subjects ... The freedom of the writer can only mean the freedom of the masses, the lowly and downtrodden.[4]

The 1949 congress of the Socialist Unity Party (SED) was even more direct and instructed writers how to build the East German state:

> The cultural task of educating people to understand social reality and develop a better attitude to work can only be achieved if writers and artists devote all their energy and enthusiasm to it ... Through their work, progressive writers can instil optimism and increased enjoyment of labour among the blue-collar workers in the factories and among those working on the land. Works of culture can reveal to ordinary people the meaning and significance of the Two Year Plan.[5]

Many returning exiles, Bert Brecht, Anna Seghers, Arnold Zweig among them, chose East Germany because here an incisive break appeared to have been made with National Socialism and a new beginning attempted. In the West, some shared the assumption that capitalism was at an end and socialism the hallmark of the post-war era, although mainstream politics took an anti-socialist course. 'Writers of the first hour' saw themselves as a new generation and claimed a voice in setting the political agenda against the established Allied and German leaders at the time. The journal *Der Ruf* (The Call) for example, whose editorial team had been groomed for democracy in American POW camps, risked losing its licence when it refused to accept Allied control of Germany, called for re-unification and the return of eastern territories, sketched a European agenda without occupiers and demanded a voice for Germany's young generation:

> For it is this young German generation, the men and women between 18 and 35, separated from their elders by not being responsible for Hitler and from the younger ones by their experience of the front and as POWs ... who are accomplishing the turn towards Europe with passionate speed.[6]

Wolfgang Borchert talked of a 'lost generation' who, returning from the war, found their previous world in ruins, relationships destroyed, orientation impossible. In the fifties, Helmut Schelsky coined the phrase 'sceptical generation' to describe a distrust of ideologies among the young and a detachment from politics after having been misled, as they saw it, by the Nazi party and its propagandists. The 'writers of the first hour' believed their generation to be honed by unparalleled destruction of the political and social system, the physical environment and moral values, and cast into a world in which only the individual could inspire innovation and renewal:

> With the material destruction and the reduction of everyone to the same level the mechanism of the economic law had obliterated the class contradictions, crushed its own economic foundations and enabled human beings to come face to face with each other. Hence it is the human being . . . who is reinstated as the centre of life.[7]

Two leading voices of this generation, Hans Werner Richter and Alfred Andersch, created the decisive forum for post-war culture: *Gruppe 47*. An annual gathering where writers would read from new works to the critical comment or acclaim of the other members, it was to become the hub of German literary culture for the next two decades. Similar to the salon more than a century earlier, the group facilitated communication and debate and gave post-war German culture a sense of purpose it might not otherwise have developed. The list of *Gruppe 47* debutantes reads like a *Who's Who* of literary culture in West Germany, among them Ingeborg Bachmann, Heinrich Böll, Hans-Magnus Enzensberger, Günter Grass, Walter Jens, Uwe Johnson and Martin Walser.

Culture and democracy: West German developments

In the political and economic reconstruction of Germany, there was no *Nullpunkt*, no zero hour, although essential new frameworks were created. The Basic Law, the written constitution for the West German state, laid the foundations for the future of democratic political development. It built on the structures and lessons of the Weimar years. Continuity was even more striking in the legislative field where West Germany accepted the main body of German Civil Code, albeit cleansed of overtly National Socialist additions and adjusted to the new polity by a process of legal reform over time. In the political culture, democracy gradually became accepted. While the democratic framework was being set up after 1945, the majority of Germans remained detached from politics and were preoccupied with their material welfare. According to an opinion poll in

1950 one in three claimed not to know what democracy meant nor whether the government in Bonn could be called democratic. By the 1970s, a positive endorsement of democratic institutions and principles predominated. Clearly, over the decades, a combination of economic, political and social factors had brought about a mentality change.

On re-entering the stage in the post-war years, German culture postulated a *Nullpunkt*, a zero hour of beginning afresh. In literature, cutting a clearing (*Kahlschlag*) was an attempt at cleansing the language from its National Socialist connotations. Writers like Wolfgang Weyrauch and Günter Eich took to reducing words to their context in order to reclaim the reliability of language as a reflection of direct experience. At the same time, *Trümmerliteratur* focused on ruined cities, broken landscapes and the fear and the isolation inflicted on the individual, while *Zeitroman* told of social dislocation, the impossibility of an assured future and the fear of a repetition of the National Socialist past.

Regardless of style and theme, post-war culture in West Germany shared a dread of serving society or politicians in a specified manner, but tried to carve out and protect a politics-free space for the individual. In his *Stadt hinter dem Strom* (City Behind the River) for example, a novel written in Nazi Germany and one of the first to be published after the war, Hermann Kasack stresses this detachment when, near the end of the work, he reports of his protagonist:

> Often he was asked how he saw the meaning of life after all his experiences. He could have answered: the meaning of transformation, of transformation every hour, every day, in yearly rings, in seven year rhythms, in epochs or aeons. But . . . he remained silent about these questions and left it to each individual to contribute through his own destiny to the whole where the whole meant the cosmic order of the world itself.[8]

In the 1940s, many Germans felt abandoned by politicians and thrown back on their own resources and personal resilience. Culture had a similar message. By the mid-fifties, Germany had joined the Western Alliance, rapid economic growth had more than healed the war-time devastation and West Germans enjoyed better living standards than at any time in the past. Social and political normalisation went hand in hand with the rise of the consumer society, mass culture and a general sense that a decade of post-war democracy had truly obliterated the National Socialist past and any stigma that might have been attached to being German. Two major tenets of the political culture crystallised at that time: pride in economic achievement and the assumption that West Germany was a model democracy and had obliterated the National Socialist past. Indeed, its location on the easternmost edge of the Western bloc had turned the Federal Republic (and West Berlin) into a showcase of western-style consumer society. Critical detachment from that society tarred anyone, especially writers and artists, with the brush of communism and a suspicion of harbouring anti-democratic sentiments.

The post-fascist proponents of West German culture refused to comply. They defended its focus on individual responsibility and underpinned this with a critical wariness of the state, its institutions and political actors. German politicians who hoped for a culture that would win them the support of citizens were irritated by the independent stance maintained by the representatives of culture. In the early sixties, for instance, the General Secretary of the CDU, Heinrich Dufhues, accused the *Gruppe 47* of acting like Joseph Goebbels and his Nazi propaganda machine by prescribing 'correct ways of thinking' to the detriment of all others. In similar vein, when Ludwig Erhard, the first Minister of Economic Affairs and second Chancellor of the Federal Republic, wanted to voice his disapproval of the intellectuals he called them self-important little pip-squeaks.[9]

Although culture refused to comply with the purposes of the German state when the state expected more compliance than culture could offer, this was not a re-run of the Weimar situation. First, the conservative and anti-democratic culture of yesteryear had been banished to the fringes of right-extremist book clubs and lost its impact on the centre of German society. Second, in the Weimar years, democracy lost ground as a political and social reality after the initial promise of the constitution. In the Federal Republic, democracy lasted long enough to expand and overcome authoritarian structures. Far from disavowing the democratic promises of the constitution, intellectuals tended to regard them as a yardstick for the shortcomings of German political reality. Many of their demands for 'more democracy' were heeded as younger generations invested the political process with their own expectations and their own confidence in democracy as a political system. As a democratic political culture developed in which pluralism, dissent, opposition, debate, individualism and participation in the political project were accepted forms of behaviour, and endorsing democracy became as 'normal' as rejecting it had been in the Weimar years, culture could free itself from the earlier dichotomy between individualist retreat and ideological conformity.

In the classical tradition of German culture, the artist is deemed to transcend the divisions and practicalities of daily life in his work and by doing so open vistas of innovation and liberation to the individual. In contemporary culture, the promise of situating the individual and society within larger contexts of meaning can no longer be taken for granted. Given this predicament, culture is charged more than ever with the tasks of vigilance, observation and remaining unaffiliated to party programmes. Writing in 1966, as the post-war generations of young Germans began to claim more democratic participation, Walter Jens saw culture as a guardian of democracy against its functional elites:

> The German writer of our day, commissioned by no class, protected by no fatherland, in league with no power is ... a lonely man three times over. But this position 'in between', this lack of ties, allows him to be – what a tremendous, unique opportunity! – free as never before.

No longer made to sing the praises of a ruler, the writer – and culture generally – must sound warnings:

> At a time when blind obedience rules, the 'No' of the warner, the Erasmus-like hesitation as well as thoughtfulness and Socratic caution are more important than ever before – not least in a country (such as Germany) where the 'Yes' counts more than the 'No', the government more than the opposition and the aggressor more than the defender.[10]

The failed socialist experiment

When Walter Jens identified the task of 'warning' as the prime function of culture and noted that the world of harmony between writers and rulers had irretrievably disappeared, he thought of the literature of West Germany and its uneasy place between the shadows of the past and the pragmatic reconstruction of economic and political power since the end of the Second World War. With hindsight, 'warning' also characterises the impact of dissident culture in East Germany. There, the state had expected culture to underpin its political aims and motivate the population in support of them. Walter Ulbricht, the first head of government in the GDR, dreamt of the dawn of a 'new socialist national culture' whose themes would consist of the socialist transformation and whose purpose was to 'excite people by cultural means and thus contribute to increasing the speed of development.'[11] With state backing, workers were encouraged to use their working lives as the theme for works of culture. The movement of worker writers (*Bewegung schreibender Arbeiter*) was also known as *Bitterfelder Weg* after the industrial town in the heart of the GDR where its annual conferences were staged from 1959.

Entrusting socialist culture to real workers, as stipulated in the *Bitterfelder Weg*, also implied that intellectuals who made writing their trade might not have depicted society in such a way that people learned the right kind of enthusiasm from their works. While Ulbricht and the socialist leadership overestimated the literary abilities of East German workers, they were more accurate with regard to the inability of professional artists, writers or filmmakers to glorify the socialist experience. East German culture used observation and vigilance, and produced warnings. The obstacles were formidable. No work could be published without having been screened, scanned, altered and approved by party officials. GDR culture was a censored culture. Censorship extended to academic work and research which often remained hidden in bottom drawers or vanished in the bureaucratic maze between party and publishing house.

Faced with a system of state control and Stasi intrusion, East Germans developed a dual culture: one public and official, and compliant in its language, networks and codes with the directives and organisations of both party and state, and another located in the niches of the circle of friends, the privacy of the flat or *datscha* where comparatively free communication was possible and personal opinions could be voiced. East German writers depicted this dual society and its complexities as far as they could. A literature committed to realistic portrayal based on vigilant observation rendered detailed descriptions of living conditions, conversations and social codes which, in a diction of calculated ambiguity, contained critical warnings, even though the socialist system was rarely challenged fundamentally. In the fifties and sixties, most East German writers complied with the prescribed task of propagating the socialist project. Their characters were actively involved in building socialism or found themselves persuaded to do so in the course of the narrative. In the seventies, however, East German literature moved away from the prescribed positive socialist heroes to choosing politically uncommitted individuals as protagonists. Thus in Christa Wolf's *Nachdenken über Christa T.* (Reflections on Christa T.) and Ulrich Plenzdorf's *Die neuen Leiden des jungen W.* (The New Sorrows of Young W.) the central characters refuse to comply with the optimistic view of life in the official GDR.

Based on subjectivity and the ever-changing perspective of personal experience, but fired by the ideas of socialism, the best of East German culture reflected a reality where distrust of functionaries, officials and production targets added to the shortages and frustrations that were typical of everyday life in the GDR. To the extent that the representatives of this dissident culture asserted a commitment to individual, critical perspectives, they implicitly challenged the state authorities to abide by their oft-proclaimed socialist principles. Although the GDR government tried to repress diversity and individualism by muzzling or expelling irksome intellectuals such as Wolf Biermann, Jurek Becker or Sarah Kirsch, it signally failed to quell dissent.

It is evident that on neither side of the Cold War divide could German culture be taken in tow by the state or used as an instrument to legitimate official policy and ensure the conformity of citizens. The non-conformist intellectuals of the West and the dissenters of the East concurred in measuring the state apparatus against the respective promises of democracy and socialism. Creative culture thus became a prominent terrain for the paradigmatic exploration of critical citizenship. Far from being a representative function of state authority, culture upheld a wary distance from *Macht*. For all the differences of style and subject matter, the shared commitment to the independence of *Geist* afforded bonds of solidarity in the cultural sphere long before political unification was realised in 1989–90.

This newly united Germany, for the first time in history, represents a state of affairs where both the state authorities and the vast majority of the citizenry are fundamentally committed to democracy and pluralism. Arguably, the post-war cultural intelligentsia provided role models for critical citizenship and thus expanded the parameters of civil society. This has now largely incorporated the critical energies of culture, replacing the old antagonism between *Geist* and *Macht*. In such an environment, culture is neither coerced into allegiance with politics nor relegated to an outsider position. The protagonists of culture are now free to explore not only the relationship between citizen and state but also the diversity of cultures and the range of identities that are alive in contemporary German society.

NOTES

1. Friedrich Georg Jünger, *Der Aufmarsch des Nationalismus*, Leipzig 1926, quoted from Kurt Sontheimer, *Antidemokratisches Denken in der Weimarer Republik*, Munich: Nymphenburger Verlagsanstalt, 1992, p. 67.

2. Thomas Mann, 'Offener Brief für Deutschland' (18 August 1945), quoted from Klaus Wagenbach *et al.* (eds.), *Vaterland, Muttersprache. Deutsche Schriftsteller und ihr Staat von 1945 bis heute*, Berlin: Wagenbach Verlag, 1979, p. 48.

3. From 'Drei Manifeste des Ersten Deutschen Schriftstellerkongresses' in Wagenbach, *Vaterland, Muttersprache*, p. 74.

4. Stephan Hermlin, 'Wo bleibt die junge Dichtung?' in Klaus Jarmatz *et al.* (eds.), *Literaturkritik der DDR 1945–1975*, vol. I, 1945–1965, Halle-Leipzig: Mitteldeutscher Verlag, 1978, pp. 53–4.

5. 'Entschliessung der Ersten Parteikonferenz der SED' (1949), reprinted in Jarmatz, *Literaturkritik der DDR*, vol I, p. 80.

6. Alfred Andersch, 'Das junge Europe formt sein Gesicht' in *Der Ruf*, 15 August 1946.

7. Hans Werner Richter, 'Warum schweigt die junge Generation?' in *Der Ruf*, quoted from the 1962 reprint edited by Hans Schwab-Felisch, Frankfurt/Main: Fischer, p. 32. Translation by R. Burns and W. van der Will, *Protest and Democracy in West Germany*, Basingstoke: Macmillan, 1988, p. 25.

8. Hermann Kasack, *Stadt hinter dem Strom*, 1946 (written 1942–4), quoted from the revised edition published by Knaur, Munich in 1956, p. 318.

9. Burns and van der Will, *Protest and Democracy*, p. 39.

10. Walter Jens, 'Der Schriftsteller und die Politik', in Wagenbach, *Vaterland, Muttersprache*, p. 238.

11. Walter Ulbricht, 'Schlusswort zur Ersten Bitterfelder Konferenz', in Jarmatz, *Literaturkritik der DDR*, p. 327.

1

The citizen and the state
in modern Germany

20   Since 1871 Germany has had five different constitutions and six different forms of the state – monarchical and republican, democratic and dictatorial, federal and unitary, divided and unified. There are no countries where the exercise of political authority and the perception of civil rights derive solely from the letter of the law or the structure of institutions; they depend as much on mentalities, traditions and conventions. It is difficult enough to maintain a consensus on such matters in countries with stable constitutional systems, like Britain or the United States. It is therefore hardly surprising that the roles of the state and the citizen and the rival claims of order and liberty are subject to dispute and misunderstanding in a country like Germany, with its broken constitutional history.

Imperial Germany, 1871–1918

The Empire that was proclaimed in the Hall of Mirrors at Versailles on 18 January 1871 was the first approximation to a nation state in German history. Yet it had come into being not through popular acclamation or plebiscite, but through Prussian military victories. It was a nation state in that the great majority of the German-speakers of Europe were included in it; except for a Polish minority in the East and smaller Danish and French minorities in the North and the West, its population was homogeneously German. But the people had played little part in its creation, except as conscript soldiers. The new state was a gift to the nation on which the recipient had not been consulted: its constitution was a contract among the princes of the existing German states, who retained their crowns until 1918. Unlike the draft constitution drawn up by the revolutionaries of 1848–9, or the constitution of the United States or those of the various French Republics, it contained no catalogue of human rights.

Nevertheless the Empire had significant democratic elements. The Imperial parliament, the *Reichstag*, was elected by universal male suffrage. It had legislative powers over a wide range of commercial and judicial matters, over the annual budget and over the military budget at seven-year intervals. But there were certain things the Reichstag could not do, or at any rate do on its own. Because the Empire was a federation, the constituent states, which retained limited sovereignty, shared in the legislative power through the *Bundesrat*. This was not an elected body, but a committee of state governments. Moreover, the internal arrangements of the individual states were not affected by the events of 1871. Their parliaments had no democratic legitimation. The franchise for the parliament of Prussia depended on the taxes one paid. The top five per cent of tax-payers had one-third of the votes. The bottom 85 per cent also had one-third of the votes. Those who paid no taxes had no votes. In the two duchies of Mecklenburg there were no elected parliaments at all. Indeed their constitutions survived almost unchanged from 1775 until 1918. Only after the turn of the century did the Southern states of Bavaria, Württemberg and Baden introduce universal male suffrage.

All of this mattered not only because the *Bundesrat* shared the legislative competence of the Empire, but because many policy areas remained within the remit of the individual states, including law and order and education. They employed many more bureaucrats than the Empire; the budget of Prussia alone exceeded the Imperial budget. It mattered all the more because one state, Prussia, with three-fifths of the Empire's population, dominated the federation. The King of Prussia was *ex officio* German Emperor (*Deutscher Kaiser*). The Prime Minister of Prussia was almost always the chief minister of the Empire, the Chancellor. The first holder of that office, Otto von Bismarck, from 1871 to 1890, established it as a major power base, though none of his successors managed to juggle the democratic and authoritarian elements of the constitution with quite the same skill as he. The armies of the various states came under the command of the Emperor, except – in time of peace only – that of Bavaria. That meant, in effect, a Prussian military monopoly.

The need to maintain the prerogatives of the existing states inevitably put a brake on the powers of the Reichstag. Federalism, in which power was shared between the Empire and the states, was incompatible with parliamentary supremacy on the British or French model. The Chancellor, the appointee of the Emperor, could be required to explain his policies to the Reichstag, but he could not be overthrown by a vote of no confidence. A parliamentary right to dismiss the Chancellor would have diminished the role of the *Bundesrat* and thereby the privileges of the states. Nor did the Chancellor rule with a cabinet; that again would have been at the expense of the *Bundesrat*. The Imperial departments, which expanded as time went on, were run by subordinate state secretaries. As long as the federal structure of the Empire operated at the expense of the one democratic feature of the constitution, the Reichstag, and as long as the internal arrangements of the individual states remained undemocratic, the prospects of a thorough-going constitutional reform were poor.

There were, however, other respects in which the rights of the individual citizen were protected. The Empire was a *Rechtsstaat*, a state subject to the rule of law. Judges and bureaucrats had some prerogatives and discretion, but these were strictly defined. They could not act arbitrarily. The laws on the press and publishing were, by the standards of the day, quite liberal. True, censorship existed and subversion, sometimes generously interpreted, was punishable with imprisonment, but in general speech, thought and avant-garde art flourished in Imperial Germany. The law of association, too, was permissive, as was business regulation. Education was universally available and illiteracy a rarity. Careers were open to talents; where there were barriers, these were psychological and social, not legal.

Practice inevitably fell short of theory. Officials could abuse their powers, especially in rural areas. Although an 1869 law guaranteed religious equality, discrimination continued in state employment. In many sectors a Protestant had a better chance than a Catholic, and a Jew, unless he converted, had no chance at all. Women had no political rights and only restricted property rights, but their educational opportunities improved and by 1914 they were beginning to enter the professions. Above all, even democratic legislatures can pass discriminatory laws. Fears of the growing power of the Socialist movement led to an anti-Socialist law, in force from 1878 to 1890, which banned Socialist meetings and gave the police unlimited powers of search, arrest and banishment. Some years earlier, the government's fear that the Catholic Church, whose members were a minority in the new Empire, could not be trusted to be fully loyal to it, led to the *Kulturkampf* – a series of Prussian and Imperial laws that imposed compulsory civil marriage, dissolved all religious orders except medical ones and drastically reduced the self-government of the churches.

During the life-time of the Empire its institutions hardly changed, but their workings evolved, providing new opportunities for citizen participation. With urbanisation, the growth of commerce and the expansion of industry, the patchwork of the old German states became a memory and the Empire more of a reality. The politics of Munich, Dresden, Karlsruhe and Weimar still mattered. Disputes about schools and the arts, the right to vote and the hope of jobs were close to everyday life. But the politics of Berlin, which were about free trade and tariffs and therefore the price of bread, and about the size of the army and the navy and therefore about taxes, came to loom larger. Elections to the Reichstag became major political events. In 1871 barely half the electorate had turned out to vote. In 1912, the last pre-war election, the turn-out was 84.5 per cent. Political parties, which in 1871 were led by local notables and run by committees of volunteers, had nation-wide organisations by 1912, professionally staffed. As the social structure changed, the Conservative Party, representing Prussian rural interests, gradually declined. The more moderately Conservative *Reichspartei* and the National Liberals, who had been Bismarck's mainstay in the first decade of the Empire, also lost ground. The various Progressive parties, split off from the National Liberals and favouring free trade and constitutional reform, recovered after the turn of the century. The *Zentrum*, which came to prominence during the *Kulturkampf* to defend Catholic interests, stagnated once that dispute lost salience. The great beneficiary of these changes were the working-class Social Democrats (SPD), who grew by leaps and bounds once the discriminatory laws lapsed in 1890. With a third of the votes and a million paid-up members, they became the largest party in the 1912 Reichstag.

This transformation in party strengths made the Reichstag more difficult to manage. For most of the time the government succeeded in gaining electoral majorities for its policies. Bismarck managed this in 1878 in favour of a turn from free trade to protection and in 1887 for an increased military budget. Chancellor Bülow managed it in 1907 over colonial policy. But by 1912, when free trade and constitutional reform were the issues, this proved too difficult. The contrast between an increasingly left-leaning public opinion and the conservatism of the Prussian and other North German states threatened a crisis.

A further complicating factor was the increasing role of the Empire in regulating economic and social relations. The turn towards tariffs in 1878, which favoured agriculture and heavy industry, re-established the role of the state as an adjudicator between interests. The introduction of a compulsory social security insurance scheme in the 1880s made Germany the world's first welfare state. These measures greatly encouraged a trend already under way, the organisation of occupational interest groups which represented heavy industry, manufacturing industry, agriculture, artisans, shopkeepers and labour. They were joined by promotional groups like the Colonial Society, the Navy League and the Hansa League, the last of which stood for free trade and against the remaining agrarian–aristocratic dominance of public and social life. Most of these lobbies had close ties with one or other of the parties – the main trade union federation, with 2.5 million members, was close to the SPD – but they also had negotiating clout of their own and often dealt directly at ministerial level with the bureaucracy.

The outbreak of the World War in 1914 exacerbated all these latent conflicts. On the one hand it strengthened the authoritarian elements in the Imperial regime, but it also, in the long run, stimulated discontent and protest. The Emperor's assurance at the beginning of the war, 'I know no parties, I know only Germans', was meant to conciliate. It ushered in a civic truce (Burgfrieden), which held for some two years. But the war also gave the military their chance to claim a primacy in policy matters. The whole of Germany was placed under a state of emergency, effectively suspending the rule of law. Military dominance was further enhanced by the creation of a supreme Army command in 1916 under Paul von Hindenburg. He and his Quartermaster-General, General Ludendorff, became the real rulers of the state, even securing the dismissal of Chancellor Bethmann Hollweg in 1917.

However, the longer the war dragged on, the more this regime was challenged. The Reichstag was not entirely eliminated. Wars cost money and the credits needed parliamentary approval: these were forthcoming, but with increasing difficulty. In particular they divided the SPD, which split in 1917, the anti-war left wing forming the USPD. As the war imposed increasing sacrifices, demands for political reforms could not be stifled, in particular for parliamentary control over the government and an end to the anomalous Prussian franchise. The question of German war aims was equally divisive and in July 1917 a majority of the Reichstag voted for a negotiated peace. The pro-peace parties were the Social Democrats, Progressives and Zentrum, Bismarck's old enemies. The war, far from sealing the fault-lines of the Empire's politics, as its leaders had hoped in 1914, opened them wider. Nor was protest restricted to parliamentary resolutions. Widespread strikes in the winter of 1917–18, initially occasioned by hunger and cold, soon escalated into demands for democratisation and a negotiated peace. They were led by unofficial shop stewards who created workers' councils (*Räte*) – ominously like the Soviets that had made their appearance in Russia in the previous autumn and gave a foretaste of developments in Germany as defeat loomed.

The end of the Imperial constitution came as Germany faced military collapse in September 1918. On 3 October the Liberal Prince Max of Baden became Chancellor, heading a government based on the three 'peace resolution' parties, after the High Command had urged a transfer to civilian rule. On 28 October the constitution was amended to subject the military to the decisions of the Chancellor and the appropriate ministers. They in turn were subject to the confidence of the Reichstag, which also gained participatory powers over war and peace and the conclusion of treaties. In the dying days of the World War the German Empire had become a parliamentary monarchy.

Revolution and the Weimar Republic, 1918–1933

War and defeat had exposed the structural weaknesses of the Empire. Those who took over its government in the autumn of 1918 were the men who had led the demands for reform, whether moderate or radical. But side by side with their new and insecure authority came revolutionary stirrings. These began with a naval mutiny, spread to the retreating army and then engulfed mines and factories. The councils of the preceding winter re-emerged. Meanwhile the Emperor Wilhelm II had abdicated on 9 November, Philipp Scheidemann of the SPD had proclaimed the German Republic and Max von Baden had handed the seals of office to Friedrich Ebert of the SPD. Ebert now formed a Socialist government of three SPD and three USPD ministers. Representatives of the councils meanwhile met at a congress in Berlin and proclaimed the Ebert government a Council of People's Commissars, answerable to them. There was now a dual sovereignty, constitutional and revolutionary, with Ebert acting as both Chancellor and co-chairman of the People's Commissars. The provisional government lifted the war-time state of emergency and proclaimed an amnesty for all political offenders. Beyond that the constitutional future of Germany was clouded. Most Germans wanted democracy, at any rate for the time being, though in what form was less certain. Most Germans accepted the republic, with or without enthusiasm. Whether most Germans wanted full-blooded Socialism is more doubtful, though the People's Commissars proclaimed 'the realisation of the Socialist programme'.

The democratic options fell into three categories. The new Germany could become a parliamentary democracy along the lines of the constitutional changes of October 1918. Alternatively it could become a revolutionary democracy, as favoured by the extreme Left of the USPD, the Spartacus League (*Spartakusbund*), led by Rosa Luxemburg and Karl Liebknecht. Their slogan, following the model of the Soviets in Russia, was 'all power to the councils', with no intermediate representative institutions and no separation of powers. To most Germans, including the SPD, this looked like a Leninist dictatorship. The USPD favoured a third model consisting of the parallel existence of parliamentary institutions and the councils to consider the specific interests of workers.

The path that was chosen was the parliamentary one, for two complementary, but unconnected, reasons. The first reason was that even on the Left this was the preferred option. Though the councils were a revolutionary institution, they were not manned by revolutionaries. The majority of their members were sympathetic to the SPD and on 20 December the congress of councils voted against a Socialist republic of Soviets and in favour of the election of a Constituent Assembly. The second reason was that the provisional government of Ebert feared that it might not be able to maintain public order against the threat from the revolutionary Left and therefore entered into a secret agreement with the General Staff, whereby the army would support the new republican order against subversion. When the Spartacus League, now renamed as the Communist Party (KPD), launched an ill-conceived rising in January 1919, this was crushed with great brutality by the regular army and irregular volunteers (the *Freikorps*), culminating in the murder of Luxemburg and Liebknecht. A series of revolutionary regimes in Bavaria ended in a similar bloodbath. These events were to weigh like an albatross on the new republic.

The Constituent Assembly, elected on 19 January 1919, met in Weimar, partly to escape the risk of mob rule, partly because of Weimar's association with the classical culture of Germany. All Germans, men and now women, too, over the age of twenty were entitled to vote. Proportional representation replaced the old unequal constituency boundaries. All later elections, national and local, took place under the same system. Except for a distinct but not overwhelming swing to the Left, the party spectrum was not too different from that of the Empire. The two Social

Democratic parties won 45.5 per cent of the vote, 11 per cent more than the SPD in 1912, but short of an absolute majority. The *Zentrum* retained its stable support at 19 per cent. The left-Liberal Democrats (DDP), successors to the old Progressives, won 18.6 per cent; the German People's Party (DVP), which had developed from the old National Liberals, won 4.6 per cent. The new monarchist Nationalist Party (DNVP), which incorporated all the old right-wing parties including the Conservatives, won 10.3 per cent. The parties on whose support the Republic depended, SPD, *Zentrum* and DDP, held over three-quarters of the seats and were able to form a government. This combination, the continuation of the old 'peace resolution' majority, came to be known as the 'Weimar Coalition'.

The 'Weimar Coalition' was not, however, able to dominate the Republic's politics. In 1922 the USPD, which had made great gains in the 1920 Reichstag election, split and the majority of its voters went over to the Communists, who had not contested the election to the Constituent Assembly, but who were to become a major force in Weimar politics. Even earlier the conservatively inclined Bavarian branch of the *Zentrum* had split off to form the Bavarian People's Party (BVP), which was a less reliable prop of republican institutions than the *Zentrum*. Above all, the DDP's electorate turned out to be fickle and drifted off to the right. The right-of-centre scene fragmented, giving rise to small regional and special-interest parties, as well as the National Socialist (Nazi) party, which made its first break-through in May 1924, though it fell back at the two subsequent elections.

Before any of these developments took place, the Weimar Assembly completed its task of drafting a constitution for the new Republic – hence known as the Weimar Republic. Its purpose was to secure a democratic basis and a democratic consensus on behalf of the new state. In this it was only partially successful. The constitution proclaimed the principle of popular sovereignty. In contrast with the Imperial constitution it also contained a long Bill of Rights, guaranteeing, *inter alia*, equality before the law, equality of the sexes, freedom of conscience and religion and freedom of association. In other respects the Bill of Rights confirmed the existing social structure, thus reflecting the compromises inherent in the Weimar Coalition. Marriage and the family were placed under the special protection of the state. In economic relations the Bill of Rights recognised the rights of property and inheritance and of freedom of contract.

The Weimar Republic's system of government, like the catalogue of citizens' rights, reflected the completion of the liberal-democratic programme rather than the Socialist demands of the council movement. The Weimar Republic was less of a federal state than the Empire had been, since the claims and vetoes of the various dynasties had disappeared in the Revolution. The Reichstag now had legislative supremacy. The Chancellor and his ministers were responsible to it, and not to the successor of the *Bundesrat*, now re-named *Reichsrat*. The original proposal of the Assembly's constitutional adviser, Hugo Preuß, that the old *Länder* be abolished, came to nothing. Now that all their constitutions had been democratised, their new governments acquired a legitimate interest in the status quo. The *Länder* retained their policy autonomy in education and public order, but in general the Weimar Republic is best described as a decentralised unitary state, not a federation. Two of the constitution's innovations proved less helpful to the democratic security of the Republic. The head of state was to be a popularly elected President with a seven-year term and considerable reserve powers. Potentially this made the holder of the office a rival to the democratic legitimacy of the Reichstag. His powers were further enhanced by Article 48, which granted him considerable emergency powers, admittedly subject to the Reichstag's veto. The implications of these two provisions will be seen below.

While the constitution dealt with civil rights and the organisation of the state, there were changes in social relations which recognised the increased power of organised labour. The old pre-war demand for an eight-hour working day was realised at the end of the war and in 1927 the Bismarckian welfare state was supplemented with a comprehensive scheme of unemployment insurance. Neither of these measures survived the economic crisis of 1929; they nevertheless symbolised the aspiration that the Republic was to belong to all citizens.

The reasons why the Weimar Republic lasted only fourteen years are complex and the world economic crisis of 1929, which hit Germany particularly hard, must be the chief one. Yet just as the war had merely highlighted the defects of the Imperial structure, so the Depression brought out the Republic's latent weaknesses. The Republic was the child of defeat: its government had been obliged to accept the terms of the Versailles peace treaty with its burden of reparations. Its statesmen became 'November criminals' in the eyes of the irreconcilables. The Republic was also the child of revolution. All revolutions are divisive. They alienate those for whom the changes they bring about go too far; they disillusion those for whom they do not go far enough. These dual discontents ensured that the Weimar Coalition failed to gain majorities at any of the

Reichstag elections from 1920 onwards. Above all, neither the supporters nor the opponents of the Republic fully understood the role of political parties in a parliamentary system. The parties' organisations had grown under the Empire; they found it difficult to transform themselves from their role as sectional agitators to that of bearing governmental responsibility. Too often it was the extra-parliamentary organisation or the Reichstag back-benchers who determined policy and cabinet personnel. Too often 'non-political' experts were drawn in to govern instead of elected politicians. One-third of the Republic's Chancellors and cabinet ministers were recruited in this way. In the election for President after Ebert's death in 1925, victory went to the war-time hero, Field Marshal Hindenburg, a man of doubtful loyalty to the democratic Republic. It was an irony, in view of the original intentions of the Republic's founders, that the maintenance of its stability depended increasingly on the Länder, especially on Prussia, where the pro-republican parties had majorities for almost all the time and were therefore able to protect the democratic order over three-fifths of the country, including the capital, Berlin.

The consequence of party fragmentation and anti-Republican sentiment was that coalitions, some of them only minority governments, were unstable and mainly short-lived. The Communist party grew steadily, from 10.6 per cent in 1928 to 16.9 per cent in November 1932. Under the impact of the Depression the Nazi party mushroomed from 2.6 per cent in 1928 to 37.4 per cent in July 1932. For the last year of the Republic the parties committed to destroying the Republic held majorities in both the Reichstag and the Prussian *Landtag*. Yet even before then parliamentary government had ceased. From 1930 onwards Germany was ruled under the emergency powers of Article 48. In the whole of 1932 the Reichstag met only thirteen times. It passed five laws, while the President issued fifty-nine decrees. The last republican stronghold fell in July 1932 when Chancellor Franz von Papen used Article 48 to topple the SPD minority administration of Prussia. Weimar was not, as has sometimes been said, a Republic without republicans. It was a Republic with not enough republicans.

The 'Third Reich', 1933–1945

The National Socialist regime is unique in German history for its denial of individual and public rights, yet it came into being entirely in accordance with the rules of the constitution. After the November 1932 election, in which the Nazi party had fallen back, the Communists had made further gains and the 'Weimar' parties won only one-third of the seats, President Hindenburg's advisers persuaded him that a government in which Adolf Hitler was Chancellor, but a majority of the cabinet non-Nazi, was the best way out of the impasse. Accordingly, Hitler was appointed Chancellor on 30 January 1933. That the Nazi party enjoyed popular support was not in doubt. Its share of the vote had been exceeded only once, by the SPD in 1919. Yet the signs that this was not just another government re-shuffle were unmistakable. A Nazi, Wilhelm Frick, was appointed Minister of the Interior; another, Hermann Goering, took over the Interior Ministry of the now non-existent Prussian government. Fifty thousand of the Nazis' streetfighters, the brown-shirted SA, and of the party guard, the black-shirted SS, were recruited as 'auxiliary police'. The second sign was that Hitler demanded new elections in which, helped by considerable intimidation, the Nazis and their DNVP allies won 52 per cent. Hitler now had a mandate to govern, though not necessarily for his particular intentions.

The 'seizure of power' (*Machtergreifung*), which was the Nazis' own term for their take-over, was a process, not a single event. Hitler's appointment was at best a condition for it. The process, which developed rapidly and was complete by the summer of 1934, had begun even before the election of March 1933. Following the Reichstag Fire in February, which the Nazis falsely blamed on the Communists, the 'decree for the protection of the state and the people' was proclaimed under Article 48, which effectively suspended all the civil liberties guaranteed under the Weimar constitution and granted powers of arbitrary arrest and imprisonment. In so far as the Third Reich had a constitution, it was contained in this document. Following the election, the new Reichstag passed the 'law for the relief of suffering of the people and the state' (the 'Enabling Act'). With only the SPD voting against, the Communist members having been suspended, the government was granted full emergency powers for four years.

Both measures remained in force for the whole length of the regime. In the two months following Hitler's appointment, political violence reached unprecedented dimensions. Between January and March there were sixty-nine politically motivated murders and up to 30,000 political opponents were incarcerated and maltreated in hastily erected concentration camps. On 1 April 1933 a boycott of Jewish businesses was ordered, enforced by the strong-arm tactics of the SA. Other measures quickly followed: powers to purge the civil service of the politically or racially undesirable; the blacklisting and public burnings of 'un-German' books, including the works of Einstein, Freud, Heinrich Mann and Erich Kästner; the abolition of trade unions; the prohibition of the SPD, followed by the 'voluntary' dissolution of the remaining parties and the proclamation of the Nazi party as the sole legal political organisation; the abolition of the Länder as separate units and of the *Reichsrat*; the direct appointment of mayors by the state and the creation of the 'People's Court' (*Volksgerichtshof*) for the prosecution of political offenders.

Hitler was determined to rule not only through the party, but over it. A condition of securing absolute power was the crushing of oppositional forces in the SA around its leader Ernst Röhm, who hoped that his 600,000 men would form the nucleus of a future German army. On the 'night of the long knives', 30 June 1934, Röhm, his supporters and other potential regime opponents – a total of ninety-six persons – were murdered. On 2 August, on the death of President Hindenburg, the offices of President and Chancellor were merged. Hitler was henceforth to be referred to as the *Führer*, not only of the party and the state, but of the entire people.

Eighteen months after Hitler's appointment the organisational structure of the new regime was in place. What it displaced was not merely the parliamentary constitution of Weimar, but the entire concept of the rule of law that had characterised not only the Republic, but the German Empire, and most of the German states even before 1871. Yet Hitler had been careful to use the path of legality to attain his absolutism. His monopolisation of power had a plebiscitary basis. The abolition of all checks and balances went through the appropriate procedure, even though the Enabling Act had done little more than confirm the powers already granted by decree after the Reichstag Fire. After the Röhm purge the radicalisation of the regime slowed down for a time, but it never ceased. The most powerful potential challengers to it were initially appeased – the Catholic Church with a Concordat, granting it religious autonomy in return for abstention from politics; and the Army by the elimination of Röhm. In neither case did the regime keep its side of the bargain. It had less to fear from the Protestant Churches. The Confessing Church, founded to oppose ideological interference by the Nazi party, never embraced more than a minority of pastors and parishioners.

The acquisition of absolute political power was a means to several ends. One of these was the complete integration (*Gleichschaltung*) of the life of civil society in that of the state, indeed the abolition, as far as possible, of the distinction between the social and the political. All autonomous associational life came to an end. Membership of monopolistic, party-dependent bodies became compulsory and their nominal representatives were also agents of the state. Walther Darré was not only *Reich* peasant leader, but Minister of Agriculture; Josef Goebbels was not only head of the *Reich* Chamber of Culture, but Minister of Propaganda. Most significant for the merging of the official and unofficial forces of coercion was the position of Heinrich Himmler, head of the party militia, the SS, who in 1934 became general inspector of yet another extra-legal body, the secret police (*Gestapo*), in 1936 head of the police in the Ministry of the Interior and in 1942 Minister of the Interior. Within the SS, Himmler's subordinate, Reinhard Heydrich, rose to be head of the Security Service (SD), which became responsible for public morale and, along with the Gestapo, for countering domestic threats to the regime. The concentration camps, whose inmates had in the main broken no law, were at all times outside the control of the normal state apparatus.

It would be wrong to assume that the regime's hold on the population rested entirely on terror, though awareness of the potential of terror was always there. Even though independent trade union structures and free collective bargaining were abolished, there were jobs where there had previously been none. A combination of cyclical factors and the regime's economic policies ensured that unemployment fell from six million at the beginning of 1933 to under half a million at the beginning of 1939. Real wages rose little, but there were more benefits in kind, from child care to holidays. Nazi propaganda made much of the unity of the people (*Volksgemeinschaft*), transcending the class struggle and the privileges of the traditional elites. The economic recovery lent some credibility to this propaganda.

However, not everyone was included in the *Volksgemeinschaft*. The dismissal of Jews from public employment and the boycott of Jewish businesses were early signs of what was to come. The Nuremberg Laws of 1935 restricted German citizenship to persons of 'German or related blood' and prohibited marriages between Jews and non-Jews. The escalation of official anti-Semitism received a boost with the annexation of Austria in March 1938, which added 200,000 Jews to the population and a much more radically anti-Semitic Nazi organisation. Anti-Jewish measures reached a climax in the *Kristallnacht* pogrom of 9–10 November 1938, following the murder of a German diplomat in Paris by a young Polish Jew. Ninety-one Jews were killed, some 25,000 deported to concentration camps, over a hundred synagogues were destroyed and Jewish-owned shops vandalised. This was followed by the imposition of a collective fine of one billion *Reichsmark* on the Jews of Germany and their formal exclusion from most economic activities, a trend already well under way by then.

It was with the outbreak of war on 1 September 1939 that the Third Reich came truly into its own. In preparation for this conscription had been introduced in 1935 and Hermann Goering had been appointed Plenipotentiary for the Four-Year Plan in 1936, giving the state further powers of economic direction, while continuing to leave industry in private ownership. In 1938 Hitler appointed himself Commander-in-Chief of the armed forces, having purged those generals who were sceptical of his strategy. In August 1939, as the war approached, a Special Criminal Law was proclaimed, greatly expanding the applicability of the death penalty. From 1940 to 1944 15,993 death sentences were carried out in Germany, quite apart from the millions of executions and murders in the occupied states and concentration camps. Yet it was beyond the borders of Germany that the terror of the Third Reich reached its full potential and that its rulers set about realising their utopia of world empire ruled by a master race. In the occupied territories of Eastern Europe Himmler was entrusted with ensuring 'political security'. Even those remnants of legality and administrative routine that were still in place in Germany did not apply here. It was in Poland that the extermination camps were set up in which six million Jews met their deaths, and along with them gypsies, homosexuals and Russian and Polish slave-labourers. Even in Germany itself the value of human life declined sharply. Under the shadow of war the 'euthanasia' of the incurably mentally and physically ill became policy; indeed, the gas chambers developed for this purpose were a trial run for the Holocaust. When news of the 'euthanasia' programme leaked out, Catholic bishops protested publicly and it was officially stopped. Unofficially it continued, claiming some 150,000 victims.

The action of the Catholic bishops showed that even under the conditions of terror, some opposition was possible; organised resistance less so. Efforts along these lines, culminating in the attempt on Hitler's life on 20 July 1944 by a group of army officers and highly placed civilians, all failed. How much public support the conspirators would have gained if they had been successful is in doubt. Despite war-weariness and other discontents, many – possibly most – Germans still felt that their country had to be defended to the end.

The German states since 1945

The military defeat of the Third Reich and its unconditional surrender on 8 May 1945 necessitated not merely economic recovery but a fundamental reconstruction of the political system. The scale of the crimes which the Hitler regime's agents – most of them ordinary Germans – had wrought on the world now became slowly apparent. Following a failed democracy and a dictatorship of unparalleled ferocity the mentalities supporting the political process required to be altered. The politics of post-1945 Germany, at both the individual and the institutional level, was defined by reference to Weimar and the Third Reich. The Third Reich had laid claim not only to total obedience and the subordination of the individual to the group, but to ideological monopoly. It had proclaimed one single, undisputed public truth and, however sceptical individuals might have been towards particular aspects of the official ideology, they had become unaccustomed to a world in which political or moral values conflicted openly. Indeed their unfavourable experience of such conflicts in the Weimar Republic had led many of them to embrace the promise of national harmony that National Socialism held out. A second legacy of the Third Reich was the destruction of associational life. Whereas in politics the individualism of opinion and conscience was discounted and indeed suppressed, in economic life policy ran in the opposite direction. The pressure to produce was exerted on individuals; the rewards system went quite a long way to undermine established status hierarchies. There was therefore a desolidarisation of life. The only community that was recognised was that of the whole people; solidarity was commanded from above, not evolved from below or among equals.

In the political vacuum that followed the end of the war, associational life revived only slowly. The only non-state institutions that had survived relatively intact were the churches and it was to these that many Germans now turned for support and reassurance. The government of Germany was for the time being in the hands of the Allied Control Council, representing the victorious powers of the USA, the USSR, Britain and France. The military occupation, the upheavals caused by the stream of millions of refugees and the shortage of many of the basic necessities of life all served further to reduce the citizen's interest in politics. Under these circumstances it was little short of amazing that four years after the end of the war two German republics were in existence with considerable powers of self-government and, in one case, an emerging stable party system. They were the German Federal Republic, covering the three Western zones of occupation, and the German Democratic Republic (GDR) in the Soviet zone. The credit for this development goes partly to the occupiers, partly to the German politicians, most of them veterans of Weimar. The four zones of occupation into which the Allies had divided Germany were meant to be administrative units only; given the growing incompatibilities of Western and Eastern policies, they soon became mini-states. Unwilling to contemplate a single German state at this stage, each of the occupiers created a number of Länder in its zone; these have remained the basis of the second tier of government to this day. Some of the Länder corresponded with historic units, like Bavaria or Saxony, others were new creations to fit the zonal boundaries. Except in South-West Germany, where the merged *Land* of Baden-Württemberg came into being in 1952, their boundaries have remained virtually unchanged. By mid-1947 elections to local authorities and Land parliaments (*Landtage*) had taken place in all zones.

Elections require a party system and while each of the occupation authorities reserved the right to license parties, they did so within the parameters of German political traditions. On the Left both the SPD and the KPD began to reconstruct their organisations informally even before the war was over. The first official licensing took place in the Soviet zone in June 1945 when, in addition to the SPD and KPD, two right-of-centre parties appeared: a Christian Democratic Union (CDU) as a successor to the old *Zentrum* and the predominantly Protestant Conservative parties, and a Liberal Democratic Party (LDPD) as a successor to the pre-1933 Liberal parties. A similar pattern emerged in the Western zones, where the new Liberal party became known as the Free Democrats (FDP). Other parties have come and mostly gone; it is the four original formations that have dominated the post-1949 party scene.

What led to the division of Germany was not only the growing strategic rivalry of the two super-powers, but their diverging recipes for fashioning post-war society. In particular they differed on how to learn from the lessons of Nazism. The Soviet authorities applied a Marxist analysis of the causes of fascism: for them it was the last resort of monopoly capitalism to the threat of proletarian revolution. To prevent its recurrence they expropriated at an early stage both the large landed estates of

Eastern Germany and the major industrial corporations. They also enforced the merger of the SPD with the KPD into the Socialist Unity Party (SED) as the first step towards a single-party state. The thesis that big business was to blame for the rise of Nazism was not restricted to the Soviet authorities or Marxists. It was widely held in the Western zones also. The British Labour Government favoured the nationalisation of the coal and steel industries, as did the British zone CDU. A referendum in the Land of Hesse, in the US zone, favoured a constitution that permitted nationalisation. The US authorities, however, took a diametrically opposite view of what was required. A functioning civil society, they argued, required a right to property: this was the only sure defence against the omnipotence of the state. When the British and US zones were merged at the beginning of 1947 this principle applied to the whole of this 'bi-zone'. With the implementation of a currency reform in the Western zones in June, 1948, which replaced the inflated *Reichsmark* with the *Deutsche Mark*, and the accompanying liberalisation of prices, a market economy was firmly in place.

It was from these three zones that a Parliamentary Council met, based on party strengths in the *Landtage*, to draw up a constitution for a West German state. Its remit was formidable – to establish what had previously proved impossible in Germany: a stable democracy with effective government. Yet because there was a consensus among West German politicians on the desired ends, even if not the means, and because there was considerable overlap in priorities between them and the Allies, a document was agreed within eight months. Because it applied to only a part of Germany and because its authors looked forward – or claimed to look forward – to national unification, it was named the Basic Law. The Basic Law it has remained. In its dual purpose of making possible the exercise of power and averting the abuse of power it has been successful, almost certainly beyond the expectations of its authors.

The Basic Law describes the Federal Republic as 'democratic and social', but its structure is really more complicated than that. The federalism ensures the dispersion of power. It is the Länder that are responsible for much of the execution of policy, even of measures that originate with the central government. They have limited powers of taxation, but above all they have retained control over their traditional policy areas, law and order and education, as well as radio and television broadcasting. Through the *Bundesrat* they have a vote on all legislation that affects their rights and responsibilities, including above all the federal budget. The main legislative chamber is the directly elected *Bundestag* and it is the *Bundestag* that exercises parliamentary control over the executive. However, it does so in a way that is designed to avoid the misuse of this device under Weimar. It elects the Chancellor by an absolute majority. It cannot demand the resignation of individual ministers. It can dismiss the Chancellor only through the 'constructive vote of no confidence', i.e. by electing another in his place. How these rules have worked out in practice we shall see below.

Like the Weimar constitution, the Basic Law contains a Bill of Rights. It comes at the beginning and is much more explicit in its requirements. It proclaims the sanctity of life, the abolition of the death penalty and the right of political asylum. A major innovation is the establishment of a Federal Constitutional Court to interpret the Basic Law and above all to adjudicate on the application of the Bill of Rights. The emphasis throughout is on the diffusion of power and on the responsibilities that go with rights. There is a distinct disinclination to trust the maturity of an electorate that had given its mandate to Hindenburg and Hitler. The Federal Republic's President is a figure-head only, and not popularly elected. There is no provision for nation-wide referendums. Popular sovereignty was to be exercised through representative institutions only.

Many of the other requirements of the Basic Law and of effective government were settled by ordinary legislation. In contrast with Weimar, the electoral system was not constitutionally anchored. After a number of amendments the electoral law has remained virtually unchanged since 1956: half the *Bundestag* is elected by simple majority in single-member constituencies, half by lists (drawn up and published by the political parties in each of the federal states) to compensate for any distortions. This means, in effect, proportional representation subject to two provisos: a party can claim seats only if it gains 5 per cent of the vote nationally or wins at least three constituencies outright. The Basic Law also permits the banning of any party that threatens the constitutional order, a provision used against the neo-Nazi Socialist Reich Party and the KPD in the 1950s and a number of extreme right-wing groups more recently.

The social component of the Basic Law's requirements was fulfilled gradually. Industrial co-determination, i.e. the presence of elected workers' representatives on the supervisory boards of the coal and steel industry, came in 1951. It was extended to other firms with over 500 employees in the 1970s. The extensive welfare state that the Federal Republic inherited was further extended by the adoption of index-linked retirement pensions in 1957. The constitutional requirement to ensure the equality of living standards throughout the federal territory has, however, led to increasing difficulties. Before unification it entailed transfers on a growing scale from the richer to the poorer Länder; since 1990, in light of the much greater gap between the Eastern and Western Länder, the equalisation imperative has led to higher taxation and a greater role for the federal government as redistributor. This in turn has led to a tilt in the power balance from Länder to federation and growing resentments among both donors and recipients about the weight of burden-sharing. In addition the Federal Constitutional Court has itself taken on the role of adjudicator of social justice by ruling on the equity or otherwise of the government's budgetary measures.

While many of the developments in the political structure of the Federal Republic have been the result of constitutional amendment, court rulings or legislation, some of the most important have resulted from changes in attitudes and conventions. The first of these has to do with the stability of government. The 'constructive vote of no confidence' has been used only twice, and only once with success – in 1982 when Helmut Kohl replaced Chancellor Helmut Schmidt. The party fragmentation that had bedevilled Weimar and that the Parliamentary Council wished to guard against has not recurred. Between 1957 and 1990 there were never more than four parties in the *Bundestag*; between 1961 and 1983 there were only three; since 1957 coalition governments have consisted of two parties only. Since German unification the number of parties in the Bundestag has risen to five, the SED's successor, the Party of Democratic Socialism (PDS), having won seats in both 1990 and 1994. The reason for this stability has been a revolutionary change in electoral behaviour. In contrast with Weimar, both politicians and voters came to realise that in a parliamentary system the effective contest should be not between legislature and executive, but between a governmental majority and an opposition. This is symbolised at election time by the duel between an incumbent Chancellor and his challenger, the 'chancellor candidate' (*Kanzlerkandidat*). Critics who witnessed the emergence of this system under the first post-war Chancellor, Konrad Adenauer, dubbed it 'chancellor democracy'. It is, however, one of the main reasons why Bonn is not Weimar and it enables citizens to feel that they have a direct say in the composition of the government.

An even more significant change in public life has been the loss of deference towards authority. The era of post-war political quiescence, in which reconstruction took precedence over all other concerns, came to an end in the mid-1960s. While the student protests against the proposed emergency legislation and the Vietnam war were the most spectacular symptoms of this, they were part of a deeper cultural change. Citizens' initiatives sprouted, generally on environmental questions, which developed into the Green Party that first entered the Bundestag in 1983. Increasingly, items for the political agenda were set from below, resulting in administrative changes that were by no means always based on formal legislation. These relate to environmental care, data protection and a growth of civic participation generally, whether in school government, planning decisions or the selection of candidates by political parties. Reforms introduced in the late 1960s improved the legal position of homosexuals and the illegitimate. The biggest change of all has taken place in the position of women. The Weimar constitution had proclaimed the equality of the sexes, but that was honoured more in the breach than the observance, while in the Third Reich women had been deliberately relegated to subordinate roles. Even in the immediate post-war years, when women had to take on much of the burden of reconstruction, they were hardly represented in the higher reaches of public life. This, too, changed from the late 1960s onwards. Women have been particularly prominent in the leadership and membership of the Green Party, but have also risen elsewhere in the party spectrum. Following the 1994 election 26 per cent of Bundestag members were women, compared with 7 per cent in 1949. Not all feminist demands have, however, been met. German legislation on abortion remains restrictive by the general standards of Western Europe. A darker side of the new politics was the emergence of urban terrorism in the 1970s by the Red Army Faction, also known as the Baader-Meinhof group after its founders, which engaged in a number of spectacular assassinations of public figures. This led, as might have been expected, to an increase in state coercion, of which the most controversial was a resolution by the federal and state governments not to employ suspected extremists in the public services – the so-called Decree on Radicals (*Radikalenerlaß*).

For most of its history the relationships of citizens and the state in the GDR were the opposite of those in the West, yet ultimately the two converged. By the time the GDR was founded it was virtually a single-party state. Following the creation of the SED the remaining 'bourgeois' parties had no independent electoral role. The state soon became a 'people's democracy' of the Soviet type, with the nationalisation of industry and the collectivisation of agriculture almost complete by the end of the 1950s. Those GDR citizens who disapproved of these measures had only two weapons at their disposal. The first was a strike, which rapidly became a national workers' rising, on 17 June 1953. It was initially a protest against higher production norms, but rapidly expanded to political demands, including free elections. This was crushed by Soviet military intervention. The second was to vote with their feet, which over two million of them did by escaping to the Federal Republic. That escape route came to an end with the building of the Berlin Wall on 13 August 1961, which was soon extended to a fortified frontier between the two German states. The GDR regime used this isolation to improve the performance of the economy, in which it was successful for a time, and to create a new state identity. The adoption of a new legal code in 1968 and of a revised constitution in 1974, which made no mention of a single German nation, was designed to put an end to any affinity the citizens of the GDR might feel with those of the Federal Republic.

Although the two German states exchanged diplomatic representation and joined the United Nations in 1973 as a consequence of Chancellor Willy Brandt's *Ostpolitik*, the GDR's external legitimacy was greater than its domestic acceptance. However, as long as there was no prospect of change in the international configuration, the population was quiescent, compensating for a lack of political liberties by a retreat into privacy. The infection of *perestroika* changed all this in 1989. The fraudulent local election in the spring, manipulated by the ruling party, led to protests. The turn to the West by the reformist Communist government of Hungary enabled East German tourists to escape over the frontier into Austria. Dissident movements began to organise openly, demanding thorough-going reforms of the entire political system. From September onwards increasingly large protest processions took place, culminating in a mass meeting in Leipzig on 9 October. When this passed off peacefully it was evident that the regime had lost the will or the capacity to crush dissent.

After a change in the SED leadership the Berlin Wall was opened on 9 November. A series of interim administrations, which contained members of the dissident movements, culminated in free elections on 18 March 1990. These were won by the CDU and its allies on a platform of national unification. Currency and economic union of the two states took place on 1 July; a Treaty of Unification, under which the GDR acceded to the Federal Republic, came into force on 3 October. On 2 December all-German elections took place. The division of Germany was at an end.

Unified Germany

Throughout modern times there has been a tension between national unity and democracy in Germany. The failure of democratic self-determination in 1848–9 has weighed heavily on the traditions of German political thinking. The partial unification of the nation in 1871 was imposed militarily from above. The two more recent experiments in democracy, those of 1918–19 and 1949, were the outcome of military defeat and national humiliation. Those who preached the primacy of the national interest were therefore feared as enemies of public liberties; those who preached the primacy of domestic reform as 'scoundrels without a fatherland' (*vaterlandslose Gesellen*). This tension was unquestionably one of the reasons for the weakness of the Weimar Republic. In contrast the much more successful and stable democracy of the Federal Republic evolved under the conditions of national division. For the first time in modern German history there was widespread, even overwhelming, support for the prevailing political institutions, so much so that the political scientist Dolf Sternberger coined the term 'constitutional patriotism' to describe the new allegiance that West Germans felt towards their non-national state.

Allegiance of this kind applied only to a diminishing minority of the GDR's citizens. Indeed, the ease with which German unification happened on the basis of a take-over of the GDR by the Basic Law and socio-economic system of the Federal Republic suggests that more GDR citizens identified with the Bonn Republic than with their own. For the first time Germans now live in a nation state based on the free vote of a majority; for the first time national unity was achieved by going with the grain of democracy, not against it. Yet the fact that this one state contains two populations with different histories, assumptions and expectations is the biggest challenge to its survival. Its society is less homogeneous, and the gap in living standards is greater than in either of its predecessors. After nearly a decade of unity there may be strong discontent with particular aspects of the new state, but there is no widespread alienation from the political system, least of all its most distinctive characteristics, the wide autonomy of the Länder and the rule of law. The gap between the citizen and the state is there: no political system has been able to abolish it. But the gap does not assume those proportions that have led to the collapse of so many regimes in Germany.

FURTHER READING

The most comprehensive introduction to German history of the period up to 1945 is Gordon Craig, *Germany 1866–1945* (Oxford: Clarendon, 1978), while Peter Pulzer, *Germany 1870–1945: Politics, State-Building and War*, (Oxford: Oxford University Press, 1997) concentrates on system change and state power in the German context. The only modern constitutional history is Hans Boldt, *Deutsche Verfassungsgeschichte*, vol. II (Munich: Beck, 1990). John Breuilly (ed.) *The State of Germany* (London: Longman, 1992) contains a number of useful essays on constitutional topics.

For the imperial period there is Hans-Ulrich Wehler's influential but controversial *The German Empire 1871–1918* (Leamington Spa: Berg, 1985) and Volker Berghahn, *Imperial Germany 1871–1914* (Providence: Berghahn, 1994). The Weimar Republic is covered by A. J. Nicholls, *Weimar and the Rise of Hitler* (3rd edn., Basingstoke: Macmillan, 1991), Edgar J. Feuchtwanger, *From Weimar to Hitler 1918–33* (Basingstoke: Macmillan, 1995) and Heinrich August Winkler's detailed and magisterial *Weimar 1918–1933. Die Geschichte der ersten deutschen Demokratie* (Munich: Beck, 1993). Useful books on special topics include Gordon A. Craig, *The Politics of the Prussian Army 1640–1945* (Oxford: Oxford University Press, 1955), Lother Gall, *Bismarck. Der Weiße Revolutionär* (Munich; Propyläen, 1980), John C. G. Röhl, *The Kaiser and his Court. Wilhelm II and the Government of Germany* (Cambridge: Cambridge University Press, 1994) and Peter Pulzer, *Jews and the German State. The Political History of a Minority 1848–1933* (Oxford: Blackwell, 1992).

The literature on the Third Reich is voluminous. The classical interpretations in Franz Neumann, *Behemoth. The Structure and Practice of National Socialism* (London: Gollancz, 1942) are still worth consulting. Among more recent works Karl Dietrich Bracher, *The German Dictatorship* (London: Weidenfeld & Nicholson, 1971), Martin Broszat, *The Hitler State* (London: Longman, 1981), Ian Kershaw, *The Nazi Dictatorship. Problems and Perspectives of Interpretation* (3rd edn. London: Longman, 1993) and Norbert Frei, *National Socialist Rule in Germany. The Führer State 1933–1945* (Oxford: Blackwell, 1993) stand out. The apparatus of repression is covered by Robert Gellately, *The Gestapo and German Society* (Oxford: Clarendon, 1990) and Helmut Krausnick *et al.*, *Anatomy of the SS State* (London: Collins, 1968). The resistance is covered by, among others, Michael Balfour, *Withstanding Hitler* (London: Routledge, 1988) and Hedley Bull (ed.), *The Challenge of the Third Reich* (Oxford: Clarendon, 1986).

For the post-1945 period books that cover the whole period include Henry A. Turner, *Germany From Partition to Unification* (New Haven: Yale University Press, 1993) and Peter Pulzer, *German Politics 1945–1995* (Oxford: Oxford University Press, 1995). Ralf Dahrendorf's *Society and Democracy in Germany* (London: Weidenfeld & Nicholson, 1968) brilliantly puts the post-war experience into historical and sociological perspective. The making of the Basic Law is covered by Peter H. Merkl, *The Origins of the West German Republic* (Oxford: Oxford University Press, 1963). For general surveys of the West German and unified German systems of government the best books are William E. Paterson and David Southern, *Governing Germany* (Oxford: Blackwell, 1991), Gordon Smith *et al.* (eds.) *Developments in German Politics 2* (Basingstoke: Macmillan, 1996) and Klaus von Beyme, *Das politische System der BRD nach der Vereinigung* (Munich: Piper, 1992).

All are likely to be updated periodically. For the German Democratic Republic, see David Childs, *The GDR: Moscow's German Ally* (London: Allen & Unwin, 1983) and Hermann Weber, *Die DDR 1949–1990* (Munich: dtv, 1993); of the many books on unification and its consequences Gerd-Joachim Glaessner and Ian Wallace (eds.), *The Unification Process in Germany. From Dictatorship to Democracy* (Oxford: Berg, 1992) and Michael G. Huelshoff *et al.* (eds.), *From Bundesrepublik to Deutschland* (Ann Arbor: Michigan University Press, 1993) may be singled out.

On the history of political parties, see Susanne Miller and Heinrich Potthoff, *History of the German Social Democratic Party from 1848 to the Present* (Leamington Spa: Berg, 1986), James J. Sheehan, *German Liberalism in the Nineteenth Century* (Chicago: Chicago University Press, 1978), and Eleanor Evans, *The German Center Party 1870–1933* (Carbondale: Southern Illinois University Press, 1981). Larry Eugene Jones and James Retallack (eds.), *Elections, Mass Politics and Social Change in Modern Germany* (Cambridge: Cambridge University Press, 1992) contains a wealth of interesting material. The development of the electoral system is covered by Peter Pulzer in Vernon Bogdanor and David Butler (eds.), *Democracy and Elections. Electoral Systems and their Political Consequences* (Cambridge: Cambridge University Press, 1983). For the Federal Republic and beyond, see Stephen Padgett and Tony Burkett, *Political Parties and Elections in West Germany* (London: Hurst, 1986) and Stephen Padgett (ed.), *Parties and Party Systems in the New Germany* (Aldershot: Dartmouth, 1993).

JOHN BREUILLY

2

German national identity

Introduction

This chapter addresses three closely related questions: Where was/is Germany? Who were/are Germans? What kind of a nation state was/is the German state? The discussion will concentrate on politics and their impact on 'ordinary' Germans, leaving aside the well-studied subject of nationalist doctrines.

Nationalism is modern. As a doctrine it asserts a connection between culture and politics. First, it claims to identify and describe a particular nation, an all-encompassing group of people, usually concentrated into a particular territory, which is constituted variously through common language, history, sentiments, customs, racial characteristics, etc. The precise form of the claim varies from case to case and within each case. The German National Assembly of 1848–9 had a different conception of the nation from that of the Third Reich but there was a common assertion of the existence of a nation.

Second, nationalism demands that the nation should be self-determined. This normally means that the nation should have its own territorial state. There are disagreements concerning the type of autonomy and how the nation state should be organised. Nevertheless the 'core' doctrine of nationalism combines assertions about cultural identity with demands for self-determination. The manner in which this core doctrine is elaborated into particular forms of nationalism is most easily and frequently studied through the writings of nationalist intellectuals and the programmes of nationalist movements. More difficult to estimate is the impact of such ideas upon state and society.

The unification period, 1848–1871

No single German state existed in 1848. In the popular movements of March, a constant refrain was the demand for a German parliament. Once this demand had been granted, elections had to be held. The decision as to *where* to hold elections implied a view of national boundaries. The obvious and practical decision was to take the boundaries of the German Confederation with the addition of the Prussian provinces of East and West Prussia.

Schleswig was outside the Confederation although ruled, under personal union, by the King of Denmark with the twin duchy of Holstein which was inside the Confederation. Logic and realism suggested there be no 'German' elections in Schleswig. However, there was a sharp reaction to the decision of the Danish government to incorporate Schleswig into Denmark. This led to the demand by the *Vorparlament* (an assembly of political activists meeting in Frankfurt in April to prepare for a German parliament) that Schleswig be incorporated into the Confederation. The Federal Diet did not do this but local Germans formed a provisional government for Schleswig-Holstein and returned representatives to the Frankfurt Parliament. From late May military intervention by Prussia on behalf of the Confederation brought Holstein and southern parts of Schleswig under German control.

The Grand Duchy of Posen (Poznan) was ruled in personal union by the King of Prussia and had a majority of Polish speakers. Logically the decision that Germany consisted of the territory of the Confederation meant there should be no 'German' elections in Posen. However, the Prussian government requested that western parts of Posen be incorporated into the Confederation. The *Vorparlament* supported and the Federal Diet complied with this request.

Thus the boundaries of 'Germany' had been extended beyond those of the pre-March Confederation. The Prussian population in the Confederation now exceeded that of the Habsburg Empire. In Posen and Schleswig local Germans reacted against counter-national claims and looked to German states and public opinion for support. In Posen liberals favoured the restoration of a Polish state which meant returning territory acquired through the partitions of Poland, including Posen. The ethnic demarcation line drawn in 1848 was a way of limiting the impact of this policy upon local Germans. In Schleswig the German view was that this was indissolubly tied to Holstein. Germans and Danes resisted ethnic partition. German nationalists argued that succession to the Duchies went through the male line and that on the extinction of this line the personal union with Denmark should cease and the Duchies be brought under the rule of a German prince.

Different boundary problems were posed by the Habsburg Empire. In the Confederation were the historic crownlands (the Archduchy of Austria), the province of Tyrol and the Kingdom of Bohemia-Moravia. The eastern half of the empire and the Italian provinces of Lombardy and Venetia were excluded. There was a German-speaking majority in the crownlands, a substantial Italian minority in the Tyrol and a Slav-speaking majority in Bohemia and Moravia. There was no difficulty with elections in the Tyrol but a Slav boycott in Bohemia and Moravia.

The boundaries for the elections – excepting Schleswig and part of Posen – conformed to an 'historic' and institutional definition of Germany. No national demands were made upon territories ruled by states outside the Confederation but where many German speakers lived, such as the Baltic provinces of Russia. Conversely, no territory was surrendered because a majority of its inhabitants were not native speakers of German.

Who could vote in the elections? The problem is identifying any modern notion of citizenship, let alone national citizenship. If citizenship means equality before the law, this did not exist in societies structured by privilege. If citizenship means political participation, this did not exist where the few elected institutions were estate-based diets. If citizenship means state membership (*Staatsangehörigkeit*), it did not exist as many states did not clearly define membership. The only point of such a definition would have been to ration claims to poor relief but in most states this was the responsibility of local government (*Gemeinde*). In 1842, when the Prussian government overrode that local power, it also introduced a law defining state membership.

German states made no distinction between people from other German states and non-German states. The Confederal Act of 1814 had stipulated that people moving between member states be freed from any emigration tax, but without a corresponding freedom of immigration, this provision had little significance.

'National citizenship' in 1848, therefore, meant only eligibility to vote in national elections. It was considered so self-evident that only men could vote that this was not even made explicit. The definition of 'men' varied; within different parts of Prussia the age of majority was set variously at 21, 24 and 25. The *Vorparlament* decided that large numbers of men could vote. The key qualification was that men should be 'independent' (*selbständig*). It was agreed that this excluded domestic servants and those in receipt of poor relief. However, some states included many wage-labourers and defined domestic service very broadly. One cannot construct a usable category of German citizenship from the extraordinary events of early 1848.

Article I of the Imperial Constitution of 1849 declared:

> The German Reich consists of the territory of the former German Federation. The position of the Duchy of Schleswig remains to be determined.

The first article (Art.131) of Part 6: 'The Basic Rights of the German People', declared:

> The German people consists of the citizens of the states which make up the Reich.

Subsequent articles stipulated that every German had the right of German citizenship which could be exercised in every German state, including voting for the national parliament, freedom of movement, settlement and the acquisition of property. No state could discriminate in its civil, criminal and litigation rights between its citizens and those of other German states. Other articles established equality before the law.

So the constitution defined a national territory and outlined a vision of national citizenship which combined equality before the law with political and social rights.

The territorial definition meant little. The parliament offered the hereditary Emperorship of the new state to the King of Prussia, thereby ensuring the exclusion of the Habsburg Empire. The constitution left regulation of freedom of movement, settlement and residence for later.

German unification meant *a union of German states*. Boundaries and membership were tied to individual states. The attempted solution of the Frankfurt Parliament is called *kleindeutsch* (little-German; Germany with Austria being called *großdeutsch* or great-German) because power was vested in the Prussian state. The relationship between the two major states determined the boundaries of the new state. The members of the national state were the sum of the members of the individual German states, not the other way round.

This view of the German national state – a new term in 1848 – I call federalist. Federalism was rooted in the tradition of the Holy Roman Empire. It left most power with individual states, including those concerning the everyday lives of most people. Within individual states much was left to the *Gemeinden*. The Imperial Constitution was a radical advance in that it vested such powers as declaring war and making peace in a national state, but it was still based on pre-industrial, federalist and imperial assumptions.

This radical advance was unacceptable to most states and many groups. Catholics rejected Prussian dominance; Protestants Habsburg dominance. Guildsmen, nobles and clergy rejected the abolition of their privileges. *Gemeinde* members were unhappy with erosion of local control. By May 1849 the idea of national unity was less popular than it had been in March 1848.

Debates on the German state made few references to culture. A Czech-speaker from Bohemia or a Polish-speaker from West Prussia was a citizen of a German state and, therefore, a German citizen. However, many such people rejected German citizenship. The idea of the German state was based indirectly and implicitly upon a notion of German culture. The constitution recognised this in Article 188:

> The non-German speaking people of Germany are guaranteed their national development, namely, equal rights for their languages, in so far as they exist in their territories, in ecclesiastical matters, in education, in administration of local affairs and of justice.

German-speakers assumed that the language of government and higher education would be German. Non-German speakers participating in these institutions were expected to learn German. Educated Germans distinguished between historic, 'high' cultures and non-historical, 'low' cultures. The first were associated with the German but also the Italian, Polish and Magyar languages, as languages used by nobles, state officials and academics. The second were equated with German dialects, perfectly acceptable for domestic and local use but no more. 'Nationality' meant membership of a high culture.

This view commanded broad agreement amongst educated Germans but also educated Britons and Frenchmen. There was little support for 'small' nation nationalism in mid-century Europe, apart from special cases like Belgium and Greece. This did not imply contempt for 'folk culture'; there was much interest in folklore and custom. However, nationality was linked to the existence of societies led by cultured elites with a tradition of statehood. Nationality and ethnicity were separate matters.

An ethnic view of nationality was irrelevant to most Germans. It did matter to Germans in borderland areas who encountered rival claims from non-Germans. When the conflict turned into violence – as in Schleswig, Posen and Bohemia – that led to German nationalist demands being put more sharply and extremely. Such borderland disputes could temporarily dominate the national question and introduce an ethnic tone into the language of nationality. They also provided Germans with causes on which they could unite, whereas questions of sovereignty and citizenship divided Germans.

The Imperial Constitution was never implemented. The only people who fought in its defence were democrats who were anti-monarchical and anti-Prussian. The crushing of radicalism in the spring of 1849 and continuing counter-revolution into the 1850s largely destroyed democratic nationalism.

Failure clarified matters. Nationalists had hoped to combine a national state with the Habsburg Empire through devices such as personal union: the Habsburg Emperor as Archduke of Austria and King of Bohemia and Moravia would belong to the German state, but as, for example, King of Hungary, would be outside the German state. Because the idea of the state as a unitary and sovereign institution with a clearly defined territory and subject/citizen population was not very well developed, the problem of sovereignty as something indivisible was not apparent.

The resistance of Austria either to internal division or any surrender of influence over the rest of Germany made the problem clear. The federal and imperial idea continued to attract many in the national movement, especially in the smaller German states, but the *großdeutsch* tradition tended thereafter to become an eclectic group of interests mainly united by their opposition to a Prussia-dominated Germany.

There were major changes in the way the national idea was projected in the 1850s and early 1860s. The suppression of democratic nationalism, Habsburg opposition to anything stronger than the restored Confederation and the lack of popular support or unity within the national movement persuaded many nationally minded Germans, especially if they were Protestant and Prussian, to look to Prussia for a lead in creating a stronger national authority. Prussia flirted with the idea in early 1848 and pursued such a policy in 1849–50 until forced to abandon it by Austria. Nevertheless, for liberals this *kleindeutsch* policy required liberalising Prussia and surrendering many of its powers to a national state. The Prussian monarchy of the 1850s rejected such changes.

The national idea took on a materialist character. Liberal nationalists looked to the Prussian-dominated Customs Union (*Zollverein*) as providing means and motive for greater unity. The *Zollverein* bound states more closely to one another. It created mutual dependency and interaction between Germans of different regions and thereby stimulated a stronger sense of common identity. Economic development meant one could envisage national unity not only as an end in itself but as something which promoted prosperity as well as power. Such advances were equated with moral progress. The whole prospect, although presented in a realistic tone, possessed utopian features.

These ideas were taken up by a substantial minority movement in the late 1850s and early 1860s which was organised in choral societies, gymnastic associations, sharp-shooting clubs, educational associations and professional organisations and found political expression in the *Nationalverein* (established 1859), the Prussian Progressive Party (1861) and other liberal parties. Outside Protestant, especially urban, regions this movement was not very popular.

Social changes fostered a popular sense of national identity. Economic development brought in its wake greater geographical and job mobility. Cross-border migration pushed governments towards bilateral agreements, reducing the tendency to treat each other's subjects as foreigners. Large numbers of Germans could now move from one German state to another more easily. Arguably such mobility did more to stimulate a national sense of identity amongst Germans than any amount of nationalist propaganda.

Prussia was neither willing nor able to lead the national movement. Dynastic conservatism accounted for the unwillingness; lack of power for the incapacity. By the time Bismarck became Prime Minister in September 1862 the incapacity was disappearing thanks to military reforms, diplomatic and military setbacks for Austria, increased dominance over the *Zollverein*, rapid economic growth and the mobilisation of a pro-Prussian national movement. However, Bismarck opposed this movement for nearly four years. The war against Denmark, leading to the acquisition of Schleswig-Holstein in 1864, alienated nationalists because it was a dynastic war in which Austria and Prussia cooperated and the Duchies were occupied by the two powers rather than being made a Confederal state. The approach of war between Austria and Prussia in 1866 was regarded with horror.

Only after Prussian victory was a positive relationship established between Bismarck and the national movement, in particular through the 'nation-building' work of the dominant party of the new North German Confederation, the National Liberals. A form of common citizenship (*Bundesindigenat*) including rights of movement, settlement and occupation was devised, along with common rules on currency, weights and measures, commercial and industrial legislation. The association of national development with economic development, civilisation, Protestantism and the Prussian state meant a rejection of federalist, imperial and Catholic national traditions.

The war against France in 1870–1 further promoted a common sense of nationality, including the predominantly Catholic South German states which had not been members of the North German Confederation but whose soldiers fought in the war. The war increased the xenophobic and ethnic elements in nationalism, with denunciations and vicious stereotyping of the French and brutal justifications offered for the annexation of Alsace-Lorraine.

The nation-state period, 1871–1945

One should not exaggerate the long-term impact of the war upon national sentiment. Catholics, democrats, labour activists and state loyalists were unhappy with a Prussian-dominated, dynastic, authoritarian state. Some liberals accepted it only as the starting-point for extensive reform. People from these camps found themselves in opposition to the new state and from the 1880s Bismarck was having difficulties obtaining a pro-governmental majority in the Reichstag.

The boundaries of the 1871 Reich were both more and less than those of the 1849 constitution. War against Denmark secured Schleswig in union with Holstein as a Prussian province. Posen was included as a part of Prussia. Alsace-Lorraine was brought under Prussian control. These extended boundaries were Prussian rather than German. Most of the subjects gained were non-German speakers opposed to incorporation into a German state. This expansion promoted a sense of national identity, but principally amongst non-Germans. Tension in these areas radicalised local German nationalism, especially against Poles.

Austrian Germany was excluded, contrary to all national traditions. There was no 'national' content to the southern boundary of the new state. For many Germans on both sides of the boundary the new state was truncated and mutilated by this loss. That Bismarck made a virtue of the boundary, as preserving the legitimate and stabilising Habsburg Empire, and insisted that Germany was a 'satiated' power with no thoughts of further expansion, simply exacerbated the offence. Both where the state was larger and smaller than that envisaged in 1849, it was less national. Whereas Article I of the 1849 constitution defined the territory of the new state as national, Article 1 of the 1871 constitution simply listed its member states.

The 1871 constitution contained no section on the basic rights of German citizens. There was the political right of all men to vote in Reichstag elections. There was also Article 3:

> For the whole of Germany one common nationality exists with the effect that every person (subject, State citizen) belonging to any of the federated States is to be treated in every other of the federated States as a born native and accordingly must be permitted to have a fixed dwelling, to trade, to be appointed to public offices, to acquire property, to obtain the rights of a State citizen, and to enjoy all other civil rights under the same presuppositions as the natives, and likewise to be treated equally with regard to legal prosecution or legal protection . . .

This did not create common rights throughout Germany. Rather it meant that all Germans enjoyed the same rights in any German state. However, it was the individual state which determined what those rights were. There were also limitations such as access to poor relief in the *Gemeinde* and the exclusion of Bavaria from many provisions. Given that things regulated by governments which concerned people most, like education, religion, poor relief and personal and property taxation, were state competences, this made the Empire a remote institution.

There was no attempt to harmonise state constitutions. Only in 1873 did the government provide a more explicit definition of national citizenship, building on the North Confederation *Bundesindigenat* and an 1869 law. The principle was that of *ius sanguinis* (the law of the blood), meaning that citizenship was automatically acquired through descent. This has been regarded as an 'ethnic' principle in contrast to the 'civic' principle of *ius solis* (the law of the soil) used by France which made place of birth the criterion for the acquisition of citizenship. This is to misunderstand the contemporary significance of the law which took over principles used by German states; it was a codification of state practice, not a statement of principle for a new nation state. It automatically included Polish speakers in Prussian provinces and automatically excluded German-speaking Austrians. Article 3 and the 1873 codification made it easier for Germans to move between states but this meant that Prussians going to Saxony would be treated like native Saxons, not that they would be subject to the same German law in both states.

All this fitted a federalist structure. Yet the state offended federalist tradition because one state – Prussia – made up over two-thirds of the total population and territory. Novel methods were developed for coordinating Prussian and German institutions. The new state had difficulties finding national symbols and ceremonies to legitimise itself. It could not adopt radical, unitary or greater-German national symbols like the black-red-gold flag or the anthem *Deutschland, Deutschland über alles*. (This phrase asserted national power over the states, an anathema to Bismarck who defended state particularism.) Equally it could not use Prussian symbols which would offend non-Prussians. The result was a series of uneasy compromises, as with the issue of a national flag. Something was required for German shipping, embassies and consulates. The issue was approached in this practical way. Article 55 in the section dealing with shipping and navigation abruptly declared: 'The flag of the navy and of the merchant shipping is black-white-red' – a compromise between the German black-red-gold and the Prussian black and white.

There were many such tensions. What title should the King of Prussia adopt as head of the Imperial state and what relationship should he have to the princes of the individual states (including himself!)? Liberals were unhappy about the adoption of terms such as *Kaiser* and *Reich* as hangovers from a discredited imperial tradition. At the ceremony of proclamation at Versailles in January 1871 there were disputes as to the wording of the *vivat*. The Grand Duke of Baden avoided constitutional complications by crying: 'Hail Emperor Wilhelm!' The preamble to the 1871 constitution referred only to the King of Prussia who, in the name of the North German Confederation of which he was President, concluded a treaty with other German princes. The first substantial reference came in Section 4 of the constitution, where Article II declares: 'The Presidency of the Federation belongs to the King of Prussia who bears the name of the German Emperor.' There followed an enumeration of the powers of the Emperor. The title *Deutscher Kaiser* is simply the name used by the King of

Prussia in his capacity as President of the Federation! There was no pomp and ceremony and a deliberate avoidance of the contentious alternative formulations: Emperor of Germany or Emperor of the Germans. 'German' did not describe a territory or people but a quality of the Emperor.

This personal focus recurs in the ways in which celebrations of the Battle of Sedan, Wilhelm I and Bismarck became the major festivals and symbols of the new Germany. For the nationalist middle class the truly national symbol of Germany's power was not its army – that remained too Prussian, aristocratic and conservative for their tastes – but the navy, a creation of the new state. Dynastic tradition jostled uneasily with new national sentiments in the symbols and institutions of the Second Empire. A flight into a distant history, like the great monument to Hermann (who had defeated the Roman legions) in the Teutoburg Forest, combined with the traditionless nationalism of navy building and *Weltpolitik* (world politics).

At the political level national identity was increasingly contested. The National Liberals lost their dominance and tended to an increasingly conservative position, using national arguments in lieu of other guiding principles to defend the status quo. Catholics, socialists and left-liberals, who by 1912 represented a majority of German voters, rejected official nationalism and argued that the Empire would only be truly national when more parliamentary and democratic. Such views were dismissed by those in power as anti-national. On the Right there developed a radical nationalism which stressed ethnicity at home and aggression abroad and was critical of the cautious and conservative qualities of the state. New demands were raised for the acquisition of overseas empire and the assertion of German power over a broader zone within Europe.

This greater stress upon ethnicity can be seen in the *Staatsangehörigkeit* (citizenship) law of 1913. Pressure for such a law had come since 1900 from the Reichstag which was concerned about the treatment of immigrants, protection of emigrants, and the problems created by varying policies on citizenship in different states. The law eventually passed reflected official and radical nationalist views and was only reluctantly accepted by the Reichstag. The principle of *ius sanguinis* was reiterated with an ethnic twist, aimed at promoting Germandom abroad and preventing Polish immigrant labour gaining citizenship.

Institutional and social changes had a greater impact on national identity. The Imperial state acquired new functions not envisaged by its founders. Protectionism made tariff policy important and led to political parties and pressure groups lobbying in Berlin. Social insurance legislation made the Empire responsible for large-scale redistribution of resources. Navy building was an imperial responsibility. The imperial government laid down guidelines on public health. The proliferation of new functions brought in its wake new imperial agencies and an imperial civil service. This had to be paid for, leading in 1909 to a crisis, the resignation of the Chancellor and the assumption of new fiscal powers by the Empire. Imperial legislation increased in significance. Politicians and voters adjusted to the increased powers and mass franchise for the Reichstag. Electoral participation increased from 50 per cent to 85 per cent; three times as many people voted in 1912 as in 1871. They voted almost entirely for national parties. By 1914 there was clearly a mass political nation.

Between 1871 and 1914 Germany became an industrial society, accompanied by massive east–west migration, large-scale urbanisation and a shift from net emigration to net immigration. People moved around more, crossing state boundaries as they did so. Mass literacy was achieved. This all increased awareness of common membership of a single society and state. Even if critical of how that state and society were organised, people were bound to it in many ways. General standards of living increased for most people in the last decade before 1914; state welfare benefits reached millions of people; the increased importance of the Reichstag meant that even the most oppositional party, the Social Democratic party, engaged in making deals to advance its interests. While some Germans supported their state in August 1914 as expansionist nationalists, most did so out of a sense that 'their' country, with all its faults, was threatened from outside, especially by reactionary Russia. The common sense of national identity temporarily masked different understandings of the war from official, radical right and democratic positions and contributed to an appearance of enthusiastic unity.

The war was a nationalising experience. Millions served in the armed forces. The Imperial state extended its control over the economy. The Auxiliary Service Law of December 1916 turned civil society into a branch of the army; all workers were regarded as conscripts. People were bombarded with propaganda which stereotyped and demonised Germany's enemies. The everyday experiences of death, injury and deprivation made clear to Germans that they belonged to a 'community of fate'.

That did not mean Germans agreed about the war. From 1916 increasing numbers of Germans came to believe that their government bore much of the responsibility for the war and stood in the way of a reasonable peace settlement. A widespread and intense sense of national identity does not mean consensus but rather that every conflicting element takes national identity for granted and believes that it better represents the national interest than its opponents.

The revolution of 1918–19 was based on the assumption that the war was lost. The right-wing legend of the 'stab-in-the-back', apart from being objectively untrue, misrepresented the feelings of those who acted to bring about an armistice, the downfall of the monarchy, the formation of a parliamentary republic and the conclusion of a peace treaty. The values of the 'Weimar coalition' (left-liberals, the Catholic Centre Party and the majority Social Democrats), based on political and social reform and on the fighting of a defensive war, were as firmly rooted in national traditions as those of General Staff or the Fatherland Party.

Germany became ethnically homogenous through the loss of Alsace-Lorraine, part of Schleswig, and Polish areas. Germans moved from those areas into Germany, increasing the sense of ethnic homogeneity. Austria, reduced to a rump state, ethnically German and bereft of imperial pretension, demanded union with Germany, appealing to the principle of national self-determination being applied elsewhere by the Allies. The idea of Germany as an (incomplete) ethnic nation state was much stronger in 1919 than it had been in 1914.

The preamble to the Weimar constitution declared it to be the product of:

> The German people (*das Deutsche Volk*), united in every branch and inspired by the determination to renew and establish its realm in freedom and justice . . .

Article 110 declared:

> Nationality in the Reich and the States is acquired and terminated as may be provided by the law of the Reich.

The constitution of 1871 had been an agreement of princes on behalf of the German nation, and the constitution of 1849 declared itself to be the work of a parliament, not of a people.

Article 3 declared the colours of the Reich to be black, red and gold. By 1924 Weimar had an official national anthem, *Deutschland, Deutschland über alles*. This was a state which proudly declared its national character and used the term *Volk* to mean nation and people.

Although a federal state the Weimar Republic imposed common principles for state constitutions. The central state arrogated to itself a wider range of powers than its predecessor and reserved many rights of intervention in the affairs of individual states. The national parliament was the sovereign institution. Legal equality, welfare rights, and political participation were all components of national citizenship and partially included women in their scope.

Yet this unitary nation state with an ethnically homogenous population and an intense and widely shared sense of national identity was deeply divided. The Right condemned the 'November criminals' for treachery; the Left believed that the real crimes were those of an irresponsible monarchy opposed to the true feelings and interests of the nation. With the exception of the communists all parties agreed that the Treaty of Versailles was iniquitous but blamed others for its imposition and completely disagreed on how it was to be undone.

The strong sense of national identity, coupled with the depth of division, created a great longing for national unity. Especially in the wake of the Depression that started in 1929, large numbers of people concluded that democratic institutions could not achieve that unity. However, few Germans supported a return to monarchical government. Only communists believed in class and internationalist solutions to the problems. What alternative national principle could be invoked?

Hitler and the National Socialist party offered a clear and simple answer. They took the strong ethnic sense of nationality and twisted it in the direction of race. Race ideology had a long pedigree but had remained on the right-wing fringe. More important than race ideology, which Hitler played down in the propaganda drive of the last years of Weimar, was the leader principle (*Führerprinzip*). Max Weber (died 1920) had presciently distinguished three principles by which a state could claim legitimacy: tradition, rationality, charisma. Under this third principle legitimate power was acquired not by inheritance or election but by virtue of a special leadership quality. Hitler developed this principle within the National Socialist movement and then projected it to the national electorate. The principle was quasi-democratic (people wanted the charismatic leader) and authoritarian (the leader would command the people). Only about 40 per cent of those voting in a free election supported Hitler, many for reasons other than those proclaimed in Nazi propaganda, and they could not know that their votes would destroy the Weimar Republic, but this desire for unity imposed by a leader was crucial to Hitler's success.

It also provides a key to Hitler's conduct after January 1933. He did not seek to establish new institutions, having no faith in institutions. The Weimar constitution was never officially revoked but simply ignored. Principles which enshrined institutional over personal power, such as the rule of law or the division of powers, were violated. Race ideology became an incessant theme of propaganda. The idea of national community (*Volksgemeinschaft*) justified the destruction of institutions representing class, ideological or other interests, such as political parties (except the National Socialists) and trade unions. Language which drew attention to social divisions was banned. There were no employers and employees but workplace leaders and followers; society was not divided along class lines but consisted of functional groups, each contributing to the organic whole.

It is difficult to estimate the impact of this. The abolition of elections, freedom of speech, press and assembly, and the brutal treatment of anyone who protested, deprive the historian of evidence on popular attitudes. However, the regime became obsessed with ascertaining the popular mood, as did the exiled Social Democratic party. Evidence from these sources suggests there was no simple acceptance or rejection of official propaganda. Many Germans rejoiced in the ending of political conflict, the return to full employment and a string of bloodless foreign policy successes. However, many also experienced continuing social inequality which gave the lie to the language of national community; they feared war; they often objected to the arbitrary exercise of power by officials; they disliked policies which conflicted with their personal interests or morality. Responses varied: workers were less positive about the regime than the bourgeoisie; older people were less influenced by propaganda than youths; Catholics displayed more solidarity than Protestants.

Open resistance was impossible. There could be no public discussion of alternatives. People grumbled and sometimes this pushed the regime into policy changes. It seems likely that increasing numbers of people, especially younger people who had known little before the Third Reich, gradually came to believe that there must be 'something' in what the regime preached, even concerning matters which had not initially concerned them. Hitler appeared a genius, especially when successful. One was told so often, without any contradiction, that problems were caused by Jews, communists, foreigners, etc. So long as these scapegoats were 'others', people tended to believe what they were told or at least became indifferent to the fate of those 'others'.

People projected their own national values on to Hitler. Hitler was a 'good German', bourgeois, kind to animals, Christian, man of the people; brave front-line soldier. So long as foreign policy was confined to revising Versailles and avoided war and domestic policy focused on reducing unemployment and imposing unity through persecution of the Left and the 'coordination' (*Gleichschaltung*) of other organisations, Hitler lived up to these images. A distinction was made between *the* Führer and the little *Führers* who climbed upon the National Socialist bandwaggon. Hitler could retain popularity by distancing himself from unpopular policies such as the removal of crucifixes from schools or the euthanasia campaign (which Hitler had actually initiated!). However, Hitler could become a captive of these images, instead of leader of the assault on traditional values in the name of the harsh creed of race struggle.

There was a complex mix of ideological conversion, retreat into indifference and privacy and projection of existing values on to Hitler. Probably only a minority held stubbornly to a sense of national identity explicitly opposed to that of the regime and few turned that into active resistance. Most resistance until the last years of the regime came from communists, and was both ineffectual and anti-national. Only in 1944 did conservative nationalists attempt to overthrow the regime.

The last years of the Third Reich saw a dramatic radicalisation and implementation of its race and imperialist ideology. The main brunt of this was felt by those living beyond Germany, but German minorities, especially Jews but also gypsies, homosexuals, Jehovah's Witnesses and others were hunted, imprisoned, exploited as slave labour and murdered. Most Germans were not directly involved in such persecution but many were indirectly involved and had some inkling, if not irrefutable knowledge, of what was happening. It is difficult to judge the extent of positive commitment to these barbaric policies. There were fanatical minorities, often well-educated, who served in organisations like the SS. There were opportunists who sought to benefit from the terror and thereby contributed to its upwards spiral. Beyond that there is controversy. Even where 'ordinary' Germans were involved in mass murder, some historians have emphasised situational pressures rather than beliefs. Others argue that such pressures were aspects of a peculiar German culture producing deference to authority no matter what it ordered. It has been suggested that race propaganda and war converted many Germans to Nazism. The most negative argument is that National Socialism was an extreme expression of values already widespread within German society.

The definition of the nation as a racial community implied a radical transformation of the relationship between nationality and citizenship. In the first couple of years of the Third Reich the regime had passed some piecemeal anti-Jewish laws (e.g., to purge the Civil Service). This did not satisfy enthusiastic anti-Semites who, through the SA, SS, Gestapo and other bodies, pursued their own campaigns against Jews. Both to accommodate this anti-Semitism as well as to channel it into legal forms, Hitler agreed in September 1935 to the passing of two laws, known as the Nuremburg Laws, dealing with citizenship and the 'protection of German honour'.

The Citizenship Law made a fundamental distinction between *Reichsbürger* (citizens of the Reich) and *Staatsangehörige* (subjects of the state). Only the former, deemed to be 'of German or racially affiliated blood', had full political rights (§1,3). The Law for the Protection of German Blood and Honour, passed on the same day, was intended, amongst other things, to prevent marriage as well as any sexual relationships between Jews and Germans.

The laws were shot through with the language of blood and race and expressed Hitler's conviction that race and nationality were identical. However, state lawyers required a clear definition of the term 'Jew' in order to implement the laws. This was provided in a supplementary law in November 1935. It did not use racial criteria (which, being absurd, were also inoperable) but defined a Jew primarily according to the confessional identity of grandparents. (A 'full Jew' was one with at least three Jewish grandparents.) The real significance of the laws was that, armed with this legal distinction (itself frequently and arbitrarily extended), the regime was able to take further measures against Jews, for example ones designed to drive Jews out of business and the professions. Such policies of *Sonderbehandlung* ('special treatment', Nazi-speak for the liquidation of racially undesirable groups) habituated Germans to anti-Jewish measures as everyday state policy and were to culminate in systematic mass murder.

Apart from reducing Jews to the status of 'subject', the Reich Citizenship Law of 1935 did not advance legally beyond the *Staatsangehörigkeit* law of 1913. There had been an intention of issuing Reich citizenship certificates but this was never put into practice. All people, other than Jews, defined as German citizens prior to the Reich Citizenship Law continued to be provisionally classified as such up to 1945. In any case, the very principle of citizenship was destroyed. The 'privilege' of political rights accorded to Reich citizens was hardly significant in the Third

Reich. Equality under the law meant nothing when the rule of law was abandoned, state or quasi-state agencies with special privileges created, police powers expanded at the expense of the courts, and the word of Hitler regarded as having the force of law. Lawyers tried in vain to define the *Führer* principle but, as Weber had insisted, charismatic rule resists institutionalisation. Bureaucracies operated their routines but in an increasingly lawless and arbitrary world.

Just as rational definitions of statehood and citizenship were destroyed and replaced with arbitrary power, so too was the definition of national boundaries. In the early years of the Third Reich many Germans believed Hitler was undoing the injustices of Versailles. When national claims extended to Austria and the Sudetenland, it was possible to appeal to the principle of 'greater Germany'. However, the extension of German rule over much of Europe made national boundaries irrelevant. The idea of living space (*Lebensraum*) and racial empire replaced that of a plurality of territorially defined nation states.

It is debatable whether most Germans found this attractive. Few were keen to be pioneer settlers in the east. Most were unenthusiastic about war unless it led to quick victories. Once the war effort faltered in the east, the idea of racial empire lost its superficial attraction. More important was the creation of a racially divided society in Germany through the mass importation of foreign labour. Many Germans participated in the subordination and exploitation of these foreigners.

From defeat to unification, 1945–1989

With Germany's defeat National Socialism was discredited by its failure and its irrationalism and barbarism. How far there was a future for moderate national values was to be worked out between Germany and the victors.

At the end of the First World War positive views of the nation state were sufficiently strong to prevent German partition. After 1945 the Third Reich had so discredited the national idea that it was continuity for the German nation state which was inconceivable. The notion of unconditional surrender implied that the Allies intended to destroy utterly what had gone before. Nevertheless, the loss of German territory to Poland and the partition of Germany into three parts (Austria, the three western zones of occupation, and the Soviet zone of occupation) were not agreed policies but developed along with the Cold War.

There were few protests about partition. Many Germans felt shame and horror at what had been done in their name during the war. Many more accepted Allied power as a brute fact and were preoccupied with survival. Germans were forced out of areas which were incorporated into states like Poland, Czechoslovakia and Hungary. This created a focus of national resentment in the Federal Republic. Austria became neutral and Austrians tried to forget or to deny that Austria had ever been a willing part of the Third Reich. The German Democratic Republic, officially socialist and tied to the USSR, grounded its legitimacy upon class, although until the 1974 constitution it officially subscribed to the 'two states, one nation' doctrine and proclaimed national unity as a distant goal.

In the Federal Republic of Germany national identity was addressed in terms of boundaries and citizenship. The Preamble to the Basic Law of 1949 declared itself the product of the inhabitants of the Federal States (Länder) who also acted 'on behalf of those Germans to whom participation was denied'. The constitution called upon: 'The entire German people . . . to achieve in free self-determination the unity and freedom of Germany'.

German citizenship was defined by descent according to the 1913 law and this was projected on to the territory of Germany as of 31 December 1937, i.e. excluding Austria but including some Polish territory as well as all of the German Democratic Republic. The Basic Law also offered citizenship to the *Volksdeutsche*, ethnic Germans who continued to live in other parts of eastern Europe.

This could look like expansionist and ethnic nationalism. It was nothing of the kind. The Basic Law was enacted with the full support of the western Allies. The Federal Republic defined itself as a liberal democracy within the western alliance. Its claim to speak for other Germans was grounded on liberal democratic assumptions in relation to the German Democratic Republic. So far as the *Volksdeutsche* were concerned, the concern was to offer refuge to Germans, often forced to settle in eastern regions under the Third Reich, for whom the Federal Republic felt responsibility. The very term 'Basic Law' attested to the provisional character of the state being constructed.

Liberal democratic identification with the west was more important than national principles. For Adenauer the priority was to integrate the Federal Republic into the supra-national institutions of the west. The government rejected neutralism as the basis for unification, as Stalin suggested in 1952. The Berlin Wall in 1961 hardened separation between the two states.

Neither the Federal Republic nor the Democratic Republic encouraged positive attitudes towards nationality, but emphasised a supranational idea – liberal democracy and socialism respectively. Nationality was given a positive accent only within that broader value system. The recent history of Germany was largely neglected in both countries although for different reasons and in different ways. In the Democratic Republic the focus was on the 'toiling masses', not national elites. The nationalism and barbarism of the Third Reich were attributed to the death-throes of capitalism. In the Federal Republic conservative historians sought to detach the history of the Third Reich from what had happened earlier.

All this helped promote negative views of nationality. When, from the 1960s, there was an increased engagement with the Third Reich in the Federal Republic, the effect on younger Germans was to increase that negativity. Many young west Germans in opinion surveys defined themselves as *west* Germans, Europeans, or in regional terms, and agreed to the proposition that the Democratic Republic was *Ausland*, its inhabitants foreigners. Liberal intellectuals argued that political commitment should take the form of 'constitutional patriotism'.

Ostpolitik had contradictory meanings in relation to national identity. By taking separate states as its starting point it accepted the legitimacy of continued political division, but justified this by the need to bring together members of a divided nation. The contradiction was resolved by decoupling nationality from statehood and politics. Anxious conservative intellectuals bemoaned the decline of national identity and the abandonment of the goal of unification. Although governments led by Kohl from 1982 accepted much of *Ostpolitik* they also cultivated a cultural sense of nationality. The Democratic Republic also cultivated positive attitudes towards national history, arguing that certain individuals and events (e.g. Luther and the Reformation; Bismarck and unification) had contributed towards progress.

More important and difficult to assess was what was happening at the everyday level. Stable institutions generate their own 'identity' amongst people in the form of shared habits and assumptions. The two states, merely by surviving for forty years, created distinct identities. There were cross-border elements to this. *Ostpolitik* stimulated contacts between the two states, ranging from family visits to major economic subventions, flowing from west to east. This, coupled with access to citizenship offered by the Basic Law to the citizens of the Democratic Republic, meant that west Germans were inclined to regard east Germans as less fortunate fellow-nationals for whom they assumed some responsibility. In the Democratic Republic, the failure of the regime to generate popular support, combined with constant exposure to the superior life-style of western Germany, led many to focus their dreams upon joining that western world.

Unification and beyond, 1989 to the present

None of this directly brought about the collapse of the Democratic Republic and German unification. That was part of a larger process involving crisis in the USSR and its communist satellites. But it explains why no alternative regime could establish itself in the Democratic Republic as east Germans looked to union with the west rather than internal reform. West Germans found it difficult to deny their sense of obligation and were persuaded in 1990 to set aside their reservations about the costs.

Those costs soon became apparent and accounted for a rapid swing from optimism to pessimism. It also became clear that the two states had produced different values and identities. The coining of the terms *Wessis* and *Ossis* and accompanying stereotypes revealed this vividly.

The dream of unification under liberal democratic auspices had come true. The historian can only plot the forms national identity has assumed in the past. In the present there are many problems associated with national identity. The project of developing national pride, which plays down and 'relativises' the crimes of the Third Reich and draws attention to 'positive' aspects of national history, seems likely to grow in strength. This could be worrying if associated with a stress on ethnic identity, reinforced by the application of the citizenship principle of *ius sanguinis* which incorporates *Volksdeutsche* from eastern Europe but rejects second and even third generation descendants of immigrant workers from southern Europe. There are, however, many Germans who continue to stress the notion of 'constitutional patriotism', demand modifications of citizenship law to take account of long-term or permanent settlement, and who watch vigilantly over any revival of racism. Germany remains the most generous provider of asylum and shelter to people from eastern Europe, even after recent restrictions.

Study of the past suggests that more important than explicit policies will be subterranean changes. A unified and powerful Germany will assert itself more and be less patient with countries which stand in the way of its policies, even where the goal is greater European integration in order to bind the German nation state more tightly to supra-national institutions. If the European integration project falters, that will increase the tendency in Germany to assert national interests. The ways in which national identity will be shaped in the foreseeable future – whether in ethnic and restrictive or in civic and inclusive terms – will owe as much to economic success and international relations as to ideological arguments about nationality. Whatever happens, it is likely that national identity, having been a latent issue after 1945, or regarded as 'natural' and beyond politics, will be a matter of debate and conflict for some time to come.

FURTHER READING

Much of the reading cited by Pulzer for chapter 1 is equally relevant to the question of national identity. For English translations of the Constitutions of 1849, 1919 and 1949 see G. Hucko (ed.) *The Democratic Tradition: Four German Constitutions* (Leamington Spa: Berg, 1987). English-language introductions to the subject include: M. Hughes, *Nationalism and Society in Germany 1800–1945* (London: Edward Arnold, 1988) and H. James, *A German Identity 1770–1990* (2nd edn., London: Weidenfeld & Nicholson, 1990). In German, O. Dann, *Nation und Nationalismus in Deutschland 1770–1990* (Munich: Beck, 1993) is a good survey while two collections of essays cover key aspects of nationalism and national identity: O. Büsch and J. Sheehan (eds.), *Die Rolle der Nation in der deutschen Geschichte und Gegenwart* (Berlin: Colloquium, 1985) and B.-J. Wendt (ed.), *Vom schwierigen Zusammenwachsen der Deutschen. Nationale Identität und Nationalismus im 19. und 20. Jahrhundert* (Frankfurt/Main: Europäische Verlagsanstalt, 1992).

There are two superb but very different general histories of the national question before unification in 1871: J. Sheehan, *German History 1770–1866* (Oxford: Clarendon, 1989) and T. Nipperdey, *From Napoleon to Bismarck 1800–1866* (Dublin: Gill and Macmillan, 1996). The national movement in the period leading to unification is the subject of J. Breuilly, *The Formation of the First German Nation-State 1800–1871* (London: Macmillan, 1996) and A. Biefang, *Politisches Bürgertum in Deutschland 1857–1868. Nationale Organisation und Eliten* (Düsseldorf: Econ, 1994). Of the seminal work by H.-U. Wehler, *Deutsche Gesellschaftsgeschichte*, the third volume (Munich; Beck, 1995) on the period 1849–1914 covers nationalism in Wilhelmine Germany. G. Eley, *Reshaping the Right. Radical Nationalism and Political Change after Bismarck* (New Haven: Yale University Press, 1980) and R. Chickering, *We Men Who Feel Most German: A Cultural Study of the Pan-German League* (Boston: Harvard University Press, 1984) examine nationalist movements before 1914.

Recent studies link the discussion of nationalism as citizenship to problems of migration and immigration. R. Brubaker, *Citizenship and Nationhood in France and Germany* (Boston: Harvard University Press, 1992) examines developments since the early nineteenth century while the collection of essays edited by D. Cesarani and M. Fulbrook, *Citizenship, Nationality and Migration in Europe* (London: Routledge, 1996) and especially the contribution by M. Fulbrook, 'Germany for the Germans: Citizenship and Nationality in a Divided Nation', takes the story to the present.

Finally, two bibliographical guides offer a detailed introduction to research and further reading: H. U. Wehler (ed.), *Bibliographie zur neueren deutschen Sozialgeschichte* (Munich: Beck, 1993) and Dieter Langewiesche, 'Nation, Nationalismus, Nationalstaat. Forschungsstand und Forschungsperspektiven' in *Neue Politische Literatur*, vol. 40, 1995, pp. 119–235.

3

Elites and class structure

In the roughly 150 years between the middle of the eighteenth century and re-unification, German society faced two major economic and
socio-structural revolutions. The industrial revolution, which lasted
from the early 1840s to the eve of the First World War, turned a still predominantly feudal society into a largely industrial society. The second
revolution, which one might call a material revolution, transformed
post-war German society between 1950 and 1970 from a society deeply
scarred by dictatorship, defeat, and destruction into one of the most affluent societies in Western Europe. Despite the structural similarities of the
two revolutions, their outcomes were radically different. The industrial
revolution ended in totalitarian dictatorship and the most destructive
war in European history; from the second revolution, the vast majority of
the divided nation emerged as a stable and increasingly pluralist democracy.

Historians and social scientists have proposed a number of interpretations to explain how a combination of various 'peculiarities of German
history' in the nineteenth century led to the catastrophes of the first half
of the twentieth century. Although the notion of a German *Sonderweg*
(idiosyncratic development) has been significantly modified and to some
extent discredited, it still retains some validity with respect to at least one
problem: namely, that in Germany in the nineteenth century, the transformation of the social and political structure failed to keep pace with the
progress of industrialisation. In Germany, unlike other industrialised
countries, pre-industrial elites retained their predominant social and
political position against the newly emerging industrial classes, stifling
societal modernisation and inhibiting the evolution of a democratic
political culture. It was not until the collapse of the Hitler dictatorship

and the founding of the Federal Republic that rapidly rising mass affluence and the emergence of a broadly based middle class laid the foundation in which democracy could take roots in Germany. The disintegration
of the East German regime followed by unification successfully completed Germany's democratisation.

Industrialisation

The key characteristics of German industrialisation were its late start and
its relatively rapid expansion in the second part of the nineteenth century, accompanied by explosive population growth. The industrial
revolution in Germany occurred in two phases. The first 'wave' of
industrialisation started in the early 1840s, accelerated in the 1850s, and
turned into a boom in the 1860s before giving way in 1873 to a prolonged
recession which has become known as the Great Depression. Between
1850 and 1870, industry, handicraft production, and mining grew by
almost 4 per cent annually. Despite such impressive growth of the industrial sector, Germany remained a predominantly agrarian country. As
late as 1871, about half of the German population was engaged in agriculture and two-thirds lived in rural communities. Industrialisation was
limited to a few provinces in the north and west, and although there was
a growing number of factories, most were small enterprises employing
only a handful of workers.

The second and decisive phase of industrialisation started in 1895
with the recovery from the Great Depression, from which Germany
emerged with a much larger and significantly altered industrial sector.
The sectors that had dominated Germany's first phase of industrialisation – mining, iron production, railways and textiles – experienced a relative decline in favour of the new 'leading sectors' – chemicals, machine
tools and electrical engineering, which made Germany the dominant
industrial and military power in Europe.

The period of 'high industrialisation' lasted from 1895 to 1913. During
this time, German GDP rose by 43 per cent. Overall production in industry and handicraft more than doubled; in some of the newer industries –
e.g. metal working or chemicals – it more than tripled. Energy consumption, perhaps the best measure of a country's pace and intensity of
industrialisation, increased by more than 250 per cent and was, in 1913,
only marginally below the British level. Germany's rapid industrial
expansion was also reflected in its growing importance as a major export-

ing nation. Between 1890 and 1913 exports tripled; two-thirds of them consisted of finished goods.

A decisive factor behind Germany's explosive economic growth was the sharp increase in its population. In 1850, the population living within the borders of the future Reich already stood at roughly 35.5 million, about as much as in France and far more than in Britain. Between 1850 and 1910, the population rapidly increased by roughly 70 per cent. Especially in rural areas overpopulation brought unemployment, misery and hunger. Prior to the 1890s demographic pressures induced migration. Beginning in the 1860s, a growing number of the rural population started to migrate west, first to Berlin, then, in the 1870s, to the emerging industrial centres in central Germany. Others chose to emigrate. Between 1846 and 1855, more than 1.1 million left Germany, mostly bound for the United States. In the decade after the American Civil War, another 1 million left the country while the last wave of mass emigration between 1880 and 1893 encompassed more than 1.8 million people. Between 1820 and 1910, some 5.1 million Germans settled in the United States.

East–west migration in the period of high industrialisation represented the largest instance of mass migration in German history. In 1907, only about half of the 60.5 million who lived in the German Reich still inhabited their place of birth. The result was a reversal of traditional demographic patterns. Whereas in 1871, almost two-thirds of the population lived in rural areas, in 1910, 60 per cent lived in urban areas with a population of more than 2,000. At the same time the number of large cities with a population of more than 100,000 grew from eight to forty-eight, with a combined population of almost 14 million.

The social structure of Imperial Germany

In Germany, industrialisation proceeded more gradually than the term 'revolution' might suggest. It was not until the closing years of the nineteenth century that Germany was transformed from a largely agrarian into a mainly industrial society while its social structure shifted from a society based on estates to one based on classes. In 1800, German society had still been a feudal society organised along rigid hierarchical lines. In the first half of the nineteenth century this traditional society gradually disintegrated, not least as a result of the social reform policies. The most significant of these were the land reform measures enacted in 1807. They freed all peasants who met certain criteria from personal service and dues in exchange for payments of rents or the surrendering of a portion of their land to the landlord. Smallholders and landless peasants were excluded from both the general reforms and the distribution of communal lands. Land reform converted land into private property, which could be bought and sold in the market, and transformed agriculture into a capitalist enterprise. At the same time it swelled the ranks of agricultural wage labourers. The result was an excess of labour which, pushed into the emerging industrial centres, gave rise to the plight of lower-class pauperism.

Compared to the agrarian reforms, the impact of the dismantling of the traditional guild order was considerably less dramatic. Although Prussia introduced *Gewerbefreiheit* (freedom of trade) as early as 1810, the guilds managed to maintain many of the restrictions until well into the 1860s. It was not until 1869 that unrestricted freedom of trade was introduced in the North German Federation.

The dissolution of the feudal order and the emergence of a class society was the result of a gradual process which lasted well into the second half of the nineteenth century. Whereas in the past, positions in the social hierarchy had been based on laws and conventions, in the new industrial social structure they were largely based on economic factors, although remnants of the old system continued to survive.

The social structure of the German Empire at the end of the nineteenth century was dominated by the old pre-industrial aristocracy and a newly emerged upper bourgeoisie. In 1895, these two groups, with their families, accounted for not more than 1 per cent of the population. Together with the *Bildungsbürgertum* (educated bourgeoisie), which with their families also numbered 1 per cent of the population, nobility and upper bourgeoisie formed Imperial Germany's elite. Below this elite was a group of smaller entrepreneurs in industry, trade and commerce, which has been called the propertied bourgeoisie, and which accounted for between 3 and 5 per cent of the population. Below this group ranked the so-called middle strata consisting of small craftsmen, merchants and peasants, who had survived the onslaught of industrialisation but were constantly threatened by proletarianisation and therefore were among the most ardent defenders of the traditional order. The overwhelming majority of the population belonged to the lower classes, which included domestic and factory workers, rural and casual labourers, servants, journeymen, and similar groups. In 1895, they constituted about 70 per cent of the population. The largest group among the lower classes were factory workers who, in 1907, accounted for about 14 per cent of the population, and 32 per cent of the full-time employed.

The persistence of traditional elites

By the end of the nineteenth century, at least statistically, Germany's social structure closely reflected the country's transformation from a predominantly agricultural society to a leading industrial power. However, numbers and statistics can only capture one, and not always the most important, dimension of social reality. The distinguishing feature of Germany's development in the nineteenth century was the fact that despite successful industrialisation and despite the emergence of an entrepreneurial bourgeoisie, political power and social eminence rested with the aristocracy whose pre-industrial ethos continued to inform German society, obstructing social modernisation and inhibiting the evolution of a democratic political culture.

One of the major reasons for the nobility's survival as a class was its ability to adapt to changing circumstances. Particularly in the wake of the land reform a significant number of East Elbian Junker (large East Prussian landowners) switched to capitalist agriculture in order to preserve their base of power. The excess amount of rural labour created by the reforms as well as by the rapid increase in the overall rural population provided them with a continuous supply of cheap labour well into the 1860s. Favourable market conditions helped the landed aristocracy to consolidate its economic position. In 1856, of the 12,339 *Rittergüter* (large estates) that existed in Prussia more than half still belonged to noble families.

A second reason was unification. Victory against France and the creation of a united Empire were largely credited to the Prussian officer corps which was heavily dominated by the Prussian nobility. The result was a significant rise in prestige. Its consequences were felt even among the bourgeoisie and leading members of the liberal establishment such as Hermann Baumgarten, who exhorted his readers to rethink their negative attitudes towards the nobility since, as the war had shown, 'the much despised Junker knows how to fight and die for the fatherland'.[1]

Finally, even if the nobility gradually lost its formal privileges, it retained its dominant position in the upper echelons of the ministerial bureaucracy, diplomacy, the military, and, to a remarkable degree, also on the local level. In 1865, about two-thirds of the Prussian officer corps and almost 90 per cent of colonels and generals belonged to the aristoc-racy. As late as 1913, noblemen were still vastly over-represented in the officer corps of the most prestigious regiments. The situation was similar in the civil service. In 1910, of the 1,858 senior-level Prussian civil servants, almost one-third came from the old agrarian aristocracy.

If the aristocracy showed a surprising ability to adapt itself to chang-ing conditions, the objective of adaptation was primarily to preserve its traditional values and the old order. This was perhaps nowhere as evident as in its 'marriage policy'. While the aristocracy was increasingly pre-pared to marry its sons to rich daughters from the upper bourgeoisie, marriages between noble daughters and members of the upper bour-geoisie remained the exception. Whereas a noble family could only profit from the first option, the second option would have entailed a loss of sta-tus and occurred rather seldom.

If the aristocracy proved remarkably able to preserve its status and position under radically changing conditions, the industrial bour-geoisie largely failed to assert itself politically and thus become an inno-vative force for social and political change. Until recently, German historians and social scientists have attributed the German industrial bourgeoisie's failure to act as a political class to a process of 'feudalisa-tion'. Instead of challenging the aristocracy's power, the industrial bourgeoisie drew increasingly close to it in style and aspirations. A growing number of its members sought social recognition by purchas-ing estates or erecting representative villas, aspiring to join the ranks of the reserve officers, gaining titles of nobility and other honours bestowed by the state, and finding for their sons positions in pre-stigious regiments or high-status posts in the civil service. By thus assimilating the values and life style of the aristocracy, the industrial bourgeoisie not only contributed to the preservation and consolidation of elements of an outmoded feudal order, it also 'considerably slowed down or stopped the development towards a humanistically deter-mined, democratic social order'.[2]

Recent empirical studies have significantly modified the feudalisa-tion thesis. They show that processes of assimilation, if they happened at all, were relatively limited in scope. Unlike in Great Britain, in Germany only a very small minority of the members of the industrial or financial bourgeoisie was elevated to the ranks of the aristocracy. Despite the fact that by 1885, 67 per cent of East Elbian estates were owned by members of the industrial bourgeoisie, most of their owners remained active entrepreneurs, as did their sons and even a considerable number of their sons-in-law. A majority of German entrepreneurs married the daughters of other entrepreneurial families or at least those from the upper bourgeoisie. Only a tiny minority married into the aristocracy. This suggests that the German industrial bourgeoisie, like the aristocracy, constituted a class with a high degree of self-recruitment.

If these findings have significantly revised important aspects of the feudalisation thesis, they have not weakened its central point of critique, namely the failure of the German bourgeoisie to challenge the power of the pre-industrial elites. Hans-Ulrich Wehler coined the phrase *Staatsnähe*, closeness to the state, to describe the mentality of the German entrepreneurial middle class.[3] This state orientation was perhaps not surprising. As a relative latecomer, German industry had to rely on the financial, organisational, and political resources of the state much more than nations that had industrialised earlier. This was reflected in the close links between enterprises and state administration as well as the large number of civil servants who, after a successful career in the bureaucracy, became entrepreneurs or managing directors. In addition, the bourgeoisie increasingly needed the traditional military and bureaucratic elites in order to check the demands of organised workers. Bismarck's anti-Socialist laws, as well as his paternalistic social policies, fitted well with the industrial bourgeoisie's belief in the need for authority in the state and at the workplace. From its perspective, the industrial bourgeoisie's étatiste orientation was hardly irrational given the prevailing social and political realities. Its adoption, however, made it susceptible to the authoritarian values espoused by the monarchical state, in which the aristocracy played a pre-eminent role.

By the end of the nineteenth century, the aristocracy had largely preserved its position of social prestige and political power while the industrial bourgeoisie had reached a position of economic and social prominence, which was diminished only by its political subordination to the traditional power elites. By contrast, the third elite group, the academic and professional *Bildungsbürgertum* such as senior administrative civil servants, university professors, secondary school teachers and judges was in full crisis. More than any other class in Imperial Germany, the *Bildungsbürgertum* had remained a status group. Its social position and prestige rested on *Bildung*, a combination of formal education in the classics and a life-long process of intellectual, moral and aesthetic cultivation. Its survival as a distinct group depended on the continued acceptance of *Bildung* as socially superior to modern 'functional knowledge'. It is for this reason that industrialisation posed a fundamental threat to the *Bildungsbürgertum*. On the one hand, industrialisation led to the rise of a competing bourgeois elite which commanded both economic and educational capital. On the other hand, industrialisation led to a progressive devaluation of the ideals of a universalist humanistic education in favour of more narrowly defined scientific and technical formation. This was reflected in the growing popularity of 'reality-oriented' secondary schools (*Realschule, Oberrealschule, Realgymnasium*) as well as technical universities. Increasingly, the traditional academic *Bildungsbürgertum* saw itself surpassed not only by entrepreneurs and managing directors, but also by the rapidly growing number of engineers, technicians, and other 'specialists'. In response, the *Bildungsbürgertum*, which in the first part of the century had been the most fervent proponent of liberalism, became increasingly conservative, not only seeking its peace with the monarchical state and the aristocracy, but exalting their economic and military successes. Large parts of the *Bildungsbürgertum* interpreted the erosion of their status in terms of a cultural crisis, caused by the assault of *Zivilisation* (civilisation) and *Gesellschaft* (society) on *Kultur* (culture) and *Gemeinschaft* (community). One form of escape was the illiberal politics of cultural despair reflected in the writings of Paul de Lagarde or Julius Langbehn, whose tremendous success and influence were an indication of the extent to which cultural pessimism had spread among the educated strata. A second form of escape were the social movements that sprang up at the turn of the century, ranging from the youthful rebellion of the *Wandervogel* (youth rambling clubs) to the search for communal, vegetarian and other alternative life-styles. These movements represented in part a genuine revolt against the stifling conventions of Wilhelmine society, in part a flight into utopian romanticism and esoteric mysticism characteristic of a trans-national 'occult underground'. Most of them evoked an idealised past against the crass materialism of the present and thus shared strong anti-modern, anti-capitalist and anti-democratic tendencies, occasionally with strong anti-Semitic overtones.

Despite internal conflicts and growing pressures from below, the elite of Imperial Germany managed to maintain its dominant position until the First World War. United in their fear of the lower classes aristocracy and upper bourgeoisie remained fundamentally hostile to democracy. It was not until the end of the First World War that the symbiosis between the two groups was finally destroyed.

The war eliminated the monarchy and with it the political power of the aristocracy, without, however, substantially weakening their privileged positions in the officer corps and the diplomatic service. The ensuing hyper-inflation bankrupted a significant number of the capitalist class. Those few who managed to take advantage of the situation by multiplying their assets emerged as the new Weimar elite, together with the holders of senior positions in the administration and the new republican leadership. Unlike the elite of Imperial Germany, however, the new elite of the Weimar Republic not only lacked internal unity and a sense of purpose, many of their representatives never accepted the new order. Confronted with a determined and militant group of Nazi revolutionaries, the Weimar Republic's elites offered little resistance.

The new middle class and the rise of National Socialism

When Theodor Geiger published his well-known study (1932)[4] of the stratification of the German people in 1925, he found that 75 per cent of the gainfully employed belonged to the proletariat, 24 per cent to the middle strata, and roughly 1 per cent to the capitalist class. Compared to fifty years earlier, little had changed. When self-perception was taken into account – Geiger called it 'mentality' – a different picture emerged: 48 per cent regarded themselves as middle-class, 51 per cent as working-class. Even this more differentiated profile omitted some important developments: the emergence of the new middle class. It consisted of white-collar employees, civil servants and members of the professions and constituted 18 per cent in Geiger's analysis of social structure. The new middle class had grown nearly as large as the old middle class and was soon to overtake it.

White-collar employees had begun to emerge in the second half of the nineteenth century. In 1882, they accounted for 4.7 per cent of the workforce; by 1907, their share had risen to near 11 per cent. From the outset, employers clearly distinguished between white-collar employees and ordinary workers. Generally, employees had higher qualifications, their positions were more secure, their working conditions were better than those of workers, and they were paid a salary rather than a wage. These distinctions shaped the self-understanding and mentality of employees who thought of themselves as a status group like the civil servants whose prestige they were eager to borrow in order to distance themselves from ordinary workers. With the introduction of a separate social security insurance for employees in 1911, in response to demands from their professional associations, these distinctions were endorsed by law.

Starting already in the pre-war period, and intensifying during the Weimar years, however, employees saw much of their privileged position eroding. Technological and organisational changes increasingly exposed them to the business cycle; social policies extended privileges, which had previously been reserved for employees, to workers as well; improvements in material conditions and reduced wage differentials led to a convergence of consumption patterns. The employees interpreted each of these changes as a symptom of a more general process of levelling (*Nivellierung*) and proletarianisation. They responded with protests directed as much against the capitalist system and its proponents as against the proletariat into whose ranks they feared to fall. What motivated this protest was a perceived threat to status and material insecurity. As Geiger shows, this united the employees with other strata of the middle class, such as the lower ranks of the civil service, remnants of the old *Bildungsbürgertum*, and parts of the old middle class, who shared their status-group orientation. Despairing in the face of economic crisis and disillusioned with the state's inability to respond to their particularistic demands for protection, they were increasingly attracted to the Nazi movement's economic programme with its strong corporatist overtones. It was these groups which accounted in large part for the rise of the NSDAP in the 1920s and early 1930s.

As Ralf Dahrendorf has perhaps most forcefully argued, National Socialism 'completed for Germany the social revolution that was lost in the faultings of Imperial Germany and again held up by the contradictions of the Weimar Republic'. With tremendous brutality, the National Socialists broke with tradition and pushed Germany towards modernity.[5] Within less than two years of taking power, the Nazis had replaced the representatives of the Weimar elite with a clique of marginalised petty bourgeois outsiders supported by remnants of the imperial elite, drifting intellectuals, and technical and scientific specialists. The proportion of outsiders was particularly large among the key groups of the Nazi elite, such as propagandists, party functionaries, and the police, whereas it was considerably lower in the military and among prominent party supporters, many of whom retained their positions in the administration or the foreign service. In an ironic twist of events, many representatives of the old elite thus subordinated themselves to a new ruling class of previously marginalised 'plebeians'.

Within a few years, the new elite was swept away by total defeat in the war and the complete collapse of the Hitler regime. With it were swept away the last remnants of the old Prussian aristocratic elite who had managed to retain their influence in the military and the higher civil service. Many lost their lives in the war, others were put to death after the failed attempt on Hitler's life in July 1944. But perhaps most important was the loss of the eastern territories and the Soviet occupation which destroyed the economic basis of the East Elbian Junker and ended their dominance in German society and politics.

West Germany's middle-class society

In 1945, few observers could have foreseen that it would take less than twenty-five years for the West German state to re-emerge as the leading European industrial power and one of the most prosperous countries in the world. And yet, in the roughly twenty years between the founding of the two German states and the late 1960s, West German society experienced a second socio-economic and socio-cultural revolution which, at least with respect to its speed and magnitude, was comparable to the industrial revolution. However, whereas industrialisation had proved to be a constant source of instability, the massive modernisation of West Germany's economy and society was remarkably free of social and political disruption.

Between 1950 and 1970, the economy grew at an average annual rate of almost 5 per cent; real GDP rose by roughly 280 per cent. That was about the same as during the entire period of industrialisation, spanning more than sixty years from 1850 to 1913. Much of the rapid economic recovery was due to the ready availability of relatively cheap labour and an upsurge in investment. Labour was provided above all by the millions of expellees (*Vertriebene*) and refugees (*Flüchtlinge*) who settled in West Germany from territories lost to Eastern European countries after the war or from Soviet controlled Eastern Germany after 1945. The excess supply kept wages down and allowed enterprises to reinvest their profits. Between 1950 and 1973, West Germany's stock of machinery and equipment per employee more than tripled while exports grew from 11 per cent to 27 per cent of GDP.

Although the massive economic gains of the immediate post-war period only gradually improved the material well-being of the average citizen, individual gains were still substantial. Between 1950 and 1970, the median net income of working-class households more than quadrupled, despite the fact that West Germans worked more than 500 hours less per year in 1973 than in 1950. The gradual rise in individual affluence was reflected in rising household savings rates, which rose to 12.6 per cent in 1970, as well as in improved quality of life. Between 1950 and 1970, the proportion of West German homes without a bath or shower decreased from 80 to 28 per cent, whilst the number of households that owned a car increased from 27 per cent (1962) to 55 per cent (1973).

Post-war economic modernisation had a decisive impact on West German social structure. Perhaps most significant was the rapid decline of West German agriculture, from almost a quarter of the total workforce in 1950 to roughly 9 per cent in 1970. It was reflected in the decline of the number of the self-employed (including family members who helped them), which dropped from 28.3 per cent in 1950 to 17.1 per cent in 1970. Those set free were quickly absorbed by a rapidly expanding economy, which suffered from a chronic labour shortage. In response, West Germany began actively to recruit growing numbers of foreign labourers to serve as temporary 'guest workers'. Between 1961 and 1973, their number grew from 280,000 to more than 2.3 million.

A second significant development was the rapid growth of the tertiary sector and with it the expansion of the number of white-collar employees and civil servants. Between 1950 and 1970, the proportion of the workforce employed in the tertiary sector, both private and public, increased by more than 10 per cent, from 32.3 per cent to 42.6 per cent. At the same time, the number of white-collar employees and civil servants increased from 20.6 to 36.2 per cent of the workforce.

The massive socio-economic and socio-structural changes of the post-war period gave rise to the notion that West German society was fundamentally different from the class-based societies of the past. The new society was, in Helmut Schelsky's words, a *'nivellierte Mittelstandsgesellschaft'*, a levelled society largely dominated by the middle strata.[6] Although sharply criticised for its negative view of levelling as levelling down, the concept did capture significant developments such as the expansion and increasing importance of the new middle strata, improved access to consumer goods, and the spread of middle-class values and mentalities. However, the concept also obscured the continued and increasing importance of social differences and inequalities. As a number of studies showed, West Germans persisted in seeing society as hierarchically structured and had no difficulty in placing themselves in that social hierarchy. In 1950, 50 per cent of West Germans considered themselves part of the middle strata, 45 per cent placed themselves in the lower strata, 1 per cent in the upper stratum, and 4 per cent at the bottom of society.

Empirical measures of stratification strongly suggest that in West Germany, the distribution of life chances continued to be substantially unequal. Income distribution for instance shows a persistently large gap between the top and bottom households, which remained remarkably stable. In 1950, the top 20 per cent of West German households received about 45 per cent of all income, the bottom 20 per cent less than 6 per cent. In 1980, the top received 43 per cent, the bottom 7 per cent. The self-employed continued to earn substantially more than workers.

The persistence of inequality was most striking in the realm of education. In all advanced societies, access to higher education has become a necessary precondition not only for social mobility but, increasingly, for a career. West Germany was one of the last industrial societies to expand its educational system, starting in the 1960s. The so-called '*Bildungsexpansion*' led to a dramatic redistribution of educational opportunities. Between 1950 and 1989, the number of children obtaining only basic education (*Volksschule*) dropped from roughly 80 to little more than 30 per cent. At the same time, middle schools and especially secondary schools (*Gymnasien* and *Gesamtschulen*, comprehensives) saw a dramatic increase in enrolment. Between 1960 and 1989, the number of young Germans completing a range of A levels (*Abitur*) rose more than four-fold to one quarter of an age cohort.

However, the expansion of the education system failed substantially to improve access to university education. As in the past, it was the higher social strata which gained most from the *Bildungsexpansion*. Of those attending grammar schools in 1989, 58 per cent of 13- and 14-year-olds were from civil-servant and 44 per cent from white-collar families, but only 11 per cent came from working-class families. University enrolments revealed a similar picture. In 1988, 38 per cent of 19- to 21-year-olds enrolled at university had a civil-service family background, but only 5 per cent came from a working-class background.

These developments are significant for at least two reasons. The restructuring of the education system led to a devaluation of lower educational qualifications. Those who had only attended the lowest type of school found it even more difficult than before to compete with their better-educated peers for higher-level positions in a shrinking job market. At the same time, higher education became increasingly a pre-condition for access to elite positions in the West German economy, in politics, and in administration. In 1981, 85 per cent of those holding leadership positions in West Germany had *Abitur*, and 69 per cent held university degrees. Only 11 per cent came from a working-class family. This suggests that education, rather than weakening the stratification of West German society, contributed to its persistence.

The social structure of the GDR

Unlike West Germany, where persisting and, in some instances, increasing socio-structural inequalities guaranteed a certain socio-historical continuity, the socio-structural history of the GDR was characterised by a radical break with the past. Starting in 1945, the newly established East German regime brought about a fundamental transformation of the political and economic system with far-reaching consequences for the social structure. It created a uniformly lower-class society. In many respects it came much closer to the image of a levelled (*nivellierte*) society than West Germany. Key events were denazification, which removed a large number of the old functional elites; land reform and the national-isation of large industry, which expropriated the large landowners and the industrial bourgeoisie; and the nationalisation of smaller enterprises in manufacture and handicraft, as well as the collectivisation of agriculture.

Many of the losers of these processes left for the West as part of a mass exodus which, between 1950 and 1960 alone, reduced the East German population by almost two million. At the same time, the transformation of the East German socio-economic system opened up opportunities for workers and peasants who filled many of the new positions. Thus, by 1948, former workers accounted for more than 50 per cent of the heads of the newly created, state-owned enterprises.

East German sociologists described society as being composed of two classes, workers and peasants plus a special stratum, the intelligentsia (*Intelligenz*). The latter was defined as comprising the 'carriers of intellectual production' and included all persons with university or equivalent degrees in politics, the military, education, research and development, the arts, etc. It also included the relatively small and concentrated power elite of not more than 350 persons who monopolised the key positions in the country. In 1961, according to official statistics, 4.8 per cent of the workforce belonged to the *Intelligenz*, 77.5 per cent to the working class, and 10.9 per cent to the peasantry. The remainder consisted of a small group of self-employed workers which, in 1989, accounted for just 2.2 per cent of the workforce. Throughout the existence of the GDR, the size of the working class hardly changed. The East German economy was similarly dominated by a disproportionately large manufacturing sector, whereas the tertiary sector remained comparatively underdeveloped.

In the immediate post-war period, it was official policy to bring about an equalisation of the material conditions of various social groups. This was particularly pronounced with respect to income differences, which were significantly less sharp than in West Germany. Those who benefited most from these policies were women and members of the working classes. As early as 1955, women constituted 44 per cent of the labour force. By the late 1980s 90 per cent of the female labour force participated in employment. Women also gained from the educational revolution. In 1989, they constituted 49 per cent of all university students and received 38 per cent of all Ph.Ds. The situation was similar with respect to the working class. In 1958, more than half of the students enrolled at East German universities had a working-class background, with less than 15 per cent coming from the *Intelligenz*.

However, starting in the 1960s, inequalities emerged which resembled those in West Germany. One feature was a growing differentiation within the working class between a relatively small elite of technically highly specialised workers and the vast majority of unskilled and skilled workers with traditional qualifications. The most important development, however, was a dramatic increase in the size of the *Intelligenz* (from 3.8 per cent of the workforce in 1952 to 15 per cent in 1985), which managed to turn itself into a new, self-recruiting and self-perpetuating socialist elite. Between 1960 and 1989, the proportion of university students from the *Intelligenz* more than quadrupled, from 19 to 78 per cent, and the differences, especially between the top level of the *Intelligenz* and the vast majority of the working class, substantially increased. Even if these differentiations did not entail significant income inequalities, the *Intelligenz*'s relative closeness to the state guaranteed them other privileges (housing, trips to the west) which, given East Germany's limited supply of consumer goods, represented the real sources of social distinction. The result of these developments was growing social fragmentation and polarisation, which the regime was unable to stop.

Post-industrial inequalities in unified Germany

The 1970s marked a turning point in post-war German social and economic history. In West Germany, as in most other advanced industrial countries, the sharp rise in the oil price known as the oil crisis put an end to what has been called the golden age of capitalism, turning optimism into gloom, and confronting governments with the seemingly intractable problem of stagflation. If West Germany proved generally more successful than other advanced industrial societies in combating inflation, it did so at the price of mass unemployment which, more than two decades later, continued to haunt the country. The crisis of the 1970s coincided with a second development which has proved even more significant. Some time in the late 1970s, West Germany ceased to be a predominantly industrial country. The rapid growth of the tertiary sector, and with it the expansion of the number of white-collar employees and civil servants, indicated that West Germany was turning into a post-industrial society.

In the 1980s, the structural transformation of the German economy provoked a growing debate among West German sociologists about whether, and to what degree, traditional models of social inequality were still adequate to analyse an increasingly complex social reality. Ulrich Beck put it perhaps most pointedly when he argued that the Federal Republic had moved beyond a class society. Despite the persistence of traditional patterns of social inequality, substantial improvements in the standard of living had changed the 'social meaning' of inequality. This had not only led to the progressive dissolution of 'subcultural class identities' but also set in motion 'a process of individualisation and diversification of ways of life and life-styles which subverts the hierarchical model of social classes and strata and questions its continued relevance'.[7]

The transformation of society in the 1960s and 1970s had generated what Stefan Hradil called 'new dimensions of inequality', unequal access to the benefits of the welfare state, to quality housing and infrastructure, an intact environment and challenging employment.[8] The degree to which an individual was affected by these new inequalities was increasingly determined by ascribed or socio-cultural factors, such as age, gender, ethnic origins, family structure and region. The result of the growing social importance of these developments was a progressive differentiation and fragmentation of society, a pluralisation of life-styles which led to the gradual disintegration and erosion of traditional ways of social organisation based on classes and strata.

The debate about new forms of inequality reflected growing social and political sensibility to the deficits of West German society. Among them were the continued discrimination against women in the job market; the deterioration in the opportunities and life chances of much of the resident population of foreign workers and their families; and the growth of pockets of 'new poverty'. Numerous studies showed to what degree relatively recent phenomena such as long-term unemployment, poverty, or the rise of right-wing extremism in the 1980s and early 1990s were connected with these new dimensions of inequality. Among the 'risk groups' most affected by long-term unemployment were the lower-skilled, the elderly, especially if they were women, and persons with health problems. Those most likely to fall below the poverty level were foreigners, single women with children, and families with three or more children. Those most likely to support the radical Right were lower-skilled men who lived in areas with low-quality housing.

However, social differentiation and fragmentation did not only contribute to the emergence of instances of marginalisation and problem groups. The transformation of West German society produced a variety of social milieus and subcultures based on shared values, life-styles, and consumption patterns. Thus, postmaterialist values pertained to the better educated and gave rise to the new social movements and the Greens. At the other end of the social spectrum, materialist values and political orientations right of centre prevailed. The end result of these developments was the emergence of a newly divided society consisting of a relatively affluent majority and a minority of marginalised problem groups. This division has frequently been referred to as a Two-Thirds Society although in reality the notion of a four-fifths society seems more accurate.

Unification did not fundamentally change the emerging post-industrial structure of German society. As East German society faced the pressures to modernise it had to adapt to the West German model. This meant above all, the reintroduction of traditional patterns of vertical mobility and socio-hierarchical structures and with it the revival of traditional patterns of inequality. The result was a period of tremendous upward and downward mobility, which affected all social groups. The losers in this process were above all the state-oriented members of the *Intelligenz*, older persons who could not be retrained, and many East German women.

The deficits of German society, however, should not detract from the fact that unification was in many ways the logical conclusion to West Germany's successful transformation into a stable democracy in the post-war period. This was due to a number of factors, not least among them the elimination of the old anti-democratic elites, the social and economic integration of the working class, and the rapid expansion of a relatively affluent new middle stratum of white collar workers and civil servants. It was above all the new middle class which in the 1960s became the vanguard of modernisation in West German society.

With unification, the German problem has finally been solved. Unified Germany is a fundamentally modern society, more modern perhaps than its western neighbours. Yet, German society is again at a turning point. Like all advanced industrial societies, it faces new challenges stemming from rapid technological change and globalisation which threaten to deepen existing inequalities while at the same time creating new ones. The degree to which German society will be able to meet these challenges without major social disruptions will most likely determine its political stability in the future.

NOTES

1. Cited in James Sheehan, *German Liberalism in the Nineteenth Century*, Chicago and London: The University of Chicago Press, 1978, p. 176.
2. Friedrich Zunkel, 'Industriebürgertum in Westdeutschland' in Hans-Ulrich Wehler (ed.), *Moderne deutsche Sozialgeschichte*, Cologne and Berlin: Kiepenheuer & Witsch, 1966, p. 337.
3. Hans-Ulrich Wehler, *Deutsche Gesellschaftsgeschichte*, vol. III, Munich: C. H. Beck, 1995, p. 724.
4. See Theodor Geiger, *Die soziale Schichtung des deutschen Volkes*, Stuttgart: Cotta Verlag, 1932.
5. Ralf Dahrendorf, *Society and Democracy in Germany*, New York and London: Norton, 1967, pp. 381–2.
6. Helmut Schelsky, *Wandlungen der deutschen Familie in der Gegenwart*, Dortmund: Ardey Verlag, 1953, pp. 218 f. See also Helmut Schelsky, 'Die Bedeutung des Schichtenbegriffes für die Analyse der gegenwärtigen deutschen Gesellschaft' in H. Schelsky, *Auf der Suche nach Wirklichkeit*, Düsseldorf/Cologne: Eugen Diedrichs Verlag, 1965, p. 332.
7. Ulrich Beck, *Risikogesellschaft*, Frankfurt: Suhrkamp, 1986, pp. 121–2.
8. Stefan Hradil, 'Epochaler Umbruch oder ganz normaler Wandel? Wie weit reichen die neueren Veränderungen der Sozialstruktur in der Bundesrepublik?' in *Umbrüche in der Industriegesellschaft*, Bonn: Bundeszentrale für politische Bildung, 1990, pp. 86–96; 'Die "objektive" und die "subjektive" Modernisierung,' *Aus Politik und Zeitgeschichte* B29–30, 10 June 1992, pp. 9–13.

FURTHER READING

A standard work translated into English is Hans-Ulrich Wehler, *The German Empire 1871–1918* (Oxford: Berg, 1985). Hans-Ulrich Wehler (ed.), *Moderne deutsche Sozialgeschichte* (Cologne: Kiepenheuer & Witsch, 1966) contains an excellent collection of essays on Imperial Germany. A detailed discussion of the German bourgeoisie can be found in Wehler's *Deutsche Gesellschaftsgeschichte* (Munich: Beck, 1995). The best analysis of elites since the Weimar Republic is still Wolfgang Zapf, *Wandlungen der deutschen Elite* (Munich: Piper, 1965).

A concise account of social transformation in East and West Germany and since unification is presented by Rainer Geissler, *Die Sozialstruktur Deutschlands* (Opladen: Westdeutscher Verlag, 1992, revised edition 1996). For key contributions on social milieus and new inequalities see Peter Berger and Stefan Hradil, *Lebenslagen, Lebensläufe, Lebensstile*, special issue no.7 of *Soziale Welt* (Göttingen: Schwartz Verlag, 1990).

ANDREI S. MARKOVITS,
BETH SIMONE NOVECK
and CAROLYN HÖFIG

4

Jews in German society

The 'German Question', however one phrases it, always involves, at least by implication, German Jewry. In its classical formulation – on national development and territorial unity – the query raises issues of citizenship, political participation and social change with immediate bearing on the Jewish communities in Germany. More recently, the German Question asks how the country could have embarked on the terrible course that led to the Third Reich, the Second World War and the Holocaust, which very nearly realised its goal of eliminating the Jewish presence in German society. In short, the story of German–Jewish relations reflects at once the hope and the horror of German history.

Jews and Germans have lived together for nearly 2000 years, and different but related tensions characterise this association – variously described as a symbiosis, a dialogue, a long quarrel and an alliance based on deception – before and after Auschwitz. The Holocaust marks a singular historical moment that has everything to do with German–Jewish relations today. But one damages the past by conflating all of German–Jewish experience with the Holocaust, or by reading events of the last centuries as simply a prelude to National Socialist atrocities. For an adequate understanding of the meaning and direction of the German–Jewish history, one must consider the longer record of Jews in Germany.

German–Jewish history

The first evidence of Jewish settlements in the region that would become Germany dates at least to the time of the Roman Emperor Constantine, who in December 321 issued a decree that referred to a well-organised

Jewish congregation in Cologne. Jewish artisans and tradesmen arrived in the Roman settlements along the River Rhine; Jewish soldiers may well have served in the armies that secured the area for the Empire. By the fourth century, Jews had established themselves – and important schools of Jewish learning – in Trier, Mainz, Worms and Speyer. (The legendary Bible commentator Rashi, for example, left his native Troyes to study in both Mainz and Worms.) By the ninth century, the Jews in Charlemagne's realm enjoyed imperial privileges and esteem; they owned houses and participated in public life. The population spread northward and eastward.

The First and Second Crusades (in 1096 and 1146) heralded the end of this peaceable coexistence, as did the Black Death in the fourteenth century, for which the popular imagination held the Jews responsible. Religious persecution of the Jews – widespread massacres and forced conversions – marked the Middle Ages in Germany, as in much of western Europe; even a 1422 bull of Pope Martin V that forbade the bringing of trumped-up ritual-murder charges against Jews could not quell the hatred and violence.

Some Jews did rise to positions of importance; as the age of absolutism unfolded, the numerous German princes and dukes welcomed the financial expertise of their individual 'court Jews' – *Hofjuden*. The Holy Roman emperors and later German kings issued explicit patents to Jewish communities, making them wards of the crown and, in principle, granting them special protection. But even these communities – now mostly living in ghettos that separated them from the general population – were subject to capricious taxation and restrictive laws on everything from travel to dress to occupational access. As such, Jews remained visibly foreign elements in German cities and villages with little contact with Christian society. Religious anti-Semitism persisted as institutional discrimination and popular violence well into the modern era.

Enlightenment and emancipation

The gradual secularisation of society, which began in the aftermath of the Reformation and the Thirty Years War, gathered full force with the Enlightenment in the second half of the eighteenth century. With watchwords like 'rational unity' and 'egalitarianism', the Age of Reason encouraged Jews to move into the larger community. In Germany, this process found its most forceful proponent in Moses Mendelssohn, father of the *Haskala*, as the Jewish Enlightenment is called. Mendelssohn admonished his co-religionists to 'be a Jew inside your house and a man outside', calling for an end to distinctions in citizenship and participation. Emanating from Berlin, the *Haskala* provided the intellectual impetus for emancipation, acculturation and modernisation of the Jewish communities. The *Maskilim*, Jewish Enlighteners, had some allies among German thinkers of the time, notably Gotthold Ephraim Lessing, whose friendship with Mendelssohn promised an affinity between cultivated Jews and the German intelligentsia. Since the 1780s, Jewish hostesses had presided over salons that attracted aristocrats, artists and the upwardly mobile. Strikingly, already by the end of the century, Jews turned in unprecedented numbers to conversion to further their integration, a rate of flight from Judaism – an 'epidemic of baptism' – that even the advent of the Reform Movement, with its vernacular religious services accompanied by organ and choir and loosened traditional tenets and practices, could not stem.

In 1782, the Habsburg Emperor Joseph II issued his Edict of Tolerance, but Germany faced a more radical programme of integration in the next decade. The Revolution in France brought legal emancipation to Jews there, and when Napoleon spread French rule through Europe, including Germany, Jews lost their special community status and became individual citizens. After Napoleon's defeat in 1814, however, German national sentiment rejected foreign 'impositions'. The emancipation enactment was largely rescinded, despite the efforts of Prussian Reformers like Prince Karl August von Hardenberg and Baron Wilhelm von Humboldt. Moreover, German intellectual sentiment turned to Romanticism, with its emphasis on the essential unity of the *Volk*, the racial community, in opposition to the rationality of citizenship. Anti-Semitism became in some circles a kind of nationalist imperative, and by 1819, the so-called Hep Hep riots saw renewed large-scale violence against Jews in the German-speaking lands.

To be sure, German nationality appealed to German Jews, who continued the trend of acculturation and conversion. Around 1820, for instance, the communities dropped their practice of calling themselves 'the Jewish Nation in Germany', preferring 'German Citizens of Jewish Faith' to emphasise their primary allegiance. One need only consider the poems of Heinrich Heine, who meant to correct the flaws of the fatherland, to see the extent to which German Jews prized their German-ness. Even Heine's efforts did not bring societal acceptance, however, and the greatest German lyric poet since Goethe never shed the onus of foreignness, of uncongeniality to German minds, as the nationalist historian Heinrich von Treitschke later asserted.[1]

Empire and modernity, 1850–1918

Just twenty years later, however, on 3 July 1869, the North German Confederation of states led by Prussia, promulgated a law that declared an end to 'all limitations of civic and citizen rights deriving from differences of religion'; when Germany was unified as the Second Reich in 1871, the statute applied throughout the Empire. What had changed? The first two Prussian victories in what would become the three Wars of Unification brought a considerable number of Jews into Berlin's purview with the newly won territory, which made more immediate the long-brewing question of integration. Moreover, the Liberal Party dominated politics in the union at the time, and its platform included equality for Jews. A pragmatic political thinker, Prince Otto von Bismarck, Prussian Chancellor and after 1871 Imperial Chancellor, accepted the strongest party's programme. In the interest of preserving Prussian national unity, Bismarck had in 1847 spoken unambiguously against full citizenship for Jews, although he maintained personal associations with prominent Jews all his life; now the exigencies of consolidating a rapidly industrialising empire prompted him to include all the productive and sympathetic forces in German society. To expedite assimilation, the 1876 Law of Withdrawal allowed Jews to remove their official affiliation with the Jewish religious community without necessarily converting to Catholicism or Lutheranism.

Throughout the Jewish population, the process of Germanisation that integration entailed became an increasingly obsessive preoccupation with conformity. Jews in Germany numbered 512,158, and they represented 1.25 per cent of the total German population in the first year of the Empire. In 1890, there were 567,884 registered Jews comprising 1.15 per cent of society. By 1910, the actual number of Jews rose to 615,000, but the proportion dropped to 0.95 per cent. Baptism, mixed marriages and emigration accounted for the steady decline of Jewish tradition; Jews who intermarried tended to abandon Judaism entirely, which left the observant community ever more distinct.

Jews counted disproportionately among the poor, as impoverished immigrants from Eastern Europe arrived in the big cities. These *Ostjuden*, or Eastern Jews, also formed a distinct body in Jewish and German society, and their stubborn foreignness and apparent poverty drew disparagement and discrimination from Germans and the native Jewry alike. To many German Jews, the *Ostjuden* represented the older, segregated life-style that they sought to overcome, and the newcomers' resistance to the forces of assimilation threatened the whole programme of Jewish integration. By the turn of the century, foreign Jews accounted for almost 20 per cent of the German Jewish population, and tensions increased both among Jews and between Jews and Germans.

Jews were also over-represented among the wealthier classes of German society; they were increasingly urban, and they had particular visibility in the professions: medicine, law, journalism and academe. (Eleven of forty German Nobel Prize winners before 1933 were Jewish.) Successful German Jews in this period adopted the refinements, manners, tastes and conventions of the Christian elite, whose world they soon regarded as their own.

Ironically the social mobility and economic achievement of Jews created as many tensions in the relations between Jews and Germans as it relieved. In the late nineteenth and early twentieth centuries, in other words, German–Jewish integration proved sufficiently successful to fix popular envy to a conspicuous elite *and* sufficiently incomplete to leave Jews vulnerable to a growing wave of anti-Semitism and a *völkisch* racism updated from Romantic notions of an allegedly endangered national ideal.

Indeed, the further Jewish integration progressed – the more Jews blended into German society – the more pronounced anti-Semitism became. Now, however, racial prejudice assumed a new, 'scientific' character and an anchoring role in politics. An economic depression of worldwide proportions in 1873 and after heralded this fundamental transformation of anti-Semitism, when anti-capitalist sentiment converged with ascendant integral nationalism. Soon respected public men openly espoused their hatred of Jews, which lent political anti-Semitism an air of respectability. Treitschke, for one example, turned a phrase of Heine, who had lamented his *own* Jewishness as a barrier to full acceptance in German society, against German Jewry, declaring in 1880 that the Jews are 'our misfortune'.[2] With a bitter and accusatory essay titled 'Jewishness in Music', Richard Wagner inaugurated in 1850 a career as a racist that influenced German cultural development in the Second Reich as much as his music did. The Protestant court preacher Adolf Stöcker launched the Christian-Social Workers Party and later a League of Anti-Semites. Initially, Stöcker meant to attract workers to a conservative clerical cause but his programme consisted almost entirely of a call to exclude the Jews from a purified German nation. Political anti-Semitism did not represent a phenomenon of the extremes, however, but a general trend that reflected the decline in Imperial Germany of liberalism, intellectual home to toleration, equality and emancipation.

A segment of German Jewry met this prejudice with a return to its heritage. At the turn of the century, the Reform movement flourished. The neo-Orthodox reaction to the Reform movement continued to promote a more traditional Judaism. Overall, the social aspect of Jewish life diversified and even prospered. A Central Welfare Agency and other organisations ran Jewish hospitals, nursing homes, schools and libraries. Jewish academic societies and religious groups such as B'nai B'rith appeared. The overarching Central Association of German Citizens of Jewish Faith published its own newspaper and boasted a membership of many thousands.

And when Theodor Herzl, the Viennese advocate of a separate Jewish state, died in 1904, the centre of Zionist activities moved from Austria to Germany. The quest for an independent Jewish homeland had German–Jewish roots, with the publication in 1862 of *Rom und Jerusalem, die letzte Nationalitätsfrage* (Rome and Jerusalem) by Moses Hess and *Derishat Zion* (Care for Zion) by Zebi Hirsch Kalischer. Certainly, Russian Jews most actively pushed for the colonisation of Palestine, but the rise of nationalism in the Second Reich, as elsewhere in Europe, prompted many Jews to shift their civic desires to a nation of their own. Martin Buber's *Der Jude*, among other Zionist periodicals, enjoyed a wide circulation, and various groups arose to support the movement.

When World War I broke out in 1914, Germany's Jews took up arms for their country. Some 100,000 Jews fought on the German side – one Jewish man in six – of whom 12,000 died.

The Weimar Republic, 1919–1933

Germany's defeat, the perceived humiliation of the Versailles Treaty and the economic and social instability in the first five years after the war wrought almost perpetual strife and discontent in the nascent democracy. The 'liberal Jewish press' and 'Jewish war profiteers' figured prominently among the alleged perpetrators of the 'stab in the back', by which, according to any number of anti-republican spellbinders, the treasonously weak-willed civilian leadership had robbed the German army, the true representatives of the natives, of victory. Capitalist–Bolshevik–liberal–Zionist conspiracy theories abounded, accommodating the multiplicity of 'reasons' for which anti-Semites hated Jews. While, on the one hand, the explicitly anti-Jewish political groups of the late nineteenth century had disappeared, few of the myriad parties in Weimar Germany remained entirely free of anti-Semitism. Even the German Democratic Party, the old Progressive Party that earlier defended Jewish integration and acceptance, distanced itself from Jewish causes as it grew more nationalist.

Against this background, however, Jews did finally permeate all levels of German society. In 1922, Walther Rathenau, whose father had brought the first electrical street lighting and telephone service to Berlin as founder of the Allgemeine Elektrizitäts-Gesellschaft, acceded to the office of foreign ministry after having served as the minister of reconstruction and attempting to renegotiate the war-reparations treaties that bound Germany to pay billions of gold marks to France and Britain, despite the grinding poverty and skyrocketing inflation that wracked the country. He presided, among other assignments, over the signing of the Treaty of Rapallo, a friendship agreement between the Soviet Union and Germany. The Right, to say nothing of the disaffected men and women on the streets, abhorred this very public Jew representing Germany in the world. On 24 June 1922, a group of assassins opened fire on Rathenau's open car. Political violence – putsches and street fights – haunted the Weimar Republic from its inception, but the assassination of Walther Rathenau marked a tragic milestone. With that act, political anti-Semitism in modern Germany became lethal.

Nationalist extremists – and gradually ever more of mainstream opinion – equated Jewish influence with the Weimar system and the experimental culture that Berlin witnessed in the late 1920s. (By the end of the decade, nearly one-third of the Jewish population in Germany lived in the capital.) As the republic lost public approval, anti-Semitic sentiment became more common and virulent. Between 1923 and 1932, 128 Jewish cemeteries and 50 synagogues were desecrated; in the early 1930s, during the worldwide depression, physical attacks against Jews increased. Right-wing students led the violence. By this time, Adolf Hitler's National Socialist German Workers Party attracted more than six million voters. The Nazis became Germany's strongest party in 1932 – and its only party in 1933.

The Holocaust

On 1 April 1933, the Nazi party organised the first large-scale anti-Jewish demonstration and boycott. It met largely with stunned disapproval from a German public that had not taken Hitler's anti-Semitism seriously enough to expect such violent disorder. That same year, however, German officialdom adopted the designation 'non-Aryan' for its dealings. Starting in September 1935, a series of measures that became known as the Nuremberg racial laws deprived Jews of sundry civic rights and prohibited marriage and sexual relations between Jews and non-Jews. A Jew, according to these measures, was anyone of Jewish descent, regardless of personal identification with Judaism; an elaborate table of family trees established the hereditary threshold of Jewishness. The Law Respecting Reich Citizenship declared Jews to be non-Germans without rights, unwelcome guests of the German nation. Only the Olympic Games of the summer of 1936 provided a respite from the *Ausgrenzung*, or systematic exclusion from society, of the Jews; for as long as foreign spectators were on hand, signs prohibiting Jews from entering certain cities and towns disappeared.

In the first years of the Third Reich, Nazi racial policy concentrated on forcing Jews out of the country. Naturally, the emigrants had to leave most of their property and assets behind. By 1938, nearly half of the 500,000 Jews had left Germany. Those who remained faced ever more fateful racial strictures.

On 23 July 1938, a new law required all Jews to carry special identity papers so that police could readily spot the 'unwanted aliens'. On 17 August, the Nazis compelled all Jews to adopt distinctly Jewish given names, such as Sara or Israel. Then in the autumn, a young Polish Jew living in France, Herszel Grynzpan, sought revenge on the Germans for deporting his parents. As his target, he randomly selected Ernst von Rath, a diplomat in Germany's embassy in France, whom he shot on 7 November. Nazi leaders quickly declared the assassination as evidence of an international Jewish plot against their regime. On 9 November, after an inflammatory speech by propaganda minister Joseph Goebbels, brown-shirted Stormtroopers and other armed party units received orders to mount a nationwide pogrom, the *Kristallnacht*, or Night of the Broken Glass. The rampage left 91 Jews dead and 300 in 'protective custody'. Some 7,500 Jewish-owned businesses were burned and vandalised. Over 25,000 Jewish men were sent to concentration camps.

After 1938, Jews could no longer attend schools with Germans, possess drivers' licences, own businesses or employ Germans. At the time, only about 15 per cent of the Jews in Germany still held jobs; the rest survived on their dwindling personal resources or relied on the organised welfare of the Jewish community. Ghettoisation proceeded, once the Nazis conquered Poland in 1939; now they had the territory to which they could deport the native Jews, and the millions of Polish Jews thus subject to Nazi rule rendered the question of confinement more pressing.

The *Schutzstaffeln*, or SS, assumed primary responsibility for managing the lot of Jews in Nazi-held Europe. A Reich Security Main Office handled the bureaucratic organisation, drafting the plans for the concentration of all Jews in sealed areas of Polish cities. When the occupation of Poland required larger-scale action, the SS formed special strike forces – *Einsatzgruppen* – to realise these plans. By the time Germany invaded the Soviet Union in 1941, the *Einsatzgruppen* had turned increasingly to on-the-spot mass executions, with plunder or torture according to the group leaders' inclination. In two years, by some estimates, the murder units killed a million Jews.

Even so, Nazi leaders began to search for a more effective way to address their 'Jewish Question'. Crudely put, there remained far too many people to murder individually, and Germany needed its men to fight its expanding war. On 31 July 1941, Hermann Göring, as head of the economic war effort, instructed the Reich Security Main Office to conceive a 'final solution'. A meeting of agency and party leaders followed in December 1941 and January 1942 in a lakeside villa in the Berlin suburb of Wannsee. The plan that emerged from this Wannsee Conference called for the construction of extermination facilities – top-secret camps not for concentrating but for killing European Jewry – in and around Poland. Six death camps commenced operations by 1942: Auschwitz, Belzec, Chelmno, Majdanek, Sobibor and Treblinka. Railroad lines brought Jewish men, women and children to the camps, where, in an efficient, factory-like fashion under the guard of the armed *Schutzstaffeln,* the *Waffen-SS,* they were stripped, shorn and gassed with carbon monoxide or the pesticide Zyklon B; batteries of crematoria disposed of the bodies. In this industrial process, six million Jews lost their lives; Auschwitz, the most developed death camp, accounted alone for about two million Jewish deaths between early 1942 and late 1944. The Nazis manned their murder machines until Red Army troops closed the camps in their advance.

The aftermath

The Final Solution changed the ways Jews everywhere conceive of their past, and it obviously changed relations between Jews and Germans in fundamental ways. Some significant continuities connect the German–Jewish experience before and after the Holocaust, however. Most importantly, the relationship continues.

Contemporary German Jewry reassembled itself from the individuals who remained in the country after the war as a matter of conscious choice; 1945 marks *the* historical conjuncture in the formation of the Jewish presence in Germany today. To be sure, only some 43,000 people identify themselves officially as part of the all-German Jewish community at present, and estimates add, at best, another 15,000 to 20,000 unaffiliated Jews to that population. (The total population in united Germany tops 80 million; the registered Jewish community represents a bit more than one twentieth of one per cent of this total.) As it was earlier in the century, the German–Jewish community is concentrated in a few major cities. Berlin, home to 8,000 or so Jews, and Frankfurt/Main, with about 5,000 Jewish residents, rank as the two largest Jewish centres. Munich, Düsseldorf and Hamburg each maintain a Jewish population of a few thousand, while communities numbering perhaps two or three dozen practising Jews hang on in the urban centres of the former German Democratic Republic, such as Dresden, Leipzig and Erfurt. In all, the Federal German community after unification on 3 October 1990 absorbed 250 to 400 practising East German Jews.

A minority of Jews in the Federal Republic are native Germans; indeed, one could only characterise the community in the post-war period as Jews who happen to live in Germany, rather than German Jews. Immigrants from the erstwhile Soviet Union comprise more than half of the German–Jewish community today; in the last several years, Berlin and Frankfurt especially have witnessed a sharp increase in the Jewish population thanks to the influx of these Soviet Jews. These recent arrivals present the German community with new challenges, particularly because they tend to be little versed in Jewish tradition and religious practices.

In contrast, Jews who came to Germany from other East Central and Eastern European countries right after the war subscribed to a more traditional Judaism than their pre-war German counterparts, a fact reflected in the conservative essence of the religious community. (With very few exceptions, most famously the synagogue in Berlin's Pestalozzi Street, the Orthodox liturgy prevails.) Though Liberalism and Orthodoxy organised separately before the war, all aspects of Judaism and Jewish life now fall into the purview of the single German–Jewish community. Strikingly, native German Jews – who represent about 10 per cent of the community's population – continue to dominate the positions of leadership in Jewish organisational life.

Given the small numbers of Jews in the Federal Republic, one might question the influence if not the prospects of the Jewish community in contemporary Germany. In fact, a good many Germans today have never met a Jew in their lives; they experience Jews in films, monuments, museums, newspapers and books, but never at school, the grocery store or the dentist. Jews represent less real beings than abstracted artefacts of an equally abstruse guilt. Certainly one can name no post-war German–Jewish figure who can claim anything like the cultural influence of Mendelssohn or Heine or Meyerbeer or Tucholsky.

Nonetheless, German–Jewish relations retain a societal significance in the Federal Republic, for the Holocaust has lent both Jews and Germans their identity in today's Germany, a unique aspect of the long German–Jewish relationship. If the German–Jewish interactions after Auschwitz are largely a dialogue about a dialogue – about the whole of their mutual history – this conversation has a spiritual, cultural and intellectual import. Since its foundation on 23 May 1949, the Federal Republic has worked through its Nazi legacy spasmodically and to mixed effect; the struggle to come to terms with the past continues to this day. To that end, as in the century or so before World War II, the record of the Jewish–German relationship since 1945 parallels the development of the Federal Republic.

Transition and reconstruction, 1945–1949

Immediately after the war, the estimated number of Jews left in displaced persons camps in the Allied zones of occupied Germany surpassed 200,000. Many Jewish refugees could not or would not go back to the places where the violence and destruction of the National Socialist regime first reached them, so they stayed in the camps in Germany. Further, anti-Semitic excesses continued in the territories that the Nazis had occupied, notably in Poland, where in the summer of 1946, Europe bore witness to its last full-scale pogrom in the town of Kielce. Without question, displaced German and Eastern European Jews found in the DP camps safety from physical attack. Just the same, German guards policed the grounds, rations consisted of black bread and coffee, quarters were inhumanely cramped and refugees could not leave the camps.

In all, nearly 90 per cent of the Jewish refugees ultimately emigrated, largely to the United States or to the fledgling nation of Israel. Slightly more than 20,000 Jews, a majority of whom came from Poland, accounted for the new German–Jewish community in this period. Some hundreds of Jews took up residence in the Soviet sector of Eastern Germany, mostly out of political affinity for the emergent communist regime.

The initial response to German atrocities in the early years of the Federal Republic tended clearly toward forgetfulness and silence rather than an honest, collective confrontation. People busied themselves rebuilding their cities and their lives and accommodating the exigencies of defeat and occupation. A self-proclaimed successor party to the NSDAP – the *Sozialistische Reichspartei*, outlawed in 1952 and reorganised as the *Deutsche Reichspartei* – agitated among the former Nazis who had lost status, jobs and power to a democratic order to continue Hitler's national programme for Germany under a strongman leader. Acts of vandalism in Jewish cemeteries punctuated the DRP's 1953 campaign.

At the same time, the Allies began their programme of denazification, the effort to remove from positions of influence active supporters of the Third Reich. (Immediately after the war, the Allied programme for conquered Germany came down to the so-called Four D's – democratisation, demilitarisation, decartellisation and denazification.) The Nuremberg Trials of 1945–6 resulted in death sentences and prison terms for all but three of the twenty-four ranking members of the Nazi hierarchy, including Hermann Göring, Rudolf Hess and Julius Streicher. The charges before the International Military Tribunal included crimes against peace, war crimes, waging an aggressive war and crimes against humanity; the evidence for this last charge marked the first large-scale public treatment of German atrocities and the Holocaust. When the Nuremberg Trials ended in the autumn of 1946, the commanders in each of the four zones of occupied Germany and regional courts assumed the task of dealing with the lesser Nazi officials, with uneven results. By 1949, the escalation of tensions between the West and the Soviet Union – and the newfound strategic appeal of a functional federal German republic as an additional western ally – encouraged a hasty abandonment of the denazification process.

The record of denazification in what would become East Germany hardly augured better for collective contrition and historical self-reflection. Without a doubt, the Soviet Union initially took the process most seriously, that is to the furthest extent, in its zone of occupation. Before the 1940s ended, hundreds of thousands of people had been purged, in the non-lethal sense, from influential positions because of their earlier affiliation with the Nazi party. The Soviets converted concentration camps in Eastern Germany to prisons, and some 120,000 people served time, of whom more than a third died while interned. In 1946, however, the Socialist party softened its policy to attract the 'little Nazis' to its membership rosters, or at least to gain their support for the new political order.

Reparations and reckoning, 1949–1960

The western Allies passed to the new Federal Republic the responsibility of denazification, which the Germans pursued through the years with a similarly waning enthusiasm. It is in the context of the diminished urgency of denazification that reparations and restitution emerged as a likely approach for German atonement, to which the FRG's leaders attached a moral importance as well as a certain pragmatic expediency: thus could the Federal Republic integrate itself more fully with the western community of nations. This dual dynamic – of at least an initial reckoning with the past, on the one hand, and, on the other hand, the redefinition, collectively and individually, of an untainted republican culture – characterised the first decade and a half of West German history.

Jewish and German elites alike considered a programme of reparations to victims of the Holocaust to be imperative for the restoration of normality in terms of both conscience and *Realpolitik*. The Allies had actually begun an indemnification process with the passage of Law 59 in the American sector in November 1947. This law provided for the individual reimbursement of illegally confiscated or forcibly sold Jewish property, but it proved a partial measure. Naming itself the legal successor state to the Third Reich, West Germany proposed a more comprehensive programme of collective restitution – *Wiedergutmachung* – to Israel, as the representative of Jewish victims of the Holocaust. As Germany's economy improved so quickly, the government of Konrad Adenauer, the FRG's first chancellor, funded a series of social policies to redress the wrongs of the Second World War, including compensation for lost or damaged property and resettlement and retraining programs for German refugees. By 1966, the FRG had appropriated DM 3.5 billion for reparations to Holocaust victims and their descendants in Israel.

From the outset, the *Wiedergutmachung* raised its own set of political problems, not the least of which stemmed from the fact that the German leadership took up the scheme despite strong opposition from the general population. By and large, the German people felt no responsibility for the atrocities that the National Socialists had perpetrated in their name. Non-Jewish victims of Nazi persecution, excluded from the reparations agreement, resented the arrangement, and many observers objected to the commodification of German guilt implicit in these 'blood-money' transfer payments. On the other side, the prospect of German restitution promised a vital source of funding for the fledgling nation. Yet many Israelis rejected the idea of negotiating directly with Germany, viewing the FRG as little different from the Third Reich. Indeed, more than half a decade after VE Day, Israel refused to add its name to the forty-seven states that had declared an official end to their war with Germany.

In September 1951, though, Adenauer told the German parliament, 'The Federal Government is prepared, jointly with representatives of Jewry and the state of Israel . . . to bring about a solution of the material indemnity problem, thus easing the way to the spiritual settlement of infinite suffering.'[3] At times, the slow and secretive proceedings nearly foundered under mutual recriminations, but on 10 September 1952, Adenauer, Nahum Goldmann, representing the Diaspora Jewry, and Moshe Sharett, the envoy of the State of Israel, signed the treaty in Luxembourg.

In contrast, the government in East Berlin offered modest pensions to the few hundred Jews in the country, but as 'victims of fascism', a category which ranked somewhat lower than that of 'fighters against fascism' applied to communists or labour leaders who had suffered persecution at the hand of the Nazis. East Germany denied any connection with all but the most progressive elements of the German past and thus saw for itself no extra responsibility for Jewish welfare. Besides, the Holocaust, so the East Germans maintained, was primarily a product of capitalism; thus, the foundation of a socialist state represented the East German contribution to a better world. In the meantime, the GDR refused to recognise Israel.

Reconciliation and confrontation, 1961–1967
The 1960s witnessed some positive developments in German–Jewish relations within the Federal Republic. Temples and synagogues were rebuilt and reconsecrated in major cities; congregation halls, research institutes, administrative buildings, social services, schools and culture centres grew up with the community. By 1963, seventy-three Jewish congregations had collected under the Central Council of Jews in

Germany. Some German Jews returned from Israel, while East Central and East European Jews fled to the Federal Republic from Stalinist show trials – bloc-wide purges with a thinly disguised anti-Semitic bent – and abortive popular uprisings in Hungary (1956) and Czechoslovakia and Poland (1968). The German–Jewish community at last gained official recognition from international Jewish organisations.

German intellectuals took up the confrontation with the Nazi past, even when private society preferred denial. Already in August 1945, the philosopher Karl Jaspers spoke of the 'ineradicable shame and disgrace' of Germans, for 'we did not go into the streets when our Jewish friends were led away; we did not scream until we too were destroyed. We preferred to stay alive, on the feeble, if logical, ground that our death could not have helped anyone. We are guilty of being alive.'[4] Two years later, a number of German writers formed Group 47, which concerned itself with the future of German literature, reminding German society of the burden of German history. In particular, Group 47 addressed the problematic issue of how the language in which the Wannsee Conference was conducted could be reclaimed for artistic purposes. By the 1960s, these authors had produced a prodigious and frank body of work – Günter Grass's *Die Blechtrommel* (The Tin Drum), Heinrich Böll's *Billiard um halb zehn* (Billiards at Half Past Nine) and Uwe Johnson's *Mutmaßungen über Jakob* (Conjectures about Jacob) all became international best-sellers.

In 1965, the Federal Ministry of the Interior reported a decline in anti-Semitic incidents in the FRG, as well as a drop in the membership of left- and right-wing extremist parties. Indeed, a naive but well-meant philo-Semitism took hold among younger Germans. The Council of Societies for Christian–Jewish Cooperation dedicated itself to mutual understanding; other groups like *Drei Ringe* (Three Rings), an organisation of Protestant, Catholic and Jewish students, took interfaith cooperation as their central aim. The history of the Third Reich became a mandatory part of the German secondary-school curriculum in 1961.

And West German relations with Israel were normalised. On 12 May 1965, the two countries established full and formal diplomatic relations. The Deutsch–Israelische Gesellschaft (German–Israeli Society) appeared in 1966 to foster person-to-person contacts between the two states. The strength of the Social Democratic milieu within each country fostered union contacts, and it became almost *de rigueur* for young German intellectuals who were part of the labour movement to pay a visit to an Israeli *kibbutz*. A dedication to anti-Nazism cemented the relationship between the German Left and Jews in this period. By 1967, reparations to Israel reached a total of DM 31.3 billion.

An event in Israel stirred Germans to confront the Holocaust more explicitly in their past and present: the trial in 1960–1 of Adolf Eichmann, the ranking SS expert on the 'Jewish Question' who headed the Reich Security Main Office. Like a number of Nazi officials, Eichmann had spent the years since the war in hiding in South America until Jewish Nazi hunters brought him to Jerusalem for the trial. In Germany, the question of war crimes and the role of ex-National Socialists in the Federal Republic regained its uncomfortable currency.

From 1963 to 1965, the FRG mounted its own proceeding; the so-called Auschwitz Trials emerged as an international media spectacle. After five and a half years of preparation, including interviews with more than 400 witnesses from around the world, the case against sixteen members of the *Waffen-SS* and one camp overseer or *Kapo* began in Frankfurt. None of the defendants – doctors, guards and gas-chamber supervisors at the most notorious of the six Nazi death camps – had violated any laws of the National Socialist state that they had served. Instead, they stood before the Frankfurt Court of Assizes for the murder and torture of unascertainable numbers of people at Auschwitz, to answer to the statutes of the Federal Republic, to say nothing of world opinion, twenty years after the end of World War II. In the end, six of the accused received life sentences of hard labour, the maximum punishment permitted by the federal German constitution. (Lawmakers abolished the death penalty in Germany in 1955.) Three defendants were acquitted, and the rest faced terms of three and a half to fourteen years in prison. *Befehlsnotstand* – just following orders – represented the thrust of the defence, and the success of this exculpatory tactic, and the abdication of individual responsibility that it implied, resonated among many Germans, for the logic of it further precluded collective complicity in the worst crime in human history.

The Auschwitz trial and the international attention that it drew remained highly unpopular in German society. The defendants had conducted their post-war lives as peaceable, middle-class family men with no criminal records in the new German state; the proceedings struck many detractors as a witch-hunt. Others expressed their frustration that even this well-publicised trial, like the steady flow of denazification cases in German courts since 1949, failed to prosecute the really influential people running Nazi Germany.

Still, the trials inspired a new wave of Holocaust fiction among

German writers, moved especially by the accounts of survivors. Martin Walser's father–son drama, *Der schwarze Schwan* (The Black Swan), arose from this period; it deals with the impact of the genocide on the second generation. Rolf Hochhuth's *Der Stellvertreter* (The Deputy), a play that centres on the Vatican's passivity toward the 'Final Solution', was premiered in Berlin at this time. And Peter Weiss put the testimony into an eleven-song verse cycle, later performed as an oratorio, and penned a drama about the Auschwitz trials titled *Die Ermittlung* (The Investigation).

Changing relations, 1968–1980

A downturn in the German economy as well as some festering problems in the political leadership of the FRG heralded the three-year Grand Coalition of the Christian Democratic Union and the Social Democratic Party in December 1966. Small parties arose, which claimed to constitute the opposition that such a government lacked. One of these small parties was the National Democratic Party, a far-right grouping, with many members who had served proudly in Nazi youth organisations. The NPD wanted to put itself forward as more than an 'old-Nazi party', but its rhetoric – rejection of the thesis that Germany bore all or most of the blame for the world wars and a 'nationalist' concern for the 'penetrating alienation of German and European values and life-style' by foreigners, as the 1967 platform read – drew from the staple sentiments of the neo-Nazi movement. By the end of 1968, the NPD held parliamentary seats in seven of the eleven West German states. When the economy began to improve, however, the party lost again the seats that it had gained in state elections and narrowly failed to enter the Bundestag.

During the Six-Day War in 1967, the German public expressed over-whelming support for Israel. The established Right and the Springer Press – with its flagship tabloid *Bild*, the most circulated paper in Germany – regarded with approval the muscular land and air attacks with which Moshe Dayan (the new 'Desert Fox') and his generals defeated a much more numerous enemy. The eternal victims had posted a decisive win.

On the other hand, the conflict rent relations between Jews and the next generation in the German Left. The rising opposition to the American war in Vietnam and the increasing appeal of Third World revolutionary movements among the New Left in the Federal Republic mutated the social democratic anti-fascist ethic from specific anti-Nazism with a central concern for the Holocaust as a singular crime into a generalised paradigm for protest. As such, Auschwitz marked an epiphenomenon, a secondary manifestation of fascism and its twin evil, monopoly capitalism. To the New Left, the 'fascist' appellation applied equally to US arms industrialists, nationalists in the German government and, among other imperialist oppressors, the State of Israel.

The *kibbutz* hat fell out of fashion with the young German Left, which adopted instead the checked scarf of the Palestinian *fedayeen* (fighters). Some observers sought to characterise this 'hyper-identification' with the Palestinians not as a heartfelt rejection of Israel but rather as a symbolic displacement of blame on the victim. Yet the New Left professed to differentiate between Jews, who merited support, and Israelis, who deserved only scorn – not unlike the East German government's policy of 'anti-Zionism' in the Middle East, a very fine distinction by which the GDR hoped its rejection of Israel would not seem anti-Semitic. The New Left saw no contradiction in its rallying to various Jewish causes within the Federal Republic while it vilified Israel at the same time; after all, Israel counted among its staunchest supporters the conservative German elites. The grotesque flaw in this logic appeared at the extremes: members of the terrorist Red Army Faction trained at Palestinian commando camps, and, in 1976, Germans among the hijackers of an El Al aeroplane to Entebbe, Uganda, participated in the 'selection' of Jewish passengers, analogous to what their fathers had done at the train platforms in the death camps.

Still, one must add here that the 'cultural revolution' that rocked Germany after 1968 – a movement much more the making of the intellectual Left than its counterpart in the United States – began when students, as part of their overall criticisms of the stratified German education system, insisted that the generation of their parents and teachers had failed to reckon meaningfully with the legacy of Nazism and the Third Reich. When the Social Democratic Chancellor Willy Brandt, on a state visit to the Polish capital in 1970, spontaneously dropped to his knees before the monument to the Warsaw uprisings, he symbolically proclaimed for Germany a new readiness to confront and begin to atone for the Nazi past.[5]

The middle 1970s saw the 'Hitler wave' break over Germany, the increasing equation in German hearts and minds of Hitler and Nazism. This conception, which laid responsibility for the crimes of the Third Reich specifically with the Führer and his paladins, had the perverse corollary effect of exonerating many Germans as 'victims of National Socialism' themselves. Even the ranks of the SS could be regarded as mere pawns in an evil system of Hitler's device.

Then, of all things, the American-made television docudrama, 'Holocaust', awakened the German conscience and opened public debate on an unprecedented scale. Whereas more than a hundred previously televised documentaries and educational programmes on the Nazi period attracted but a handful of viewers beyond a self-selected intellectual audience, fifteen million people – 40 per cent of the viewing public – tuned into 'Holocaust' for each of the four nights that it was broadcast in January 1979. Thousands called or wrote to Germany's high-brow Channel Three, often with personal testimony or protestations of remorse. (One ex-SS officer sent his private pictures of a burning synagogue filled with Jews to corroborate a similar scene in the movie.) Clearly, this thoroughly mediocre Hollywood melodrama revealed the continued relevance of the Nazi past to the German present.

Not surprisingly, the mini-series also provoked negative reactions. At the extreme, protest turned to violence, when neo-Nazi groups bombed two television transmitters during the showing of a documentary titled 'Final Solution' that was broadcast three days before 'Holocaust'. Letters and editorials in some conservative newspapers disdained the film's 'kitschy' sentimentality. Other comments bespoke a desire to forget the past and to refrain from making the Germans solely culpable for World War II and its atrocities – the Allied fire bombing of Dresden came up in this context. Finally, some critics worried that the film would stir up anti-German sentiments or otherwise tarnish the international image of the Federal Republic.

Nonetheless, popular interest in the programme echoed in political developments of the time. Eleven defendants stood trial for their activities at the Majdanek death camp; when four were acquitted, an unusual display of public outrage ensued. On 4 July 1979, 355 members of the West German parliament – all but one Social Democratic delegate and a smattering of conservatives and liberals – voted to drop the statute of limitations on murder. Until then, the constitution stipulated a thirty-year limit on murder prosecutions, which meant that Nazi crimes might soon go unpunished. While lawmakers would not specifically extend the deadline for war crimes, the new law allowed the sporadic proceedings to continue.

Shifting images, 1980–1989

In 1982, Helmut Kohl won a parliamentary majority to replace the Social Democrat Helmut Schmidt as Chancellor, and in the elections one year later the centre-right Christian Democratic Union campaigned on 'traditional' German virtues. Many scholars view Kohl's election as indicative of a general increase in conservatism in Germany, and, indeed, in Europe. The 1980s in the Federal Republic confronted the post-1968 New-Left-inspired institutional order and ethos, above all in the universities, with an ascendant and updated Right. Certainly Germany's self-image was changing, and Jewish–German relations reflected this transition.

In a word, Germany in the 1980s sought normalisation – of its national image and the issue of the Nazi past in the democratic present. This trend had political as well as cultural ramifications. In a visit to Israel in 1984, Kohl, the first German Chancellor who had experienced the Third Reich only as a small child, invoked the 'grace of a late birth', which – so Kohl believed – exculpated his generation of direct historical responsibility because he was too young to have had to make conscious decisions about Nazism. The extreme right *Republikaner* party, under the charismatic direction of former SS man Franz Schönhuber, began to make its presence felt in German politics with its platform of national strength, racial purity and neutral independence between the super-powers. In 1985, a Frankfurt theatre prepared to perform Rainer Werner Fassbinder's anti-Semitic play, *Der Müll, die Stadt und der Tod* (Garbage, The City and Death). The piece continued the well-worn trope of the Jew as evil capitalist, but its planned premiere marked a momentous rethinking of the Jewish community's presence in the FRG. On opening night, demonstrators in the first post-war protest by German Jews as Jews with a domestic concern occupied the stage and prevented the performance. In the end, this direct action compelled the cancellation of the entire production.

Then came the Bitburg fiasco. President Reagan announced at a White House news conference in the spring of 1985 that he would not stop at a concentration camp site during his forthcoming trip to Germany, lest the visit awaken memories that might threaten the excellent contemporary relationship between the Federal Republic and the United States. Instead, President Reagan, accompanied by Chancellor Kohl, planned to lay a wreath at the military cemetery in Bitburg to honour Germany's war dead, a gesture of understanding after the rest of Europe had marked the fortieth anniversary of the Normandy landing and D-Day, festivities that had pointedly excluded the German Chancellor. Shortly after Reagan's announcement, the media reported that in addition to regular German soldiers, forty-nine members of the *Waffen-SS* Division *Das Reich*, known for its singular brutality in the complete destruction of the French town Oradour-sur-Glane in 1944, lay buried in the Bitburg cemetery as well. American legislators urged Kohl to release Reagan from his commitment and implored the President to forego the trip, but the German parliament voted 398–24 to have the visit proceed. The two dozen dissenting votes all belonged to the Green Party, while the Social Democrats and the liberals remained mute on the issue.

Amid acrimony and outcry on both sides of the Atlantic, Reagan did visit the Bitburg graveyard on 5 May 1985, though he also stopped at the Bergen-Belsen concentration camp, despite his initial pronouncement, thereby making matters worse by publically equating a place where Jews were murdered with one in which their murders lay buried. The Greens demonstratively journeyed to Poland to visit Auschwitz on the day that Reagan toured Bergen-Belsen, a nobly intended act that, in unfortunate fact, meant that virtually no German leftists or liberals joined the handful of Jewish demonstrators where the Chancellor and the President actually appeared.

Three days after Bitburg, the President of the Federal Republic, Richard von Weizsäcker, did what he could to soothe the situation with a moving and honest speech to commemorate the fortieth anniversary of VE Day. 'All of us,' von Weizsäcker said, 'whether guilty or not, whether old or young, must accept the past. We are all affected by its consequences and liable for it . . . We must understand that there can be no reconciliation without remembrance.'[6]

The quest for a normal national identity became an academic dispute as conservative scholars addressed the 'historicisation' of the Holocaust. Andreas Hillgruber's 1985 thesis *Zweierlei Untergang* (Two Kinds of Demise) and, above all, Ernst Nolte's 1986 article in the *Frankfurter Allgemeine Zeitung* 'Vergangenheit, die nicht vergehen will' (The Past that Will Not Pass Away)[7] represented an open call to normalise the Holocaust within the context of twentieth-century history by linking it to mass exterminations that the Bolsheviks had perpetrated. Hitler, it was claimed, learned genocide by example.

The rebuttal of such odious revisionism came most eloquently and trenchantly from the Frankfurt social philosopher Jürgen Habermas. He contended that the Basic Law had played such a decisive role in creating steady institutions in the Federal Republic as to call for a new type of democratic national pride in the shape of 'constitutional patriotism'. The quest to 'normalise' German history by relativising the Holocaust was morally and intellectually wrong. Other scholars joined either side of the controversy until President von Weizsäcker settled it to the detriment of the revisionists and German unification overtook the public discourse.

Conclusions

Ignatz Bubis, chairman of the directorate of the Central Council of Jews in the Federal Republic, insisted that 'unification had no impact on the Jewish communities in Germany'.[8] He meant that the five new states in the East revealed themselves to be as congenial to German Jews as the West had been, at least judging by the respectable frequency of their politicians' pronouncements. In reunited Berlin, in fact, the restored golden dome crowns the reconsecrated New Synagogue in the Oranienburgerstraße, which also houses the archive and exhibits of the Centrum Judaicum. A Jewish high school has resumed instruction in the building of the Jewish boys' school that Moses Mendelssohn helped found two centuries ago, and non-Jewish parents clamour for an opportunity to send their children there for the lessons of tolerance as well as college preparatory course work.

Generally, the 1990s witnessed such positive development as the well-received Jewish Museum in the City of Berlin Museum and the popular acclaim for and far-reaching public discussions of Steven Spielberg's Oscar-winning movie, *Schindler's List*, and Daniel Goldhagen's study, *Hitler's Willing Executioners*. At the same time, however, plans for a Holocaust memorial in Berlin have stalled amid increasing acrimony and official cold feet, revealing a peristent snag in the German–Jewish discourse. More troublingly, episodes of right-extremist violence continued to mar the social and political scene.

Without question, xenophobia and right-wing aggression have risen in much of Central and Western Europe, notably in France, Spain, Sweden, Italy and Austria. The spectre, however pale, is particularly ominous in Germany. Many Germans share this unease, as their candle-light vigils against racism and violence eloquently demonstrate, and neo-Nazi incidents scarcely threaten German democracy. Still, these attacks coincide with a growing rightward drift, which in the reunited Germany lends a certain legitimacy to more extreme politics – and perhaps a more equivocal historical self-conception – than the old Federal Republic deemed acceptable.

In all, the changing nature of Germany's European presence, its accumulation of power, and the passage of time will all contribute to forces that will erode the 'special' nature of the old Federal Republic's relationship with the Jews. But no matter how concerted the German effort toward normalisation of this relationship, the indelible character of Auschwitz will guarantee its continued uniqueness for Germans and Jews alike.

NOTES

1. Heinrich von Treitschke, *Deutsche Geschichte im nenzehnten Jahrhundert*, vol. IV, Leipzig: S. Hirzel Verlag, 1889, p. 423.
2. Heinrich von Treitschke, quoted in Alfred D. Low, *Jews in the Eyes of the Germans*, Philadelphia: Institute for the Study of Human Issues, 1979, p. 372.
3. Lily Gardner Feldman, *The Special Relationship Between West Germany and Israel*, Boston: George Allen and Unwin, 1984, p. 40.
4. Quoted in Gordon Craig, *The Germans*, New York: Putnam, 1982, p. 145.
5. The monument in Warsaw conflates two separate events, the uprising of the Jews in the ghetto in April 1943 and of the Polish population of Warsaw in the spring of 1944, bespeaking the fact that the Poles, too, have problems with coming to terms with their own relationship to Jews after the Holocaust.
6. Richard von Weizsäcker, *A Voice From Germany*, trans. Karin von Abrams, New York: Weidenfeld and Nicholson, 1985, pp. 43–60.
7. Ernst Nolte, 'Vergangenheit, die nicht vergehen will', in *Frankfurter Allgemeine Zeitung*, 6 June 1986.
8. Quoted in Susan Stern (ed.), *Speaking Out: Jewish Voices from United Germany*, Chicago, Berlin, etc.: edition q, 1995, p. 62.

FURTHER READING

On the nineteenth- and early twentieth-century history of Jews in Germany, particularly in cultural and intellectual spheres, see the critical essays in David Bronsen, (ed.), *Jews and Germans from 1860 to 1933: The Problematic Symbiosis* (Heidelberg: Carl Winter Universitätsverlag, 1979); and H. I. Bach, *The German Jew* (New York: Oxford University Press, 1984). For the prominent Jewish personalities, consult Jehuda Reinharz and Walter Schatzberg (eds.), *The Jewish Response to German Culture* (Hanover and London: University Press of New England, 1985).

Fritz Stern, *Gold and Iron* (New York: Alfred A. Knopf, 1977) concerns Bismarck, his relations with the banker Bleichröder and the formation of the Second Reich. In another vein, the personal memories in Monika Richarz (ed.), *Jewish Life in Germany* (Bloomington and Indianapolis: Indiana University Press, 1991) offer a glimpse at the world experienced by Jews in German-speaking parts of Europe.

The classic documentation of the Holocaust remains Raul Hillberg, *The Destruction of the European Jews* (Chicago: Quadrangle Books, 1961). For the social and political pre-history to the 'Final Solution', see Karl A. Schleunes, *The Twisted Road to Auschwitz* (Urbana and Chicago: University of Illinois Press, 1970). A succinct but thorough historiography of the scholarly debates on the origins and meanings of the Holocaust appears in Michael R. Marrus, *The Holocaust in History* (Hanover and London: University Press of New England, 1987).

On the post-war period, see the essays in Anson Rabinbach and Jack Zipes (eds.), *Germans and Jews Since the Holocaust* (New York: Holms & Meier, 1986). On the question of German and Austrian efforts to make workable sense of the Nazi past, consult Kathy Harms, Lutz R. Reuter and Volker Dürr (eds.), *Coping with the Past* (Madison and London: University of Wisconsin Press, 1990); and the pertinent chapters in Judith Miller, *One, by One, by One* (New York: Simon and Schuster, 1990).

5

Non-German minorities, women and the emergence of civil society

110   In Germany, the emergence of both civil society and political democracy followed the same trajectory of modernisation. Like democracy, civil society had a troubled start in a country where state policies continued to emulate authoritarian traditions and restrict rights of social participation. Democracy and civil society took a firmer shape after 1945 when anti-democratic forces had lost their commanding influence while unprecedented economic growth reduced inequalities.

This chapter traces the emergence of civil society with reference to non-German labour migrants and to women. Both groups were largely excluded from rights of social participation at the beginning of the twentieth century and constituted a focal point of the National Socialist agenda. In the post-war era, the East German model decreed women's equality through employment and excluded non-Germans from civil society. The West German model extended social citizenship to non-German minorities and women without overcoming all legacies of exclusion that had gone before.

Labour migration and non-German minorities in German civil society

In the eighteenth and early nineteenth centuries when German rulers tried to develop the economy of their region and boost tax yield, foreigners played a key role as financiers, engineers or specially hired technicians. Non-German minorities who sought refuge from religious persecution – the Huguenots or Jews for instance – also benefited from the interest in importing modern business practices. Including such minorities into German society invariably took the form of special privileges. Although permitted to pursue their trades, these minorities remained excluded from civil society and their special status could be withdrawn at will by the ruler.

For most of the nineteenth century, migration was in an outward direction. The German economy was too weak to support the growing population and emigration constituted a major tenet of socio-economic development. During the Great Depression of the 1880s, up to 200,000 people a year left the country. From the 1890s onwards, culminating in the decade before the First World War, the German economy grew faster than ever before and emigration fell to a trickle while the recruitment of migrant labour became a regular feature. Census data suggest an increase from 224,000 to 1.5 million between 1871 and 1914.

Labour migrants in Imperial Germany, 1871–1918

The bulk of migrant labourers were seasonal workers from Poland, Galicia or Russia and employed on the vast agricultural estates of Eastern Prussia. Here, industrial development had wreaked havoc as villagers moved into towns in pursuit of better wages. Although agricultural manpower was permanently in short supply in these regions, recruitment was strictly seasonal. Fearing what they called 'polonisation', a cultural visibility of Poles in German regions, the German authorities insisted that all labour migrants returned to their home country during the winter months. Above all, they wanted to prevent a repetition of developments in the Ruhr region. Here, Polish miners who happened to hold German citizenship – the *Ruhrpolen* – set up distinctive communities during the period of rapid industrialisation. The German (and Prussian) authorities viewed these developments as a danger to German cultural and national homogeneity.

In Imperial Germany, migrant workers had a second-class status. Unprotected against dismissal, their wages were lower than those paid to Germans and their working conditions normally harsher. Although able to return year after year, migrants were not permitted to settle. Temporary in their status, they lived in separate accommodation (which was locked up at night) and remained excluded from those citizens' rights which pertained in German society at the time. Migrant workers could be deported if they committed (or were accused of committing) an offence, lost their employment or, in the case of women, became pregnant. The exclusion of migrant workers from German civil society was borne out when more than one million who worked in Germany in August 1914 lost their liberty and were detained as labour conscripts for the duration of the First World War.

Non-German labour in the Weimar Republic, 1918–1932

In the Weimar Republic, the employment of seasonal migrant labour in agriculture continued along the same principles but on a reduced scale since many agricultural areas in the east had been lost to Poland. The pace of the Weimar economy was too uneven to create the demand for additional labour that had existed before 1914. Foreigners remained a supplementary labour force and did not benefit from the implementation of democratic structures. On the contrary, the Weimar administration tightened the system of labour market registration and stipulated that foreigners could only be employed if no German worker could be found. This principle of exclusion has remained in force to the present day. It means that non-Germans take second place to Germans on the grounds of their national origins.

Non-German labour and slave labour in the Third Reich, 1933–1945

National Socialism radicalised the exclusion of non-Germans from civil society by decreeing that Germans were superior and non-Germans inferior. The Nazis employed the language of race to justify their classification of people. In this language, Germans were called Aryans, a term used in legislation from 1933 onwards to exclude non-Germans (and Jews) systematically from German civil society. The ultimate aim of Nazi policy can be described as creating a society for Germans only. Such a society institutionalised discrimination by applying different laws to Germans and non-Germans.

In theory, Nazi society should have included fewer and fewer non-Germans as racist doctrines took root. However, the economic preparation of war and the introduction of military service in 1935 created labour shortages even before the backlog of mass unemployment had been cleared. Initially, the National Socialist labour administration redirected workers from agriculture and small businesses to work in industry while the women were left to cope with running family farms, retail shops, and the like. By 1938, labour supply in agriculture had fallen so drastically that food production and harvesting were under threat.

The recruitment of foreign labour to work inside Nazi Germany was the flip-side of 'germanising' German society and preparing for war. In 1934, the Nazis concluded intergovernmental contracts with Italy, Poland and Yugoslavia, followed by hundreds of recruitment offices and a flood of propaganda designed to entice non-Germans to work in Germany. By 1938, close to 200,000 had been hired and deployed in agriculture. In place of short-term contracts, the National Socialists relied on the Gestapo to enforce social apartheid. Friendliness towards non-German workers was explicitly forbidden; non-Germans who had social and in particular sexual contacts with Germans were imprisoned in a concentration camp or executed.

This programme of recruiting foreign labour was little more than a prelude to the use and abuse of non-German workers during the Second World War. Nazi Germany treated the territories that its armies occupied as a massive reservoir for conscript labour. Young men and women were seized and deported to Germany by the SS. Forced to work without pay, without freedom of movement or personal rights and frequently starved to death, many of these 'Fremdarbeiter' (aliens used in forced labour) in Nazi Germany suffered the fate of slaves, albeit in an industrial society of the twentieth century.

By May 1940, 500,000 Poles had been deported to Germany, adding to the 300,000 non-German workers who were already in the country. After the German advances into Russia, deportations reached new heights. Between April and December 1942 alone, 1.3 million Russian civilians were taken to Germany, an average of 40,000 people per week. In 1944, one in three workers in German industry and every second worker in German agriculture were Fremdarbeiter. From 1943 onwards, German industrial enterprises constructed their own labour camps along Gestapo lines. Forced labour extended also to several million prisoners of war, most of them Russians, and similar numbers of concentration camp prisoners. German industrial plants even chose locations next to concentration camps to exploit slave labour.

Treated as inferior on account of their national origin, Fremdarbeiter suffered total exclusion from German society. Compelled to work, their lives depended on their Nazi guards and the interpretation of Nazi ideology by those around them. In some cases, Germans treated their non-German workers humanely even at the risk of denunciation and punishment. In most cases, however, they never questioned the exclusion of Fremdarbeiter from civil society since it did not seem so different from the way in which migrant workers had been treated in the past. Overall, 14 million non-Germans had been forced to work in the German war economy. In May 1945, 7.5 million *Fremdarbeiter* remained to be liberated.

Contract workers in the German Democratic Republic

The post-war era seemed to herald a new departure. Officially, the East German state welcomed foreigners who originated in socialist countries. Leaving aside diplomats and foreign students, only a handful of political refugees held residency permits, among them members of the West German Baader-Meinhof terrorist group. Generally speaking, the GDR kept its borders closed. When state socialism collapsed in 1989, the population included 1.2 per cent non-Germans, fewer than had been living in the same region in 1939. East German society was essentially German-only in its composition. Manpower shortages were met by recruiting all adults of working age for employment. However, the problem was exacerbated as East Germans, most of them young and well trained, escaped to the West. The Berlin Wall, built in 1961, and the fortified borders that followed, had the purpose of halting the flow and stabilising labour supply.

Low productivity had always made the East German economy labour-intensive and dependent on additional supply to increase output. By the mid-sixties, women and men had been fully integrated into the labour market and further manpower could only be found outside the GDR. The GDR did what German governments had done since the 1890s and recruited from abroad. Between 1966 and 1986, it concluded agreements with the governments of Poland, Hungary, Algeria, Cuba, Mozambique, Vietnam, Angola and China to supply contract workers, *Vertragsarbeiter*. All worked in industry, especially in hazardous sectors such as lignite mining and chemical production. During their period of employment in the GDR, they lived in hostels that were guarded and locked at night. They could be dismissed at will and deported; pregnant women were deported or forced to have an abortion. In addition, the government of the home country was entitled to part of a worker's earnings while the GDR withheld up to half the wages if the home country was financially indebted to it.

The GDR authorities discouraged social contacts with non-Germans and treated them as potentially *republikfeindlich*, hostile to the Republic. Recruitment from Poland and Hungary came to a halt at the first sign of democratic developments there and shifted increasingly to Third World countries. In 1989, after the mass exodus of East Germans created severe manpower shortages in the East German economy, the GDR government responded by recruiting 60,000 additional workers from China and Vietnam and signing agreements for a further 90,000 from Mozambique.

The collapse of the SED regime caught just over 100,000 contract workers in the GDR. Within six months, most had been dismissed. Without rights, homeless and without income, they were outcasts in East German society. After the March 1990 elections, destitute contract workers received some financial assistance until they were deported. A handful of Vietnamese refused to leave and won the right to remain until the end of their original five year contract in 1994. Permitted to work only as pedlars and street traders, their presence aroused considerable public hostility in the climate of social uncertainty before and after unification. After 1989 it became evident that East Germans had no experience of living alongside non-German minorities as members of civil society.

Labour migrants in the Federal Republic of Germany

In deliberate contrast to the violation of human rights under National Socialism, and an equally deliberate attempt to protect democracy more effectively than the Weimar Republic had done, the constitutional framework for the West German state, the Basic Law, opens with a section on human rights. In doing so, it committed the policy process and the public authorities to safeguarding social citizenship for everyone regardless of nationality, background, gender, religion or culture. Although the law of origin, *ius sanguinis*, prevailed in post-war legislation on citizenship and rendered Germany a non-immigration country, the centrality of human rights enabled migrant workers to settle in German society.

By the mid-1990s, 8.4 per cent of Germany's population were non-Germans, so were one in three six-year-olds and one in five adolescents. In major cities such as Berlin, Frankfurt, Munich and Stuttgart, 20 per cent or more of the inhabitants were non-Germans. With 1.8 million, Turks were the largest non-German minority and Islam the third largest religion. About half the non-Germans had lived in the country for fifteen years or more. No longer for Germans only, German society at the close of the twentieth century had become culturally more diverse than at any point since the beginnings of the German nation state.

This change occurred unplanned. By the mid-1950s, economic recovery had healed the social dislocations of the post-war years and generated demand for additional labour. West Germany followed the familiar route of recruiting from other countries. Between 1955 and 1968, the government signed agreements with Italy, Spain, Greece, Turkey, Morocco, Portugal, Tunisia and Yugoslavia and the Federal Employment Agency (Bundesanstalt für Arbeit) administered the policy by setting up recruitment agencies and issuing contracts in the sending countries. Only workers with valid contracts could enter. Contracts were short-term, usually for one year. After that time, 'rotation' was to take effect, i.e. workers would return home to be replaced by others. Rotation was to ensure that industry had its labour supply but society did not incur the risk that non-Germans would settle. Labour recruits from abroad became known in post-war Germany as *Gastarbeiter*. In deliberate contrast to the exclusion and hostility implied in *Fremdarbeiter*, *Gastarbeiter* emphasised the status of the foreigner as a guest who would receive fair treatment. Such a worker would, of course, have to abide by the rules of the host and, most importantly, leave before too long.

The *Gastarbeiter* programme did not go to plan. Employers preferred to keep the workers they had trained while West German democracy bestowed rights of social citizenship upon non-German workers that modified the exclusion inherent in their status as migrants. From the outset *Gastarbeiter* were protected by the same labour law as Germans. The 1965 foreigners' legislation enabled non-Germans to apply for residency permits and receive unemployment and sickness benefits. Although regulations varied between German Länder, a non-German person without employment could no longer be expelled. Uncertainties persisted since the majority of non-Germans held only conditional residency permits. In 1990, a further revision of the foreigners' legislation stipulated that non-Germans who had lived in the country for at least eight years could apply for unconditional residency permits.

In 1955, 1,000 *Gastarbeiter* came to Germany. By 1960, their number had grown to 280,000. After the Berlin Wall halted the labour supply from East Germany, recruitment increased. At the end of the decade, *Gastarbeiter* numbered over two million, and 2.6 million in 1973 when a recruitment ban, *Anwerbestopp*, came into effect. Financial incentives to return home attracted just 400,000 takers. The majority decided to stay and settle. The additional and temporary workforce of yesteryear, the *Gastarbeiter*, became a non-German minority within German society, no longer migrant workers but residents.

Residency brought social 'normalisation'. The typical *Gastarbeiter* was an adult of working age, in employment and living in temporary housing or hostels. About 70 per cent were men, 30 per cent women. Few had come with their families, most had migrated alone and supported their relatives back home. The *Anwerbestopp* turned workers into residents who activated their right of bringing their families to Germany. This they could do, provided they were in work and had found suitable housing. Forced to find this at short notice, non-Germans tended to settle in run-down urban areas where rents were cheap and where German landlords accepted them. The process of family reunion generated challenges of social participation and equal treatment in civil society which had not been tested when *Gastarbeiter* were merely workers without much call on social institutions such as schools, neighbourhoods, leisure activity or the labour market after their initial contracts had come to an end.

The social developments that followed involved two processes of change. The first concerned the cultural orientations of the non-German minorities themselves. Issues such as religious orientation, social and moral values and the boundaries between mainstream and minority culture only came to the fore as families settled and set about creating an identity between their culture back home and their new living environment. This process was most apparent among Turks, partly because their cultural heritage and customs were markedly different and partly because Turks were less willing than other national groups to leave after the *Anwerbestopp*. They became the largest minority group in Germany only after the mid-seventies when family reunion had begun to take effect.

The second process of change arose from generation change. While first-generation migrants drew on the customs of their own background, second and third generations became fluent in the German language, immersed in German everyday culture, yet also rooted in their minority culture and religion. They developed a dual identity, German-Turkish, for example, or German-Greek. They expected acceptance of their cultural differences and fair opportunities of social participation within German civil society. As for their own minority group, they advocated contacts with German mainstream society and made use of opportunities to participate in advisory councils and similar institutions at local and national level.

Generation change thus promoted a new cultural proximity of non-German minorities and German civil society. It also highlighted the extent to which social inequalities persisted. Most of the original *Gastarbeiter* were blue-collar workers, most of them at the unskilled and semi-skilled levels. Forty years on, blue-collar employment still predominated among non-Germans although a slight shift from semi-skilled to skilled employment had taken place. Bearing in mind that blue-collar labour generally decreased during this period and unskilled workers are more at risk from unemployment than others, the *Gastarbeiter* and their descendants have been trapped at the wrong end of modernisation. Germans rode the crest of new white-collar opportunities and an increasing diversity of managerial and leadership positions while their non-German colleagues looked on.

Income levels reflected these uneven employment opportunities. In the mid-1990s, one out of three Germans but two out of three non-Germans lived at or below the poverty line. Social exclusion generally constituted a greater risk for non-Germans than Germans. Among Germans, just 3 per cent failed to obtain a school leaving certificate; among non-Germans, one out of three remained without educational qualifications. Twenty per cent of young Germans and three times as many non-Germans did not obtain a vocational qualification. One in ten Germans and four times as many non-Germans lived in substandard housing. Unemployment also hit non-Germans more than Germans, although in this respect, East Germans were worse affected with some 20 per cent out of work in 1996.

The first generation of *Gastarbeiter* won the right to stay and become members of German civil society. Issues of equality featured less prominently for a generation which experienced their living conditions in Germany generally as better than those they had left behind. The second and third generations developed their identity as members of their minority culture in Germany and compared their own opportunities with those of their German peers. Although most were born in Germany, they remained foreign nationals and suffered the same exclusion from employment or education as foreigners generally. Most Germans have accepted the presence of *Gastarbeiter* and their descendants, but acquiesced in their socially inferior status or benefited from it through improved chances of occupational mobility. However, half a century after the first *Gastarbeiter* set foot in post-war Germany, non-German minorities are beginning to find a voice of their own, challenging the legacies and practices of social exclusion and helping to inject civil society with cultural pluralism.

Equal opportunities and the emergence of civil society in Germany

Women and their movements in Imperial Germany, 1871–1918

When the German nation state was founded in 1871, women remained politically and socially disenfranchised. For working-class women, poverty made employment inevitable, thus suspending the social norms that developed among the middle class and came to dominate everyday culture in Germany. The German middle class evolved in the shadow of the aristocracy whose values they emulated as civil servants, administrators or public employees. The code of social respectability included role prescriptions for women. Women were confined to the home, groomed for marriage and not permitted to take on paid employment. As wife, homemaker and mother a woman was socially and economically inferior to her husband. Unmarried women were ridiculed as 'spinsters' and confined to a life as unpaid housekeepers living with relatives. The most able worked as governesses.

The uncertain pace of industrial growth between 1871 and 1890 wrought havoc with these role prescriptions. Many middle-class families found themselves impoverished and women had to earn money in secret by sewing or embroidery. For young women without a dowry, prospects of marriage were minimal. Unless middle-class families underwent social demotion and became shopkeepers, artisans or labourers, women were trapped in a world without opportunities.

The bourgeois women's movement played a major part in breaking this deadlock. The *Allgemeiner Deutscher Frauenverein* (General Association of German Women) (ADF) was founded in 1865 as an umbrella organisation for women's associations calling for women's rights of education, employment and political participation. It was replaced in 1894 by the essentially nationalist and conservative *Bund Deutscher Frauenverbände* (Federation of German Women's Associations) (BDF). It replicated the class divisions of German society by excluding the women's movement that had emerged within the labour movement from membership. The two women's movements in Germany differed in their perception of women's rights and place in society.

The bourgeois women's movement did not question the primacy of the family in a woman's life but focused its demands on the position of single women. Like German middle-class women generally, the movement wanted to create more openings that would suit women, not change the social or political system. Employment in social work, the caring professions and teaching was deemed most suitable. Rivalling men or even aspiring to leadership positions was never part of this agenda. Equality meant that women were different from men and could feel equal by being useful within their distinctive social sphere. During the First World War, this focus translated seamlessly into fervent nationalism and a belief that a woman's duty on the home front was as vital for the nation as a soldier's duty on the battlefield.

One of the most important creations of the bourgeois women's movement and for women's employment opportunities generally was the *Lette Verein*, named after its male co-founder. Set up in Berlin in 1866 in order to train young women in secretarial and commercial skills it laid the foundations for office-based female employment and the entry of women into the previously male-dominated world of white-collar work. From Berlin, the *Lette Verein* spawned a network of commercial colleges (*Handelsschulen*) turning out qualified young women who could compete in the labour market. Twenty years on and after a flood of petitions by the bourgeois women's movement, women were admitted to grammar schools, allowed to take the leaving examination and proceed to teachers' training colleges. Indeed, it was Helene Lange, a leading figure in the bourgeois women's movement, who founded the first teachers' training college in Berlin and took the essential institutional step of making teaching qualifications accessible to women. School teaching (which in Germany entailed civil service status) was to emerge as a major career for educated women. Universities agreed between 1900 and 1909 to accept women as regular students. On the eve of the First World War, the gender barrier of access to higher education and some careers had been shattered.

The 'proletarian women's movement' developed as a branch of the Social Democratic Party. Its agenda was inspired by August Bebel's *Die Frau und der Sozialismus* (Women and Socialism, 1878) and by the pressures on working-class women to seek employment. As industrialisation intensified so did the employment of women, not least since they were paid less than men. Whether they were married or not, had children or not did not matter. By the 1890s, one in four factory workers was female, and most women worked to escape poverty. The proletarian women's movement campaigned for equal pay, equal treatment at work and the enfranchisement of women. Significant sections of the labour movement, however, took women's employment as evidence of poverty and hoped for a society where working people would be affluent enough for women to be able to stay at home. While middle-class women perceived the right to employment as a step towards equality, working-class women, or at least the labour movement under whose umbrella their movement operated, did not perceive employment as a special right but as a poverty-imposed burden that diminished the quality of their lives.

In 1908, women in Germany won the right to join political parties, take part in public assemblies and address public meetings. In 1918, they won the right to vote as the last war-time government hastened to institute democracy from above in a bid for a lenient peace. Although representatives of both women's movements had petitioned for women's enfranchisement, doubts persisted in the bourgeois women's movement as to whether voting bestowed the right kind of womanly equality. These reservations were overtaken by events. During the war years, women of all social backgrounds had been drafted into the labour market. The barriers that had kept women from most paid employment before the war no longer applied. Women, it was felt, had earned the vote.

Despite their war-time contributions as workers, tram conductors and nurses, the Civil Code of 1900 remained in force and defined women as socially and economically inferior. Married women had no rights to conclude business transactions, seek employment without the consent of their husbands or determine the education of their children. In case of divorce, women lost all economic security and rights of access to their children. These restrictions were to remain in place without substantial change until the 1970s.

Women in the Weimar years, 1919–1932

The Weimar years were a new era. The 1919 constitution guaranteed active and passive voting rights for women over the age of twenty. Ten per cent of the delegates in the National Assembly were women and many former activists from the women's movement now entered parliamentary politics. The class divisions of Imperial Germany gave way to divisions between political parties. Women of the bourgeois movement tended to support conservative political parties and shared their reservations about democratic government; the proletarian women's movement split into hostile camps, with Social Democrats and Communists juxtaposed until the end of the Weimar Republic.

For the left-wing parties, the Weimar experience was a disappointment since the majority of German women supported political parties of the centre and the right. When the National Socialists became the strongest party in the Reichstag in 1930, most of their voters were men, but women followed as the party picked up electoral momentum. While political equality gave women in Germany an opportunity to participate actively in politics as voters, parliamentarians and office holders, their predominantly right-of-centre preferences contributed to weakening the democratic system that had secured them a political voice.

Socially, the Weimar years transformed women's lives. The war had put an end to long skirts and lace-up boots. Weimar women sported short hair-cuts and skirts as fashion spearheaded and reflected their new opportunities. Grammar schools included nearly 40 per cent girls; by 1930, nearly one in five university students was female. Participation in the labour market rose little compared to the pre-war years but the structure of employment now reflected the overall modernisation in the economy. Domestic and agricultural labour decreased while more and more women worked as secretaries, clerks, sale assistants or on the assembly-lines of electrical and other hi-tech industries of the day. Social work and the caring professions emerged as new occupational fields. The civil service offered valuable career tracks although the so-called 'celibacy clause', the rule that female civil servants had to remain unmarried, was rescinded only in the 1950s. Regardless of social class, the new woman of the Weimar years worked before marriage or worked for a life-time if she was single. Given the war-time losses of men, more and more women were single and gained unprecedented financial independence and social acceptance as career women.

Throughout the Weimar years, anti-modernists warned that women's new participation in education, employment and politics endangered the family, population growth and the future of German society itself. The economic crisis and mass unemployment in the late twenties and early thirties created further resentment as men were laid off in their millions and women taken on or retained as cheap labour. Driven by hardship, many women found themselves in the role of principal bread-winners while the right-wing propagandists accused democracy of destroying the family. The Weimar years, which had opened many avenues of social participation to women, closed on the sour note that more and more Germans, men and women, spurned the advances of equality and opted for the destruction of democracy and women's rights.

Mothers and workers in National Socialist Germany, 1933–1945

National Socialism imposed a women's state policy with two apparently contradictory tiers. It wished to confine women to a family role and also wished to utilise them as a labour force for the purposes of the state. Initially, Nazi women's policy was designed to redirect women from employment to motherhood and reverse the decline in the birth rate. From 1933 onwards, a marriage allowance (*Ehestandsdarlehen*) could be claimed if a woman of Nazi-approved German origin gave up her employment after marriage. The birth of each child triggered a discount on the original loan. Abortion was treated as a serious crime for German women, but forced upon women whom the Nazis regarded as inferior. The Nuremberg race laws of 1935 outlawed marriages and sexual relations between Germans and Jews and encouraged divorce of existing mixed marriages. The racist overtones of Nazi women's policy extended to the so-called Mother's Cross, an award for women who had borne four or more children and billed as the female equivalent of the Iron Cross. It was given out for the first time to three million women on Mothers' Day 1939. Only mothers who were regarded as 'German' in the eyes of the Nazis qualified for the award. Women from ethnic and national minorities and even lower class women with large families, mothers of retarded children or women who had aroused the dislike of local Nazi dignitaries were excluded.

On coming to power, National Socialism banned all organisations that had articulated social and political interests during the Weimar years. The proletarian women's movement was smashed in 1933 together with the labour movement. The bourgeois women's movement was submerged into the Nazi mass organisation *Frauenwerk* which offered apparently non-political courses in child-care and domestic skills and – from 1935 onwards – air raid training to over five million women. The *NS-Frauenschaft* saw itself as the vanguard of Nazi women's policy and gained formal acceptance as an organisational sector of the Nazi party in 1936. At the eve of the Second World War, it had 2.3 million members. Girls over the age of ten were organised in the *Bund Deutscher Mädel*, the female equivalent of the Hitler Youth. Membership became compulsory in 1936. In the BDM, preparation for motherhood took second place to an ideology of unquestioning service to the Nazi state. In 1935, a one-year work experience in the *Reichsarbeitsdienst* (Reich Labour Corps) became obligatory. Young women between seventeen and twenty-five were assigned to work in agriculture or domestic service in exchange for accommodation, board and pocket money. In 1939, this unpaid female workforce numbered 200,000, one year later close to 340,000. In 1941, the compulsory service was extended by six months and often spent in paramilitary functions such as helping to evict Poles from their homes during the Nazi programme of 'germanisation' in the east. BDM and *Arbeitsdienst* activism moulded a generation of young women who did not question the Nazi ideology of social exclusion but experienced their own Nazi years positively as collective endeavour and personal leadership challenge.

The glorification of women as mothers informed the propaganda of the Nazi years but social reality told a different story. In 1933, a vituperate campaign against 'double earners' forced married women, whose husbands were employed, out of the labour market. Since the economic crisis had left many working-class men unemployed and dependent on the earnings of their wives, the majority of women who lost their jobs were middle-class professionals such as university teachers, doctors and journalists. In 1936, women were barred from becoming judges and public prosecutors and generally from holding positions of authority over men. Overall, 800,000 women were driven out of the labour market as Nazi women's policies took effect.

Yet, the labour force in Nazi Germany never included fewer than one third women, more than in Britain or the United States at the time. By 1936 war production had led to labour shortages. Now, women could obtain a marriage loan and remain in employment, factories established day nurseries to keep women with children in the labour force, while an entitlement to maternity leave and other measures to improve the birth rate were introduced although not always implemented on the factory floor. Instead of working the permitted forty-eight hours, women, including young mothers, were forced to work up to sixty hours. With the exception of public service where equal pay came into effect in 1939, women remained a cheap labour force. On average, women's pay in the Nazi years amounted to 56 per cent of men's.

For the war economy, female labour was to be fully mobilised. From the spring of 1939 onwards, all women between the ages of seventeen and forty-five had to register for employment and in 1943 employment was ordered by decree. Still, at the end of 1939, one million single women and 5.4 million married women without children were not employed. During the war, women's employment figures barely rose from 14.6 million in 1939 to 14.9 million in 1944 and even fell by half a million between 1939 and 1941. Women who were already in employment when recruitment by decree came into operation, were prohibited from leaving. But the decree itself contained such a web of special clauses that women with good connections to Nazi officialdom could evade it. Despite official appeals to pay their duty of thanks (*Dankespflicht*) to the Reich few women enlisted to do so. Moreover, the men serving at the front strongly disliked the idea that German women and specifically their wives, sisters or mothers should be forced to work. Fearful of disaffecting German men and women, Nazi labour administrators refrained from all-out compulsion except against socially weak groups such as working-class women. Instead, they brought in more and more labour slaves – among them 1.5 million women – and diverted as much labour as the SS would hand over from concentration camps to their key industries.

Between survival and normalisation, 1945–1949

At the end of the Second World War two out of three adults were women. Most had managed on their own for several years. In the immediate post-war years, the concern for survival eclipsed all else. Few women heeded the political transformation that went on around them. Most were preoccupied with bartering goods for food (*hamstern*), clearing up the rubble in the destroyed cities (*Trümmerfrauen*) in exchange for improved food ration cards and taking on employment at the orders of the occupying powers. Post-war survival also meant living in cramped conditions, often sharing cooking facilities and bathrooms with several families and suffering worse shortages of food, clothing or fuel than at any time during the war when Nazi Germany had supplied its own population and plundered the areas under occupation.

Normalisation set in with economic recovery in the late forties. From one day to the next, women were dismissed to make room for men who had returned from POW camps or had delayed looking for work until the hour of denazification had passed. Some, of course, had yearned for material living conditions that would again allow them to be housewives and mothers. Many, however, had no intention of giving up work. In particular women of the war generations who could not expect to marry were more than ever determined to build their social status on a career, not on marriage. With the division of the country in 1949, women's equality took on two different meanings as East and West Germany each proclaimed it a corner stone of their civil society.

Equality as employment in East German civil society since 1949

In East Germany, equality had been written into the constitution of 1949 and was confirmed in amended versions later on. Central to equality was the right to work for each citizen. It amounted to a duty to work and applied equally to men and women. Those without work were despised as drop-outs. East Germany's women's policy was designed to integrate women into the labour market and keep them there even after childbirth. Targeted at mothers, it set about eliminating the conflict between employment and motherhood and persuade women to commit themselves to both.

Compared with the war-time generations, women who grew up in East Germany were better educated and qualified. From the seventies onwards, half the students throughout the education system were women. In vocationally oriented intermediate colleges, *Fachschulen,* women outnumbered men; girls were as likely as boys to obtain apprenticeships. The traditional pattern that young women would leave school at the earliest opportunity without qualifications had been eliminated in the GDR.

In 1950, women constituted 40 per cent of the labour force; in 1989, at the end of the GDR, their share had reached 49 per cent. Nine out of ten East German women were in employment or vocational training programmes. Numerically at least, equality with men had been achieved. In reality, women's pay was one third lower than that of men, and women were less likely than men to hold managerial positions and were directed to 'female' occupational fields such as health care, administration, banking, teaching and textile production.

These hidden inequalities of employment were cushioned by special concessions, most of them aimed at mothers. Incentives to marry and start a family included the allocation of an apartment, a marriage loan and entitlement to a discount on the birth of each child. A whole gamut of benefits added up to a second wage package. Relative to the low average wage for women, allowances were generous and a woman with two children could increase her income by nearly 50 per cent. In addition women (not men) were entitled to maternity benefit, up to three years of paid leave after the birth of a child, paid leave to care for sick children, a monthly (paid) day to catch up with the housework and an increasingly comprehensive network of full-time day care for children between the ages of nought and ten at such low cost that it would have been more expensive to look after a child at home.

GDR social policy encouraged women to marry in their early twenties and to have their children before the age of thirty. In the family, traditional gender stereotypes survived. Despite their full-time employment, women performed the bulk of domestic and child-related duties and had less time for leisure than men. Discontent with these discrepancies made an increasing number of women file for divorce. In the 1980s, the divorce rate in the GDR stood at 40 per cent. Moreover, a growing number of mothers opted to remain single. About 50 per cent of newborn babies were born to unmarried women. When the GDR collapsed, one in four families was headed by a single parent, most of them women.

After unification, established practices were discontinued and hidden inequalities turned into disadvantages. Employers ceased to offer child-care facilities or leave to care for children, forcing women with children and in particular single mothers into unemployment. Since their previous low wages translated into low benefits, many faced poverty. Generally, women had drawn the shorter straw. Their qualifications, though good, had been less good than those of men; their occupational fields, though prescribed by the GDR state authorities, had been less in tune with economic modernisation than post-unification development required. Their comparatively large families, which had been an economic advantage in the GDR, now turned into a disadvantage as child-care became more expensive, less accessible or unavailable altogether. After unification, women were more likely to move directly into unemployment without the cushion of short-time working or employment on work creation schemes. In the mid-1990s, 70 per cent of the unemployed and a similar proportion of the long-term unemployed were women.

Yet, women in post-communist East Germany retained their employment motivation, took an intensely active approach to retraining and reduced their commitment to early motherhood. In the first five years after unification, the birth rate dropped by 60 per cent. Unemployed women continued to look for work. There was nothing to suggest a comeback of the full-time housewife. If women wanted to turn the clock back, it was in the direction of the GDR and a women's policy which most had perceived as protection. The hidden inequalities had gone largely unheeded in a society where the state seemed to have instituted equality and women had come to believe that they were treated equally.

In pursuit of equality: women in
West Germany since 1949

The Basic Law listed women's equality among the human rights and in doing so set the agenda for women's policies in West Germany. From the outset, there was no consensus. Conservative policy makers sought to protect the family with women's lives centred on marriage and children while the political Left continued to link women's equality to employment. In the 1950s, improved standards of living opened choices. Most West Germans then wanted married women to stay at home and single women pursued their working lives.

How little had changed since the Weimar years became evident in 1957 when the constitutional promise of equality was finally translated into legislation. Although women in employment seemed to be granted the right to equal pay, employers tended to relegate them to lower wage groups. With regard to domestic rights and divorce, women did not fare any better. The law stated that they were responsible for running the household. As in the Civil Code of 1900, a husband could force his wife to work or terminate her employment against her will. Divorce left women without a claim to joint material possessions, custody of children or other landmarks of equality. This was to change only in 1977 when the 'housewife model' was replaced by the partnership principle. Even then, it took another decade or so before German courts embraced the spirit of equal opportunities and stopped making maintenance payments and custody rights dependent on a woman's moral conduct.

Since the 1980s, European Community directives on equal opportunities and equal treatment of women prompted German legislators to outlaw discriminatory recruitment practices more vigorously. Since the mid-eighties women or men may take part-paid leave for up to one year after the birth of a child with a guarantee of re-employment at the same level within three years. Women who had given up employment in order to bring up children won some pension rights. Several Länder introduced equal opportunities legislation – some even advocated positive discrimination – and created a network of equal opportunities agencies.

With regard to electoral preferences, West Germany followed the Weimar pattern. It took until the mid-sixties for the predominantly conservative vote of the female electorate to decline. In the seventies, women who had grown up in the post-war era perceived the SPD as the advocate of equal opportunities; twenty years on, the Green Party had a similar appeal for women under the age of forty. Increasingly, women of the post-war generations insisted on parliamentary and political representation and blamed party organisations for a lack of equality. Until the seventies, the Bundestag had fewer women members than the Reichstag. In the mid-eighties, the Greens imposed a 50 per cent women's quota in politics, followed in 1988 by a similar quota in the SPD while the other political parties recommended that women be represented in accordance with their share of the party membership. The new emphasis on political equality brought more women into leadership positions, produced regional governments with a women's majority, and ensured that at least one in four members of parliament at regional and national level in the mid-1990s were women.

The changed expectations about equality date back to the mid-sixties. Then, improved access to education had closed the qualification gap. Indeed, women had staged a silent revolution of educational success. In 1950, when 5 per cent of an age cohort went to university, one in five students were women. In the late eighties, at least 20 per cent of an age cohort went to university, over 40 per cent of them women. Women's access to advanced and higher education recast their biographies. In the early sixties, most young women would be in full-time employment by the age of twenty; in the nineties most remained in full-time education. At first glance, little seems to have changed in a workforce which since the 1940s has included 40 per cent women. Yet the structure of female employment altered considerably. No longer a domain for unmarried women – although 90 per cent of single women and nearly as many divorcees and widows were active in the labour market – employment has become a normal dimension of life for married women as well. In the early 1990s, nearly 60 per cent of married women in the old Länder were in employment.

Close to half a century after the constitutional promise of equality had been formulated, many obstacles remained in place. Women's pay for full-time employment was still one-third lower than that of men. Most married women had interrupted their employment for family reasons, often more than once. Only 17 per cent had worked without career breaks. Returning to the labour market often involved accepting lower-skilled and lower-paid work. Women with children faced the challenge of combining family roles and employment without significant institutional support. Less than 5 per cent of pre-school children in West Germany had access to full-time child care (in the GDR over 90 per cent did), kindergartens opened for two or three hours in the morning or the afternoon, schools closed at lunchtime. Until adulthood, a child's life was centred on the family and women were the main carers. In the fifties, when married women with children began to venture into the labour market or were forced to work for economic reasons, their children had been pitied as latch-key children (*Schlüsselkinder*) and they themselves vilified as bad mothers. Unspoken assumptions that families and especially children suffer when women go out to work, have remained strong enough in Germany to make women feel guilty and search for compromise between family duties and employment motivation.

Young women today prefer to have both, employment and a family, without being made to choose between them. Many postpone childbirth until later in their careers, reduce family size to one child or do not have children. One in three women work part-time, usually women with children. In Germany, however, part-time employment above the unskilled level is at a premium. Faced with a social system skewed against working mothers, women in Germany have been under pressure to leave the labour market. Women with advanced education and professional qualifications are less likely to do so than women with elementary education only. Some, of course, prefer to be housewives but these mostly belong to the older generations or the lower-skilled cohorts.

In the seventies, the new women's movement shifted the debate from equality in education and employment to issues of personal identity and self-realisation. Demands to legalise abortion and allow women to 'decide over their own body' provided a clear focal point for the new movement. In 1974, the Bundestag agreed to legalise abortion but was forced to retract after the Federal Constitutional Court intervened. A further review after German unification again failed in removing abortion from the list of criminal offences and making it a woman's right. Declaring it a criminal offence for which punishment will not be enforced, current legal practice allows abortion during the first twelve weeks of pregnancy and after obligatory counselling has been obtained.

In defining equality as self-realisation, the new women's movement implied that participation in conventional employment or family roles made women play the men's game and lose their identity. Many women withdrew into women-only environments, safe houses and feminist enclaves. More importantly, the discourse on self-realisation underpinned the motivation of women from the post-war generation to aspire to leadership functions in line with their abilities and qualifications. The new women's movement sensitised the German public to gender inequalities, boosted women's social and political confidence and helped to reduce social exclusion in civil society.

FURTHER READING

As an introduction to German civil society and its uneven development, Gordon Craig, *The Germans* (Harmondsworth: Penguin Books, 1982) remains unrivalled and eminently readable. The collection of essays edited by Gordon Smith *et al.*, *Development in German Politics* (Basingstoke: Macmillan, 1992; rev. edn. 1996) places case studies of women, migration and citizenship in their contemporary political context, while Werner Weidenfeld and Hartmut Zimmermann (eds.), *Deutschland Handbuch* (Munich: Hanser, 1989) presents matching chapters on East and West Germany. Rainer Geissler, *Die Sozialstruktur Deutschlands* (Opladen: Westdeutscher Verlag, 1992) draws the strands together and offers a succinct account of German civil society since 1945 and its present-day East-West divide.

Klaus J. Bade (ed.), *Population, Labour and Migration in the 19th and 20th Century* (Oxford: Berg, 1987) examines the place of *Gastarbeiter* and non-German minorities in the broader context of labour migration and immigration policy, while his collection of essays, *Migration, Ethnizität, Konflikt* (Osnabrück: Universitätsverlag Rasch, 1996), places developments in Germany in a comparative European context. Daniel Cohn-Bendit and Thomas Schmid, *Heimat Babylon. Das Wagnis der multikulturellen Demokratie* (Hamburg: Hoffmann & Campe, 1992) argues that migrant workers and their descendants have become essential for the German economy to function while their presence allowed German workers to improve their social status.

The best introduction to the history of women, their movements, political preferences and social opportunities in Germany since the nineteenth century remains Ute Frevert, *Women in German History* (Oxford: Berg, 1989). Eva Kolinsky, *Women in Contemporary Germany* (Oxford: Berg, 1993) concentrates on post-war developments with case studies on education, employment, political involvement and the hidden inequalities in West and East Germany before and after unification. Gisela Helwig and Hildegard Maria Nickel (eds.), *Frauen in Deutschland 1945–1992* (Berlin: Akademie Verlag, 1993) contrasts women's social and economic participation in the two Germanies and also considers the effects of post-communist transformation of women in the former GDR.

6

Critiques of culture

Theoretical foundations

Most lists of the critics of modern culture would include Karl Marx, Friedrich Nietzsche, Sigmund Freud, Max Weber, Martin Heidegger, and T. W. Adorno before writers in other languages. The perceived importance of such German critics of modern culture has much to do with the desire to understand the disastrous course of German history in the first half of the twentieth century as a model of the dangers of modernity. From the Romantic period onwards many of the critiques of culture which preceded the catastrophic events reflect concerns about the destruction of tradition which became central to those events, and during the events themselves ideas about culture became dangerous political issues. It is, though, often unclear what links together the abovementioned thinkers as proponents of a 'critique of culture': neither term in this notion – which, as Adorno says of the word *Kulturkritik*, 'like "automobile"... is stuck together from Latin and Greek'[1] – is self-explanatory. The meaning of the word 'culture', with its links both to the search for permanence and to growth and development, is, for example, significantly suspended between the ideas of identity and change. 'Culture' is generally defined in terms of collectively shared values and practices that legitimate the goals of a society and imbue them with meaning. In the sense given to it by Immanuel Kant in the *Critique of Pure Reason* of 1781 'critique' refers to the legitimation of the criteria by which something is to be judged. Kant made 'critique' central to his philosophical enterprise precisely because the criteria for determining cognitive, ethical and aesthetic validity in modern society could no longer be accepted from existing traditions and had instead to be legitimated before the 'tribunal of reason'. The real problem, however, was that what constituted 'reason' had also ceased to be self-evident: it is the realisation of this fact which is shared by the main proponents of a critique of culture.

Kant's thought is 'reflexive': it tries to use the capacity of reason to legitimate reason's own operations, thereby posing the question as to the relationship of the thought that carries out the critique to the thought that is criticised. If one accepts that in modernity the foundations of value can no longer be assumed to be universally legitimate, the very idea of a critique of culture will necessarily involve a whole series of methodological difficulties arising from this structure of 'reflection'.

In the case of Kant radical ideas that played a limited historical role in changing a still largely feudal Germany paralleled many of the ideas which fuelled real political changes elsewhere, especially in France. Kant eschewed Enlightenment claims about the theological structure of nature 'in itself' and restricted truth-claims to what could be validated by empirical evidence available to rational beings. Modern humankind was to 'give the law to itself' in both the cognitive and the ethical realms, rather than receive it from theological or other traditional authorities. The autonomy of rational subjects therefore had to be its own foundation. However, because of the problem of reflection, subjectivity seems unable to explain its own status as both the subject and the object of thinking: what was the motivating ground of subjectivity itself? Kant left this question wide open, which meant that there was no final answer to why there is knowledge at all, or, indeed, to what knowledge or reason really is. It is against the background of the lack of agreed answers to these questions that modern questioning of culture in Germany is carried out.

Attempts by J. G. Fichte, Friedrich Schlegel, Novalis, F. W. J. Schelling, G. W. F. Hegel, and other German Idealist and Romantic philosophers from the 1790s to the 1840s to answer the questions left open by Kant are the main source of the conceptual frameworks of the later critiques of modern culture. These critiques, by Marx, Georg Simmel, Nietzsche, Heidegger and others are far more reliant on Idealist and Romantic philosophy than has often been appreciated. Idealist and Romantic philosophy's central concern was to overcome the split between subject and object, mind and nature suggested by Kant. Critiques of culture invariably entail an attempt to re-define the relationships between culture and its 'other'. Such critiques therefore only become possible at the moment when the sense of being 'at home' in God's nature and one's own culture is lost. 'Nature' itself thereby changes its status, and becomes a potentially dangerous concept, as later invocations of 'blood and soil' make drastically clear.

If, like Rousseau and his heirs, one regards nature as the source of the life which gives the world purpose and direction, then modern culture can, when it 'loses touch' with nature – for example by treating it as merely an object to be used – be regarded as a damaging threat to our relationship to both external and internal nature. At the same time, if modern culture could re-establish contact with nature it would become the source of a harmonious existence, which would be generated by nature itself. However, if nature is a nature of 'eat or be eaten', whose principles are power and self-preservation, as it was for Hobbes and his successors, then culture is required to enable us to subdue nature in the name of a higher purpose. In many reactionary twentieth-century theories 'authentic' culture even becomes what is needed to put us back in touch with the brute reality of nature which other 'degenerate' modern forms of 'civilisation' have repressed. An account of the relationship between culture and nature therefore requires an account of what nature is 'in itself', which is precisely what Kant refused to provide. He does, though, in the 1790 *Critique of Judgement,* make the influential suggestion that we may get a sense of nature in itself from the enjoyment of natural beauty, rather than from scientific investigation.

The perceived need for a critique of culture is, of course, not the direct result of philosophical reflections of this kind, resulting rather from a disenchantment with the dominant aspects of culture on the part of real individuals. This disenchantment and its practical effects are the product of the often agonising adjustment of German society to secularisation, industrialisation, the rise of new forms of technology, the growth of the cities, and the destruction of traditional forms of social cohesion by the processes of capitalism.

Nihilism, nature and culture

Discussion of modern culture in Germany often centres upon the 'nihilistic' consequences of natural science's capacity to give deterministic explanations of more and more aspects of the human and the natural world, a kind of explanation which, as Max Weber suggests, empties the world of mythological and anthropomorphic forms of meaning, in the process of 'disenchantment'. The ability to explain and control nature by obviating mythological and theological forms of understanding can liberate modern societies both from some of the ravages of uncontrolled nature and from many inhuman practices. At the same time, the way this liberation takes place in Germany, where active involvement in democratic politics fails to develop in the way it does in Britain and France, distances many members of society from the sense of real participation in the liberation, thereby creating new anxieties and bringing about new threats to self-preservation of the kind that are associated with the natural world. These threats can no longer be regarded as part of a painful but meaningful 'natural' order, because traditional views of such an order are undermined precisely by what produces the new threats. The term 'nihilism' – which is usually associated with Nietzsche's idea of the 1880s that, with the 'death of God', the *'highest values devalue themselves'* – already appears in this context as part of arguments concerning the status of human reason in the 1780s.

In an exchange of letters with the Enlightenment thinker, Moses Mendelssohn, on whether G. E. Lessing was a Spinozist, the writer and philosopher F. H. Jacobi articulated many of the structures used by subsequent thinkers to question modernity. Being a Spinozist was regarded at this time as much the same as being an atheist, because for the seventeenth-century Dutch philosopher the intelligibility of the world was exhausted by what the natural sciences can explain, and nature was therefore merely a rigid system of laws. Jacobi's (theologically based) claim against Spinozism was that its reliance upon the 'principle of sufficient reason' – which Jacobi reformulates as 'everything *dependent* is *dependent upon* something'[2] – leads to a regress of 'dependences', and fails to explain why the world is intelligible at all. Scientific explanation only sees the truth in terms of what it itself presupposes, because the final ground – *'Grund'* – of explanation cannot be explained, and therefore leads to the abyss – *'Abgrund'* – of nihilism.

The same account of the nature of modern science appears in Nietzsche's thoroughly atheistic critique, in the 1872 *Birth of Tragedy,* of the hopes for scientific progress in the second half of the nineteenth century, and in Weber's assertion in 'Science as Vocation' of 1919 that 'No science is absolutely without presuppositions, and no science can ground its own value for him who rejects these presuppositions.'[3] Weber sees the end of the power of Christianity over Western culture as leading to the situation where 'The old gods, disenchanted, and therefore in the form of impersonal powers, are climbing out of their graves and striving for power over our life and are beginning again their eternal battle with each other.'[4] All the scientist can do, Weber maintains, is describe this situation, there being no way in which science can now provide grounding for evaluative positions. The dilemmas for 'occidental rationality' caused by the question of the 'ground' will be central to the work of Heidegger, Adorno and many others, and attempts not to draw Weber's conclusions from the lack of an absolute ground form the substance of many theories of culture.

Jacobi also helped to give rise to a new way of thinking about the question of values in the modern world via his understanding of the Spinozist notion that what something is depends on its not being other things, rather than on something intrinsic to itself. The disturbing consequence of this is that nothing is of value in itself, because everything depends upon its relationships to other things to have a value at all. If one does not presuppose God as the self-grounding highest value, the result is that nothing is ultimately valuable. In that case there would seem to be no way of establishing foundations of value in modern secular societies, apart from via arbitrary imposition which could not command universal assent.

Kant realised that the threat entailed by this way of constituting value was already becoming manifest in the increasingly capitalistic world of his time. He therefore argued for two examples of intrinsic value: rational beings capable of giving the law to themselves in moral decisions, and aesthetic objects, which are valued for their own sake, not for their usefulness for other purposes. The suspicion that a world based on abstract relationships between material objects destroys forms of 'organic' human solidarity, via an inversion of values which replaces the living, the spiritual and the human with inert relationships between material things, informs aspects of Romantic philosophy and literature in Schelling, Ludwig Tieck, E. T. A. Hoffmann and others in the first half of the century, plays a major part in Richard Wagner's *Ring of the Nibelung*, and also underlies the sociologist Ferdinand Tönnies' distinction between 'community' and 'society' in *Gemeinschaft und Gesellschaft* (1887). The idea will, crucially, be able to be understood from both a progressive and a reactionary perspective.

In *Capital* (1867) Marx sees 'commodity fetishism' as the result of the social world becoming dependent on 'exchange values', on commodities whose value depends upon their relations to other exchange values. This dependence obscures both the source of new value – human labour – and the ground of value – the usefulness of something for real human lives:

the forms of equivalence on which the commodity system is based take precedence over the content that they are supposed to represent, so that money becomes more important than the specificity of what is exchanged via money. To this extent money can also be linked by analogy to scientific knowledge, which is indifferent to the specificity of its object, in the name of the general concept under which that object falls. Similar worries about the effects of abstract systems emerge in the critiques of Hegel's philosophical system by Schelling (in the 1830s and 1840s) and Marx, and in the doubts about rationalisation and bureaucracy in the work of Weber and his successors.

The limits of reason

Kant's separation of the world in itself from the world as it appears to us already suggested the need to find a way of re-connecting forms of thought with a basis in nature, and this need fuels many of the key critiques of culture. The controversial, often forgotten, mediating figure here is Schelling. Throughout his work, from the 1790s to the 1850s, Schelling challenges any conception of nature that regards it as just the object of natural science and technology and as opposed to 'subjective' mind. These conceptions, he maintains, lead to a dualism which makes it impossible to understand either how physical nature, including our own bodies, can also be mental, or how the mental can interact with the physical. There can in Schelling's terms therefore be no ultimate difference between 'mind' and material 'nature'. The important consequence of this view in the present context is that conceptual thought can never finally explain itself.

Questionable versions of the idea of the limits of conceptual thought will recur in later, Schelling-influenced theorists such as Arthur Schopenhauer, Nietzsche, C. G. Jung, Heidegger and Ludwig Klages. It is therefore vital to differentiate the ways in which the underlying conception of nature is presented in such theories. In his 1800 *System of Transcendental Idealism* Schelling had referred to the 'unconscious productivity' of nature and asked how this 'productivity' relates to human reason, which necessarily depends on living nature for its very existence. Exactly one hundred years later Freud would, in *The Interpretation of Dreams,* use a related model to explore the basis of subjectivity. Whereas Freud regards dreams as the 'royal road' to the unconscious, Schelling claimed that art was the means via which we can understand what cannot be explained in terms of natural science, because it requires the combination of 'conscious' and 'unconscious productivity'. The role of aesthetics in the questioning of the status of scientific knowledge is vital from the Romantics onwards.

However, the Romantic questioning of Enlightenment reason by means of art involves a prophetic danger. The concern of such questioning is with what science and philosophy cannot articulate conceptually, which has to be articulated in some other manner. In Germany the new perception at the end of the eighteenth century of music as the most important art, and the simultaneous emergence of the greatest music of the modern period, are the first signs of a concern with the non-conceptual that is most convincingly worked out in Adorno's theory of 'non-identity' in his writings on aesthetics and philosophy of the 1960s. Suspicion of conceptual thought's repression of difference in the name of identity can, though, often lead to a denial of the legitimacy of scientific and other forms of universalising rationality, in favour of 'intuitive' approaches to the world which are not open to public accountability. The potentially sinister political implications of 'intuitionist' theories become particularly apparent in the twentieth century. At the same time it is equally mistaken to try to repress inescapable aspects of ourselves which need to be understood and articulated via those aspects of culture not primarily concerned with publicly accessible conceptual determination. The need for a balance between the demands of scientific and 'expressive' types of rationality is perhaps the central concern for contemporary critiques of culture in Germany, and the lack of such a balance is a dominant feature of the history of German critiques of culture.

When criticising Fichte's approach to philosophy in the early 1800s, Schelling already revealed a danger that would emerge in the Marxist model of praxis as the progressive domination of nature for human ends. Schelling says of Fichte: 'in the last analysis what is the essence of his whole opinion of nature? It is this: that nature should be used ... and that it is there for nothing more than to be used.'[5] If nature is merely to be used it ceases to be a living resource that can be the birthplace of new meanings and a corrective to the narcissistic desire of subjects to dominate what is not themselves. Schelling is aware that the growth of the modern subject's control over nature may involve a deep self-deception. If nature, as the ground of the human will, is in fact what motivates the subject's search for knowledge, it necessarily subverts the subject's desire for total control because our own will is not fully transparent to us. Schelling's contention here would, via the assimilation of analogous ideas from Freud, underlie Horkheimer and Adorno's critique of 'instrumental reason' – the 'subordination of everything natural to the arrogant subject'[6] – which they associated with the atom bomb and with Auschwitz in the 1947 *Dialectic of Enlightenment*.

It is the work of Schopenhauer that links Schelling's conception of subjectivity and nature to the more questionable traditions of cultural critique. *The World as Will and Representation* of 1819 sets up a paradigmatic dualism: the world of knowable 'representations', including ourselves, is, Schopenhauer maintains, the product of the one underlying self-contradicting force – the 'Will' – that constitutes the world 'in itself'. Any manifestation of the Will *qua* representation must sustain itself against other manifestations, which will eventually destroy it. Although Schopenhauer himself draws Platonist and Buddhist conclusions from his position, the metaphysics both of Nietzsche's 'Will to power' and of the related Social Darwinism which is decisive for reactionary thinking in twentieth-century Germany are already made possible by the basic structure in question, as are – more indirectly – aspects of nationalist and racist conceptions of the relative strength and fitness of the 'races'. In these views a greater quantum of the underlying power, of the kind supposedly possessed by one aspect of a culture or one race rather than another, will eventually overcome a lesser quantum in an 'agonistic' battle for self-preservation. As such, 'reason' is only ever a form of self-deception that conceals the real motivating ground of human action. The problem with such irrationalist positions is that they claim more than they themselves can allow in their own premises. Any claim to reveal the real ground of reason beyond the deception must itself be true and thus rely upon a ground that would validate the claim. This, though, already invalidates the initial claim.

The question for serious critiques of culture is how to come to terms with the 'other' of reason without claiming privileged 'intuitive' knowledge of that other, for example by being part of a particular race. Knowledge can only be arrived at by interpreting how the world appears, even though we can also be aware in other ways, such as via art or dreams, that the world always transcends what we can explain or experience. Freud, for example, insists that we can never be directly conscious of the drives that subvert our attempts to understand ourselves: consciousness is only one of the 'representations' to which the drives give rise. Failure to acknowledge this structural inaccessibility of the final ground of our world is an index of the dangers in many theories of culture.

Suspicion, myth and value

Much of the most important German thinking about modernity takes the form of what Paul Ricoeur has called the 'hermeneutics of suspicion', associating the term with Marx's theory of ideology, Nietzsche, and Freud. For these thinkers the surface meaning of cultural phenomena is suspect because its genesis is 'overdetermined' by motivational factors which are not immediately accessible to the producers of that meaning. These factors need not, though, be excluded from eventually becoming rationally accessible, for example through 'ideology-critique' or psychoanalysis. The hermeneutics of suspicion relates to a generalised mistrust of the development of modernity which crystallises after the middle of the nineteenth century. The Schelling-derived critique of Hegel in the 1840s by the 'Young Hegelians', such as Feuerbach and Marx, and Nietzsche's critiques of Western philosophy's reliance on Christian metaphysics are both aimed against an idealism which thinks the truth of being is to be found in philosophical and scientific forms of thought that exist independently of the history within which they emerge. The conclusions drawn from these critiques are, however, instructively different.

Nietzsche's *Birth of Tragedy* invokes the culture of Athens in the fifth century BC as a means of questioning the legitimacy of modern culture. It does so by employing a version of Schopenhauer's central idea, terming – in the (unacknowledged) light of a Romantic tradition which goes from Friedrich Schlegel, to Friedrich Creuzer, to Schelling, and to J. J. Bachofen – Schopenhauer's Will 'Dionysus', and the world of representations, including dreams, 'Apollo'. Nietzsche's answer to the crisis of culture, which would be echoed in many subsequent demands for a re-birth of tragedy as a way of reuniting a community fragmented by modernity, such as the 'Thingspiel' movement of the 1930s, is a return to the 'healthy' public awareness of the irredeemable nature of existence celebrated in the Dionysian aspect of tragedy, the aspect made accessible via nonconceptual music. For Nietzsche existence can only be justified as an 'aesthetic phenomenon', all attempts, including those in the natural sciences, to arrive at a final truth being merely another form of 'art', because they project a meaning where ultimately there is none. The tragic approach to existence is, he claims, being revived in Wagner's employment of Dionysian music in his music-dramas, which will bring about a collective re-birth of German myth.

The topos of myth as a means of criticising the effects of modernity can be both progressive and regressive. Traditional myths manifest the values of a culture in a concrete story of the origin of that culture. The notion of a 'new mythology' that would be a 'mythology of reason' which could unite modern society played a role in the ideas of Friedrich Schlegel and Schelling around 1800. A 'new mythology' would overcome the divorce between the results of science and the awareness of the significance of those results in the general population. It was therefore an – unrealised – attempt to extend the possibilities of human communication and agreement in an increasingly abstract modern society. Related ideas would be adopted by Ernst Bloch in the 1930s as part of his critique of the failure of the Left to take account of people's need for aesthetic sources of value and meaning which do not rely on the assumption that technological progress will necessarily be accompanied by social progress. Connections of a modern mythology to a particular nation are, on the other hand, the product of the 'Romanticism' – which has little or nothing to do with what was meant by those who first established the term – exemplified in the work of Paul de Lagarde and some of the Nazi ideologues like the Germanist Alfred Baeumler, and Rosenberg, the author of *The Myth of the Twentieth Century*.

Nietzsche himself came to repudiate some of his early nationalist conceptions – and Wagner – and moved in the 1880s to a position which proposes a complete 'transvaluation of values', including the value of truth itself. Christianity is, he maintains in *Towards a Genealogy of Morality* of 1887, based on 'slave morality', via which the strong have been persuaded to deny their real nature by the weak, thereby giving rise to a neurotic culture of self-denial. Nietzsche rejects the idea that anything is inherently good or evil, because these terms inverted their meanings during the rise of Judaism. In the face of the devaluation of all ultimate values which is the result of the 'death of God', what matters is whether the new values preserve and intensify 'life'. Nietzsche wants a 'higher culture' based on 'Men with a still natural nature, barbarians in that terrible sense of the word'.[7] In the increasingly ruthless context of Wilhelmine capitalism and imperialism it is not clear to whom Nietzsche is actually referring, but there is anyway an incoherence at the heart of his argument that is characteristic of many reactionary critiques of culture.

For Nietzsche's argument to work life must be a value in itself, which already invalidates the notion of a complete 'transvaluation', and implies a merely random battle of differing kinds of life against each other. The problem Nietzsche and others who follow him fail to solve is that any attempt to 'transvalue' old values must either admit that a relativity of values is inescapable, or it must admit that at least one ultimate value must be kept in place. The former position can lead to an indiscriminate imposition of the values of the strong over the weak, of the kind Nietzsche and his most questionable Social Darwinist and Nazi successors often advocate, and the latter can involve the incoherent attempt to justify this imposition. An alternative response to a relativity of values had, though, already been mapped out by Romantic thinkers like F. D. E. Schleiermacher, namely an interpretative search for consensus, of the kind later advocated by Jürgen Habermas, based on what always already happens in non-coercive everyday communication. Nietzsche's frequent equivocations over the value we term 'truth' suggest a further inconsistency in his position. A Nietzschean assertion like 'truth is really a way of establishing dominance over the other', which wishes to subvert the notion of truth, becomes self-refuting or paradoxical, because the assertion has to rely on what it claims to deny, namely the possibility that assertions can be true independently of what motivates them. Nietzsche's problematic reflections on the status of truth relate to other important questions about language which recur in modern German reflections upon culture.

Language: 'Logocentrism' or 'World-Disclosure'?

In one of his most influential moves, whose effects have recently been visible again in post-structuralist and postmodernist thinking, Nietzsche tries to undermine the modern conception of the autonomous subject by insisting upon its dependence on the language it speaks. The important issue here is how language is conceived. In what Schopenhauer and Feuerbach termed the 'ontotheological' Platonic and Christian traditions language was supposed to be '*Logos*', the manifestation of the order of God's universe. This conception is put into question in varying ways from the Romantics onwards. In an example of the irrationalism characteristic of reactionary thinking in the first half of the twentieth century Ludwig Klages' rejection of the idea of *Logos* leads him at the end of the 1920s – thus well before the term is employed by Jacques Derrida – to the concept of 'Logocentrism'. The term refers to thinking that privileges the repressive, static concepts generated by rational *'Geist'*, 'mind', over the living reality of *'Seele'*, the 'soul'. However, as the following will suggest, Klages' theory travesties the tradition from which it derives.

From the second half of the eighteenth century onwards, in the work of J. G. Herder, Wilhelm von Humboldt, Schleiermacher and others language came to be seen as a vehicle of cultural identity: differences in the way natural languages articulated the world became valued for their 'living' capacity to disclose new ways of understanding existence, rather than for their derivation from a divine source. The positive implications of this view for tolerance and mutual enrichment between cultures already began to contrast, though, with a sense that language, as the universal condition of possibility of intersubjective communication, could also pose a challenge to the freedom of the individual subject. In its most disreputable version this idea of the 'prison-house of language' appears in Nietzsche's assertion that 'the spell of certain grammatical functions is in the last analysis (*im letzten Grunde*) the spell of *physiological* value-judgements and racial conditions': as such, 'unconscious domination . . . by the same grammatical functions' determines what can be thought by a thinker of a particular race.[8] Nonsense as this clearly is, questions about the possibly repressive nature of language are indeed vital to critiques of culture.

Avant-garde art, which emerges most vividly around the time of the First World War in Dada's attack on the confining aspects of established forms of culture, can be defined by its refusal to communicate in ways which are accepted by established culture. At the same time such art must always rely upon the orders which it rejects, as otherwise the point of its refusal is lost. Humboldt and Schleiermacher already realised that there is a necessary tension between the need for language 'schematically' to fix a world which is re-identifiable for pragmatic and other purposes, and language's 'poetic' capacity to disclose the world in new ways. Acceptance of the inherent necessity of such a tension has, though, been too rare in modern German reflections on language and culture.

Disenchantment with certain forms of language often constitutes part of a wider reaction against modern civilisation's rationalising tendency towards a reduction of differing 'locally grown' cultural forms into a sameness that empties them of their former meaning – a process which has actually become much more dominant since the emergence of the electronic media than it was earlier in the twentieth century. Like scientific and philosophical systems, and like money, language can be understood as a system of differences which has only a virtual relationship to the world. By the early part of the twentieth century this sometimes leads to the sense, present, for example, in the early work of Walter Benjamin, that language has now come apart from the world. The idea of a language which would really connect to the world – which is often associated with music – therefore becomes a means of suggesting a way beyond the alienation inherent in the destruction of traditional national or theological forms of articulation. This idea appears in a wide variety of guises, most of which are demonstrably flawed because they rely upon the notion of a former situation which can never be proved to have existed at all, most of which connect to the concomitant suspicion of other systems – from money, to metaphysics, to bureaucracy – yet all of which also point to manifestations of real discontent with modern culture. It is, though, in this area that the most dangerous critiques of culture are established.

The politics of cultural critique

In *Heritage of Our Times* Ernst Bloch summed up how legitimate ideas which began in Romanticism come to be distorted and assimilated into reactionary politics in his notion of 'non-simultaneity' (*'Ungleichzeitigkeit'*), the recurrence of superseded ideas from the past that results from the attempt to come to terms with disturbing contemporary social phenomena. Modern capitalism's application of technology and its increasing rationalisation and bureaucratisation of the labour market are inescapable factors which establish the material conditions of political decisions. A more humane social existence could only result from a radical reorganisation of these factors, that would make them function for the good of the majority, rather than for the minority who control them. However, instead of being able to seek out the real socio-economic causes of their anxieties, members of the lower middle class in particular resort to regressive 'non-simultaneous' images and ideas from pre-modern culture. These are accompanied by the idea of the working class as the enemy in relation to whom they gain a precarious sense of their superior identity, and, in the most disturbing case, of 'alien' 'races' like the Jews, who are seen as responsible for the unstable money-dominated economy. Bloch refuses just to condemn the conceptual failure present in 'non-simultaneity', because it is the result of deep-seated anxieties which have real roots in and effects on politics. How this sort of failure comes about can be illustrated in the account of modernity of the philosopher and sociologist Georg Simmel.

In 'The Concept and Tragedy of Culture', and in other writings around the time of the First World War, Simmel exemplified a mode of cultural critique which recurred in many subsequent thinkers and is echoed in certain popular responses to historical developments. In the 1905 *Philosophy of Money* Simmel asserts that 'money spares us immediate contacts with things to an ever greater extent'.[9] As such, 'The "fetish-character" which Marx attributes to economic objects in the epoch of commodity production is only a specifically modified case of [the] fate of the contents of our culture.'[10] The 'tragedy of culture' lies in the fact that this loss of contact leads to an 'autonomous logic' of culture where the 'self-objectification' of human subjects – via which the human subject is able, e.g. in art, to 'return to itself' – actually 'leads away from the purpose of culture', which is contact with what he terms 'life'.[11]

This might seem to be just another version of a defensible topos of cultural critique. Marx had suggested that the accumulation of 'dead labour', in the form of machines, institutions, capital etc., increasingly limits the possibilities of meaningful 'living labour'. Lukács takes up the Marxian idea, in the light of his acquaintance with Simmel, in *History and Class Consciousness* of 1923, claiming that machine work results in 'an ever more intense exclusion of the qualitative human-individual attributes of the worker'.[12] Simmel, however, uses his notion of culture in a paradigmatically different way. In *The War and the Spiritual Decisions* of 1917 he maintains that 'the "machine of war" has a completely different, infinitely more living relationship to him who uses it [i.e. the soldier fighting for his country] than the machine in the factory'.[13] 'Life' – in the form of a *war* – is therefore what overcomes culture's moves away from direct contact with reality, because it breaks through the abstractions which govern modern civilisation! Thomas Mann makes much the same point in *Reflections of an Unpolitical Man*, seeing the war as a process of the 'self-recognition' of German culture.[14]

In the light of such contentions it is no coincidence that the dominant metaphors for the war in this period, such as the metaphor of the storm which releases an accumulated tension, are metaphors of natural, not social events, or that theorists like Spengler in the 1917 *Decline of the West* (second volume 1922) see the history of culture in terms of Goethe's notion of morphology, cultures being essentially organisms which grow and decay. In the most striking example of 'non-simultaneity' prior to widespread collusion with the Nazis, many German intellectuals enthusiastically greeted the onset of war in 1914 on the basis of this strange inversion of nature and civilisation. How, then, can a critique of culture lead to an attitude where the mass destruction of human life on an unprecedented scale via the utilisation of new military technology is seen as 'spiritually' preferable to attempts to render modern societies more humane?

Faced with the fact that many of the processes that really lead to the crises of war and inflation take place in the 'abstract' realm of capital exchange, the desire to grasp what is going on led, especially in the Weimar period, to the public success of theories which explain 'the crisis of culture' in a 'mythological' manner by the use of concrete images derived from a supposedly more tractable reality. The predominant strategy entails an enlisting of nature or 'life', which is connected to the '*Volk*', on the side of what is to be preserved, against the 'degenerate' other side, a procedure which was, of course, part of the Nazi attempt to divide art itself into 'healthy' and 'degenerate' products. Mann's and Spengler's opposition of 'culture' to 'civilisation', where the former is on the side of 'life' or 'soul' and is the location of the '*Volk*', and the latter of rigidity and stasis (of Klages' 'logocentrism') and is the location of the 'mass', turns the dualist topos into a potentially even cruder political weapon. Spengler's combination of his theory of morphology with an evaluation which ranks the new products of technology above modern art (as though they could validly be compared in this manner) suggests just how confused thinking on the part of those interested in the 'conservative revolution' could become. A related combination of enthusiasm for the technological modernisation of society and an antagonism towards the questioning of traditional values by aesthetic modernism has, incidentally, also been characteristic of the American neo-conservative thinking about culture that has influenced the German Right during the Kohl years.

The task of the most important critiques of culture from the Weimar period onwards is to find ways of opposing irrationalism without forgetting that irrationalist theories are distorted expressions of real problems. How, though, is one to oppose irrationalism without invoking an 'absolute' value like 'scientific progress' which can just as easily lead to other kinds of oppression and exclusion? Weber already suggested in 'Science as a Vocation' that: 'The fate of our age, with its characteristic rationalisation and intellectualisation and above all the disenchantment of the world, is that the ultimate, most sublime values have withdrawn from public life, either into the nether-worldly realm of mystical life or into the brotherliness of immediate personal relationships between individuals.'[15] The really significant difficulty involved here appears, though, not in the reactionary theorists like Spengler, whose ideas are often merely symptomatic, but in the divisions on the Left over the relationships between culture and politics.

In the face of the alienation felt in relation to modernity, art would seem to have to offer a sense of meaning lacking in reality itself, hence the tendency in Romanticism for it to be regarded as an answer to nihilism, which preserves something beyond what can be explained by science without recourse to traditional theology. In Germany, however, this assumption too easily feeds into an obfuscation of the real conflicts in the name of the values of education ('*Bildung*') exemplified in the works of Goethe, Schiller and other producers of classical bourgeois art. When the values of *Bildung* – as the 'organic' expression of 'German culture' – turn out not only to be capable of being employed as they were in relation to the First World War, but also to be apparently useless in preventing the Nazi descent into barbarism, the very idea of a culture based on the edifying function of art becomes harder to sustain.

There is a three-way division in response to this situation on the Left, which is represented by Lukács, Brecht, and Adorno. In the 'Expressionism Debate' at the end of the 1930s, which concerned the role of art in revolutionary politics in the light of the Nazi threat, those like Lukács who accept at least some of the line of the Moscow-dominated Third International see the aim of progressive art as a 'realism' which 'reflects' social reality, thereby performing an educative function. A version of this approach would later play an important role in the cultural politics of the GDR. Lukács' idea of realism is exemplified in the classic bourgeois traditions of the novel, in which the actions of individuals and the movement of the historical 'totality' are integrated by the form of the work. Avant-garde art, on the other hand, makes manifest the widespread feeling of disruption of any continuity between individual experience and the wider course of events. The assessment of the cultural significance of such works depends upon what role art is supposed to play in progressive politics. Brecht and Bloch regard the classical realist tradition as likely to block contact with social reality because it sustains the uncritical aesthetic dimension of *Bildung* by encouraging contemplation and identification with the main figures in the work. Brecht's response is pragmatic: it is a question of theatrical and other praxis, not of a particular form of art, as to what enables people to see through ideological deception and get in touch with reality. Artistic practice will change according to the historical and political situation: the very idea of art which transcends its social and historical context is therefore put into question.

For Brecht cultural questions become questions of the critique of ideology: the goal of art is the uncovering of a truth concealed by dominant cultural forms. This perception of culture poses a dilemma which is explored in the 'Critical Theory' of Benjamin and Adorno. The problem they confront is the one with which we began: if culture wishes to criticise itself there must be some way in which this criticism can be grounded. The point of the Romantic aesthetic tradition for many thinkers was that it relied upon cultural forms which resisted integration into the realm of merely relational values: the work of art had intrinsic value and therefore in some sense legitimated itself, albeit by partially separating itself from the rest of the social world. This idea of art had led the Romantics to the idea that truth itself, as a further intrinsic value, was inherently linked to what was revealed in art. Heidegger takes up this idea, from a politically indefensible perspective, in his 1935–6 *Origin of the Work of Art,* and it plays a role in both Benjamin and Adorno. In the view particularly associated with Adorno the fact is that if art is to be directly used for political ends it becomes just another part of the world of 'instrumental reason' and its effect will be potentially of the same order as any other kind of effect.

The dilemma for the defence of the aesthetic tradition is already clear from the divergent political affiliations of the main thinkers who advance philosophical positions relating art to truth. Not long before his tragic death trying to flee the Nazis Benjamin asserted that 'There is never a document of culture which is not at the same time a document of barbarism',[16] because the values embodied in existing culture in fact more often mask the oppression which inaugurated that culture than lead to social transformation. Benjamin's early reflections on art and culture had relied upon the theologically inspired idea of a language that would have a more than arbitrary relationship to what it signified, which was manifested in the truth of the unique literary text. Under the influence of Brecht and in the face of the course of German history Benjamin had moved to an analysis of the effects of modern technology on the destruction of traditional notions of the unique work of art, attempting to see this destruction as a positive political opportunity for a new kind of revolutionary culture.

Adorno protested against this surrender of the possibility of truth residing in works of modern art like those of Schönberg or Kafka in an exchange of letters with Benjamin. Benjamin's view, Adorno maintains, leads merely to a rejection of 'autonomous art' because of its failure to possess 'immediate use value'.[17] Instead of modern technology, of the kind used in movie film, being a way of demystifying traditional forms of art in the name of political change, film itself, as is evident in the products of Hollywood, is part of what Adorno and Horkheimer would later term the 'culture industry', which turns art into merely a commodity. This view is, though, ambiguous, even with regard to the autonomous art it wishes to defend. By using forms derived from existing society in order to articulate utopian possibilities, art is indeed, as Benjamin had suggested, always also in complicity with what it opposes, and, as such, is ideological. However, it is not just ideological: 'The promise of the work of art to institute truth by imprinting shape (*Gestalt*) into socially transmitted forms is as necessary as it is hypocritical.'[18] The refusal to resolve the conflicts inherent in this dual status of art makes Adorno's position of enduring importance in diagnoses of the ills of modern culture.

Adorno's gloomy overall view of modern culture does depend, though, upon an over-emphatic interpretation of the role of subjectivity in the modern world, which is shared at the other end of the political spectrum by Heidegger. This interpretation also plays a significant role in the recent Foucault-, Derrida-, and Lyotard-influenced debates in Germany about modernity and post-modernity. It was via the assimilation of recent French theory that the tradition of Nietzsche- and Heidegger-inspired cultural critique gained new impetus in Germany, after being rejected for its links to Nazism by the Marx-oriented generation of 1968. Like the authors of *Dialectic of Enlightenment*, Heidegger views the modern era as an era of 'subjectification', in which nature becomes merely an object for the manipulating subject, in the application of modern technology. This contentious view makes the same links between the commodity system, systematic natural science, and 'Western metaphysics' as were inherent in many aspects of the critiques we have already examined. Heidegger himself was active as a Nazi from 1933 onwards and remained in the party until 1945: like many others, his way of interpreting the problems of modern culture led him to a complete political and ethical failure. What, then, led Horkheimer and Adorno to advance a view which is so similar, despite their opposition to the Nazis and their crucial role in restoring radical critical thinking to post-war German society?

In his 1985 *The Philosophical Discourse of Modernity* Habermas, the foremost heir to the tradition of Critical Theory, claims that Horkheimer and

Adorno 'surrendered themselves to an unrestrained scepticism with regard to reason, instead of pondering the grounds which make one doubt this scepticism itself'.[19] In his version of the story the failure to ground modern reason since Kant that underlies the positions we have been considering is based on a false paradigm, shared by Nietzsche, Horkheimer and Adorno, Heidegger, and post-structuralism, which is generated precisely by the search for a ground of subjectivity. This leads either to the irrationalist pursuit of the intuitively available ground of the world's intelligibility, or to an exclusive concern with the negative effects of the domination of subjective rationality over the object world, at the expense of a failure to recognise the real advances made possible by modernity. Habermas's alternative paradigm is based upon the claim that it is only through the processes of *intersubjective* communication that subjects gain an identity at all. This identity is therefore dependent upon the acknowledgement of others. The dilemmas of the modern tradition of 'subject philosophy' can be overcome by the realisation that there is no ultimate solution to the problem of subjectivity's relationship to nature: this relationship must therefore be continually re-negotiated within society.

Habermas, then, makes a distinction between what may be argued in philosophical accounts of the ground of human culture, and the consequences that may be drawn from these accounts for political action within a democratic public sphere, where consensus can only ever be provisional. However, his admirable attempt to overcome the problems that underlie modern German critiques of culture often tends to assume there is no further need to engage with the old questions. The desire to have done with the issue of nature 'in itself' is, of course, not surprising. Many of the Nazi or proto-Nazi irrationalists, like Klages, were also notable for their expressly ecological 'Romantic' concern for non-human nature, a concern which is also, though, linked precisely to the sources of the worst indifference to human suffering. Habermas's suspicion of 'Romantic' thinking is part of a widespread suspicion on the Left. However, the rise of a democratically oriented German Green movement would have been impossible without a Romantic tradition whose often forgotten early history is now being re-written, for example in the impeccably democratic work on Romanticism by the philosopher Manfred Frank.

The search for ways of legitimating a critique of technological domination and commodification in the newly united Germany must rely both upon the radically new perspectives opened up by feminist critiques of male domination, and upon a renewal of already existing critical resources. Perhaps only now will the fear resulting from the way those resources were perverted begin to be overcome in the name of the potential they still possess. In a recent text Habermas himself rejoins the tradition of cultural critique in a manner startlingly appropriate to the Schelling about whom he wrote his doctoral dissertation in 1954: 'It is true that the timebombs of a ruthlessly exploited nature are quietly yet stubbornly ticking away. But while outer nature broods in its way on revenge for the mutilations we have inflicted on it, nature within *us* also raises its voice.'[20] The consumer-dominated new Germany, like the rest of the developed West, is as yet still unlikely seriously to heed this renewal of Romantic concerns. However, the question for the future will be whether aspects of a tradition that contributed to catastrophic political failure might yet prove in different circumstances to offer resources that now make disaster less likely.

NOTES

1. T. W. Adorno, *Gesellschaftstheorie und Kulturkritik*, Frankfurt/Main: Suhrkamp, 1975, p. 46.

2. In Heinrich Scholz, ed., *Die Hauptschriften zum Pantheismusstreit zwischen Jacobi und Mendelssohn*, Berlin: Reuther und Reichardt, 1916, p. 271.

3. Max Weber, *Gesammelte Aufsätze zur Wissenschaftslehre*, Tübingen: J. C. Mohr, 1988, p. 610.

4. *Ibid.*, p. 605.

5. Friedrich Wilhelm Joseph Schelling, *Sämmtliche Werke*, ed. K. F. A. Schelling, I Abtheilung vols. I–X, II Abtheilung Bde. 1–4, Stuttgart: Cotta, 1856–61, I/7, p. 17.

6. Max Horkheimer and T. W. Adorno, *Dialektik der Aufklärung*, Frankfurt/Main: Fischer, 1971, p. 5.

7. Friedrich Nietzsche, *Sämtliche Werke*, eds. Giorgio Colli and Mazzino Montinari Munich: dtv, 1980, vol. V, pp. 205–6.

8. *Ibid.*, vol. V, p. 35.

9. Georg Simmel, *Philosophie des Geldes*, Frankfurt/Main: Suhrkamp, 1989, p. 531.

10. Georg Simmel, *Das individuelle Gesetz*, Frankfurt/Main: Suhrkamp, 1987, p. 140.

11. *Ibid.*, p. 147.

12. Georg Lukács, *Geschichte und Klassenbewußtsein*, Amsterdam: Thomas de Munter, 1967, p. 99.

13. Georg Simmel, *Der Krieg und die geistigen Entscheidungen*, Munich and Berlin: Duncker & Humblot, 1917, p. 49.

14. Thomas Mann, *Betrachtungen eines Unpolitischen*, Frankfurt: Fischer, 1960, p. 86.

15. Max Weber, 'Science as a Vocation', translated by Michael John, in Peter Lassman, Irving Velody and Herminio Martins (eds.), *Max Weber's 'Science as a Vocation'*, London: Unwin Hyman, 1989, p. 30 (translation amended).

16. Walter Benjamin, *Gesammelte Schriften* I.2, Frankfurt/Main: Suhrkamp, 1980, p. 696.

17. Henri Lonitz (ed.), *Theodor Adorno; Walter Benjamin. Briefwechsel 1928–1940*, Frankfurt/Main: Suhrkamp, 1994, p. 171.

18. Max Horkheimer, and T. W. Adorno, *Dialektik der Aufklärung*, Frankfurt/Main: Suhrkamp, 1971, p. 117.

19. Jürgen Habermas, *Der philosophische Diskurs der Moderne*, Frankfurt/Main: Suhrkamp, 1985, p. 156.

20. Jürgen Habermas, *Vergangenheit als Zukunft*, Zürich: Pendo-Profile, 1991, p. 125, quoted in Peter Dews, *The Limits of Disenchantment*, London, New York: Verso, 1995, p. 165.

FURTHER READING

There are numerous histories of German philosophy and cultural theory. Frederick C. Beiser, *The Fate of Reason: German Philosophy from Kant to Fichte* (Cambridge, Mass.: Harvard University Press, 1987) gives a detailed philosophical history of the period in which the terms of the debate on modern culture in Germany were first established. Andrew Bowie, *Aesthetics and Subjectivity: from Kant to Nietzsche* (Manchester: Manchester University Press, 1993) investigates the Romantic exploration of subjectivity, and Andrew Bowie, *From Romanticism to Critical Theory. The Philosophy of German Literary Theory* (London: Routledge, 1997) looks at reflections on language and truth in modern culture from Kant to the Frankfurt School.

Manfred Frank's two volumes *Der kommende Gott* (Frankfurt/Main: Suhrkamp, 1982) and *Gott im Exil* (Frankfurt/Main: Suhrkamp, 1988) offer new perspectives on myth and modernity. While Louis Dumont, *German Ideology* (Chicago/London: Chicago University Press, 1994) offers a valuable analysis of the differences between French and German approaches to modern culture, Martin Heidegger, *Vorträge und Aufsätze*, (Pfullingen: Neske, 1954) includes key essays on science, technology and modernity from a more inner-German perspective. Albrecht Wellmer, a leading contemporary philosopher, also tackles issues of modernity and culture in his *Endspiele: Die unversöhnliche Moderne* (Frankfurt/Main: Suhrkamp, 1993).

Perhaps the most significant critic of modern culture, particularly with regard to Germany after National Socialism, is T. W. Adorno. The best introduction to the style and complexity of his critique of the 'culture industry' is *Minima Moralia* (Frankfurt/Main: Suhrkamp, 1978), a collection of short essays and aphorisms which he calls explorations of the 'damaged life' of modern culture. A more conventional analysis of German culture before 1933 is Fritz Stern, *The Politics of Cultural Despair* (New York: Anchor Books, 1965), which explores the links between German cultural thought and reactionary politics.

The attempt to re-define the relationship between rationalism and irrationalism in German culture plays a central role in Herbert Schädelbach, *Zur Rehabilitierung des 'animale rationale'* (Frankfurt/Main: Suhrkamp, 1992), which contains an important essay on 'Kultur und Kulturkritik' (Culture and Cultural Criticism), and in Oskar Negt and Alexander Kluge, *Geschichte und Eigensinn* (Frankfurt/Main: Zweitausendeins, 1981), which is a monumental attempt to re-think the idea of German identity in relation to the notions of work and the public sphere.

7

The functions of 'Volkskultur',
mass culture and alternative culture

The three concepts of *Volkskultur*, mass culture and alternative cul- $\quad$
ture are seminal for an understanding of the history of German modernity. They reflect different conceptions of the popular and it is important
to outline their functional significance within the development of German cultural, ideological and political history. Special attention is to be
paid to the authors of high culture as both promoters and critics of popular culture in order to highlight the negotiation of attitudes between the
educated classes and the rest of the population. Paradoxically, the varieties of 'low' culture are in some respects creations of the same elites who
otherwise insist on keeping the sophisticated and reflexive culture of the
minority separate from that of the majority. Just as folk culture, mass culture and alternative culture spell out distinct phases within the trajectory
of modernity, so the relationship between the cultural intelligentsia and
the mass of the people changes. While the three basic forms of popular
culture today stand for parallel and intermixing trends within the
diversification of contemporary civilisation, they arose within successive
historical conjunctures which were laden with both liberating and fatal
potential. The ideological functions of popular culture reveal most
conspicuously the contradictory set of hopes and prejudices as well as the
antagonistic discourses which accompanied civil society as it unfolded in
Germany during the past couple of centuries.

The importance of 'Volkskultur' for
the formation of national identity

Settled within today's broad spectrum of a mass entertainments culture
German folklore festivals include groups from Austria and Switzerland,

preserve regional customs and costumes, and project German minority culture in other continents. At the inception of modernity *Volkskultur* was not so ostensibly depoliticised but played a vital part in the formation of nationhood and became a prefigurative notion for political unification. The development of German national culture in the nineteenth and twentieth centuries is unthinkable without the initial retrieval of local and regional folk traditions and their incorporation into the national heritage. From the second half of the eighteenth century until deep into the nineteenth sections of the literary intelligentsia acted as collectors and custodians of forgotten German documents and folk traditions with a view to promoting a sense of nationhood which embraced all social classes. Justus Möser, a North German advocate of the Enlightenment, influenced by the spirit of the English moral weeklies, stressed the necessity of a history of rural customs and, somewhat provocatively, held that a nation's main 'body' was made up of its peasant families.[1] Möser's views made an impact on subsequent German writers keen to discover the peculiarities and distinctions of a spiritual German nationhood while Germany remained politically divided into kingdoms and a plethora of petty principalities. The collection of popular German songs and fairy tales by such writers as Johann Gottfried Herder at the end of the eighteenth century and Clemens Brentano, Wilhelm Tieck and the brothers Grimm (Wilhelm and Jacob) in the early nineteenth century lifted a substantially oral tradition into the national consciousness by disseminating it through the printed word. They popularised a heritage which had hitherto been the collective property of the 'ordinary folk' in different parts of the German-speaking lands. It thus became consolidated into a record destined to represent the foundations of a national cultural history.

At its inception, this process required that the notion of *Volk* be no longer merely connoted with the common, the parochial or regional, but allied to the concept of nation. This significant semantic shift was achieved by Johann Gottfried Herder who in his two-volume collection of *Volkslieder* (1778 and 1779) laid the accent neither solely on folk-songs nor exclusively on Germany. Horace and medieval Latin poems, texts of songs by Shakespeare, Opitz and Goethe as well as those by anonymous authors, literary pieces originating from Greenland in the north to Italy in the south, from Iceland in the west to the Baltic in the east are brought together under six regional European categories, followed for good measure by a seventh book devoted to songs from the 'hot latitudes' (Madagascar, Brazil, Peru). In other words, Herder tried to establish the notion of cultural nationhood within an exercise of comparing and contrasting different national traditions. He believed that the distinctiveness of a national voice could best be demonstrated by the typical variety of folk-poetic artefacts that a language community was capable of producing. Hence he developed the idea of the uniqueness and difference of 'national bodies' and the excellence of their respective 'national creations'. Herder regarded the ordinary people as both the ferment of cultural creativity and the prerequisite of a national public and a sense of nationhood.

It is the last third of the eighteenth and the beginning of the nine-teenth century that gave rise to notions of *Volkskunst, Volksmusik, Volksli-teratur, Volkskultur, Volkstheater* (folk or national art, music, literature, culture, theatre), *Volkstum* (folkdom) and *Volkskunde* (popular culture). The term *Volksbuch* (popular narrative) was coined by Joseph Görres (1807). At about the same time Achim von Arnim and Clemens Brentano edited three volumes of German folk-songs (some of them adopted from other languages) entitled *Des Knaben Wunderhorn* (1805–8). Jacob Grimm who, with his brother Wilhelm, collected and edited fairy tales (*Kinder-und Hausmärchen*, 2 vols., 1812–15) and legends (*Deutsche Sagen*, 2 vols., 1816–18), formed the notion of *Volksdichtung* (folk or national poetry), assuming that there was a collective genius at work which gave the nation organic wholeness and identity of character. While this postulation of an actually existing creative national genius is testimony to the fact that even the greatest scholar can be misled by the lodestar of ideology, Jacob Grimm, far from being alone in making such an assumption about the *Volksgeist* (national spirit), was only expressing notions typical of many of the greatest university teachers at that time. The brothers Schlegel thought likewise. Earlier on, Friedrich Carl von Savigny (1779–1861), the founder of the 'historical school' and Jacob Grimm's most influential pro-fessorial mentor and friend, had affirmed his belief in the wholeness and continuity of the national spirit in a programmatic essay:

> Wherever we find original historical documents the common law (*das bürgerliche Recht*) has already assumed a certain character which is peculiar to the nation (*Volk*), just as its language, customs and constitution. Moreover, these phenomena do not have a separate existence, they are but different powers and activities of the one nation, inseparably connected by nature . . . [2]

The law, like language, was seen as 'organically connected with the nature and character of the people'. 'The law' and 'the people', appearing in the singular here, encapsulated a silent longing for unity, while the area in central Europe where German was the native language actually remained a political patchwork of more or less independent states. There was neither a unified law nor a unified people. Given the political charge in the dreams of the nation of 'poets and thinkers', as Madame de Staël had called the Germans, it is too harsh to judge, as this otherwise perceptive French intellectual had done, that the educated classes left the political reality exclusively to the princely powers while fighting their own wars in the heavens of pure theory. The subsequent career of the term *Volk* showed that it could express the claims to constitutional and political agency by the mass of the people and, conversely, serve as a manipulative instrument in the rhetorical arsenals of nationalistic politicians. In the first half of the twentieth century National Socialism provided extremes of the latter, while in 1989 the authority of the rulers of the GDR was undone by the demonstrating crowds in Leipzig reclaiming their constitutional sovereignty with the vehemently democratic slogan 'Wir sind das Volk' (We are the people). The demonstrators later voiced their central political demand by stating 'Wir sind ein Volk' (We are one people).

In their construction of a German cultural identity the educated elites of the late eighteenth and early nineteenth centuries had to battle against two immense obstacles. Not only were the German people divided by the political geography that was anchored in a variety of feudal and feudal-absolutist dynasties, but it was also the case that German cultural traditions, both popular and educated, had for long periods been relegated to a secondary status, first by the Latin culture of the Holy Roman Empire and later by the ascendancy of France as a cultural model. The collation of German folk narratives, songs, plays and customs provided evidence for the cultural elite of an essentially common German culture existing within a variety of regional forms. There were of course those who believed the common to be identical with the vulgar, equating *Volk* with *Pöbel* (plebs). Even while Herder was trying to establish the idea of *Volk* as something that quintessentially expressed the deepest and most comprehensive basis of nationhood, there were those (e.g. Christoph Friedrich Nicolai early in the nineteenth century) who rejected the blurring of distinctions between the poetry of the literary genius and the songs of the plebs. Yet the growing internal trade amongst the politically divided parts of Germany, the common cause of the Germans against the Napoleonic armies, and the gradual introduction of modern industry made it possible, and increasingly necessary, that a sense of trans-regional identity giving expression to a yearning for nationhood be developed. The wished-for unity of German culture demanded a historical pedigree and the assumption of a common rootedness of all things German in an essentially uncorrupted collective genius gained ground.

In this context the foundation of Germanic Studies (*Germanistik*) as a proper university subject in the first half of the nineteenth century remains a major achievement of the educated bourgeoisie in helping to establish the cultural identity of an emergent nation and of culture as a crucial factor in affirming its existence. Political unification came much later, although there were powerful rhetoricians and thinkers in its favour at the beginning of the nineteenth century, such as Johann Gottlob Fichte, the philosopher, who held that the petty princes would all have to abdicate before unity was possible. In Germany the idea of the *Kulturnation* preceded that of the *Staatsnation*. One practical instrument for the dissemination of ideas was the development of publishing houses and the evolution of a literary market, with Leipzig hosting the most important European book fair. From 1825 it was also the seat of the German book trade organisation. As Goethe observed, it was especially in terms of ideas that Germany had become a 'market where all the nations offered their wares'.[3]

The Romantic movement in Germany, fired by a belief in the continuity and unity of the *Volksgeist*, was able to trace and retrieve the historical forms of the German language down to its Indo-European origins and documented German literature from the early Middle Ages onwards. Following British and French precedent, Germany too wished to stress its distinctive national character. This was difficult in a country where regional patriotism even amongst merchants and scholars was stronger than their allegiance to the nation. For example, Jacob Grimm, who laid the foundation stone of German philology and, together with the Dane, Rasmus Rask (1787–1832), counts as the founder father of Germanic philology, had in mind both his regional attachment to Hesse and his patriotic sense of belonging to a larger Germany when in his inaugural lecture he spoke about the feeling of being homesick. In his letters he frequently referred to Hesse compatriots with special affection. Not surprisingly, in the Germany of the early nineteenth century the term *Vaterland* had two meanings, indicating either a German region together with the sense of belonging to a *Landsmannschaft* (provincial fellowship), or, alternatively, referring to all the regions together in which German was spoken, and thus providing some evidence of a feeling for a more general, loosely German identity. Apart from the collections of German fairy tales, legends, descriptions of customs and legal practices the Grimm brothers also edited medieval high-culture literature. It was in Savigny's private library that Jacob Grimm first came to know Bodmer's edition of minnesingers (the German troubadours). These texts showed that even the cultivated language was subject to strong regional inflections. In helping to demonstrate the historical depth and variety of German literature and legal tradition Jacob and Wilhelm Grimm were at one with a large section of the professional classes that worked for a cultural and, by implication, political identity of Germany, preferring parliamentarism to absolutist rule. Although by no means anti-aristocratic the Grimm brothers joined five other Göttingen professors in 1837 and signed a famous protest against the suspension of the Hesse constitution which had been granted in 1833. They promptly lost their jobs and left for Berlin. Like the Grimm brothers many Germans began to feel that collective deference to an absolutist prince stifled both individuality and the emergence of a civil society in which the distinction between public and private spheres and constitutionally guaranteed rights were recognised.

Yet the emergence of a national public invested Germany with a double legacy. Certainly, the growth of a nation-wide culture carried with it the promises of bourgeois emancipation, the advance of individual liberty and the vision of unifying the diversity of the German-speaking lands into one political entity in the heart of Europe. However, feelings of patriotic civility were problematically paralleled by militant convictions that the *Volk* must stand together against the alien otherness of neighbouring nations. The patriotic sentiments that were forged in the early nineteen hundreds were quite contradictory. On the one hand, they included a xenophobic mix which was mobilised in the Napoleonic Wars and, on the other, an imagined national commitment to civic virtues shading over into notions of world citizenship (Wieland, Goethe, Schiller), shining examples of humanism and a vision of universal harmony between peoples as augured in Friedrich Schiller's 'Ode to Joy'. Another poet of the time, Friedrich Hölderlin, understood patriotism as a noble sentiment which was as yet lacking in the majority of Germans. Plainly, the high-minded love of the nation, which since the late eighteenth century went together with demands for republicanism and representative democracy, was always in danger of being swamped both by the princely denials of civic freedoms and the xenophobia whipped up during the Napoleonic Wars. As the nineteenth century progressed an anti-republican, inward-looking ideology, while not peculiar to Germany alone, became particularly strong there and formed the mainstay of a widespread, though by no means generally accepted, authoritarian culture. By the middle of the nineteenth century intellectuals like Heinrich Heine, a consistent and biting critic of francophobia, were outnumbered by such compatriots as Ernst Moritz Arndt, Friedrich Ludwig Jahn (i.e. *Turnvater Jahn*, founder of a paramilitary gymnastics movement), Wolfgang Menzel and others who combined their hatred of France with subservience to the German princes.

In other words, the intelligentsia was by no means uniformly republican or liberal. However, it was united in believing that there was a genius of the *Volk* whose voice must be preserved and articulated by transposing oral traditions into a written record of folk tales, folk plays, fairy tales and folk-songs; by establishing an historical record of German legal and high literature; and by using the tone and form of the folk-song as a template for popular literary production. One of the remarkable features of Germany in the first half of the nineteenth century is that conservative, liberal and revolutionary poets alike, unconcerned by possible allegations of bad taste or kitsch, strove in some of their work for the stark, simple forms of expression that folk-songs and fairy tales had. As Ludwig Uhland observed, in this kind of poetry the individual genius committed itself to expressing the common experience, from everyday feelings to the longings and protests of those suffering under conditions of oppression. Examples of the former are Matthias Claudius's 'Der Mond ist aufgegangen' (The moon has risen, the golden stars are sparkling; set to music by Schubert), poems by Joseph Freiherr von Eichendorff (e.g. 'In einem kühlen Grunde' – In a cool valley; 'O Täler weit, O Höhen' – O valleys wide, O hills; set to music by Schubert, Mendelssohn and Schumann), Ludwig Uhland ('Am Brunnen vor dem Tore' – At the well outside the gates; 'Ännchen von Tharau') and Heinrich Heine (e.g. 'Ich weiß nicht, was soll es bedeuten' – I do not know what it means); while Heine's 'Die Weber' (The weavers; with the bitter refrain 'Germany we're weaving the cloak for your hearse, we're weaving into it a threefold curse . . .') and Hoffmann von Fallersleben's 'Deutschland, Deutschland über alles' are illustrations of the latter.

The history of the *Deutschlandlied*'s use is instructive for the tortuous course of German culture itself. Distinctly republican in sentiment the poem could not enter on an official career in Imperial Germany although, ironically, it was effectively combined with a tune of homage to a monarch, taken from Joseph Haydn's 'Emperor' Quartet. The song was chosen as democratic Germany's national anthem in the Weimar Republic, only increasingly to serve as a nationalistic expression of defiance against the borders imposed on Germany by the Versailles Treaty. For this reason, and because the first stanza was further discredited after acquiring connotations of an insufferably domineering German nationalism, only the third stanza with its stress on 'unity and right and freedom' is sung at official occasions in the Federal Republic. The fate of the *Deutschlandlied* mirrors the hopes of Germany as a civil society, the depth that German culture and politics had sunk to in the Third Reich and the eventual victory of liberal-democratic traditions from whence the poem originated.

The 'Volk' as mass

In the run-up to the 1848 revolution the term *Masse*, suddenly virtually interchangeable with *Volk*, acquired a particularly positive charge. Up until then it had been used mainly negatively in reference to the allegedly base and detestable instincts of the 'lowly folk'. However, as is evident from a letter in 1838 by Georg Gottfried Gervinus, one of the Göttingen Seven, the people were now conceived as a mass proponent of republican national sentiment who, regrettably, were as yet accorded no political honour: 'In our lands the mass has no honour, and without this it cannot be part of the political state of affairs.'[4] In 1841 Johann Jacoby added another concept to the political debate in close semantic proximity to *Volk* and *Masse*, that of the independent citizen. He provocatively asked what the chief desire of all the German social estates was. 'Legitimate participation of the independent citizen in the affairs of state,' he answered and went on to argue that the *Volk*, having reached a certain 'ethical-intellectual standing' through education, must be given a legal status that corresponded to its degree of culturedness. Referring to the provinces of Prussia, and to those of other parts of Germany by implication, he rightly pointed out that, 'even in the eyes of our enemies, the French and the English',[5] there was a high level of general education. Jacoby was but one of many who judged the existing framework of politics and public administration to be out of phase with the degree of culture and education that had in fact been achieved. The spread of education and information nurtured demands amongst scholars, the liberal professions, merchants, entrepreneurs, tradesmen and industrial workers for participation in political decision making. The battle for the mind of the masses as the central drama of modernity had begun and it developed in Germany with particular ferocity, producing typical instruments of governance as well as responses of resistance and self-protection.

Before the foundation of the Empire the disjuncture of authoritarian government and a better informed mass public led to a situation where at best only the increased application of censorship, at worst the persecution and emigration of outspoken citizens, could keep the people silenced in order to sustain the powers that be. Emigration was a fate that had indeed to be faced by many Germans who believed that they should speak up for their own people: Heinrich Heine (Paris), Karl Marx (London), August Heinrich Hoffmann von Fallersleben (Italy and various German provinces), Georg Herwegh (Zurich and Paris), Ferdinand Freiligrath (Belgium, Switzerland, England), Karl (later: Carl) Schurz (USA) and many other, lesser known publicists. It was largely because of the actual or assumed popularity of a literary elite committed to democratic-republican ideals that pre-Bismarckian Germany became the classic country of public censorship. The absolutist administrations and the intelligentsia siding with them regarded the *Volk* both as a dough to be kneaded into a submissive mass and as a source of unrest, anarchy and revolutionary ferment necessitating reactive legislation and autocratic police regimes. In 1835 the German Federation issued a decree forbidding or restricting the publications of those belonging to Young Germany (*Junges Deutschland*, a loose grouping of liberal-democratic writers). All German governments were thereby obliged to bring to bear their respective criminal codes and the laws restricting the freedom of the press. The decree named Heinrich Heine, Carl Gutzkow, Heinrich Laube, Ludolf Wienbarg and Theodor Mundt, but additionally bookshops, publishers and printers were targeted. Nineteen years later, in 1854, a police handbook appeared which contained a blacklist of 6,300 individuals who were rated as enemies of the government and exponents of revolutionary ideas, naming amongst others Hoffmann von Fallersleben, Dr Arnold Ruge, David Strauß and Karl Schurz. Censorship and ideological discrimination were well-worn practices that haunted writers in various degrees of severity practically until the middle of the twentieth century when at least the constitution of the West German Federal Republic simply stated that 'censorship does not take place'. It had not been particularly acute under the Wilhelmine emperors, nor in the Weimar Republic.

Hitler's Third Reich had no official censor, nor did the German Democratic Republic, but these two regimes sustained practices of all-pervasive ideological control, through the organs both of the State and the governing Party, allowing critical material to be published only if one or other faction of the governing elite protected it. Intellectuals who did not conform had to emigrate, were stripped of their nationality or, in the case of the GDR, became awkward dissidents.

Censorship and ideological exclusion were crudely coercive instruments for ensuring the subaltern accommodation of the mass of the people, particularly because their arbitrary application could easily bring about a further loss to the state of the very loyalty that these instruments were supposed to secure. The maintenance of legitimacy intensified as a problem beyond any censor's control through the rise of mass literacy and the development of political parties and pressure groups within increasingly urbanised environments. These gnawed away at established authority moored in hallowed tradition. Nineteenth-century Germany followed the basic trajectory that characterised European societies in general, namely the transformation from feudal-agrarian communities to industrial mass societies. This brought with it what Max Weber later identified as a secular process of disenchantment. The growth of the cities was not merely a quantitative phenomenon. It meant incisive changes in legal status and life-styles, notably those of the urban settlers. The traditional towns had been corporate communities, with a hierarchical structure of estates and a privileged core of burghers amidst a majority of merely tolerated folk without civil rights. By contrast, the modern towns were sprawling in the open landscape, internally divided by the possessive individualism of the bourgeois class and the pauperism of the proletariat. They were statistical aggregates of anonymously gathered citizens, held together by little more than civic bureaucracies and transport systems. The inhabitants, involved in struggles for equal rights and social betterment, were concentrated around industrial, administrative and trading activities. In other words, modern society disaggregated the old corporate cohesion, dissolved the fusion of church and state and through the enlightening effects of its secular tuition reduced the ideological hold of organised religion. While the modernisation process pushed for political and cultural diversity, the overriding issue of mass culture was how to stabilise the cohesive identity of the population by non-coercive means.

One way of doing this was by imbuing society with a feeling of national superiority. This was certainly attempted in the Empire of the Prussian kings which otherwise lacked convincingly unifying symbols, not least because it had been created from above and failed to unite all the German-speaking regions. Nevertheless the achievements of German culture were functionalised in the nineteenth century and much of the twentieth for the purposes of triumphalist nationalism. But modern German culture was never short of people with critical potentials of anti-authoritarian watchfulness. For example, the blind belief in military prowess was classically exposed as barbaric by Nietzsche in the opening paragraph of his *Untimely Meditations* (1875). Culture, he stated, had nothing to do with stern discipline, efficient generalship and the obedience of the ranks. Contemporary German culture, he held, lacked originality and inspiration and was at best only an execrable jumble of copied styles, at worst the smug acquisition of an all too numerous class of philistines bragging with their encyclopaedic education (*Bildungsphilister*). As long as these mistook the victory over France in 1871 for a defeat of French culture they would hasten the further destruction of aesthetic productiveness and bring about the 'extirpation of the German spirit (*Geist*) for the benefit of the German Reich'.[6] The latter's nationalistic appeals to the citizens' patriotic sentiments were unmasked both by class-conscious politicians like August Bebel and Karl Liebknecht and by critical literati as cynical propaganda ploys of the ruling elites. Famously, the seventeen-year-old Brecht, when he had to write a school essay on the Latin saying that it was allegedly 'sweet and honourable to die for the fatherland', simply pronounced this to be a piece of interested propaganda, invented by the imperial ruler's fat court jester before he hastily departed the battle (at Philippi in 42BC). In short, throughout the course of modernity society divided into a majority which saw culture as serving the greater glory of the nation and a minority which cherished critical independence from authority, both secular and ecclesiastical.

The diversity and division of the cultural and political heritage manifested itself further in the different mass organisations that vied for majority allegiance in Imperial Germany and thereafter. The political and ideological rhetoric became particularly shrill in the newly founded German Reich because of the presence of Social Democracy which was critical not only of the Reich's aggressive imperialism but also of its monarchical authoritarianism and lack of democratic legitimation. The SPD rapidly grew into Europe's largest political party and, despite being suspended by law between 1878 and 1890, was an oppositional force to be reckoned with as much for its threats to the established order as for its accommodations with the modernising dynamic of capitalism.

The foundation of the Social Democratic Party was the product of initial collaboration between radical intellectuals, workers and sizeable sections of the bourgeoisie committed to social justice, first realised within the worker educational associations formed from the 1840s onwards. There were one hundred and four of them by 1862. Against a background of the 'apathy of the masses' (Lassalle) these provided the most active recruits for the first party-political organisation of workers in 1863. At that time the liberal-bourgeois dream of a peaceful accord between the classes was still alive. Apart from poets like Freiligrath, Heine, Herwegh and Georg Werth who set to verse proletarian experience there were Rhenish industrialists and financiers like Friedrich Harkort (1793–1880) and Gustav Mevissen (1815–99) who argued that knowledge was a capital that had to be shared by all classes both to heal dangerous social rifts and to increase wealth and well-being for all. Bebel and Liebknecht were products of the Leipzig workers' educational council and sought drastic improvements in the position of the workers through the spread of education.

However, as Liebknecht pointed out in his famous speech 'Wissen ist Macht – Macht ist Wissen' (Knowledge is Power – Power is Knowledge, 1872), the ruling class had an interest in sustaining its hegemony by keeping the mind of the masses in darkness through entertainment, a trivial press, the discipline of the barracks and the limitations of primary education. The commitment to realising a general humanitarian civilisation was guaranteed, according to Liebknecht, only through the Social Democrats gaining power. Apart from educative non-fiction it was indeed a vast production of pulp novels, edifying tracts, calendars and almanachs which satisfied the tastes of the mass readership. Liebknecht regarded it with suspicion. His speech made it clear that the workers' educational associations had indeed become what Friedrich Bosse in the 1890s would call the 'unruly child' of initially well-intentioned efforts by an enlightened bourgeoisie. That class had gained social recognition post–1848 and it had subsequently been integrated into the establishment of the Wilhelmine Reich, leading to a shrinkage of its national-liberal orientation in favour of a more radically nationalistic one. The festivities in honour of Friedrich Schiller illustrate this change. Having been a hero of liberal humanism for the many Schiller societies before 1848, he had become a prophet of German unity by 1859 (his centenary) and a forerunner of Bismarck by 1905 (the hundredth anniversary of his death)!

By the end of the nineteenth century this development had exacerbated a situation where the meaning of the cultural and political heritage and the acquisition of education had a tendency to divide on class lines, with conscious efforts being made by the different ideological factions to deploy both the print media and forms of mass organisation for their respective aims. The nationalist-imperialist factions agitated effectively through the Pan-German League and such mass organisations as the Naval League (1.1 million members by 1913, of which 790,000 were corporations) and the Kyffhäuser fraternity (with some 2.9 million members by 1910). There was a distinct preponderance of educated, Protestant men in all these associations, pointing to a further fissure within Wilhelmine society, that between Protestants and Catholics. During the 'culture war' (*Kulturkampf*), which marked the whole of the Bismarckian era, 1871 to 1890, liberals as advocates of a clear separation between church and state sided with statist conservative forces against a Centre Party that for more than merely tactical reasons became committed to parliamentarism and social issues.

The strength of political Catholicism was not diminished by the *Kulturkampf* nor was that of Social Democracy, the biggest bogey of all the conservative forces, when it emerged from the suspension of its activities between 1878 and 1890. By the turn of the century the Party had a membership of over one million and was flanked, unofficially, by a number of large cultural associations with national umbrella structures, notably the worker gymnast, worker singer and worker theatre organisations. These had all grown out of the worker educational councils in various industrial towns but, for legal reasons, could not openly declare their affiliation to a political party. Social Democracy imitated and adapted the outward forms of bourgeois association in an attempt to cultivate distinctive life-styles and compensate for the economic and cultural deprivations of the working class. The cleavage between militant nationalism and Socialism was highlighted in exemplary fashion by their respective calendar of festivities. The organised working class celebrated March 1848 as the first attempt at parliamentary democracy, then the beginning of Spring as a symbol for the rise of a better society, the First of May as international Labour Day and the commemoration of Ferdinand Lassalle's death as a great socialist leader. By contrast nationalist Germany focused on quite different dates and events: the victory at Sedan in the Franco-Prussian War, the Emperor's birthday or the Germanic tribes' victory over the Romans in AD9 (the battle in the Teutoburg woods).

The way that Germany had internally become a major battleground of ideas which competed for a mass following was also documented by the development of the illustrated weeklies. The most famous and largest of its kind in Europe was *Die Gartenlaube* which began in 1853 with a distinct national-liberal slant, committed, like the bulk of the bourgeois press, to spreading education and enlightened knowledge amongst all social classes. However, reaching a circulation of over 380,000 in the 1870s, it showed itself in tune with the imperialist desires of the German Reich and became a byword for kitsch and smug conservatism. Similarly, *Kladderadatsch*, an acidly anti-aristocratic and anti-militarist weekly founded in 1848, later toned down its political satire when it sided with the politics of Bismarck, reaching a circulation of 50,000 copies in the 1870s. The ideological conformism of these periodicals was to some extent counterbalanced by the stinging satire of *Simplicissimus*. Founded in 1896 it targeted, like the later political cabaret *Das Überbrettl* in Berlin, both the actual and the typical figures of established society. The quality and impact of its presentation changed during the many phases of its existence until after the Second World War. In its heyday, undoubtedly the years before 1914, with a circulation figure topping 65,000 copies, it remained tellingly critical of the authoritarian stiffness so typical of the pillars of Wilhelmine society both in Berlin and in the provinces. It was from the ranks of Social Democracy, however, that the most biting humour was produced. Their satirical journal, *Der Wahre Jacob*, was founded in 1879 and, under various editorial regimes, survived until Hitler's seizure of power in March 1933. It reached its peak circulation figure of 380,000 copies in the two years preceding the First World War, reflecting strong anti-imperialist feelings within the working class. Yet, when Germany joined the War, *Der Wahre Jacob*, along with the rest of the German press, lined up with the chauvinism that had gripped the masses.

Despite this spell of ostensible harmony between the classes, made into an ideology of the united *Volk* by working-class poets like Karl Bröger, it would be false to assume that this World War did more than temporarily mask the existing ideological divisions in German society. Weimar Germany was repeatedly on the brink of civil war. Apart from the many ideological divisions appearing in the bourgeois camp, the German working class movement tore itself into three major factions (the Majority Social Democrats, the Independent Social Democrats and the Communists) plus a string of minor groupings. Within socialist-proletarian culture these fractures were less evident. The German Empire's repressive laws of association were liberalised by the Weimar Constitution so that cultural organisations could openly declare their party-political affiliations. This proved particularly valuable for the socialist youth movement and for the unhindered collaboration of the various branches of what came to be known as the worker culture movement. By the end of the Weimar Republic this had attracted a membership of many hundreds of thousands, embracing anything from proletarian nudist clubs with over 60,000 members to the worker sports association which had over a million members. There was proletarian mass theatre and international worker Olympiads took place in Frankfurt (1925), Vienna (1931) and Antwerp (1937). Worker culture cartels were formed in many cities and the goal of providing a socialist cultural environment for men and women of all age groups and interests was realised to a considerable degree, offering compensations for physical and intellectual deprivations. In its more militant sections, this movement openly and programmatically challenged bourgeois culture. Before 1933 the German and Austrian worker culture movements were the most extensive attempts by socialists and communists, despite their increasingly bitter divisions, to develop a counter culture within capitalism.

However, the size and the allures of non-socialist mass culture in the Weimar Republic proved more powerful. The Belgian socialist, Hendrik de Man, had argued in his well-known *Psychology of Socialism* (published in Germany in 1926) that the mass of the workers, far from being attracted to a distinctive proletarian culture, were looking for the gratifications of bourgeois mass entertainment and consumption, not least because it gave them a sense of upward social mobility. In any case, the relentless forces of competition for jobs worked against the virtues of solidarity which the trade-union and proletarian cultural organisations aimed to practise. Sociologists and psychologists analysed modern society less in terms of class than as a mass of isolated individuals. Le Bon, whose theories became very influential in Germany, had talked of a transformation of society into a mass of individuals, without cohesion and without ties.[7] Ferdinand Tönnies had described the long-term process of the vanishing warmth of village community (*Gemeinschaft*) and its replacement by the cold anonymity of urban society (*Gesellschaft*).[8] The increasing incredulity of religious faiths produced a feeling of 'transcendental homelessness' (Georg Lukács) that made society rife for secular ideologies. Theorists of mass society, including Friedrich Nietzsche, considered such developments as necessary preconditions for the emergence of a strong leader. The prime quality of such a leader, who might himself emerge from the masses, was a fanatical faith in the cause he was pursuing in order to gain recognition as a superfather of the crowd. Sigmund Freud concurred with Le Bon that once infected by the leader's hypnotic powers the individuals in the crowd identified with him, suspended their own personal interests and beliefs and thus descended several rungs in the order of civilisation. It is difficult to dismiss the relevance of such theories for the crisis situation at the end of the Weimar Republic, although it was the profound economic insecurity visited on German society which triggered the mechanisms of mass psychology. Only then did a rhetoric playing on the desire to stand together against actual or imaginary enemies prove to have a broader appeal than the merely class-cultural basis of socialism. The National Socialist leaders, while not averse to talking about the masses either flatteringly or with cynical contempt, revived the notion of the *Volk* as an organically and racially homogeneous body and made it the basis of an anti-modernist ideology of integration. It was in the name of the *Volk* that the corporate property of the worker culture movement, along with the property of the trade unions and, of course, of individuals deemed to be inimical to the Reich or the *Volk*, was confiscated. Culture itself became the preserve of manipulation on a vast scale both by the National Socialist Party under Alfred Rosenberg and by the Ministry of People's Enlightenment and Propaganda under Joseph Goebbels. His Reich Culture Chamber saw to it that all the arts and the media of mass communication were synchronised with the interests of the Nazi movement. The modernist process of the diversification of culture was thus halted.

The pluralisation of culture

In their famous book *Dialectic of Enlightenment* (1947) Max Horkheimer and Theodor W. Adorno argued that mass culture under conditions of advanced capitalism and fascism was but a manipulative instrument for the deception of the masses. It reduced everything to the sameness of stereotypes. While the coercive aspects of fascism had vanished with its military defeat, two ideological blocs now competed for influence. In the

Soviet Zone, later the German Democratic Republic, this was done by a partial revival of the proletarian-socialist culture of the Weimar Republic. This culture claimed to represent the interests of the majority of workers in industry and on the land. It was steered by a party (*Sozialistische Einheitspartei Deutschlands*) which, to all intents and purposes, was in sole command of the state without submitting to free elections. A similar situation of reduced tolerance seemed to hold in the Federal Republic. The protection of an affluent society on a capitalist basis and the frontline engagement in a Cold War with the Soviet Union were the chief concerns of the media. An atmosphere of stifling conformism characterised West German mass culture in the first two decades after the Second World War. However, politicians committed to parliamentary democracy could control neither culture in general nor the media in particular. A vociferous literary intelligentsia engaged in scathing criticisms of post-war West Germany by way of both narrative portrayal and public pronouncement in the media, thus testing the tolerance the new political culture would allow.

In the course of the 1960s subcultures of subversive artists (provos, situationists) and student communes (*Kommune 1* in Berlin) began to challenge the affirmative mass culture in which affluent West Germany had settled. In the eyes of both the ideologically non-conformist writers and the young student intelligentsia German society was manipulated by a core of established politicians and mass media like the tabloid-type daily *Bild-Zeitung*. The Germans had failed to face up to their fascist past and displayed an 'incapability to mourn'.[9] But far from falling back into old patterns of authoritarianism German society was, as Alexander Mitscherlich had recognised earlier, on the way to a 'fatherless society'. The non-acknowledgement of the fathers was both a problematical attempt at escaping from their crimes and a liberating annulment of Freud's fatal mechanism whereby a mass regressing to the status of the primeval horde would crave for the authority of a superfather. A culture of protest by feminists, environmentalists, ecological researchers, liberationist theologians, peace marchers and refusenics allergic to the 'Coca-Cola and Karajan culture'[10] demanded recognition, at first as an open challenge to clichéd mass culture and state-subsidised high culture, later as a retreat into alternative niches. Fresh ways of thinking were offered which proved capable of infiltrating and changing mainstream culture. Men began to adjust to the increased self-confidence and alterity of women, established political parties started to recognise the virtues of ecological arguments and the mass media themselves, far from showing the one-dimensionality of an unreflectedly manipulative culture, fractured in the service of different tastes in an ever broadening spectrum of interests and market opportunities. The alternative culture of the 1970s and 1980s has had a gateway function in preparing the German public for the acceptance of yet greater diversification.

The pluralisation of culture is driven further by the multiculturalism concentrated mainly in the large towns but radiating out into the countryside. It issues from the presence in the Federal Republic not only of migrant workers, but also of third-generation immigrants from inside and outside Europe. The enormous variety with which individuals from different nations acculturate, or fail to do so, makes generalisation impossible. Some manage to settle into the life-style of their German environment, others make for subcultural enclosures allowing a greater or lesser interface with the host culture. While the variety and militancy of the alternative scene belies any notion of German contemporary culture being homogeneous, there is no question that its mainstream and marginal varieties are set in a German or European heritage whose possibilities and limitations they explore. It is therefore not surprising that the greatest difficulties of reconciling German and immigrant mentalities is to be found in the literature of the largest contingent of non-Europeans living in Germany, the Turks, some of whom write in German as their mother tongue. Counter to widespread German prejudice they do not present any kind of monochrome image either of themselves as Turks or of Turkey which, despite being mentally and physically distanced from it, they still often regard as their home country. Within the united Germany Turks and other migrants have become targets of xenophobic attacks, a situation that is not helped by high levels of unemployment, particularly in the new Länder, the erstwhile German Democratic Republic. While there is no question that immigrants both as individuals making an indispensible contribution to the German economy and as communities forming migrant subcultures extend the range of contemporary culture in Germany, their tolerance by the host and the fortification of their identity is often no more substantial than the texts they offer as a bridge for understanding.

NOTES

1. Justus Möser, *Osnabrückische Geschichte* (1768), quoted in Friedrich Stroh, *Handbuch der Germanischen Philologie*, Berlin: Walter de Gruyter & Co., 1952, p. 51.
2. Friedrich Carl von Savigny in *Zeitschrift für geschichtliche Rechtswissenschaft*, quoted in Stroh, *Handbuch*, p. 55.
3. Johann Wolfgang Goethe in a letter to Thomas Carlyle, 20 July 1827, quoted in Hans-J. Weitz, *Goethe über die Deutschen*, Frankfurt: Insel Taschenbuch 325, 1978, p. 207.
4. Eduard Ippel (ed.), *Briefwechsel zwischen Jacob und Wilhelm Grimm, Dahlmann und Gervinus*, vol. II (Berlin, 1886), p. 159, quoted in Karl Obermann (ed.), *Einheit und Freiheit. Die deutsche Geschichte von 1815–1849*, Berlin: Dietz Verlag, 1950, p. 160.
5. Johann Jacoby, *Vier Fragen, beantwortet von einem Ostpreußen* (Mannheim, 1841, p. 6), quoted in Obermann, *Einheit und Freiheit*, p. 166.
6. Friedrich Nietzsche, *Unzeitgemäße Betrachtungen* in Karl Schlechta (ed.), *Friedrich Nietzsche, Werke in drei Bänden*, Munich: Carl Hanser Verlag, 1966 ff., vol. I, p. 137.
7. See Gustave Le Bon, *Psychologie du Socialisme*, Paris: Librairie Félix Alcan, 1899 ff.
8. See Ferdinand Tönnies, *Gemeinschaft und Gesellschaft* (1887, rev. 1912), translated as *Community and Association*, London: Routledge and Keegan Paul, 1955.
9. See Alexander and Margarete Mitscherlich, *Die Unfähigkeit zu trauern. Grundlagen kollektiven Verhaltens* (1967), Munich: Piper Verlag, 1977.
10. Quoted in Wolfgang R. Langenbucher, Ralf Rytlewski and Bernd Weyergraf (eds.), *Kulturpolitisches Wörterbuch Bundesrepublik Deutschland/Deutsche Demokratische Republik im Vergleich*, Stuttgart: J. B. Metzler Verlagsbuchhandlung, 1983, p. 30.

FURTHER READING

The complex cultural and political processes involved in the emergence of a bourgeois public and in the transitions from tradional to modern society are admirably analysed by Jürgen Habermas, *Strukturwandel der Öffentlichkeit. Untersuchungen zu einer Kategorie der bürgerlichen Gesellschaft* (Neuwied and Berlin: Luchterhand Verlag, 2nd edn., 1965). Analyses of modernity by German thinkers are discussed by David Frisby, *Fragments of Modernity* (Cambridge: Polity Press and Oxford: Basil Blackwell, 1985). Theories of mass culture and mass society are critically reviewed by Alan Swingewood, *The Myth of Mass Culture* (London and Basingstoke: Macmillan Press, 1977). The political influence of the educated bourgeoisie is traced in Jürgen Kocka (ed.), *Bildungsbürgertum im 19. Jahrhundert. Teil IV, Politischer Einfluß und gesellschaftliche Formation* (Stuttgart: Ernst Klett Verlag, 1989). For a specific analysis of the worker culture movement see Wilfried van der Will and Rob Burns, *Arbeiterkulturbewegung in der Weimarer Republik* (Frankfurt/Main, Berlin, Vienna: Ullstein Verlag, 1982). A comprehensive cultural history is attempted by Hermann Glaser, *Die Kulturgeschichte des Bundesrepublik Deutschland* (Frankfurt/Main, Fischer Taschenbuch, 3 vols., 1990). Alternative culture is developed by the 'new social movements' which are analysed in sociological and political terms in Roland Roth and Dieter Rucht (eds.), *Neue soziale Bewegungen in der Bundesrepublik Deutschland* (Frankfurt/Main and New York: Campus Verlag, 1987). Aspects of multiculturalism are dealt with in David Horrocks and Eva Kolinsky (eds.), *Turkish Culture in German Society Today* (Providence and Oxford: Berghahn Books, 1996).

8

The development of German prose fiction

The novel in the belated nation

There is a widespread view of German culture generally which says that it is, in all kinds of ways, thoughtful, sophisticated and profound; but that it is curiously bereft of any sustained relationship to the familiar, empirically knowable facts of daily living. Instead of concerning themselves at all vigorously with outward things, the Germans, so the argument runs, attend to such pursuits as music (that supremely non-referential art), speculative philosophy, and theology (particularly when it assumes the guise of radical inwardness). This problematic condition of inwardness reveals its shortcomings nowhere more clearly than in the bulk of narrative prose works that issued from the German-speaking lands in the great age of European realism (that is, from the mid-eighteenth century onwards): whatever distinction may inhere in that body of prose writing, it cannot be claimed to be the distinction of common-or-garden realism.

However overstated such a view of German culture may be, there are elements of truth to it. Certainly its prose literature from Goethe on does pose an acute evaluative problem. The dilemma is felt by both non-German and German critics alike. Wolfgang Preisendanz speaks for many commentators when he writes:

> If one takes as one's yardstick the contribution made [by German writers] to the definition of their contemporary age, then there seems to be much justification to the frequently voiced reproach that the assertion of 'poetry's direct access to the highest court of appeal' caused a withdrawal from – or at the very least a lack of contact with – the urgent, burning problems and realities of politico-social life, and

that – yet again – the social integration of the creative writer in Germany was prevented.[1]

The phrase 'poetry's direct access to the highest court of appeal' ('Reichsunmittelbarkeit der Poesie') which Preisendanz quotes is taken from the great Swiss writer Gottfried Keller; it figures in a letter in which Keller takes the traditional notion according to which, within the Holy Roman Empire, certain territories had direct access to the Emperor, and applies it to the aesthetic privilege of poetry – even in the modern age. Hence, Priisendanz is invoking the notion that the literature of the German-speaking lands is deeply in love with poetry – to the virtual exclusion of prosaic and quotidian matters. 'Poetic realism' is, as it were, the artistic compensation for – and transfiguration of – backwaterdom. Hence that constant debate in German discussions of the theory of narrative forms: with an urgency that does not obtain in either English or French aesthetics of the period, German commentators of the nineteenth century constantly pit 'poetry' against 'prose'. (To these issues I shall return later.)

One explanation of the peculiar character of German culture refers us to the political and social history of the German-speaking lands. The argument runs as follows. German literature prior to 1871 was of necessity provincial because before that date what we now know as Germany did not exist as a national entity in the way that other European countries did – that is, as a unified nation state. The 'Holy Roman Empire of the German Nation' meant provinces, small territories – in a word, particularism – rather than a cohesive demographic unit with its centre of gravity in a capital city. Up until the last three decades of the nineteenth century, Germany existed only in its language and culture; it was, to invoke hallowed terms, a 'cultural nation' rather than a 'political nation'. And, even when a coherent political unit did emerge on German soil – and Prussia is the obvious example from the eighteenth century onwards – the institutionalisation of Pietism as to all intents and purposes the official state religion (with weighty consequences for education) produced a culture of intense, passionate inwardness which was furthered by the state because it could be relied upon never to call the secular order seriously into question. As Wolf Lepenies puts it, 'isolation from power produces melancholy that turns to inwardness, and precisely this turning away increases the separation from society'.[2]

In much thinking about the course of German history and culture there is an often unspoken norm that is invoked. As far as history is concerned the norm asserts the following doctrines. The proper course of historical development traced by the modern nation entails a gradual process of bourgeois self-assertion in the name of increasing economic power and social mobility. Gradually the middle classes win forms of political recognition for themselves by challenging feudal structures and by achieving influence and representation within an ever more democratic, participatory form of government. The German lands fail to obey this model in the eighteenth and nineteenth centuries; 1830 and 1848 mark dismal failures. Hence, when Germany does finally come into line and join the European norm in 1871, she does so in a condition of curious disequilibrium. By the end of the nineteenth century she is, economically, a formidable power, but in terms of her social and political structures and attitudes, she is out of synchrony with the times. This is the curse of the 'belated nation'; this is the time-bomb at the heart of, to invoke another canonical term from the historiography of the German-speaking lands, the 'idiosyncratic development of German affairs'. The upshot is the monstrosity of the Third Reich.

A not dissimilar category of normative thinking is also applied to the argument about the evolution of the European novel. The central tenets can be summarised as follows. The birth of the modern novel is linked to the increasing self-assertiveness and self-confidence of the middle classes. It expresses a sense of rapid economic change and development. The prevailing ethos derives from the revolutionary energies of capitalism, and the emphasis falls unashamedly on the individual. The bourgeois novel is a narrative form that may be termed realistic precisely because it is concerned with the interplay of the characters' inner, psychological life and the palpable facts (*res*) of society. The realistic novelist exploits the traditionally sanctioned amplitude and untidiness of the novel form to acknowledge the simple 'thereness' of the material world. The upshot is what Roland Barthes has described as the 'effect of the real'[3] – a rhetoric of descriptive plenitude which pays tribute to material facticity, not for its potential aesthetic transformation into some realm of higher – that is, symbolic – import, but simply as an act of constatation of what is. J. P. Stern speaks of the realist's delight in descriptive abundance, in those 'emblems of plenty'[4] whose acknowledgement of simple 'thereness' conjoins the literary text and the extra-literary world. By contrast, many German novels are concerned, so the traditional view suggests, with the inward realm to the virtual exclusion of outward practicalities.

These are complex issues. Parts of the orthodox view of the historical and literary heritage of Germany ring true. But there are certain features I wish to challenge.

I begin with the argument about the historiography of the German lands. The challenge to the schematic historical view of Germany's cankered development has been mounted most vigorously by David Blackbourn and Geoff Eley in their study *The Peculiarities of German History* (Oxford, 1984). They point to a number of ways in which the historiographic stereotype obscures features of German economic and social life which express a measure of bourgeois emancipation and enterprise. It should, for example, be stressed that the territorial particularism of the Holy Roman Empire produced an urban culture[5] sustained by a profusion of institutions – universities, concert houses, theatres, churches, chapels, publishing houses, book fairs, libraries – where intellectual and cultural life flourished with great vigour. To say that culture was emasculated by bureaucratic apparatuses is to capture only a half-truth. The very extent and energy of German cultural and intellectual life did on many occasions provide a context for thorough-going critical debate.

I now turn to that particular form of literary mimesis which dominates both the theory and the practice of novel writing in Europe throughout the nineteenth century. It is noteworthy that much critical discussion of literary realism over the past thirty years or so has sought to highlight the degree of artifice, even on occasion of self-consciousness, that is present in the so-called 'classics' of European realism. In this sense, then, realism entails not only mirroring, reflecting, but also reflectivity. When, therefore, Klaus-Detlef Müller refers to 'the high level of reflectivity, in both poetological and aesthetic terms',[6] of German realism, he must not be understood as making the (European) best of a (German) bad job – if for no other reason than that the definition of literary realism is now able to accommodate the whole dimension of reflectivity. In this context, it is pertinent to consider Hegel's brilliant commentary on the modern novel as both a re-creation and an interrogation of bourgeois society:

> In its modern sense the novel presupposes a reality which has already taken on the condition of *prose*, in the context of which it then – having regard both to the liveliness of events and to the individuals and their fates – seeks to reclaim for poetry its forfeited entitlement, in so far as that is possible within the obtaining presuppositions. One of the most familiar confrontations, and one ideally suited to the

> novel, is therefore the conflict between the poetry of the heart and the resistant prose of external circumstances, the contingency of external affairs. [7]

Here, it seems to me, the notion of interplay (that is: both conflict and mediation) between poetry and prose produces not German provincialism but the first commentary of real range and scope on the novel as a European form. Artistic mimesis emerges not simply as a replication of the outer world; rather, it entails reflection of and on that world. To borrow an aphorism of Bertolt Brecht's: 'Realism is not the way real things are, realism is the way things really are.'[8] In the survey that follows of German prose from the mid-nineteenth century to the present time, I shall be concerned to suggest how perceptively and cogently German narrative prose, not in spite of but because of its dimension of reflectivity, manages to mediate and to analyse the complex experience of unfolding modernity.

Poetic Realism

In the 1850s Poetic Realism was very much in the ascendancy as far as aesthetic prestige was concerned. The dominant voice in matters of aesthetic taste as applied to prose narrative was Julian Schmidt, who became the editor of the influential magazine known as the *Grenzboten* (Frontier Messenger) in March 1848. The year is, to put it mildly, significant. Schmidt was acutely aware of the revolutionary turmoil all around him; and, in his theory of Poetic Realism, he is strenuously concerned to assert the necessity of literature's allegiance and responsibility to the practical social world. Yet he is opposed to critical stridency in prose fiction, to ugliness of theme and literary mode. Rather, the humble world of prose is to receive the validation of poetry. Schmidt never tires of insisting on the necessity of the process of mediation – and in this sense, the implications of his theory are soothing and essentially conservative. Yet, as we shall see, many of the finest writers of the second half of the nineteenth century bear witness less to the mediations between poetry and prose than to the tensions that obtain between them, and to the critical illumination thereby afforded.

This is nowhere more powerfully the case than in the work of Adalbert Stifter. In the latter half of the 1840s he published a number of stories in a collection entitled simply *Studien* (Studies) which show him at the height of his powers. Time and time again, in prose of extraordinary gravity and emphasis he invokes the gradualness of natural processes, the unremarkable sequences of familial and village life as generations succeed one another. Yet he also recognises the pain of human individuation and subjectivity. In Stifter's hands the stark processes of particular human tragedy coexist with an acknowledgement of the implacable thereness and integrity of the laws of human and natural generality (*Der Hochwald* (The High Forest), 1843; *Abdias*, 1842; *Das alte Siegel* (The Old Seal), 1843; *Der Hagestolz* (The Old Bachelor), 1844). The revolution of 1848 initially produced elation in Stifter, but then he was appalled by what he could only see as tumult and chaos. He responded with a collection of tales entitled *Bunte Steine* (Coloured Stones, 1853), which opens with a famous Preface ('*Vorrede*') asserting his belief in the truth, dignity, and beauty of the 'little things' in both art and life. Yet the willed didacticism of the author's stance promises more than it can deliver. Time and time again the stories acknowledge painful, inadmissible experience. The weighty cadences of litanesque narrative fracture as the resistant aberrations of human wishing and thinking make themselves heard. Towards the end of his life Stifter sought ever more single-mindedly to stylise his art and the lives of which it speaks into patterns of secure sublimity. The result is an extraordinary, monomanic prose; not quite believable, or, more accurately, only believable at those points where the flux and energy of unbiddable experience makes itself felt (*Der Nachsommer* (Indian Summer), 1857; *Die Mappe meines Urgroßvaters* (The Papers of my Great-Grandfather), last version 1867).

If Stifter offers us a glimpse of the complex field of force in which poetic prose (as ordering, redemptive principle) and unregenerate prose (as constatation of the human all-too-human) are locked in dispute, his contemporary Gustav Freytag, with *Soll und Haben* (Debit and Credit, 1855) offers us the egregiously successful mediation between the two. The novel is, within the German-speaking lands, one of the supreme best-sellers of all time. And it is so because it addresses – and offers a placebo for – one of the key anxieties of modernity. Constantly the novel speaks of the emergence of a new form of mercantile and economic life, one which is no longer grounded in the solid integrity of goods and services but is, rather, sustained by forms of volatile, speculative, high-risk capitalism. All the unsettling tendencies are identified, thanks to the appalling schematism that runs right through the novel, with Jewish practices. By contrast, the hero, Anton Wohlfarth, manages to combine energy, practical good sense, and efficiency with idealism. This, then, is poetry triumphant, but poetry endowed with the comforting solidity of a decent balance sheet (to which the title of the novel refers).

The sense of social and economic change which is omnipresent – although firmly contained – in Soll und Haben also makes itself felt in the novels of one of the most successful writers of the last four decades of the nineteenth century: Friedrich Spielhagen. The history of European realism in the nineteenth century is not without examples of novels which seek to combine a prose of detailed observation and constatation of social life with fiercely melodramatic moments of high passion and grandiose utterances. Balzac and Dickens are obvious examples. Yet, in the case of their novels, there is a sense in which the melodrama is part of the social diagnosis. The very luridness of the imagination derives from, and interlocks with, the energy with which modern culture displaces older, more pacific, more familial and secure forms of living.[9] In one sense, something similar ought to apply to Spielhagen. Yet the texts never quite sustain the promise which they hold out. The overheated imaginings merely provide distraction from – rather than illuminating – the undoubted socially diagnostic intention which animates whole sections of the writing. It is almost as though the imagination, once aroused, loses its purchase on the economic and social detail which the text conveys so scrupulously. Precisely this issue, namely the interplay of imagination and facticity, is central to the work of the great Swiss writer Gottfried Keller. Keller's principal achievement is the two-volume collection of stories which explore the socio-cultural identity of a fictitious Swiss community – Die Leute von Seldwyla (The People of Seldwyla, 1856, 1873–4). The stories vary in theme, mode and register. But what they have in common is a sense of the complex interplay between the individual consciousness and the corporate pressures and demands of the social world. Time and time again Keller registers the inventiveness, the creativity, the sheer quirkiness of the individual imagination; and he understands the need for prosaic checks and restraints, while also fearing the loss of vitality entailed. Keller is masterly in his presentation of the processes of socialisation – and in his clear-eyed appreciation of the price that it exacts in terms of individual creativity. His great novel, Der grüne Heinrich (Green Henry, first version 1845–5, second version 1879–80) is unforgettable in the astringency with which it debates the rights and wrongs of the mechanisms that convert Heinrich Lee from an aspiring painter into a psychological wreck (in the first version), and into a somewhat monosyllabic and joyless civil servant (in the second version).

Like Keller, Wilhelm Raabe is concerned with the complexity and pain of socio-cultural change. Raabe does not always steer clear of sentimentality. But at his best, he can be wonderfully dispassionate and even-handed. *Pfisters Mühle* (Pfisters Mill, 1883–4) shows him at the very peak of his powers. Ebert Pfister, the main character and narrator, finds himself spending the summer holiday at the mill which was his birthplace, having to make arrangements for it to be sold. In all kinds of ways, the pull of nostalgia is strong; yet Ebert himself, and the text of which he is the fictional author, also acknowledges the liberation which the modern world provides – for all its destructive energies – from the claustrophobia of village life. Poetry is not the exclusive prerogative of the past. Similar themes exploring time and historical change inform the oeuvre of Theodor Storm; hence his fondness for framed narratives in which the act of recalling proves to be the chief catalyst for the account which the text puts before us. Storm is a master of the *Novelle* form. In his greatest work – and it is his last – *Der Schimmelreiter* (The Man on the Grey Horse, 1888) he relates the narrative mode of recall to the central theme which concerns him. The story is told of Hauke Haien, an intellectually gifted, fiercely ambitious man who single-mindedly pursues his goal of becoming Dykemaster in his community. He re-designs the shape of the dykes, and he seeks to carry through a number of reforms in the teeth of opposition from the largely superstitious and mistrustful villagers. As the telling of the tale makes clear, the truth about Hauke is no simple matter – because the themes at the centre of his story are constantly being re-enacted as the community confronts processes of flux and change.

Appropriateness of form is one of the supreme virtues of the work of Theodor Fontane. He is the chronicler *par excellence* of Wilhelmine Berlin. He is in many ways the most unemphatic of novelists. Explosive events and grand passions are rare in his work. For the most part, he is content to eavesdrop on the characters in their social existences. He is a master of conversation. And the conversations he reports are wonderfully revealing of the characters – precisely because, in psychological terms, they rarely get away from the complex pressures, texts, and sub-texts of their society. In a sense, they carry society around with them; they are always literally or metaphorically in dialogue with their society. Fontane is the most subtle of eavesdroppers; above all, in his use of symbols he explores the psychic mechanisms of repressed selves. The symbols often reveal but also conceal the implicit drama of the inner life. Sometimes the characters perceive their entrapment; at other times they abstain from reflection and self-interrogation. Precisely this interplay of knowing and not knowing, of seeing and not seeing is at the heart of Fontane's narrative and symbolic mode. The poetry of his carefully crafted texts offers critical – and compassionate – analysis of the prosaic lives of socialised creatures. Like his characters, Fontane is tactful. But that tactfulness should not be confused with half-heartedness or flaccidity. His diagnosis may be understated; but it is mercilessly perceptive. At the centre of his greatest novel *Effi Briest* (1895) is a duel which is fought by Innstetten the husband in order to avenge his wife's adulterous affair. The duel is only outwardly a great moment of life-and-death confrontation; more truthfully, it is the result of an elaborate, tortuous acquiescence in convention, a weary grasping at straws, a charade in which all parties go through the motions. The theme of inauthenticity takes us forward into the twentieth century; to Arthur Schnitzler and Thomas Mann.

Modernity and crisis

Mann's *Buddenbrooks* (1901) has as its subtitle 'Decline of a Family'. That decline is enacted through the waning fortunes of a patrician North German family over three generations and spanning the period from 1835 to 1877. As Germany emerges from the German Confederation, that last relic of the Holy Roman Empire which survives Napoleon's inroads, into existence as a unified nation state (and by the end of the century that new state will be a formidable economic power), so the Buddenbrooks find that they are less and less able to cope with the strains of economic – and other – modernity. The new world is one of speculative, high-risk investment capitalism in which their static, patriarchal version of family and firm has little place. The 'decline', of which the novel's subtitle speaks, unfolds both in socio-economic and in physical terms. The inward texture of these processes is held in conceptual focus by means of a governing opposition of, on the one hand, strong, brutal, efficient living and on the other weakness, vulnerability, scrupulousness – in a word, thoughtfulness. The outer decline is matched by a growth in inner life. And that inner life, for all its repudiation of the practical world, is linked to the outer world. When Thomas Buddenbrook discovers philosophy in the Schopenhauerean-cum-Nietzschean mode, when Hanno Buddenbrook improvises at the piano in what is unmistakably the mode and mood of Wagnerian chromaticism, we recognise that inwardness is linked to outwardness, mentality to history, reflectivity to practicality, poetry to prose.

In part at least, *Buddenbrooks* is a Naturalistic novel. A more radical, reductive form of Naturalism is, however, achieved by Arno Holz and Johannes Schlaf in short prose sketches, the finest of which is the collection of stories entitled *Papa Hamlet* (1889). The almost claustrophobic concentration on the flow of sense-impressions second by second produces a prose that is discontinuous in its immediacy. What is particularly intriguing is the fact that the (putatively) 'documentary' prose of these sketches oscillates uneasily between a condition of punch-drunk constatation on the one hand and on the other vividly evocative mood pictures. It is, to put it mildly, an odd collision of poetry and prose; and I shall want to return to it at the end of this chapter.

Austrian literature of the early twentieth century seems to be very much marked by that 'overcoming of Naturalism' of which Hermann Bahr spoke in a famous volume of essays of that name, published in 1891. Much of the early prose writing of Hugo von Hofmannsthal speaks insistently of complex states of mind and being – none more suggestively than *Ein Brief* (A Letter, 1902), a fictitious letter that purports to be written by the young Lord Chandos to his mentor and protector Bacon as an explanation of a particular crisis of language and cognition. Words have, it seems, lost their purchase on the world; conversely, humble things and objects seem to assert their radiant there-ness with an epiphanic intensity that is (as yet) beyond language. A more astringently realistic and socially critical perspective is provided by Arthur Schnitzler. His *Leutnant Gustl* (1901) is the first successfully sustained interior monologue in Western European literature. The form would seem to promise a journey into the rich, uncharted depths of the human psyche. But Schnitzler's masterly story is anything but that. Gustl's inwardness is of a piece with his outwardness. The mind is no untrammelled Joycean realm; rather, it is a tissue of half-truths, vanities, and prejudices, and Schnitzler mercilessly exposes the mental flotsam and jetsam that constitutes the ethos of this unremarkable (and by that token typical) member of the Austro-Hungarian army. The realistic focus that sustains his two main novels is impressive. *Der Weg ins Freie* (The Road into the Open, 1908) is painfully clear-sighted in its perception of the uncertainties of the liberal Jewish intelligentsia in the anti-Semitic climate of Karl Lueger's Vienna; and *Therese* (1926) uncompromisingly chronicles the emotionally, socially, and financially exploited life of a governess.

Time and time again in the years between the turn of the century and the outbreak of the First World War writers embody in their fiction a sense of cultural crisis and unease. In 1906 Robert Musil publishes *Die Verwirrungen des Zöglings Törleß* (The Confusions of the Recruit Törless); at one level it is a painfully accurate study of bullying at a military school; but at another level (which may not always interlock happily with the first) it understands the hero's puberty as the psychological statement of a far-reaching philosophical sea-change, one in which the demarcation lines between the real and the possible, the actual and the imaginable are constantly challenged and shifted. By contrast, it is the crisis of urban modernity that is at the heart of Rilke's *Die Aufzeichnungen des Malte Laurids Brigge* (The Notebooks of Malte Laurids Brigge, 1910). As the title, which refers to notes and jottings ('*Aufzeichnungen*') rather than the more coherent genre of 'diary' or 'autobiography', makes clear, dislocation and displacement is at the heart of the text. Malte, alone in Paris, exposed to the brutalising energy of the metropolis, is indeed a displaced person. He bears witness to, without being able to heal, the fragmentation of the modern world. That fragmentation, that loss of reassuring overview also informs the work of Franz Kafka, of which the first great example is *Das Urteil* (The Judgment) of 1912. At one level, it explores the murderous tension between father and son, and it culminates in the father's condemnation of the son to death by drowning, a verdict which the son carries out. Any attempt on the reader's part at obtaining a stable psychological causality founders. The cool, seemingly unruffled narrative perspective promises more than it can deliver; events occur, battles are fought and won, but we can find no reliable vantage point from which to survey and interpret the happenings that pass before us. As the later texts by Kafka (*Die Verwandlung* (The Metamorphosis), 1915; *Der Proceß* (The Trial), on which he worked in 1914-15, although it was only published posthumously in 1925; and *Das Schloß* (The Castle), written in 1922 and published in 1926) repeatedly show, he had the extraordinary ability to generate multiple intimations of meaning – bureaucratic, institutional, psychological, sexual, theological, philosophical – without privileging any one set of significations. In Kafka's universe, everything may be out of joint; but there is no alternative and revelatory structuration of meaning available – there is only the achingly familiar, yet somehow no longer quite tenable world bounded by family, home, profession. Something similar applies to the work of Robert Walser. His prose lacks the manic dislocations of Kafka in his more spectacular modes. But underneath the modest textures of his prose one perceives a world that continues to function although it is no longer sustained by reliable, comforting structures of meaning.

The sense of order threatened by imminent chaos pervades Thomas Mann's *Der Tod in Venedig* (Death in Venice, 1912). Centrally, it is concerned with the decline and death of an artist, Gustav von Aschenbach, who goes to Venice on holiday and there becomes infatuated with Tadzio, a young Polish boy. At one level, Aschenbach falls victim to the ambiguity of beauty, the only absolute, according to Plato, which reveals itself to human senses. This worship of beauty, of perfection of form governs Aschenbach's life as both man and artist – and precisely that cast of mind prevents him from realising that he is sliding into obsession and chaos. The political reverberations of Mann's tale are sombre: that high 'poetic' culture is in no sense proof against the forces of dissolution and barbarism. The suggestion is that Germany – perhaps Europe as a whole – is waiting for the chance to cast aside all notions of order, containment, scruple in the name of some entry into intense, incandescent experience. Two years after the story's appearance, Europe was engulfed by the great fervour of what promised to be an ultimate, once-and-for-all confrontation, the War to end all Wars. That the reality was brutally different is attested by the two great novels of the war which German literature produced: Erich Maria Remarque's *Im Westen nichts Neues* (All Quiet on the Western Front, 1929) and Arnold Zweig's *Der Streit um den Sergeanten Grischa* (The Dispute over Sergeant Grischa, 1927).

The cultural crisis that precipitated (but had not been purged by) the unparalleled carnage of 1914–18 is explored by a number of novels of the immediate post-war period. Heinrich Mann's *Der Untertan* (The Subject, 1918) dissects with fierce satirical energy the grotesquely subservient mentality that abased itself before the authoritarianism of Wilhelmine Germany. Mann's cutting edge is splendidly denunciatory. But many of the subsequent novels that issued from the Weimar Republic and the Austria of the 1920s and early 1930s – and they are classics of High Modernism – are sustained by a critical enterprise of a very different kind. The key achievements of Thomas Mann, Hermann Broch, Hermann Hesse, Alfred Döblin, and Elias Canetti are animated by a two-fold concern: on the one hand, by the need to offer cultural diagnosis of the stresses and strains of modernity, and on the other by the need to find some kind of privileged consciousness or redemptive promise that points a way forward. Thomas Mann's *Der Zauberberg* (The Magic Mountain, 1924) conjoins two kinds of novel strategy: on the one hand, it is a wonderfully sophisticated exemplar of the German *Bildungsroman*, a novel genre which lovingly and expansively chronicles processes of spiritual growth and psychological maturation in the adolescent male self; on the other, it is an historical novel which explores the ideologies of pre-1914 Germany, and which ends with the 'great thunderclap' of the First World War. The implication is that German culture, in its inwardness and spirituality, is able lovingly to explore the processes by which the self comes to reflect on the nature of its experience – but is desperately inattentive to the prosaic realities of social and political life which are responsible for a war that converts a whole generation into cannon fodder. There is a sovereign, almost encyclopedic sweep to *Der Zauberberg* – and this also applies to Hermann Broch's *Die Schlafwandler* (The Sleepwalkers, 1931–2). It combines narrative and essayistic strands in an attempt to chart the paradigm shift of values that leads from the seemingly secure (Fontanesque) world of the late nineteenth century to the horror of the war. Both these novels end with a hope of emergence out of a world of destruction and despair; but that hope (in, for example, the longing for a 'new word of love' expressed at the end of *Der Zauberberg*) seems tormentingly distant. By contrast, in Hermann Hesse's *Der Steppenwolf* (1927) the hope is stronger. *Der Steppenwolf* registers the inroads of modern life (commercialism, radio, jazz) into the consciousness of high bourgeois culture. Harry Haller, the representative of that culture, is offered the chance to discover a new wholeness which embraces a multiplicity of selves (and cultures), and the novel closes on a note of personal and cultural anticipation.

By contrast, Alfred Döblin's *Berlin Alexanderplatz* (1929) speaks powerfully of the destruction of the individual self, as the protagonist is swamped by the brutalising onslaught of urban modernity. Döblin questions whether any kind of reflectivity could be even sustained let alone wrested free of the social and historical chaos. The mind is as much part of the social pandemonium as is the multiplicity of material and statistical facts which fill the pages of *Berlin Alexanderplatz*. The close of Döblin's novel envisages the solace of surrendering the individual self to some higher communal purpose and identity. But Döblin's novel is at its finest in the stylistically brilliant passages of collage which express the sensory battering that is city life; the redemptive promise seems little better than chimerical. A similar interplay of realistic and redemptive strategies informs Robert Musil's immense, but incomplete, novel *Der Mann ohne Eigenschaften* (The Man Without Qualities, volume 1, 1930; volume 2, 1933; volume 3, 1943). For much of its length it is an incomparable satirical portrait of Austria in 1913, poised on the brink of catastrophe, yet resolutely committed to a grand celebration of the overlap, in 1918, of the seventieth year of Franz Joseph's accession to the throne, and the thirtieth year of Wilhelm II's reign. In one entirely crucial sense, the novel is about a series of non-events, conceived in celebration of what, as Musil's readers knew with historical hindsight, was destined to be a non-event. Yet there is another strategy to *Der Mann ohne Eigenschaften*; above all in the depiction of the incestuous love between Ulrich, the main character, and his sister Agathe there emerges a mystical strand to Musil's great project, a mysticism which esteems (transcendental) possibility over (concrete, livable) facticity. The novel text does not close; it breaks off in irresolution as a fragment. The epitaph of all such grand, sophisticated attempts at reconciling social substantiality (prose) and spiritual redemptiveness (poetry) is to be found in Elias Canetti's *Die Blendung* (The Blinding, 1935–6). It is a ferocious text, in which the spiritual world of the bookish intellectual and the psychiatrist (the two Kien brothers) is destroyed when the unregenerate world of bodiliness is admitted. The images of books burning with which the novel closes have an ominous political ring to them.

However, not all German prose of the 1920s and 1930s is as Delphic (or apocalyptic) as the sophisticated texts we have just been discussing. Hans Fallada's *Kleiner Mann, was nun?* (Little Man, What Now?, 1932) is the touching story of the painful social and economic decline of Pinneberg, a white-collar worker in Berlin, who loses his job as salesman in a department store. Irmgard Keun's *Das kunstseidene Mädchen* (The Artificial Silk Girl, 1932) and *Gilgi* (1931) are remarkable for their ability to eavesdrop on the consciousness of young women who are in love with the bright lights and glamour of Weimar Germany, but who also have within them stirrings of criticism and intimations of morally better things. Erich Kästner's *Fabian* (1931) follows the fortunes of a man who is intelligent enough to see through the pretensions of his society, but not resolute enough to break free.

In 1933 when the Nazis came to power, a 'Reich Culture Chamber' was created by Goebbels with the express task of legislating for all aspects of cultural production. Inevitably, propagandist literature of one kind or another was the result. The 'blood and soil' ideology was embodied in the prolific output of such writers as Friedrich Griese and Hans Blunck. Yet, apart from such obviously aligned voices, other writers were also allowed to publish. Many of them were anything but Nazi hacks. Christian – especially Catholic – literature was permitted, as was writing of spiritual uplift that spoke of (largely undefined) 'higher things'. Thus, figures such as Werner Bergengruen and Ernst Wiechert were able to publish, although on occasion (most notably in the case of Wiechert) they fell foul of the regime. Ernst Jünger is a particularly problematic case. His work from the 1920s on tends to glorify an ethos of strenuousness, of spiritual and moral courage, of ontological and aesthetic transcendence. The recurring preoccupation with heroism whatever the cost is not necessarily pernicious; yet nowhere does Jünger attempt to reflect critically on the heady mish-mash of aestheticism, barbarism, and stylistic fastidiousness that characterises his own work – and the somewhat better literature that circulated in Germany post-1933.

Perhaps the most impressive engagement after the Second World War with such issues of (as one might put it) cultural guilt and complicity is offered by Thomas Mann's novel *Doktor Faustus* (1947). Like Hesse's *Das Glasperlenspiel* (The Glass Bead Game, 1943) it is essentially valedictory, in that it looks back at the particular mentality and spirituality of German culture and explores its relationship to the German catastrophe. *Doktor Faustus* tells the life of a fictitious composer; and it seeks to link him, as musical genius, with the inward genius of the German people – and also with other key entities in the cultural chemistry of the German nation, most notably Protestantism, Nietzsche, and the *Faust* legend. The novel seeks to account for Nazism in terms of a particular cultural crisis – that of lateness and spiritual emptiness, a condition in which only parody and irony can activate the last remnants of creativity and belief. Mann's text, in an act of truly anguished self-reflexivity, bears witness to the crisis that it seeks to diagnose and understand: it, too, is an aesthetic latecomer, an extraordinary compendium of references, allusions, quotations. The result is an utterly remarkable novel; graceless, often forbiddingly cerebral, but astonishingly suggestive as a feat of cultural analysis.

German prose fiction in the post-war world

In the aftermath of the war, Germany was divided into two states which developed separately for forty years. Their literatures too followed separate courses, although, as we shall see, there are points of rapprochement. Initially, the literature coming out of the occupied zones bore witness to the rubble and devastation left physically and spiritually by the Third Reich. However, in the 1950s, the Federal Republic, under the Chancellorship of Konrad Adenauer, achieved miracles of rebuilding and reconstruction. The rapidly emerging affluence prompted Heinrich Böll, who first made his name by writing the bare, sparse prose of so-called 'rubble literature' (*Trümmerliteratur*), to produce a series of novels which warn against the dangers that affluence may bring forgetfulness. *Billiard um halb zehn* (Billiards at Half Past Nine, 1959) and *Ansichten eines Clowns* (Views of a Clown, 1963) focus on family relationships as the paradigm for the health or sickness of the nation. The use of first-person narration brings into urgent focus the question of the individual and his or her relatedness to the surrounding world; the stylistic mode interlocks with the moral theme – and this remains true of Böll's later fiction, *Gruppenbild mit Dame* (Group Portrait with Lady, 1971) and *Die verlorene Ehre der Katharina Blum* (The Lost Honour of Katharina Blum, 1974). Much of Böll's critical and satirical energy is echoed in Martin Walser's *Halbzeit* (Half Time, 1960) and *Das Einhorn* (The Unicorn, 1966), which explore the anomie of mid-life crisis that afflicts Anselm Kristlein, a man marooned in the strangely antiseptic well-being of contemporary West Germany. Uwe Johnson, in particular with *Mutmaßungen über Jakob* (Conjectures about Jakob, 1959), finds a prose of pained complexity to cope with the divided psyche of a country that exists in and as two states.

Far and away the finest of all the novels to emerge from West Germany in the 1950s and 1960s is Günter Grass's *Die Blechtrommel* (The Tin Drum, 1959). At one level, the novel expresses a viscerally critical view of German society from the late 1930s, through the Nazi years and the war, to the 1950s. At another level, it uses the overtly synthetic figure of Oskar Matzerath, who obstinately refuses to grow up, to mock the tradition of the *Bildungsroman*. Oskar is both narrator and experiencing self. By arresting his physical growth he retains the child's closeness to bodily functions, to what happens below the waist and behind the scenes. Yet at the same time he is a narrator of spellbinding literary and linguistic sophistication, indeed virtuosity.

Alongside the socially critical voices of Böll, Grass, and Walser there emerge fictions whose concern, although not indifferent to the social dimension, is directed at problems to do with the knowability and definability of the individual self. Max Frisch explores these issues in *Stiller* (1954) and *Homo Faber* (1957), as do Peter Weiss, Peter Handke, and Peter Schneider in *Lenz* (1973). In the later 1970s this leads to a crop of autobiographies which uphold the site and issue of subjectivity. Such texts coexist with fictions that respond to the student radicalism of the late 1960s, the terrorism of the early 1970s, and the often injudicious reaction of the state authorities (Heinrich Böll, *Die verlorene Ehre der Katharina Blum*, 1974; Peter Schneider, *. . . und schon bist du ein Verfassungsfeind* (*. . . and* already you are an enemy of the Constitution, 1975). In Böll's cautionary tale a young woman is destroyed by the gutter press. In his enormous trilogy *Die Aesthetik des Widerstands* (The Aesthetics of Resistance, 1975, 1978, 1981) Peter Weiss seeks to fuse narrative mode, aesthetic theory and socially critical discursivity. It is a titanic attempt that tries, but probably fails, to achieve a unity that is at once aesthetic, moral, and political. More characteristic of modern German writing have been texts that constantly recognise fissures and disparities. And this is nowhere more vividly the case than with women's writing. Ingeborg Bachmann's *Malina* (1971) is a particularly striking example. The complex shifting of the levels and modes of narrative statement bears witness to the psychological, sexual and social needs of the female self, needs that conflict uneasily without reaching any kind of harmonious resolution or reconciliation. Bachmann's compatriot, the Austrian Elfriede Jelinek (*Die Klavierspielerin* (The Piano Player), 1983; *Lust*, 1989) explores the problematic territory in which the (largely male-derived) images of women in literature, film, the media and pornography are acknowledged, exploited, re-worked, and challenged. Time and time again there are extraordinary moments in Jelinek texts where the obsessive prose of sexual repetitiveness modulates into its own thematisation and interrogation. A particular contribution to women's writing also emerged from the German Democratic Republic, to which I now wish to turn.

Censorship (and self-censorship) in the GDR produced a climate that in one sense militated against the emergence of any creative literature of stylistic and thematic range; but, in another sense, the constraints generated in writers a skilfulness at creating implied statements, allegories, sub-texts beneath the surface of 'acceptable' literary discourse. Much writing in the early years (as in the work of Anna Seghers) is concerned to affirm the new state as the humane successor and counter-voice to the monstrosity of the Third Reich; the claim is that the GDR is a state sustained by a culture that harks back to, and re-animates, the great tradition of Weimar Classicism. Gradually, however, the tensions beneath the surface make themselves felt as writers such as Hermann Kant (*Die Aula* (The Lecture Hall), 1965; *Das Impressum* (The Imprint), 1972) explore the price paid (and enforced by) the social engineering of the communist state. Literature from the past is used with a critical, rather than simply affirmatory, purpose – in, for example, Ulrich Plenzdorf's *Die neuen Leiden des jungen W.* (The New Sufferings of Young W., 1972), Irmtraud Morgner's *Leben und Abenteuer der Trobadora Beatrix* (Life and Adventures of the Troubadour Beatrix, 1975) and *Amanda: ein Hexenroman* (Amanda, a Novel of Witches, 1983), and Christa Wolf's *Kassandra* (1983).

It is noteworthy how many significant titles of GDR literature have been produced by women. There are a number of factors that may have contributed to this state of affairs. One is that, in theory, the GDR was committed to equality of the sexes, and provision in respect of maternity leave and crèches was admirable. On the other hand, the reality was very different – not least because the mentality that informed GDR culture was in some ways conservative, betraying more than a few traces of Prussian inheritance. Women thus felt acutely the conflicting norms within which they had to function. Moreover, many of them were frequently in touch with, and mindful of, each other – and this resulted in a network of critical, as it were interactive, voices. Christa Wolf is in all kinds of ways a key figure. Her *Nachdenken über Christa T.* (Reflections on Christa T, 1968) is a decisive work in that, in defiance of the tenets of socialist realism (which prescribes positive, that is socially productive, heroes and heroines), it seeks to validate the unaligned gaiety, good humour, and poetic subjectivity of a young woman, Christa T., who is in quest of a fuller realisation of the self than her prosaic culture allows her. The reflectivity of the narrator, her strenuous attempt, through her account, not to lose touch with the qualities of her friend after her death from leukaemia, amounts to a quest to wrest poetry from the conformist dreariness of GDR orthodoxy. In *Kassandra*, Wolf re-tells the story of the Trojan War from the perspective of the marginalised (and prescient) consciousness of Cassandra, of a female subjectivity trapped in a world informed and deformed by the ethos of male heroism. And in *Kindheitsmuster* (Patterns of Childhood, 1976) she explores through part-autobiographical, part-fictitious narrative her own, her family's, and her country's past. With Wolf the quest for the self, for an authentic instance of humanity, always reverberates with social and political implications. In *Was bleibt* (What Remains, largely written in 1979, but published, apparently with some revisions, in 1990) she produces a semi-fictional account of her surveillance by the Stasi, and of her own internalisation of that condition. The text was only published after the *Wende* (the unification of Germany), and this led to bitter accusations that she had failed to take the risk of raising her voice in criticism of the GDR when she might thereby have achieved something, that she had only published when it was convenient to do so, thereby appealing for facile sympathy. To outside observers, the ferocity directed at Wolf seems excessive – not least because the text at the centre of the furore is one that offers, precisely, criticism and exploration of the mechanisms by which acquiescence occurs and surveillance takes hold of the mentality of the victim.

Mention of the *Wende* invites one to reflect on the differences between the literatures of the two German states up to 1989. It should be stressed that a number of significant novels thematise the issue of the difference between the two states and their (psychological and other) cultures – Uwe Johnson's *Zwei Ansichten* (Two Views, 1965), Peter Schneider's *Der Mauerspringer* (The Wall Jumper, 1982), and Thorsten Becker's *Die Bürgschaft* (The Pledge, 1985). These texts explore the problems of the psychological and emotional wrench produced by the differences of mentality between citizens of the two regimes – and by the ensuing lack of understanding and trust. Differences, then, there were (and, one might add, still are) between *Wessis* and *Ossis*. Yet long before the collapse of the Wall there were signs of a measure of convergence between the two literatures. It is important to register that, when the government of the GDR revoked Wolf Biermann's citizenship in 1976, they elicited a wave of dissent from writers and intellectuals in the GDR – and a wave of literary emigration to the West, the like of which had not been seen before. But it is not simply that the flood of exiles meant rapprochement in the sense of East going West; the rapprochement had already been there in that, increasingly, from the early 1970s a concern for the artistic expression of the self had been an urgent feature of both literatures (Peter Handke, *Die Stunde der wahren Empfindung* (The Hour of True Feeling), 1975; *Langsame Heimkehr* (Slow Homecoming), 1979; Christoph Meckel, *Suchbild* (Picture Puzzle), 1980; Peter Härtling, *Nachgetragene Liebe* (Grudging Love), 1980; Volker Braun, *Hinze-Kunze Roman* (Tom, Dick, and Harry), 1985; and Christoph Hein's *Der Tangospieler*, (The Tango Player), 1989). Time and time again (for writers from both West and East) the delimiting and constricting agencies are mental as much as physical and institutional. The inwardness of German prose, to which I have constantly drawn attention, is vitally part of that enterprise which comprehends social reality not so much as a set of outward events, settings or circumstances but as a cast of mind.

One final observation by way of conclusion. In 1989 the Austrian writer Thomas Bernhard died. He left behind an oeuvre that is single-minded in the ferocity with which it denounces his native country in a veritable litany of disgust and outrage. Not, admittedly, that Bernhard is alone in this savagely critical enterprise – witness the work of Gert

Friedrich Jonke, Felix Mitterer, Norbert Gstrein, Gerhard Roth, Peter Rosei, and Peter Turrini. Similar perceptions of the strains and deprivations behind the idyll can be heard from the Swiss writers Peter Bichsel, E. Y. Meyer, and Hansjörg Schneider. But nobody can equal Bernhard for sheer monomanic intensity. There is something obsessive about his texts, whether we consider the autobiographical works (*Die Ursache. Eine Andeutung* (The Cause, an Intimation), 1997; *Der Keller. Eine Entziehung* (The Cellar, a Withdrawal), 1979; *Der Atem. Eine Entscheidung* (The Breath, a Decision), 1981; *Die Kälte. Eine Isolation* (The Coldness, an Isolation), 1984; *Ein Kind* (A Child), 1985) to the fictional writings from *Frost* (1963) to *Das Kalkwerk* (The Lime Works, 1970) and *Auslöschung. Ein Zerfall* (Extinction, a Degeneration, 1986). Given the stultifying subject matter, one would expect Bernhard's work to be boring and/or merely offensive (it is this, admittedly, to some of his compatriots). Yet it seems to me that the work is none of these things; and this is because of the language which has, in defiance of the brutalising, deadening subject matter, an extraordinary vitality, even elation to it. The bitter prose of referentiality is transmuted into heavily accentuated, rhythmic prose; the article of faith that sustains Bernhard's creative enterprise is one that validates not the world of which the text speaks but the words in which the text speaks. I have been at pains to suggest that German writers from Stifter, Keller, and Raabe, via the Naturalists and the classics of High Modernism to our contemporaries have consistently, in their different ways, sought to make their work embrace both the prose of referential constatation and the poetry of reflectivity. The dialectic is, as I hope this survey has suggested, an animating one. And perhaps nowhere more laceratingly and miraculously so than in the achievement of Thomas Bernhard.

NOTES

1. Wolfgang Preisendanz (ed.), *Wege des Realismus*, Munich: Fink, 1970, p. 90.

2. Wolf Lepenies, *Melancholie und Gesellschaft*, Frankfurt/Main: Suhrkamp, 1972, p. 99.

3. Roland Barthes, 'L'effet du réel' in Gerard Genette and Tzvetan Todorov (eds.), *Littérature et réalité*, Paris: Seuil, 1982, pp. 81–90.

4. J. P. Stern, *On realism*, London: Routledge, 1973, p. 5.

5. See Mack Walker, *German Home Towns*, Ithaca and London: Cornell University Press, 1971.

6. Klaus-Detlef Müller (ed), *Bürgerlicher Realismus*, Königstein/Ts: Athenäum, 1989, p. 11.

7. G. W. F. Hegel, *Aesthetik*, quoted in Hartmut Steinecke (ed.), *Romanpoetik in Deutschland: von Hegel bis Fontane*, Tübingen: Narr, 1984, p. 46. Steinecke's compilation is superb and gives one a sense of the resonance and thoughtfulness of the aesthetic debate in Germany.

8. Bertolt Brecht, *Gesammelte Werke in zwanzig Bänden* (Werkausgabe, edition Suhrkamp), Frankfurt/Main: Suhrkamp, 1967, vol. 16, p. 837.

9. See T. W. Adorno, 'Balzac-Lektüre', in *Noten zur Literatur*, Frankfurt/Main: Suhrkamp, 1981, pp. 139–57, and Christopher Prendergast, *Balzac: Fiction and Melodrama*, London, 1978.

FURTHER READING

The link between Germany's division into small states and the emergence of a modern industrial society is the common theme of Mack Walker, *German Home Towns* (Ithaca and London: Cornell University Press, 1971); David Blackbourn and Geoff Eley, *The Peculiarities of German History* (Oxford: Oxford University Press, 1984); Helga Grebing, *Der 'deutsche Sonderweg' in Europa 1806–1945: eine Kritik* (Stuttgart: Metzler, 1986) and Jürgen Kocka, *Geschichte und Aufklärung* (Göttingen: Vandenhoeck & Ruprecht, 1989).

Of the many studies of literary realism, the following are especially good introductions: Stephan Kohl, *Realismus: Theorie und Geschichte* (Munich: Fink, 1977); J. P. Stern, *On Realism* (London: Routledge, 1973); Christopher Prendergast, *The Order of Mimesis* (Cambridge: Cambridge University Press, 1986) and two volumes by Lilian Furst: *Realism* (ed.) ('Modern Literatures in Perspective', London: Longman, 1992) and *All is True: the Claims and Strategies of Realist Fiction* (Durham and London: Duke University Press, 1995).

Other works offer a more detailed discussion of realism in German prose writing from the nineteenth century to the present. See in particular Hugo Aust, *Literatur des Realismus* (Stuttgart: Metzler, 1981); Clifford Albrecht Bernd, *German Poetic Realism* (Boston: Twayne, 1981); Andreas Böhn, *Vollendete Mimesis: Wirklichkeitsdarstellung und Selbstbezüglichkeit in Theorie und literarischer Praxis* (Berlin and New York: de Gruyter, 1992) and Ulf Eisele, *Realismus und Ideologie* (Stuttgart: Metzler, 1976).

Hans Vilmar Geppert, *Der realistische Weg: Formen pragmatischen Erzählens bei Balzac, Dickens, Hardy, Keller, Raabe und anderen Autoren des neunzehnten Jahrhunderts* (Tübingen: Niemeyer, 1994) offers a comparative perspective while Werner Hahl, *Reflexion und Erzählung* (Stuttgart: Kohlhammer, 1971); Robert C. Holub, *Reflections of Realism: paradox, norm, ideology* (Detroit: Wayne State University Press, 1990); Hermann Kinder, *Poesie als Synthese* (Frankfurt/Main: Athenäum, 1973); Klaus-Detlef Müller (ed.), *Bürgerlicher Realismus* (Königstein/Ts: Athenäum 1981); Gerhard Plumpe (ed.), *Theorie des bürgerlichen Realismus: eine Textsammlung* (Stuttgart: Reclam, 1985); Wolfgang Preisendanz (ed.), *Wege des Realismus* (Munich: Fink, 1970) and Bernd W. Seiler, *Die leidigen Tatsachen: von den Grenzen der Wahrscheinlichkeit in der deutschen Literatur seit dem achtzehnten Jahrhundert* (Stuttgart: Metzler, 1983) link a thorough discussion of German concepts of literary realism with interpretative pointers to key works. The full-length study by Martin Swales, *Studies of German prose fiction in the age of European realism* (Lewiston, Queenston, and Lampeter: Mellen, 1995) allows the reader to follow up the themes, works and authors discussed in this chapter in a German and European historical and cultural context.

9

Modern German poetry

The lyric poetry in German culture since the 1870s is caught between polarities of aesthetic and political allegiance perhaps more extreme than in any other genre. Between an ethically responsible poetry engaged with the real and a poetry of privileged inwardness, there can, it seems, be little common ground. The conflict between these impulses is demonstrated with unique clarity in reactions to the Holocaust. Yet, reviewing the period as a whole, it is striking how this central opposition is reformulated time and again in shifting constellations. What links these different impulses is a knowing reflection on the self and the character of poetic creativity. That, it might be argued, defines the crucial signature of the modern.

A new poetry: paths out of the *'Gründerzeit'*

The period from 1870 to 1890 saw a definitive change in German poetry. Wide-scale literacy programmes, technical innovations in printing and paper-production and the popularity of lending libraries and mass-circulation family magazines created a new appetite for culture among the middle classes. The great names of the dominant *Erlebnislyrik* (poetry of experience), Theodor Storm and Gottfried Keller, published their final collections; the moral poetry of popular anthologies remained decorative but trivial; nationalist poets like Emanuel Geibel produced hymns of patriotic fervour and heroic cliché. Torn between inflated idealism and salon culture, the central problem for poetry as a genre was how to negotiate between public and private demands in a rapidly changing world.

The death of Theodor Storm in 1888 effectively marked the passing of that lyric inwardness which had characterised the first half of the nineteenth century, and the beginnings of a poetry for the modern age. Two strands of poetry emerged to counter the complacency of bourgeois culture: a poetry of social reality and a poetry of Symbolist transcendence. Conrad Ferdinand Meyer and Friedrich Nietzsche can be seen, in their different ways, as figures of transition. Although Nietzsche's primary importance is as a philosopher, the rhapsodic vitality and provocative imagery of his poetic language were nevertheless influential. Although experience still formed the basis of Meyer's late poetry, his repertoire of concentrated symbols – boats, the evening star and statues (famously, the Fontana Trevi in Rome) – brought German poetry close to the esoteric currents of European modernism which had begun with Baudelaire in France.

The beginning of the new century saw a plurality of simultaneous reactions to the instability of society. Alongside the work of Arno Holz (the only poet of significance to emerge from the Naturalist movement), the rise of workers' poetry, the developing Berlin cabaret scene and Frank Wedekind's satirical chanson and ballad forms, all offered a counterpoint to the complacency of bourgeois culture. At the same time there were the beginnings of an ecstatic, vital poetry which would pave the way for Expressionism (Else Lasker-Schüler, Franz Werfel, Theodor Däubler, Yvan Goll). Dominant, however, was a highly wrought poetry which grafted the inspiration of French Symbolism on to the mystic inwardness of the German Romantic tradition.

Rejecting the spiritual impoverishment of modern living, writers like Rainer Maria Rilke, Hugo von Hofmannsthal and Stefan George sought redemption in a transcendent realm. They created a poetry of symbols which are not explained or adduced but rather intuited though emotional experience. What Hofmannsthal calls 'Zauberworte' (magic words) offer an echo of a pre-verbal condition and promise access to the secret correspondences of the universe.

Hofmannsthal's lyric oeuvre is very small. His best work celebrates – and enacts – those haunting moments of privileged being, where the music of poetry offers glimpses of a primal unity which has been forfeited by humankind. An account of the poetic crisis which led to the end of his lyric production is given in his celebrated essay 'Ein Brief' (A Letter) of 1902. Purporting to be a letter written in 1603 by Philip Lord Chandos to Francis Bacon, it records the break-down which has robbed him of all coherent and stable relation with the phenomenological world. It has become a paradigmatic text of the crisis of modernism and expresses the dislocation and fallibility of language with unique intensity.

Rilke and George, on the other hand, looked to poetic language as the only possibility to express a truth about human experience. A distinguished translator from French and Italian, George drew especially on Baudelaire in his use of symbols and synaesthesia and his 'art for art's sake' aesthetic. But, unlike Baudelaire's indulgence in the vulgar or shocking, George crafted instead a cult of beauty and death which was marked in the early years especially by striking symbols, like the celebrated black flower. All aspects of his life and work were divorced from social reality: from his exclusive literary circle to his ornamental private publications and his distinctive punctuation and typography. Although his later poetry demonstrated an increasingly vatic sense of mission and classical discipline, his continuing eclecticism distinguished him fairly absolutely from the incipient chauvinism and thuggery of National Socialism.

After early collections marked by the neo-Romantic cult of feeling and Russian orthodox piety, Rilke's *Neue Gedichte* (New Poems, 1907 and 1908) represents a move away from effusion to a new lucidity and plasticity influenced by the visual arts – especially Rodin, and later Cézanne. Nonetheless, it is a mistake to see his 'Dinggedichte' (Thing Poems) as exclusively concerned with those objects which many of the famous poems feature in their titles: 'Der Panther', 'Blaue Hortensie' (Blue Hydrangea), 'Römische Fontäne' (Roman Fountain). In focusing on the integrity of being belonging to plants, animals and inanimate objects (often works of art), Rilke is most concerned to explore the relation between the object and inner human states. The poems are also notable for their sensuous realisation of movement, transition and metamorphosis. The *Duineser Elegien* (Duino Elegies), begun in a rush of lyrical intensity in 1912 and finished after years of creative crisis, in 1923, are the high-point of his work. Characterised by a movement between lament and aspiration (reminiscent of Hölderlin) they reproach the degradations of the modern world, while simultaneously intimating a deep consonance between man and the earth. Here, as in his *Sonette an Orpheus* (Sonnets to Orpheus, 1923), Rilke ultimately celebrates the redemptive power of art.

The Expressionist revolt

It is in Expressionism that German poets first pass beyond the poetic transcendence of Rilke, Hofmannsthal and George, and seek to encounter directly the crisis of modern industrial capitalism. This was essentially the movement of a young artistic avant-garde who congregated in Berlin cafés, notably the Café des Westens, to create a bohemian milieu of artistic collaboration and progressive thinking manifested in a host of journals and creative projects. Although originating in the visual arts, poetry was at the forefront of the Expressionist movement in Germany. It was a poetry marked less by a community of style than a community of attitude.

Jakob van Hoddis's famous poem 'Weltende' (End of the World) uses a collage technique and fine ironic phrasing to set the portents of apocalypse in grotesque contrast with the cynical insouciance of the bourgeoisie. One of the most well-known poets of the period, Georg Heym, draws on Hölderlin and Rimbaud to present gothic accumulations of images depicting a city presided over by monstrous deities. While Alfred Lichtenstein balances no less grotesque images with a mordant wit borrowed from cabaret, the observations of bodily decay and death made by the young Berlin doctor, Gottfried Benn, in *Morgue und andere Gedichte* (Morgue and other Poems) of 1912 shocked his readership with a grisly and apparently cynical voyeurism. August Stramm condensed explosive inner states into a clipped and dislocated syntax often close to the limits of intelligibility, while Anton Schnack and Ernst Stadler explored human misery in sonnet forms with sprawling lines, reminiscent of Walt Whitman.

Central to almost all the poetry, however, was the conviction that the cerebralised facade of social order should be destroyed in order to unleash a purging eruption of some vaguely conceived 'essence'. In this it can be seen to anticipate the debacle of the First World War. Confronted with the reality of mechanised warfare, the mood darkens and many poets struggle to locate some transcendent reconciliation. Like the exotic melancholy of the bohemian Else Lasker-Schüler, Georg Trakl's work opens on to a very individual poetic soul-scape. But where Lasker-Schüler eschews distortion to concentrate on non-alienated fantasy states, Trakl explores a realm of sickness and decay. Strangely compressed images coexist without causal connections. Striking adjectives of colour, complex metaphors, parataxis and distorted syntax enact the collapse of order into chaos. Trakl's final poem 'Grodek' invokes his experience of the First World War as a medical orderly in the Galician town of that name. It is a major document of Expressionism both in the brutal dislocation of language and in the image of the silent sister, a fragile intimation of redemption retrieved from chaos.

The best Expressionist poetry turned on a paradox. For while the preceding generation saw themselves as the last guardians of a culture coming to an end, the Expressionists felt themselves to be at an intersection, at once looking backwards and forwards, at once mystical and revolutionary. By the time the best-known anthology *Menschheitsdämmerung* (Twilight (or Dawn) of Humanity, 1920) was published and had brought Expressionism a wider public, it had already become an historical document. Heym, Stadler, Trakl, Stramm and Lichtenstein were already dead; others had matured in different directions or fallen silent. Very quickly the movement lost much of its imaginative density and passed into a final phase of large gestures, rhetoric, and (after 1918 especially) left-wing pathos (Stadler, Franz Werfel, Johannes R. Becher).

The energy which had typified the early years of Expressionism passed to a movement of anti-sense and anti-art under the randomly chosen name *Dada*. Coming out of the 'Cabaret Voltaire' group founded in 1916 in Zurich, artists like Hans Arp, Kurt Schwitters and Hugo Ball established groups all over Europe. Unlike Expressionist writers, they recognised the bankruptcy of modern civilisation but neither lamented it nor wanted to anticipate something new. The focus was instead on an anarchist, and often parodic, sense of creativity which issued into a multitude of experimental forms and events. The movement had some forerunners, in the work of Wedekind and Christian Morgenstern for example, and its energies would be resurrected to a certain extent in the Austria of the 1950s and the 1980s GDR. However, the historic importance of Dada is that it made nonsense into a founding principle of poetry for the first time.

After Expressionism: Brecht and Benn

Germany's defeat in the First World War and the collapse of the second Reich resulted in a state of demoralisation which precipitated a new cultural sobriety. The ways out of that crisis followed two distinct directions: on the one hand an attempt to secure tradition, and on the other, the development of a socially critical line.

Rilke, George and Hofmannsthal published their final works during this period, but were very much on the periphery of the Weimar scene. In their wake came the continuation of a reactionary transcendental poetry by writers like Hans Carossa, Rudolf Alexander Schröder and Ina Seidel. These poets rejected what they considered the devalued currency of modern living and sought a return from the 'paradis artificiels' of Symbolism to the 'paradis naturels' of traditional religious or landscape poetry; the stability of their forms offering a counterpoint to the increasing instability of the times.

At the opposite end of the spectrum was a move to encounter the times directly, and to democratise and politicise the genre. Here political cabaret and its related forms (chanson, Moritat (gruesome ballad) and review) are of crucial importance. Texts were written with performance in mind – often for notable 'diseuses' like Trude Hesterberg. The direct contact with the audience and the public nature of the poem began to determine its structure. Berlin was the centre of the cabaret scene, most famously the 'Schall und Rauch' (Sound and Smoke) cabaret opened by Walter Mehring in 1919. Forms and attitudes varied. Joachim Ringelnatz and Klabund (Alfred Henscke) became noted for satirical role-poems and social vignettes, while Mehring parodied any number of forms from baroque litany to jazz.

There was also a more politically explicit poetry ranging from Erich Kästner's vehement attacks on the Weimar establishment to Kurt Tucholsky's pioneering newspaper poems or the anarchist journalist and poet Erich Mühsam's revolutionary songs. The year 1928 saw the extension of workers' poetry and the foundation of 'The Union of Working Class Revolutionary Writers' (BPRS). Johannes R. Becher proclaimed his ambitious communist agenda in volumes of traditional forms and high pathos. In contrast, Erich Weinert's widely recited political verse drew on cabaret forms and the tradition of Heinrich Heine to develop an operative poetry which would appeal to the masses. These, and others like them, were often disappointed by the possibilities open to poetry for political change. Nevertheless, the Weimar Republic saw one of the most important attempts to re-function the genre.

In a sense these developments were recognisable continuations of directions which had already been present in the early years of the century. However, during the years of the Weimar Republic, two figures, Bertolt Brecht and Gottfried Benn, created distinctive poetic modes which came to represent the extreme alternatives of poetic and political allegiance. The positions from which they started were similar: a rejection of the formal Classical–Romantic consensus which had provided the foundation for German poetry since Goethe and the mixture of nihilism and vitalism which marks the early years of the modern era. Their diverging models were to shape the poetic landscape for the next half-century.

After his early Expressionist years, Benn developed an essentially monologic, inward-looking poetry marked by a deep cultural pessimism. The crux of his poems is a longing to escape the anguish and deprivation of the cerebral and to recapture a primal unity. Floods of procreative images rub shoulders with a montage of the abrupt, often recondite, jargon of the modern age. Benn's open disparagement of the human condition led to a willed isolation from other trends, and indeed from public communication. This is exemplified in a radio dialogue with J. R. Becher of 1931, 'Können Dichter die Welt ändern?' (Can Poets Change the World?), where he argued that poetic form alone was capable of harnessing the chaos of life.

Bertolt Brecht is now recognised as one of the most important German lyric poets of the twentieth century, and yet he too is one who distrusted the traditional forms and feelings of lyric poetry. In direct contrast to the self-sufficiency of Benn, Brecht's first collection, *Die Hauspostille* (The Household Breviary) of 1927 announced an energetically communicative and emphatically 'useful poetry' which he dubbed 'Gebrauchslyrik'. At this stage Brecht generally refrains from direct political comment, preferring instead a satirical re-working of naive and traditional forms. The collection is chiefly remarkable though for sheer range, both formal (from broadside ballad and song to hymn and chronicle), and emotional – from the raucous sensuality of the songs to the elegiac 'Liturgie vom Hauch' (Liturgy on Breath) or the posturing of 'Vom armen B. B.' (Of poor B. B.). Gradually this multiplicity of voices issued into the more rational sobriety and the explicit political commitment of his later 'learning-poems'.

Looking back, in 1938, Brecht accounted for this development by recalling the times he was writing in. Those times, which saw the rise of National Socialism and the marginalisation and vilification of progressive writers and intellectuals, triggered a political and poetological schism. Benn's increasing solipsism would have a profound effect on the development of poetry after the Second World War; Brecht's 'Gebrauchslyrik' set the agenda for committed writing of the 1960s and beyond.

'Bad time for poetry': poetry in the Third Reich and exile

The legacy of the Third Reich is the centrally determining factor in the development of post-war German poetry, even for those strands of literature seeking to oppose or evade it. The Nazis plundered German Classicism in support of their literary monumentalism and looked to pious turn-of-the-century *Heimatdichtung* (patriotic provincial poetry) to furnish their atavistic 'Blut und Boden' (blood and soil) archetypes. On the street and at rallies the new order resounded to a declamatory poetry in Classical forms, replete with the symbols central to Nazi ideology: heroic peasants, honour, the mission of the poet and the rebirth of *Volk* and Fatherland. Goebbels hailed the 'stählerne Romantik' (steely Romanticism) of the era which, he hoped, would combine fervour and discipline to intoxicate and politicise a disoriented populace.

There were few forms of direct literary protest within the Third Reich; the majority of the poets who remained in Germany choosing instead the path of 'inner emigration'. Notwithstanding highly organised mechanisms of censorship, a relatively large number of poets were able to survive in Germany, as long as they published in tiny editions or alternative journals. The writers whom one associates most readily with inner emigration, Wilhelm Lehmann and Oskar Loerke (along with Carossa, Schröder, Seidel, Werner Bergengruen, Gertrud von Le Fort), were traditionalists who had been on the periphery of the Weimar Republic. They were joined by a group of mainly younger and more interesting (also more restless) poets who crystallised around the journal *Die Kolonne*: Günter Eich, Peter Huchel, Elisabeth Langgässer and Gertrud Kolmar.

For the older writers Nazism represented an acute manifestation of tendencies within modern society. They sought solace in Christian or mystical beliefs and the traditions and forms of the nineteenth century. For almost all of them the experience of nature became the source of poetic inspiration, but also a refuge from the pain of reality. Brecht's famous complaint about the times 'when a conversation / about trees is almost a crime, / because it includes a silence about so many misdeeds',[1] touches the heart of the dilemma. These poets believed that humane hope could only be salvaged in personal circles: their guardianship of bourgeois cultural tradition they regarded as a defiance against the barbarism of the Nazi spirit; their modulated language they saw as a rejection of the *Lingua Tertii Imperii*. But while the poetry perhaps offered tacit forms of resistance, there is a danger, publicly at least, that it lent National Socialism the appearance of poetic diversity.

The erstwhile Expressionist Gottfried Benn initially greeted Nazism as a natural extension of his earlier attitudes – his primitivism and suspicion of reason seemed to be answered by the vitalism and irrationalism of the new order. Tensions soon developed between the poet and the authorities though, not least because of his continued defence of Expressionism, officially declared degenerate. He developed instead an aesthetic of coldness, discipline and hermeticism based on the 'absolute poem', as an antidote to the absurdity of existence. This development was exemplified in his *Statische Gedichte* (Static Poems) of 1948 which gathered poems from over a decade and established his reputation after the war. Benn's apolitical stance and his willed indifference to Nazism was not exceptional, but rather symptomatic of a tendency among writers and thinkers at this time to prefer the mythological to the historical, and with that, finally, to devalue the human.

Hitler's accession to power in 1933 precipitated a mass exodus from Germany, which gained momentum after the Reichstag fire was followed by a wave of book burnings and the imprisonment of 'undesirable' authors. The exile poets are far from a homogenous group, however.

Generally writers took up where they had left off in the Weimar Republic: from a poetry of counter-propaganda by Mehring in the United States or Weinert in the Soviet Union, to the solitary lament which makes up the bulk of exile poetry. It is a commonplace of criticism that the poetry of exile as a body is formally and thematically conservative. Writers were concerned to rescue the German cultural heritage from misappropriation by Nazism and the sonnet in particular enjoyed a renaissance as therapeutic talisman against chaos and contradiction. Criticism has long been divided as to whether aesthetic rather than moral judgements can rightfully be brought to bear on such a literature *in extremis*. For many, poetry was simply a means of surviving.

Central to much of the poetry is a sense of loss: loss of personal, cultural and political identity and, more fundamentally perhaps, loss of language. Divorced from their mother tongue, it is no surprise that, for many writers, poetological texts become central. In writers as different as J. R. Becher, Max Herrmann-Neiße, Berthold Viertel or Theodor Kramer, the German language even becomes a quasi-sacred substitute for a lost homeland.

Nostalgia for home remained a defining theme for many exiles. This was made more complex for those who were Jewish and many of those who survived, including Paul Celan, Erich Fried, Else Lasker-Schüler and Nelly Sachs, chose to remain abroad permanently. Sachs left Germany in 1940 for Sweden where she was awarded the Nobel Prize for Literature in 1966. Her poetry finds its definitive voice 'in the habitations of death', also the title of her 1947 collection. For her the suffering of Israel becomes a paradigm of universal suffering and inspired incantatory hymnic poetry with a mosaic of cryptic – although sometimes unsettlingly arbitrary – symbols.

There is one poet, more than any other, for whom this 'bad time for poetry' ('Schlechte Zeit für Lyrik' is the title of one of his poems) produced a direct and innovative response. Unlike the conservative and intensely personal poetry of most exile writers, Brecht continued to exploit a range of personas (particularly that of sage and teacher), and forms (sonnet, epigram, satirical song, hymn, ballad) in the service of an essentially communicative poetry. For him, strategy was everything. If his language lost some of its metaphoric density, his work on a muscular reflective verse without rhyme and in irregular rhythms (and his 1938 essay on that subject) would prove definitive in his development. Alongside his diction it is the dialectical movement of his texts which most characterises his achievement. This is nowhere more evident than in 'An die Nachgeborenen' (To Posterity), his haunting invocation of a humane world to be born out of 'the dark times', which has become a key inspiration for the postwar era.

Poetry after Auschwitz

The devastation of the Second World War at first encouraged a belief in a 'Stunde Null' (Zero Hour), a *tabula rasa* which might permit a totally new start. Wolfgang Weyrauch coined the term *Kahlschlag* (clearing of terrain), defining the need, felt especially by younger writers, to purge the German language of the political distortions of the past and to start afresh with a language cleaned and simplified. The premium placed upon the truthful documentation of war and its aftermath is exemplified by Günter Eich's celebrated 'Inventur' (Inventory). It is a bald stock-taking of existence which leaves behind metre, rhyme and traditional metaphors almost completely. But aside from this poem, the programme was not as influential as at first supposed. On the contrary: far from a fundamental caesura, German poetry is striking for those continuities which established themselves across the years of the Third Reich.

Community with the pre-war years was immediately supplied by the nature poetry of Lehmann and the conservative poets of inner emigration. This made itself felt in the dominance of inherited formal traditions (critics even complained of 'sonnet frenzy'), remoteness from time and the world, an increase in Christian motifs and a pre-occupation with the natural world as salvation. At the time this poetry was widely read and acclaimed; its almost total retreat from the empirical reality provided comfort and distraction for a people desperately evading the horrors of fascism. It was against this restorative tendency that the philosopher Theodor W. Adorno directed his celebrated dictum that to write poetry after Auschwitz was barbaric. His polemic was not intended as a ban on poetic utterance, but rather as a challenge to the insularity of a poetry which had not been contaminated by the shock of the mass destruction.

The dominant trend of poetry during the 1950s up until about 1970 is generally identified as hermeticism. A key influence was Gottfried Benn, whose *Static Poems* of 1948 and 1951 lecture, 'Probleme der Lyrik' (The Problems of Poetry), set the poetic agenda for almost a decade after the war. His belief that art obeys its own rules regardless of social context secured an apparently inevitable development towards an ever greater abstraction and elitism. Formally that process is manifested in an increased inwardness, the reduction of poetic forms and the cultivation of closed metaphors. For other writers, Paul Celan, Ingeborg Bachmann, Rose Ausländer, Karl Krolow and Marie Luise Kaschnitz, a similar movement comes explicitly as a reaction to fascism. Although Adorno's negative dialectic allows for an interpretation of the withdrawal from everyday comprehensibility as a political gesture immanent in the structure of the poem itself, more generally this strand of poetry has little to say about the world of which it is part.

Celan is the exemplary representative of hermetic poetry in Germany after the war. His work is a response to the Holocaust, to which his parents fell victim, but more specifically to the legacy of the Holocaust as it marked the German language. The celebrated 'Todesfuge' (Death Fugue), written in 1945, has become perhaps the classic poetic document of the Nazi atrocities. He later rejected this poem and his work underwent a drastic reduction of formal options. This gradual 'straightening' ('Engführung', the musical term, is the title of an important poem) issued into a chastened terseness, especially in the late poems, which seems designed to resist comprehension. In his Büchner Prize speech of 1960, 'Der Meridian' (The Meridian), he claimed that poetry was distinguished by a 'Neigung zum Verstummen'. His own writing (and translation) demonstrates an unshakable belief in the poem as possible dialogue, but it also seeks to give utterance to that 'tendency towards silence'. One of the most important factors in his work is his Jewish heritage, which conditions his negative mysticism, his juxtaposition of elemental images and the negation of traditional linguistic or Biblical structures. Celan took his own life in 1970.

Bachmann, although her poetry is often bracketed with Celan's work as hermetic, is more accessible and more attached to a recognisable contemporary experience. Her first collection, *Die gestundete Zeit* (A Respite for Time) was a major media event, and challenged the restorative consumerist thinking of the 1950s by illuminating an altogether darker side of progress. She managed to create a new modern poetic language which was at once of its times yet did not obscure its roots in German tradition. While her poems reiterate her own passionate belief in poetry as an intimation of utopia, the links between loss of love, loss of identity and loss of language which dominate her later work in increasingly disturbing variations have recently been highlighted by feminist interpreters, for whom she has become something of an icon. Amongst her handful of final poems 'Keine Delikatessen' (No Delicacies) of 1963 records a decision to abandon the lyric mode.

Revolutionary poetry and the poetry of revolution

The work that emerged in the transition to the 1960s heralded a fundamental paradigm shift in lyric poetry. The monologic and elitist tendencies of hermetic poetry were rejected and two very different and equally radical possibilities emerged.

The first is a revolution of the poetic project at the level of language itself. The highly diverse texts that are classifiable under the heading of 'concrete poetry' (Eugen Gomringer, Helmut Heißenbüttel, Franz Mon) represent an attempt to diminish or even abolish the primary referential function of language. Elements of language are liberated from systems of grammar or 'sense' then recombined, either mechanically, or according to the creative will of the experimenter. This programme was enhanced by the use of optical and acoustic elements.

A rather different understanding is to be found in the *Wiener Gruppe* (Wiener Group), named after its leader Oswald Wiener, the most important members of which are probably Ernst Jandl and Friederike Mayröcker. Turning to the traditions of Dada and Surrealism they understood themselves as an anti-bourgeois avant-garde for whom the removal of the hierarchic structure of the sentence was a token resistance against the power of social structures. In the provincial climate of the late 1950s concrete poetry was regarded not simply as a new idiom but as a completely new genre. Aside from odd exceptions (Jandl's ludic sound poems, for example), it failed to reach a broader public.

At the same time other writers set about recording the unpoetic inconsistencies of the factual world, exactly in the hope of reaching as wide an audience as possible. Poetry 'after its return from silence', in Krolow's phrase, quickly developed a radical agenda. Hans Bender's anthology *Mein Gedicht ist mein Messer* (My Poem is My Knife) of 1961 provides perhaps a useful motto for an aggressive new writing which culminated in the propaganda poetry associated with the student uprising of 1968. Different directions of political poetry up until 1968 can be exemplified by the lapidary didacticism of Erich Fried on the one hand, and the political folk-songs of the *Liedermacher* (singer-songwriter) Franz Josef Degenhardt on the other.

In any analysis Hans Magnus Enzensberger must stand as the key figure in this new orientation. His *verteidigung der wölfe* (defence of the wolves) of 1957 established him almost immediately as voice of angry youth challenging the complacency, bureaucratisation and distorted values of the affluent post-war society. Both in theme and mode he is indebted to Brecht; indeed with Enzensberger begins a reception of Brecht which will become influential in the 1960s and decisive for writers like Erich Fried, Peter Rühmkorf, Hilde Domin, Yaak Karsunke and F. C. Delius. Enzensberger's conviction that the poem was a necessary 'object for use' ('Gebrauchsgegenstand'), his rhymeless speech and stretched syntax bear witness to his direct engagement with political reality, but also to his debt to modernism. An acute awareness of impending ecological or nuclear catastrophe increasingly coloured his thinking, to the point where he gave up poetry for a while, as a medium no longer capable of serving the cause of survival, and endorsed the (much misunderstood) 'death of literature' in the pages of the journal *Kursbuch*, which he edited.

Literature *after* the death of literature saw a boom in sales of lyric poetry. What was billed variously as 'New Subjectivity' or *Alltagslyrik* (poetry of the everyday) was interpreted at the time as a return from the doctrine of usefulness and as a reaction against the political exigences of the student movement. A mood of prevailing disillusionment, exemplified by Nicolaus Born's poem 'Ausgeträumt' (Finished Dreaming), tends to support the theory that this is essentially a poetry of withdrawal. Nonetheless, the tendency to see it as a straightforward reaction to overpoliticisation is a mistake. On closer inspection it is as much alive to the transforming power of the imagination as it is to the empirical reality of the everyday and it is as much a rejection of the hermeticism which culminated in Paul Celan as it is to the extreme didacticism of the 1960s.

Influenced by the Beat Generation and popular culture from the United States, writers (Born, Günter Herburger, Rolf Dieter Brinkmann, Jureck Becker, Jürgen Theobaldy and Michael Krüger) responded with work in which apparently random details from the intimate sphere of everyday living furnish the poem. A new generation of women writers also made their mark (Karin Kiwus, Ursula Krechel and Christa Reinig, who had left the GDR). Disappointed by the failure of the political movements of the late 1960s to address women's concerns explicitly, their work was quickened by, and fed into, the emancipatory energies of the Women's Movement. Traditional forms, symbolism and metaphor were rejected for an emphasis on directness, the spontaneity of a 'snapshot' (Brinkmann), free forms and a sometimes abrasive contemporary slang. An exception to this is Reinig's provocative re-working of the ballad tradition. The best texts of this period demonstrate a simplicity that is precisely calculated. However, not all of the poetry could rise above the banality of its origins.

Poetry of the German Democratic Republic

One of the most striking facets of post-1989 reassessments of GDR literature is the new and deserved prominence given to lyric poetry. Because poetry is the genre most sensitive to the acute tensions between the desire for individual self-realisation and the pressures to conform, it was arguably in this genre, above all others, that GDR writers found a distinctive voice.

Although the 1960s and 1970s can be seen as the decisive period, the poetry of the early years did not consist only of the production lyricism and tractor-verses of the *Bitterfelder Weg* (Bitterfeld Path). Right from the beginning there were other voices too. On the one hand there was a recourse to the Classical German heritage which followed directly from developments in exile and was intended to legitimise the GDR as the rightful extension of a humanist Enlightenment tradition. This is exemplified by the work of J. R. Becher, installed as the first Minister of Culture in 1949. But there were also voices who often controversially introduced and extended modernist impulses: Peter Huchel, Stephan Hermlin, Erich Arendt. A quite different approach is seen in the work of Erich Weinert, Louis Fürnberg, and KuBa (Kurt Barthel), who produced cult anthems to leaders of the new society, in the prescribed new vernacular, or 'cadre Latin' ('Kaderwelsch'), as Brecht labelled it.

Brecht's own work of this period is marked by a sobriety and a laconicism derived from study of the Oriental forms and of Horace. His *Buckower Elegien* (Buckow Elegies) of 1953 present often melancholy reflections on what had been achieved in the GDR, and warnings about the dangers of fascism and the bureaucracy of the new state. This collection includes some of his most simple and moving poems which combine meticulous observation and reflection in almost aphoristic form: 'Der Rauch' (Smoke), 'Der Radwechsel' (Changing the Wheel), 'Böser Morgen' (Bad Morning).

At first, it was on the tradition of Brecht that the younger GDR poets of the 1960s were to build. Günter Kunert's epigrammatic learning poems, for example, owed much to his model and earned him official approval until his early tendency to irony and his uncompromising refusal to skate over inconsistencies led to clashes with the authorities. Soon, the emergence of a younger generation of poets changed the direction of GDR poetry. These were writers who had learned from Brecht but also from other traditions, often under the tutelage of the poet Georg Maurer at the J. R. Becher Institute for Literature in Leipzig. A key influence was Johannes Bobrowski, whose confessional explorations of landscape and memory enriched GDR poetry with an uniquely humane and elegiac sensibility.

The fact that a large number of the younger poets hailed from the province of Saxony prompted the label 'Sächsische Dichterschule' (Saxon School of Poetry). But more than geographical provenance, these writers were united by the desire to make poetry once more a vehicle for the submerged potential of the individual. Although their bid to rehabilitate subjective experience had very little to do with the more solipsistic tendencies of New Subjectivity in the West, hostile official reactions to their work nevertheless made their poetry an unprecedented focus of debate. Here Volker Braun must stand as a single example for this group which encompassed such diverse signatures as Sarah Kirsch's associative elegiac, Heinz Czechowski's nostalgic melancholy, Reiner Kunze's minimalism, Karl Mickel's satires, Elke Erb's elliptical prose poems and Wolf Biermann's humour and fury. From the beginning, Braun understood his poetry as provocation, and the declamatory, nonchalant, drastic impatience of his early poems can be compared to that of Enzensberger in the West. In Braun the tension between socialist commitment, the influence of international modernism and expression of personal dissatisfaction epitomises the dilemma of GDR poetry as a whole. The withdrawal of the operative pathos of his early work to make way for more subtle reflection and an increasing range of form, metaphor and reference (Klopstock, Hölderlin, Rimbaud) are also typical.

Despite the hopes initiated by Honecker's famous 'no taboos' speech of 1971, the development of GDR poetry tells of increasing disillusionment and despair. The turning point was the expatriation of the exuberant poet and singer Wolf Biermann in 1976. His poignant but outspoken collection *Die Drahtharfe* (The Wire Harp) published in 1965 (in the West) had led to over a decade of harassment and censorship. His departure initiated a mass exodus of writers including Kunert, Kunze and Kirsch.

If the 1980s, in the words of Günter Kunert, marked 'the end of the principle of hope', they also saw the liberalisations of *glasnost,* which allowed a greater scepticism to be tolerated in the public realm. Poetry by critical writers brought the banality and brutality of everyday life into sharper focus and treated previously taboo themes such as sexuality and suicide. The posthumous publication of the terse but raw poetry of Inge Müller, who had committed suicide in 1966, also proved influential in East and West. Significant too is a bleak nature poetry by writers like Wolfgang Hilbig and the Sorbian Kito Lorenc which is filled with the refuse landscapes of a radical last days' consciousness. The rejection of utopian thinking is particularly evident in the work of older writers like Czechowski, Braun, Arendt and Erb. A prevalent sense of living in an historical limbo, and the widespread thematisation of silence as well as montage techniques, fragmentation, and stylistic terseness signal a definitive 'modernisation' of GDR poetry.

This is most extreme in the work of the very youngest generation of writers; writers who were 'born into' the established socialist state. They greeted the system, not as a reaction against fascism, or as the hope of a humane society, but only as a deformed reality. Many existed on the periphery of regimented GDR society in artistic communities, like the Berlin district of Prenzlauer Berg, which has given its name to the experimental counter culture which developed across the country. Beyond the playful aspects of work by Uwe Kolbe, Stefan Döring or Bert Papenfuß which drew on the traditions of Dada, Expressionism, Russian Futurism and the insights of French post-structuralist theory, was a serious bid to undermine or escape the ideologically determined structures of language. The dissolution of this subculture was already under way before the fall of the Wall brought the end of the GDR itself. The fact that at least two of those central to the creative impetus of the scene were secret police informants has all but destroyed the myth of the postmodern enclave at the heart of the authoritarian state. Many of the poetic innovations of these years have, however, been continued in the new Germany.

Apocalypse and experiment: the 1980s and beyond

The loss of faith in socialism across a broad spectrum of poets and a growing anxiety about the costs of technological progress bring GDR poetry very close, in the 1980s, to the poetry of the West. This decade saw a wave of poetry which chimed in with the insecurities of global politics and issued into a topos of *Abschiednehmen* or 'taking leave of a disappearing world'. As with any poetic fad, the results were mixed. Wastelands of ice and stone are widespread synechdoches for a condition which proclaims the end of Enlightenment thought. The figure of Hölderlin, whose 'Hälfte des Lebens' (The Half of Life) becomes the almost obligatory signature of left-wing melancholy, stands alongside references to Walter Benjamin's 'Angel of History' as a representative of the collapse of the belief in progress. Reactions are manifold: from the irony and willed nihilism of late Peter Rühmkorf, to the retreat into laconic detail of Kunze, the mobilisation of an idealist past in the work of Rolf Haufs or the mystic romanticism of Rose Ausländer.

The poetry of Kirsch, Kunert, Enzensberger, and Krüger is perhaps exemplary of the dominant mood. Krüger's perceptive records of damage to the social and natural environment focus on 'the simple things', but are now disturbed by radical linguistic doubt. The abrasive rhetoric of Enzensberger's early work sharpens into the historical scepticism of the long narrative poem *Der Untergang der Titanic* (The Sinking of the Titanic, 1978) and the grim irony of *Die Furie des Verschwindens* (The Fury of Disappearance, 1980). More recent collections retire into a more gentle melancholy or technical virtuosity. Kirsch's numerous collections, published in the West since 1977, have also darkened in tone, as they chart the decline of a damaged natural landscape and a hunger for stability in a dislocated world. Odd syntactic shifts, frequent enjambment and the deliberate fluctuation between tenses and grammatical moods of a collection like *Bodenlos* (Groundless, 1996) create a stylistic indeterminacy which is both challenging and distinctively resonant.

The historical pessimism of the 1980s has found its most consistent expression in the work of Günter Kunert, however. From *Abtötungsver-fahren* (Mortification Procedures, 1980) his poetry has recorded visions of decline and the inevitability of ecological collapse. Most recently he has revived a poetic of pure form in the tradition of Benn and Rilke and has looked to traditional forms to fix the fleetingness of his surroundings.

Formally, the poetry of the 1980s has tended in two distinct directions. In part as a reaction to the prosaic banality of the 1970s, there was an extraordinary renaissance of classical forms and metres and a re-installation of the poet as prophet and seer. For some this has gone hand in hand with a culture of feeling reminiscent of the apolitical attitudes of the post-war years, notably in the best-selling poet Ulla Hahn. A related phenomenon is the consolidation of the powerful tradition of religious poetry written by women (Christine Lavant, Elisabeth Borchers, Christine Busta). On the other hand, a poetry of linguistic experiment has proliferated and been taken up especially by younger writers like the Romanian German Oskar Pastior or Thomas Kling. Kling, like Papenfuß from the former GDR, turns to language as material and deconstructs traditional discourses through intertextual montage, typographical effects and lack of semantic stability.

In the years since the end of the GDR lyric poetry has been the genre most immediately called upon to absorb the shock of transition and dispossession. An extraordinary wave of poetry sought to fix the euphoria of the *Wende* of 1989 and the disillusionment, existential homelessness and consumerist frenzy which followed. One poem in particular, Volker Braun's 'Nachruf' (Obituary) became a rallying point, and secured what has become the dominant paradigm of the 1990s. Braun's moving testament mourns not only the loss of those utopian ideals which inspired the GDR, but also the historical identity of all those who lived out its realities. This lament, which also characterises some extraordinary final poetry by Heiner Müller, is not confined only to poets from the GDR and Günter Grass's *Novemberland: 13 Sonette* (Novemberland: 13 Sonnets) marks the return of this West German novelist to the lyric mode. It is perhaps too soon to see clearly what has distinguished the developments since unification. Almost inescapable, nevertheless, is a focus on the fractured and multiple identities of the new Germany and beyond – enriched by distinctive new voices like the young Turkish German poet Nevfel Cumart. Noticeable too is a reluctance to ascribe to poetry the visionary authority and resonant voice of classical tradition. This is shared by two of the most innovative writers to have made their mark since 1989: Durs

Grünbein and Barbara Köhler. Grünbein's hard-edged postmodern ironies and Köhler's restless, yet precise passion belong to different ends of the poetic spectrum. Both poets, however, exploit a variety of traditional forms and an emphatically contemporary idiom; both write with insights won from theory, and a rigorous self-consciousness. Both, finally, share an understanding, common perhaps to all the most important poets of this period, of poetry as the intimation of a fuller, richer existence enacted in the fabric of language.

NOTE

1. 'Was sind das für Zeiten, wo / Ein Gespräch über Bäume fast ein Verbrechen ist / Weil es ein Schweigen über so viele Untaten einschließt!', from Brecht's poem 'An die Nachgeborenen' (To Posterity).

FURTHER READING

One of the best introductions to modern German poetry for the English reader remains Michael Hamburger's dual-language anthology *German Poetry 1910–1975* (Manchester: Carcanet, 1977). This, along with his many essays on individual poets and movements, offers an excellent insight into the development of poetry during the twentieth century. Walter Hinderer's volume *Geschichte der deutschen Lyrik vom Mittelalter bis zur Gegenwart* (Stuttgart: Reclam, 1983) offers an authoritative overview epoch by epoch, each chapter written by a leading expert in the field, while Klaus Schmumann's stimulating *Lyrik des 20. Jahrhunderts: Materialien zu einer Poetik* (Reinbek: Rowohlt, 1995) collects the key poems, essays and documents which have shaped the era.

A number of very useful texts trace particular strands of development during the period. Hugo Friedrich, *Die Struktur der modernen Lyrik* (Reinbek: Rowohlt, 1956) became hugely influential in defining an understanding of the modernist project in Germany, and transmitting its energies to post-war German poetry. Hitrud Gnüg, *Entstehung und Krise lyrischer Subjektivität: Vom klassischen lyrischen Ich zur modernen Erfahrungswirklichkeit* (Stuttgart: Metzler, 1983) presents a detailed account of the manifestations of poetic subjectivity since the Classical era, while the complex interrelationship between poetry and politics is examined in the essays of Heinz Ludwig Arnold (ed.), *Politische Lyrik*, 3rd. edn. (Munich: edition text + kritik, 1984). Gisela Brinker-Gabler (ed.), *Deutsche Literatur von Frauen*, 2 vols. (Munich: Beck, 1988) is a useful source text for women poets who are often marginalised in accounts of the period.

Of the many studies of specific turning points in the development of German poetry, three in particular deserve mention here. The anthology edited by Kurt Pinthus, *Menschheitsdämmerung: Ein Dokument des Expressionismus* (1920, reprinted Hamburg: Rowohlt, 1959) is a key document of German Expressionism, while Karl Riha and Jörgen Schäfer (eds.), *DADA total: Manifeste, Aktionen, Texte, Bilder* (Stuttgart: Philipp Reclam jun., 1994) offers an insight into the anarchic world of Dada, and Patrick Bridgwater, *The German Poets of the First World War* (London: Croom Helm, 1985) explores the response of poets to war experience and its impact on poetry in the Weimar years.

Much has been written about the poetry of the two German states after 1945. Siegbert Prawer, *Seventeen Modern German Poets* (Oxford: Oxford University Press, 1971) provides an excellent introduction to the student, with an introductory analysis and detailed notes on individual poems. For a provocative account of the post-war period, with an excellent bibliography, see Hermann Korte, *Geschichte der deutschen Lyrik seit 1945* (Stuttgart: Metzler, 1989). In the GDR, the best poetry defied the officially prescribed themes of socialist endeavour to find its own voice. Peter Geist's stimulating anthology *Ein Molotow-Cocktail auf Fremder Bettkante: Lyrik der siebziger/achtziger Jahre von Dichtern aus der DDR. Ein Lesebuch* (Leipzig: Reclam, 1991) provides an excellent overview while Gerrit-Jan Berendse, *Die 'Sächsische Dichterschule'. Lyrik in der DDR der sechziger und siebziger Jahre* (Frankfurt/Main: Lang, 1990) is a pioneering study of one of the most innovative groups of GDR poets.

German unification in 1990 ended the division of Germany and confronted poets on both sides of the former German border with a new political and cultural agenda. An excellent anthology and first analysis of the new impulses is provided by Karl Otto Conrady (ed.), *Von einem Land und vom andern: Gedichte zur deutschen Wende 1989/90* (Leipzig: Suhrkamp, 1993).

MICHAEL PATTERSON *and*
MICHAEL HUXLEY

10

German drama, theatre and dance

The significance of Germany's contribution

One might imagine that a nation's lack of a strong tradition in the performing arts would inhibit its ability to develop exciting and internationally acclaimed achievements in theatre and dance in the modern period. However, in the case of Germany, it may be argued that it was precisely because of this lack of tradition that the conditions were created for innovation and experiment, so that over the last hundred years the German-speaking nations have excelled in theatre, dance, opera and dramatic literature, in both theory and practice, in ways that have been both adventurous and influential. The story of modern theatre could not be told without reference to Brecht, nor that of dance without mention of Laban, and these are merely the best-known names of the many practitioners who worked in German-speaking nations to transform the performing arts of this century.

Eighteenth-century Germany had no golden age of theatre to look back on, no Shakespeare, no Racine, no Calderón. The reasons for this were several: for centuries Germany had served as the battleground of Europe; the German language itself was held in low esteem; and, most importantly, Germany did not exist as a nation, comprising in fact several hundred kingdoms, dukedoms, bishoprics, etc., with no major cultural centre like London or Paris.

The result was that until the first half of the eighteenth century the primary manifestations of German theatre were, on the one hand, the travelling players performing their crude pieces in market squares and inn yards, and, on the other, the Schools Theatre of the Protestants and Jesuits, the latter written mainly in Latin, whose major function was the propagation of religious faith. In the eighteenth century attempts were made to establish a theatre for the Germans, principally by Gottsched (1700–66) in his slavish imitation of the French, and later and more importantly by Lessing (1729–81) in his recommendation to seek inspiration in Shakespeare. Lessing was also closely involved in the important but short-lived undertaking to establish a National Theatre, significantly in the Free Town of Hamburg (1767–9).

As the eighteenth century drew to a close and the nineteenth began, a new and vigorous theatre developed, initially at the many German-speaking courts, soon spreading to the commercial playhouses of the major towns, and represented now by the names of the leading classical dramatists: Goethe (1749–1832), Schiller (1759–1805) and Kleist (1777–1811) in Germany, and Grillparzer (1791–1872) in Austria.

By the 1830s German theatre had established itself as a major cultural force and as a rallying point for German nationhood, playhouses being the one public place where ordinary German citizens could congregate and debate issues or celebrate their past in their own language. This function of the theatre continues to the present day: in the final months of the German Democratic Republic, for example, as we shall see, theatres provided the political forums which contributed to the eventual collapse of the Communist regime.

Theatre of the common people

It was in the context of the growing success and commercialism of the German-language theatre of the early nineteenth century that a brilliant young medical student, Georg Büchner (1813–37), began to write plays. Although he died at the tragically young age of twenty-three, and the three plays he wrote were not performed until many years after his death, the impact of his writing on modern German theatre is inestimable. In particular, his seminal and unfinished play *Woyzeck* (1837) is paradigmatic of the special way in which German theatre has developed.

The piece is significant in two major respects. First, this story of a simple-minded soldier who murders his lover in a frenzy of jealous despair was the first play in European theatre in which working-class figures, speaking in dialect, are treated with complete seriousness (traditionally, they, and their outlandish speech, were regarded as subjects suitable only to comedy). Dubbed the 'first working-class tragedy', *Woyzeck* was a major step forward in the growing nineteenth-century trend towards realism, associated particularly with the so-called 'bourgeois tragedy' of Friedrich Hebbel (1813–63, e.g. *Maria Magdalena*, 1844), the writer believed by Ibsen to be a finer playwright than himself. This tendency towards realism was reinforced by the innovative productions of the Duke of Saxe-Meiningen's troupe, whose style, with their carefully rehearsed ensemble work and realistic props and costumes, was acknowledged by both André Antoine and Konstantin Stanislavsky as an important influence. This increasing concern with authenticity eventually led to the Naturalist movement, represented most significantly in the theatre by the founding in 1889 of Otto Brahm's *Freie Bühne* in Berlin, an institution modelled on Antoine's *Théâtre libre* in Paris and, like its model, devoted to the staging of the new naturalist writing. The leading exponent of this new drama was Gerhart Hauptmann (1862–1946), one of those primarily responsible for rescuing Büchner from obscurity. Hauptmann's play, *Die Weber* (The Weavers, 1892), which deals with the revolt by Silesian weavers against the depression of their wages as a result of the introduction of steam-looms, is significant in two major respects: first, it took, as had Büchner's *Woyzeck*, the innovative step of treating a serious theme in dialect; secondly, there is no individual principal character as the focus of the action; the community of weavers is the collective 'hero' of the play. In a similar vein, in his 'Berlin tragedy' *Die Ratten* (The Rats, 1911), there is the statement: 'Before art, as before the law, all men are equal.'[1] This engagement with working-class life became much more firmly established in German theatre than was the case generally in Europe (the other exception – for obvious reasons – was Russia, as, for example, in Gorky's *Lower Depths* of 1902). In Britain the identification of theatre with the middle classes, and in France the continuing stranglehold of neo-classicism, militated against a similar exploration of proletarian problems. D. H. Lawrence and Zola formed two important exceptions, but significantly both are now better remembered as novelists.

This special strain in the development of German theatre is most strongly represented in the twentieth century by the political theatre of Erwin Piscator (1893–1966) and Bertolt Brecht (1898–1956). In the so-called 'New Sobriety' of the 1920s, Piscator often employed the new technology of the age, including photographic and cinematic back-projections, revolving sets and conveyor belts to present a left-wing view of contemporary society, as in productions like that of Paquet's *Sturmflut* (Tidal Wave, 1926), Toller's *Hoppla, wir leben!* (Hurray, We're Alive!, 1927), Alexei Tolstoy's *Rasputin* (1927), and Brod's and Heimann's *Die Abenteuer des guten Soldaten Schweik* (The Adventures of the Good Soldier Schweik,

1928). After the Second World War Piscator promoted documentary theatre, for example Rolf Hochhuth's *Der Stellvertreter* (The Representative, 1963), a controversial piece about the silence of Pope Pius XII during World War II about the Holocaust. For a while in the twenties one admittedly not very active member of the Piscator Collective was Bertolt Brecht, who was to emerge as the most influential figure of German theatre, arguably of world theatre, in this century.

Brecht's reputation rests not least on the fact that he excelled in three areas: as theatre practitioner, theatre theorist and as playwright (not to mention his considerable qualities as a poet). Unlike Artaud, for example, whose ideas have also had a powerful influence on the performing arts in this century, Brecht was able throughout his career to test and refine his ideas through successful practice, culminating in his directorship of the Berliner Ensemble from 1949 until his death in 1956. Unlike Stanislavsky, who often found himself in dispute with the author of the texts on which he worked, as was the case with Chekhov, Brecht was himself a major dramatist, and so could provide a continuous link from theory to dramatic writing to scenic practice.

As a theatre practitioner, especially through touring with the Berliner Ensemble, Brecht's staging techniques have influenced a whole generation of theatre designers, performers and especially directors, notably Peter Stein in Germany, Giorgio Strehler in Italy, Roger Planchon in France, and William Gaskill and Max Stafford-Clark in Britain. Clear, politically informed readings of texts, uncluttered set designs and a restrained and unemotional style of acting have become characteristic of theatre productions in post-war Europe, and much of this is due to the impact of Brecht.

As a theorist, Brecht is probably best known for propagating his notion of *Verfremdung*, which is usually and inadequately translated into English as 'alienation'. More properly, it means 'distantiation', that is, theatrical means intended not to involve the audience uncritically in the action of the play but to impel them to a fresh consideration of the issues and events presented before them. Whereas traditionally in post-Renaissance drama the spectator more or less passively observes the conflicts taking place on stage, the thrust of Brecht's ideas is to re-negotiate a new relationship between audience and dramatic action, whereby the spectator is challenged to make choices about what is observed on stage. This, within the confines of the conventional theatre context in which he was working, did not lead to actual intervention by the audience: it would have been inappropriate for a member of the audience to leap on to the stage and bar the way of Mother Courage as she trundles off with her cart. However, Brecht went some way towards establishing this new role for the audience in the staging of his *Lehrstücke* ('teaching plays'): so, for example, at the premiere of *Die Maßnahme* (The Measures Taken) in 1930, the Control Chorus was performed by 3,000 Berlin workers singing in unison. This piece, Brecht declared just before his death, pointed most decisively forward to the future of theatre, and in papers found after his death he distinguished between the 'minor pedagogy', whose object was the transformation of the spectator from passive to active observer, and the 'major pedagogy', which would have enabled the actual participation of the audience. This latter impulse has been taken up particularly by the South American director Augusto Boal, who in his Forum Theatre invites the audience vocally to comment on and even change the course of the dramatic action.

As a playwright, Brecht's work has been characterised by a combination of political commitment and refined sensibility, an object lesson for the many playwrights who learned from his work that political propaganda does not have to possess the crude caricatures and unreasoned diatribes of the agit-prop political theatre in the 1920s and 30s. In his finest work, *Das Leben des Galileo Galilei* (The Life of Galileo, 1938), *Mutter Courage und ihre Kinder* (Mother Courage and her Children, 1939), *Der gute Mensch von Sezuan* (*The Good Person of Sezuan*, 1940) and *Der kaukasische Kreidekreis* (The Caucasian Chalk Circle, 1945), Brecht was to provide models of political debate within powerfully dramatic stories that were to affect the writing of a generation of playwrights: Peter Weiss (1916–82), Tankred Dorst (1925–), Peter Hacks (1928–), Volker Braun (1939–) and Heiner Müller (1929–95) in Germany; Max Frisch (1911–91) in Switzerland; Armand Gatti in France; John Arden, Edward Bond, John McGrath and David Hare in Britain.

While Brecht's work has tended to dominate the overtly political theatre, there also existed another modern German phenomenon of theatre about ordinary people. This was the *Volksstück* (literally 'people's play'), associated with the names of Marieluise Fleisser (1901–74), e.g. *Pioniere in Ingolstadt* (Pioneers in Ingolstadt, 1929) and Ödön von Horváth (1901–38), e.g. *Geschichten aus dem Wienerwald* (Tales from the Vienna Woods, 1931), and now with more recent writing for German theatre, ironically since the 1950s to some extent under the influence of English playwrights like Arnold Wesker, Harold Pinter and Edward Bond in his *Saved*. More

contemporary images of working-class life have been depicted by Martin
Sperr (1944–), e.g. *Jagdszenen aus Niederbayern* (Hunting Scenes from
Lower Bavaria, 1966), Rainer Werner Fassbinder (1945–82), probably better known for his films, e.g. *Bremer Freiheit* (Bremen Coffee, 1971), Franz
Xaver Kroetz (1946–), e.g. *Heimarbeit* (Homework, 1971), *Stallerhof*, 1972
and *Oberösterreich* (Morecambe, 1972) and Botho Strauss (1944–), e.g. *Groß
und Klein* (Great and Small, 1978).

Theatre of the visual image

The other major strain in modern German theatre, and one that can
already be seen in the irrational atmosphere and dream-like construction
of Büchner's *Woyzeck*, is that of experimentation and imagistic adventur-
ousness. Philosophically aligned more to the irrational tradition of
Schopenhauer and Nietzsche, this other strain was initially significantly
appropriated by the opera, notably in the powerful mythic works of Wagner. Wagner's programme was not only to offer aesthetic enjoyment and
intellectual stimulation but to re-create the sacredness of the theatre of
Ancient Greece by making Bayreuth virtually a centre of pilgrimage. He
wished to create the *Gesamtkunstwerk*, 'the total work of art', which would
bring together the elements of drama, music, dance and the visual arts in
one aesthetic whole. Neither of these aspirations could succeed against
the limited bourgeois perceptions of his audiences or against the weari-
ness of the theatrical conventions of the day. Something of the same
aspirations lived on in the short-lived and largely uninfluential parallel
movements at the turn of the century, the *Neuklassik* ('neo-classicism')
and the *Neuromantik* ('neo-romanticism'). The main exponent of the first
was Paul Ernst (1866–1933), whose mythical dramas have a certain affinity
with the poetic plays of W. B. Yeats, and the main representative of the
second was the Austrian poet Hugo von Hofmannsthal (1874–1929),
whose dramatic work significantly is now best remembered as operas
scored by Richard Strauss (e.g. *Elektra*, 1906, and *Der Rosenkavalier*, 1911).

The most vibrant manifestation of imagistic exploration occurred,
however, in German Expressionism. Indeed, German Expressionism
may well remain the last artistic movement in European culture to which
a whole generation of young writers, painters and musicians subscribed.
Its dramatic manifestations were propagated by the early German cinema, notably in films like *Das Kabinett des Dr. Caligari* (The Cabinet of Dr
Caligari, 1920), and so its impact on European culture was greater than its

brief life-span might otherwise suggest; for Expressionism in German drama lasted only from 1913 to the early 1920s and in terms of theatre practice for an even shorter period, from 1917 to about 1923.

There had been significant forerunners in this major breach with naturalism, both within and outside German-speaking countries. Strindberg's dream and fantasy plays like *A Dream Play* (1902) and *The Ghost Sonata* (1907) were widely performed in Germany (1,035 performances of twenty-four of his plays between 1913 and 1915 alone) and proved hugely influential. In his Preface to *A Dream Play* Strindberg proposed a completely new approach to the theatre, an approach which was to characterise the changed view of Expressionist drama:

> In this dream play the author has ... attempted to imitate the inconsequent yet transparently logical shape of a dream ... a mixture of memories, experiences, incongruities and improvisations. The characters split, double, multiply, evaporate, condense, disperse, assemble.[2]

Character was no longer based on a nineteenth-century view of the individual – that which cannot be divided – but was seen in a process of flux, as in a dream. The world no longer seemed coherently structured, but randomly assembled. In the sciences Heisenberg's Uncertainty Principle and Einstein's Theory of Relativity made inroads into the old certainties. In politics, Europe was careering towards the blood-bath of the Great War. Nietzsche had proclaimed the death of God. Modernism had dawned.

In Germany Büchner, in this respect too, had anticipated the dream-like scenarios so characteristic of Expressionism, but it fell to another dramatist to prepare the ground for the Expressionist revolution: Frank Wedekind (1864–1918). Declared by the critic Rudolf Kayser to be the first Expressionist,[3] Wedekind expressed his dismay at what he regarded as the trivial banality of Naturalism and wrote powerful plays, often episodic and symbolic in nature. His *Frühlings Erwachen* (Spring Awakening, 1891), which contains scenes of masturbation, flagellation and homosexuality, was predictably banned for public performance for over a decade and a half (in Britain it could not be performed until the abolition of the Lord Chamberlain), but, once it had been seen in Reinhardt's staging in Berlin in 1906, was performed a further 660 times in the next twenty years. Almost everything about it prefigured Expressionism: the theme of youth in revolt against a repressive generation; its optimistic conclusion; the episodic structure; the grotesque caricatures, especially of figures of authority; and the symbolic figure of the Man-in-the-Mask in the last scene. Above all, the economy of language and the powerful imagery and variety of settings restored a theatricality which had tended to be submerged in the drawing-room settings of much nineteenth-century realist theatre.

Significantly, the next two major milestones on the path to Expressionist theatre were the work of two painters, Oskar Kokoschka and Wassily Kandinsky. Kokoschka's work, *Mörder Hoffnung der Frauen* (Murderer Hope of Womankind), a mythic struggle between a male and female warrior, was first performed in Vienna in 1909. It is interesting not least because the piece can be understood only by reference to the stage-directions: the dialogue consists in the main of ecstatic shouts, which remain meaningless without the accompanying action on stage. Similarly, Kandinsky's *Der gelbe Klang* (Yellow Sound), written 1909–10 but never staged at the time, is a deliberate attempt, as the title suggests, to bring together elements of colour, sound and movement. Again, language, with its implied assertion of coherence and meaning, becomes secondary, and theatre becomes almost indistinguishable from dance.

A similar concern with the primacy of the visual image became characteristic also of the best theatre practice in the early years of the century, notably in the work of Max Reinhardt. Reinhardt (1873–1943) was one of the most prolific directors of the twentieth century, who, partly because he never theorised extensively about his work, partly because the colossal range of his work prevented him from being identified with a particular style, has attracted less attention than he deserves. His contribution was considerable however: he worked with first-rate artists and designers, transforming stage-sets from banal living-rooms or painted backdrops into works of art; he reintroduced into the repertoire lively productions of Greek tragedies and medieval plays, displaying a sure hand in the directing of crowds that would become a feature of the Expressionist theatre; he blew the dust off Shakespeare and created a 'real' forest on a revolving stage for his production of *A Midsummer Night's Dream* in 1905. Above all, he encouraged new talent, both in actors and playwrights, even when, as was the case with Expressionist drama, he was not wholly in sympathy with it.

When we turn to Expressionism proper we find that, while the dramatists and the theatre they worked for continued to retain a strong visual element, there was an intoxication with language and a desire to communicate that militated against the relegation of dialogue to a secondary role. Except in the so-called 'telegram style' of a writer like August Stramm (1874–1915), the scripts of Expressionist plays are often quite wordy. So in the works of the major exponents, e.g. Georg Kaiser (1878–1945) and Ernst Toller (1893–1939), one finds, interspersed between the staccato utterances, lengthy speeches by the main characters. Nevertheless, the richness and variety of the visual elements remain the most distinguishing and compelling feature of Expressionist theatre. For example, Kaiser's *Von morgens bis mitternachts* (From Morn to Midnight, 1912) moves from a bank to a hotel room, then to a snow-covered landscape and the protagonist's home, finally to a cycle-race stadium, a nightclub and a Salvation Army hall, each offering exciting possibilities for stage-design in a way that makes the limited scenarios of most modern French and English drama seem cautious and bland in comparison. These visual strengths and freedoms of German Expressionism, which influenced the cinema (e.g. Fritz Lang's *Metropolis*, 1926, owed much to Georg Kaiser's *Gas* of 1917), were to characterise German theatre for the rest of the century. Thus the bold experiments of Piscator and the scenic variety of Brecht's plays would have been unthinkable without the Expressionist precedent. In the latter half of the century, alongside pieces about the common people, there have been pieces which offer theatrical excitement rare outside Germany. Some examples will suffice: Peter Weiss's monumental piece set in a lunatic asylum and depicting events of the French Revolution, which appeared under the magnificently unwieldy title, *Die Verfolgung und Ermordung Jean Paul Marats dargestellt durch die Schauspielgruppe des Hospizes zu Charenton unter Anleitung des Herrn de Sade* (The Persecution and Assassination of Jean Paul Marat as Performed by the Inmates of the Asylum of Charenton under the Direction of the Marquis de Sade, usually abbreviated to *The Marat/Sade*, 1964); Tankred Dorst's epic account of Ernst Toller's involvement in the attempt to set up a Soviet Republic in Munich in 1919, entitled *Toller* (1968); Peter Stein's staging of Ibsen's *Peer Gynt* over two evenings in a Berlin exhibition hall in 1971 and of Eugene O'Neill's *The Hairy Ape* in 1986; or, more recently, the seven-and-a-half hour performance of Heiner Müller's *Hamlet-Maschine* at the Deutsches Theater in Berlin in 1990.

Less spectacular, but also deriving from the distortions of Expressionism, have been the grotesque creations of the Swiss playwright, Friedrich Dürrenmatt (1921–90), and of the Austrian writer, Peter Handke (1942–). The best known of Dürrenmatt's plays, and possibly the most widely performed post-war drama in German, is *Der Besuch der alten Dame* (The Visit,

1955). The central figure is an ageing, grotesque millionairess, most of her body parts artificial, who revisits her home town in order to wreak revenge on the man who had wronged her in her youth. By using her wealth she manages to bribe the whole community into hounding her victim to his death. *Die Physiker* (The Physicists) of 1961 presents an equally bleak picture: three supposedly mad inmates of a mental hospital turn out to be a nuclear physicist, guarding the terrible discovery of nuclear destruction, and two rival secret agents trying to gain access to this discovery. They are all three outsmarted by the Director of the hospital, who turns out to be genuinely mad and will use the discovery to threaten the world with destruction. More experimental were the plays of Peter Handke, whose two most significant early pieces of 'speech-theatre', *Publikumsbeschimpfung* (Offending the Audience) and *Selbstbezichtigung* (Self-Accusation), both performed for the first time in 1966, question and challenge the conventions of theatre by presenting a bare stage with 'speakers' uttering repetitive and disjointed pronouncements and questions – plays without plot, character or, in any conventional sense, dialogue. There shortly followed his best-known piece, *Kaspar* (1968), based on an historical figure, Kaspar Hauser, who supposedly spent the first sixteen years of his life in complete isolation, able, on being first discovered, to speak only one sentence. Handke's Kaspar is a clown-like figure, whose original sentence is destroyed by the intervention of three voices, and who is then gradually initiated into the use of language. As Kaspar's confidence grows, he is joined by other Kaspars, but discovers that the language that he has been taught is arbitrary and without meaning; his utterances become more and more disjointed until his final pronouncement: 'I am I only by chance.'[4] It is perhaps not wholly surprising that Handke, like Dürrenmatt, has tended to write less and less for the public medium of the theatre and has retreated into the more personal utterances of prose writing.

This scepticism about language and the resultant emphasis on the visual, which has characterised so much of twentieth-century German theatre, provided a context for an expressive public art-form that dispensed with words altogether: that of dance.

German early modern dance and '*Tanztheater*'

Dance, the most ephemeral of arts, can leave the most lasting images. Fourteen masked figures, dressed in tail coats, gentlemen in black, gesticulate across a table covered in green baize, centre stage. Their discussions, becoming heated, drive them into action; gesticulations develop into physical threats until finally guns are drawn. They seem familiar, eternal gamblers with people's lives; their formal antics but a prelude to the appearance of the character who really matters, death. When he appears he does so as a man, one whose blunt, four-square stance, solid features and gestures can be both ruthless and gentle. He reminds you of a bull, of Moloch, a destroyer, as this is indeed a dance of death. Kurt Jooss's dance-drama *Der Grüne Tisch* (The Green Table) endures in performance as well as in the memory. Since its triumphant premiere in 1932 at Rolf de Maré's Choreographic Competition, Théâtre des Champs Elysées, Paris, where it won first prize, it has been performed throughout the world and has been staged by more dance companies than any other work in the modern repertory.[5] Yet it is virtually the only pre-war example of European early modern dance to have survived. This is no accident, for it distils the visual and theatre languages of the time and is the first major dance sequence on the tragedy of war.

Exactly fifty years later there is a stage covered in pink and white carnations. A group of men in coloured dresses frolic. Their hops, jumps, leaps are childlike, innocent. These rabbits are carefree. Their play is joyful, but short-lived. A man in black looks on. He is big, blunt, four-square, with solid features. He stands for no nonsense, chases the innocents. Pina Bausch's *Nelken* (Carnations, first performed 30 December 1982) is one of many of her works where the stage is literally transformed into another place for her dancers: in *1980* the stage is turfed, in *Arien* covered in water, in *Frühlingsopfer* earth. *Nelken* too survives in repertory and serves as a reminder of another era now past.

Jooss (1901–79) and Bausch (1940–) capture the spirit of the time and place in which they worked. The Germany that is at the root of their choreography has changed in the intervening half century. German modern dance has changed: what Jooss described as a dance-drama has developed into a new performance form in the work of Bausch and her contemporaries – often called *Tanztheater*. The ability of German choreographers working within this genre has endured. They distil narrative and expression in a way that distinguishes German modern dance as one of the definitive forms of modern culture. The lineage from Jooss to Bausch is clear. She was one of his later pupils who danced the role of the old woman in his 1960s Folkwang Ballet production of *Der Grüne Tisch*.[6] However, they also belong to different periods and this account takes them as the twin focuses for an exploration of the milieu out of which they distilled their particular views of the world.

The success of 1932 marked the international recognition of early European modern dance yet heralded its downfall. The new form of dance had developed on both sides of the Atlantic in the first two decades of the century. The nature of the form was remarked on by the eminent American critic, John Martin, in his definitive 1933 account of *The Modern Dance*,[7] where he characterised it as a phenomenon that arose in America *and* Europe. In central Europe, and especially in Germany, new ideas about dance had been pioneered before the First World War in choreographic experiments, especially those of Rudolf Laban (1879–1958) in Munich and Émile Jaques-Dalcroze (1865–1950) in Hellerau, Dresden. These pioneers attracted aspirant dancers to their studios and in 1913 one of them, Mary Wigman (1886–1973), made her debut. The new dance's ambassador marked out a new territory for women with a shockingly expressive solo of unrestrained power and lust, *Hexentanz* (Witchdance, 1913). Modern dance was resolutely of the twentieth century and, as such, its pioneers were part of modernity's early strivings: Adolphe Appia's stage designs were first realised for Jaques-Dalcroze's demonstrations of his Eurhythmics in 1912 and 1913; Laban's dancers performed in Dada soirées at the Cabaret Voltaire in Zurich from 1916. Another of its pioneers, Oskar Schlemmer (1888–1943), led the Stage Workshop and the choreographic experiments at the newly formed Bauhaus in Weimar, his choreography heralding a new approach with *Triadisches Ballett* (Triadic Ballet, 1922). Mary Wigman sums up how this excitement carried over into the twenties:

> Everything seemed young and novel, as if nothing had been done before. Extreme contrasts collided, controversies were brought to a head, there was constantly a meeting of minds which bore the most wonderful results. What all of them had in common was the wrestling for a personal message and its artistic expression of universality.[8]

The dancers gave it many names but most settled on either *Moderner Tanz* or *Ausdruckstanz*. Of the latter Koegler, in his definitive essay, 'Dance under the Swastika', points out that it was a dance of expression, not expressionist dance: that is to say, broader in concern than the expressionist theatre with which it was contemporary and with which it had links.[9] Two of the new dancers to emerge in the twenties, Harald Kreutzberg (1902–68) and Kurt Jooss, created roles in productions of expressionist plays – the former in Oskar Kokoschka's *Mörder Hoffnung der*

Frauen, the latter in Georg Kaiser's *Europa*, drawing on this role when creating 'death' in *Der Grüne Tisch*.[10] These dancers, Wigman, Laban and their other pupils carried all before them in the late twenties until the new modern dance was acknowledged as the dominant form.

Much of the German modern dance of the twenties and early thirties dealt with the modern condition. For Wigman this provided an opportunity to deal with a new emotional range both in choreography and performance: thus *Totentanz* (Dance of Death, 1926), *Totenmal* (Call of the Dead, 1930), *Das Opfer* (Sacrifice, 1931) contrasting with the ecstatic lyricism of her solo cycle *Schwingende Landschaft* (Shifting Landscape) of 1929, which included *Sommerlicher Tanz* (Summer Dance), *Pastorale* (Pastoral) and *Festlicher Rhythmus* (Festive Rhythm).

Jooss's *Der Grüne Tisch* and *Großstadt* (The Big City, 1932) marked the culmination of the many strands that modern dance was developing: a daring use of narrative; sophisticated character development based on Laban's principles of *Eukinetics*; an acknowledgement of Expressionism in the theatre; a cohesive technical vocabulary. *Der Grüne Tisch* was modernist and anti-war, 'a moving eternalisation of emotion' and 'a gem of formal artistry', as John Martin said in the very year that he began to define modern dance.[11] It was precisely these characteristics and Jooss's defence of his Jewish composer and dancers that led to his exile under the Third Reich in 1933. During the thirties the life blood of modernism in central European dance ebbed away. Whilst not all dancers followed Jooss and his company out of the country, those who remained, including Wigman, compromised their modernism in deference to their country.[12]

It was not until the 1970s that German modern dance fully recovered from Nazism and the war that it led to. Ballet in Germany underwent a much-needed revival in the 1960s, especially through the work of John Cranko (1927–73) and the highly acclaimed Stuttgart Ballet which put the country back on the international ballet map. The *Tanztheater*[13] that has emerged in Germany in the last three decades of the century has many exponents, most of whom studied with the early moderns Jooss, Wigman, Cébron, Chladeck or Palucca. They include Reinhild Hoffmann (1943–) in Bremen and Bochum; Johann Kresnick (1939–) in Bremen and Heidelberg; Susanne Linke (1944–) in Essen; Rosamund Gilmore and Vivienne Newport (the other major innovator, outside the European lineage, is William Forsythe (1949–) at the Frankfurt Ballet). However, it is the town of Wuppertal that has gained international recognition for the innovations of Pina Bausch.

Bausch's *Nelken* (1982), the second of the two dances that begin this essay, was made nine years after she was appointed Director of the Wuppertal Dance Theatre. Her first choreography had been for Jooss's Folkwang Ballet in nearby Essen, where she had performed with company members that included Linke and Newport. In 1971 she had her first commission from the Wuppertal Theatre for *Aktionen für Tänzer* (Actions for Dancers) and this piece for twelve dancers was danced there and on tour by the Folkwang Ballet. It looked quite different from other work of the time: her dancers performed flat out on a stage stripped of decoration in choreography that was frenetic, reckless, committed, devoid of traditional theatrical trappings and relentless.

In the following decade she was to choreograph many of her signature works including *Frühlingsopfer* (The Rite of Spring, 1975), *Blaubart* (Bluebeard, 1977), *Café Müller* (1978) and *1980 – Ein Stück von Pina Bausch* (1980 – A Piece by Pina Bausch, 1980). *1980* was made in the months following the death of her companion, the stage designer and performer Rolf Borzik. He had collaborated with her since her appointment at Wuppertal and had been responsible for the realisation of the seminal set for *Café Müller*. The wooden café chairs that clutter the stage in this autobiographical work were moved at breakneck speed by Borzik himself, as Bausch and the other dancers attempted to hold on to each other, both literally and metaphorically.

In her work Bausch presents 'people as they really are', offering interesting parallels with the *Volksstück* discussed above. Indeed, Servos likens her approach to Brecht's and reminds the reader that it was the latter who first employed this phrase when writing of choreography.[14] *Tanztheater* is characteristically large-scale (either theatrically or in length), presenting real people, real events and real emotions. The situations that explore the intimacies of life also reflect how it is socially constructed, especially through the analysis and portrayal of gender. These are facilitated by formal means that stress discontinuity, deconstruction and collage. Servos has characterised her work as a return to a 'language of the body', whilst Schmidt emphasises the 'renewal of the human image'. Bausch is unquestionably the main figure in late twentieth century German dance, her stature being comparable to that of Heiner Müller in theatre.

The relationship between *Ausdruckstanz* and *Tanztheater*, between the pre-war generation of Wigman and Jooss and a generation brought up in a divided Germany, is contested. Bausch's early German supporters, notably Norbert Servos, Jochen Schmidt and Hedwig Müller, at first argued strongly for direct historical and aesthetic continuity between the two,[15] whilst contending that *Tanztheater* has reclaimed the core of *Ausdruckstanz* and reconstructed it within a new theatrical framework that restates values, especially gender values, that were lost to Nazism. Koegler is more equivocal, suggesting that *Ausdruckstanz* in 1933 was a spent force and was therefore easily taken over and destroyed.[16] In her analysis of Wigman's work, Susan Manning sets out a challenge to the German historians, arguing that the disjuncture caused by Nazism means that the later *Tanztheater* has to be read in association with this part of its past too.[17] Schmidt later contended that

> above all dance theater distances itself from the ideology of expressionist dance that went along so blithely with the Nazi regime. Dance theater is truly a radical democratic movement, and I think that it can deal with the historical experience of expressionist dance. They know exactly what happened there and don't want it back again.[18]

The remarkable thing about Kurt Jooss is that he did not need such hindsight. *Der Grüne Tisch* stands as a testimony to those who offered a critique of war and nationalism at the onset of a regime that epitomised them.

German theatre and dance as cultural manifestations

The first British theatre-building, which went by the surprisingly uninventive name of 'The Theatre', was a commercial enterprise by James Burbage in 1576. In addition to the not wholly reliable noble and royal patronage he enjoyed, Shakespeare had to run his theatre at a profit. To this day in Britain and the United States, the performing arts are regarded primarily as entertainment; we speak of 'show-business' (a word that has no equivalent in German), and in Britain Value Added Tax will be charged on a ticket to watch a performance of *Hamlet*, while one can buy the text in a bookshop without paying a penny to the government.

The first German theatre-buildings were created and paid for by the courts: they represented a necessary part of cultured life, initially accessible only to the nobility and a select group of the bourgeoisie. Later the court theatres opened their doors wider, and municipal theatres were set up in the larger towns, and many commercial enterprises were established to undertake the management of theatres. However, the notion that theatre represented culture rather than entertainment has been preserved in Germany to this day.

This can be seen first by the location of most German theatres. Apart from exceptions like the Royal National Theatre in London, British theatres are usually set in a row of banks, offices and shops, distinguishable only by their neon signs and immodest advertising hoardings. In Germany most theatres are set apart in their own grounds, with imposing entrances, like 'majestic temples to the Muses', to borrow Peter Fischer's phrase.[19] If one were to approach the theatre, one would soon discover that, far from having just one production on offer to choose from, there was a whole variety during the week, with a different show being performed each evening. These might range from conventional theatre to opera and to dance; from a Greek tragedy to an Ayckbourn farce, from a piece by Schiller to a dance performance of a contemporary work, from Samuel Beckett to a Mozart opera. Germans expect their theatres to fulfil a library function, providing them with a range of experience from the entire European theatrical heritage. Many will buy season tickets through long-established organisations like the *Volksbühne* and will stolidly see every production in the repertoire, rather in the spirit of a pious church-goer, whose regular attendance witnesses to their desire for spiritual succour rather than to their hope of being well entertained.

This repertory system, common to most German theatres, places colossal financial and personnel demands on the management. To dismantle and erect a new set each evening, to provide and store costumes and props, to find sufficient rehearsal space, all cost enormous amounts. To cast so many different productions adequately requires a large standing ensemble of actors, directors, musicians and possibly dancers, in place of the hire and fire system prevalent in Britain and the USA. The result is that nearly all theatres in German-speaking countries are dependent on subsidies that are the envy of theatre-practitioners in the rest of the world. The range and often the excellence of both theatre and dance in Germany are due in great measure to the protection of long-standing subsidies, which they have enjoyed at least since the Weimar Republic in the 1920s. State and municipal subsidies to German theatres now stand at about seven times the amount of public funding the United States provides for all the arts, and the Berlin Opera House alone receives almost as much as the British Arts Council has at its disposal for all the theatres it supports. The German theatre-goer pays normally about a third of the actual economic cost of a theatre ticket, and in the former German Democratic Republic it was only about a tenth. As an indicator of the economic power of the German theatre, the director Peter Stein, who had helped to make West Berlin one of the major arts centres of Europe, had only to threaten to take his ensemble to another city, for the West Berlin Senate to approve the building of a luxurious new building which was to cost over DM 100 million.

Once inside the theatre, the theatre-goer will have a very different experience from that of their British counterpart. In place of the crowded foyer and appropriately named crush-bar of the typical English theatre, one will see large, candelabra-lit halls and corridors, in which the audience will parade in the intervals. The programme that is purchased will reveal something more than which firm supplied the cigarettes and stockings and which drama school the leading lady attended. The German programme, prepared by a full-time *Dramaturg*, will normally provide full documentation for the production, with historical background, critical essays and directorial commentary.

Once the curtain opens, the stage will usually be seen to be much larger than in a British theatre, the sets more opulent, the lighting more complex. The choice of play will not have been limited by an 'economic' size of cast, and the actors will perform with intelligence and discipline but will often lack that winning presence of their Anglo-Saxon counterparts, whose future livelihood, after all, depends on their need to please.

Because the theatre has traditionally been regarded as a public and cultural institution, its importance in the cultural life of Germany has been much more significant than in most other countries. Predictably, during the Third Reich theatres and theatre organisations (like the former *Volksbühne*) came under the centralised control of Goebbels Ministry of Propaganda. On 1 September 1944 all theatres were closed as a contribution to the war effort, a contrast to Britain, where theatres were being encouraged to boost the nation's morale. The difference is marked: to the German mind, the pressing needs of the war meant that the intellectual reflection associated with theatre-going was a luxury inappropriate to the urgent demands of defending the Fatherland; to the British, the chance to have fun, sing a song and see some colourful spectacle represented a brief respite from the misery of warfare.

After the war the theatre was again employed to reinforce or to challenge social attitudes. In the West, official attitudes were sometimes reflected by theatre managements, as in the 'Brecht boycott' after the building of the Berlin Wall in 1961. Equally often, especially after 1968, progressive theatre managements staged pieces which challenged western orthodoxy (notably pieces like Peter Weiss's *Vietnam-Discourse* of 1968).

In East Germany, despite the predictably more cautious policy of theatre managements and their inability to stage pieces that would attract official disapproval, the theatre, especially in the 1980s, fulfilled the function of being the debating chamber for political ideas. As the actor Ulrich Mühe summed it up: 'a kind of unspoken understanding between public and performers grew up over the years about the intentions of a production.'[20]

This provocative function of the theatre in the former German Democratic Republic bears witness to the fact that the theatre in Germany has remained a vital force in society. It was, in part at least, thanks to the 'unspoken understanding' of which Mühe speaks, that the East German theatres contributed to the removal of the Berlin Wall and the collapse of the Communist regime. So, for example, Christoph Hein's play *Die Ritter der Tafelrunde* (The Knights of the Round Table), which was premiered in Dresden in 1989, managed by using the thin disguise of its setting in the court of King Arthur to depict a government on the point of collapse. In a final confrontation with his father, Mordreth tells the old King Arthur: 'It is your kingdom, father. You and your knights made it. I don't want it ... All this here, I don't want it.'[21] Despite the fact that the East German press reviewed the piece as though it were a purely historical drama, the audience had no difficulty in seeing the parallels with their own situation.

Apart from the churches, theatres in the GDR provided the only public forums for political debate, and so it was perhaps unsurprising that it was theatre workers in Berlin who organised the first officially sanctioned protest demonstration in East Berlin on 4 November 1989. Within days the Wall had fallen, both literally and metaphorically.

Without such an obvious role to play as in the dying days of the GDR, and having to cope with the financial pressures of economic recession, theatre and dance in today's Germany are struggling to maintain their place at the centre of German culture. While theatres are forced to close or merge, especially in the new *Bundesländer,* and for the first time actors and other theatre workers face uncertain futures, it is easy to be pessimistic about the continuing significance of the performing arts in Germany. What one can say with some confidence is that they will continue to be supported by public money to a much greater extent than in any other nation and that they will repay this generosity by remaining not only sources of aesthetic pleasure but a focus for expressing the concerns of the society that funds them.

NOTES

1. Gerhart Hauptmann, *Sämtliche Werke*, Centenar-Ausgabe, ed. Hans-Egon Hass, Berlin: Propyläen, 1965, II, p. 778.

2. August Strindberg, *The Plays*, trans. Michael Meyer, London: Secker & Warburg, 1975, II, p. 553.

3. Rudolf Kayser, 'Das neue Drama', *Das junge Deutschland*, Berlin: Deutsches Theater, 1918, p. 139.

4. Peter Handke, *Kaspar*, Frankfurt/Main: Suhrkamp, 1968, p. 101.

5. Over 30 international productions since it was restaged at the Bayerische Staatsoper, Munich, 1964: see Anna and Hermann Markaard, *Kurt Jooss: Life and Work*, Cologne: Ballett Bühnen, 1985.

6. A version for the BBC, filmed in 1966, still survives.

7. John Martin, *The Modern Dance*, New York: A. S. Barnes, 1933, republished New York: Dance Horizons, 1965.

8. Mary Wigman in *The Mary Wigman Book: Her Writings Edited and Translated*, ed. Walter Sorrell, Middletown: Wesleyan University Press, 1975, p. 54.

9. Manfred Kuxdorf gives an interesting analysis, 'Expressionism and dance: a literary perspective' in *Expressionism Reassessed*, eds. Shulamith Behr, David Fanning and Douglas Jarman, Manchester: Manchester University Press, 1993.

10. Unpublished interview with the author, 1978: see also Michael Huxley and Kurt Jooss, 'The Green Table – a Dance of Death: Kurt Jooss in Interview', *Ballet International* no. 8/9, 1982.

11. John Martin reviewed *Der Grüne Tisch*, 'The dance: war satire', *The New York Times*, 2 October, 1932, p. 8, in the same year that he delivered lectures which formed his defining text *The Modern Dance*.

12. For a broader consideration of the body and Nazism see Wilfried van der Will, 'The Body and the Body Politic as Symptom and Metaphor in the Transition of German Culture to National Socialism' in *The Nazification of Art*, eds. Brandon Taylor and Wilfried van der Will, Winchester: The Winchester Press, 1990.

13. As with *Ausdruckstanz*, direct translation loses the force of the original and 'dance theatre' has other less culturally specific meanings.

14. Norbert Servos, *Pina Bausch – Wuppertal Dance Theatre or the Art of Training a Goldfish*, Cologne: Ballett Bühnen, 1984, p. 21.

15. See Hedwig Müller, *Mary Wigman*, Cologne: Ballett Bühnen, 1986, Norbert Servos, *Pina Bausch*, and Norbert Servos, 'Whether to resist or conform: *Ausdruckstanz* then, and now?' *Ballet International* no. 1, 1987, pp. 18–21.

16. Koegler restates this in a sympathetic review of Manning's book, 'Coming to terms with Germany's past – in American', *Ballet International/Tanz Aktuell*, no. 5, 1994, p. 48.

17. Susan Manning makes this case in detail in *Ecstasy and the Demon: Feminism and Nationalism in the Dances of Mary Wigman*, Los Angeles: University of California Press, 1993.

18. Jochen Schmidt, 'From Isadora to Pina: the renewal of the human image in dance', *Ballet International/ Tanz Aktuell*, no. 5, 1994, pp. 34–6 (in an issue on twenty years of Wuppertal Dance Theatre).

19. Peter Fischer, 'Doing princely sums – structure and subsidy', *The German Theatre*, ed. R. Hayman, London: Wolff, 1975, p. 219.

20. *Theater heute*, December 1989, p. 6.

21. *Theater heute*, July 1989, p. 34.

FURTHER READING

There is a substantial literature on drama and theatre in Germany. For development in the early part of the twentieth century see Michael Patterson, *The Revolution in German Theatre 1900–1933* (London: Routledge & Kegan Paul, 1981) and John Willett, *The Theatre of the Weimar Republic* (New York: Holmes & Meier, 1988). The story is taken into the post-war period by Michael Patterson, *German Theatre Today: Post-War Theatre in West and East Germany* (London: Pitman, 1976) and W. G. Sebald, *A Radical Stage: Theatre in Germany in the 1970s and 1980s* (Oxford: Berg, 1988).

Drama as a genre is the focus of Christopher D. Innes, *Modern German Drama, a Study of Form* (Cambridge University Press, 1979) while two collective volumes from the 1970s concentrate on the function of the theatre in German culture and the diversity of performance: Ronald Hayman (ed.), *The German Theatre. A Symposium* (London: Wolff, 1975) and Roman Clemens and Siegfried Melchinger (eds.), *Theatre on the German Speaking Stage* (Munich: Goethe Institute, 1971). The recent collection of essays by Derek Lewis and John R. P. McKenzie (eds.), *The New Germany: Social, Political and Cultural Challenges of Unification* (Exeter: Exeter University Press, 1995) places studies of contemporary theatre and drama in a broader cultural and social context.

On German dance theatre, the best works concentrate on leading personalities. See in particular Susan Walther (ed.), *The Dance of Death: Kurt Jooss and the Weimar Years*, Choreography and Dance vol. VII, (Yverdon: Harwood, 1994) and Anna and Hermann Markaard, *Kurt Jooss: Life and Work* (Cologne: Ballett Bühnen, 1985); Mary Wigman is the theme in Susan Manning, *Ecstasy and the Demon: Feminism and Nationalism in the Dances of Mary Wigman* (Los Angeles: University of California Press, 1993) and Walter Sorrell (ed.), *The Mary Wigman Book: Her Writings Edited and Translated* (Middletown: Wesleyan University Press, 1975), while Norbert Servos, *Pina Bausch – Wuppertal Dance Theatre or the Art of Training a Goldfish* (Cologne: Ballett Bühnen, 1984) combines a review of contemporary dance with an appreciation of the contribution made by Pina Bausch to its development.

11
_____

Music in modern German culture

Arguably one of the most conspicuous leitmotifs running through
German cultural history is the degree to which music has assumed a role
of national significance far exceeding that in any other European country.
An obvious starting-point for explaining such a phenomenon would be
the almost unbroken legacy of major German-speaking composers who
have exercised a lasting international influence over musical developments over the past 200 years. But other factors have proved equally vital
to the all-pervasive influence of music. Consider, for example, the multiplicity of opera houses and orchestras (something in the region of 150 at
the present time) that have existed in each major provincial and metropolitan centre since the nineteenth century, or the unparalleled opportunities that Germany has offered for music education, drawing students from
all over the world. Then one must take into account the strong musicolog-
ical traditions in German-speaking countries which have provided the
fundamental principles for almost all musical scholarship of recent years.
In statistical terms, this preoccupation with musical analysis, research
and theory has been exemplified by a much greater number of specialised
periodicals devoted to music than in any other country.[1] It is hardly surprising that throughout its history, writings on music have often
embraced wider philosophical and political concepts to the extent that
musical polemics, in particular the controversy surrounding modernism
and music, were invariably transformed into issues of national concern.

Modernism in the nineteenth century

In the mid-nineteenth century, the central debate of musical modernism
was conducted between the proponents of *Zukunftsmusik* (Music of the

Future), as represented by the composers Richard Wagner and Franz Liszt, and those opposed to their ideas, principally the composer Johannes Brahms (1833–97), the violinist/composer Joseph Joachim (1831–1907) and the Viennese critic, Eduard Hanslick (1825–1904). In the broadest terms, Wagner and Liszt subscribed to the belief that the music of the future should be concerned with expressing poetic and quasi-philosophical concepts as manifested in the novel genres of music-drama and symphonic poem, whereas Brahms, Joachim and Hanslick argued that music was in essence an autonomous art-form. Rejecting the superimposition of programmatic concepts upon music, they desired the preservation of abstract genres exemplified in the sonata, symphony and quartet, thereby retaining classical principles of compositional technique.

Significantly, the dispute between supporters of both schools assumed national proportions, fuelled on the one side by the publication of the 'Manifesto against the New German Music' which appeared in the *Berliner Musik-Zeitung* in 1860 with the joint signatures of Brahms and Joachim, and Hanslick's regular vitriolic diatribes in the daily Viennese newspaper the *Neue Freie Presse*, and on the other by Wagner's autobiography *Mein Leben* (initially published privately between 1870 and 1881, though appearing posthumously in 1911 in an abridged version) and his numerous polemical essays, of which the anti-Semitic tract *Das Judenthum in der Musik* (Jewishness in Music, Leipzig, 1850, revised and expanded in 1869) was the most notorious. Battlegrounds were drawn up almost on geographical lines. For example, Leipzig – home to the internationally famous music conservatoire founded by Mendelssohn in the 1840s – remained a bastion of conservative musical thinking well into the twentieth century, whereas Weimar, where Liszt and later Richard Strauss were engaged as court composer and conductor respectively, provided the environment for musical experimentation.

Given such polarised musical attitudes, it would be all too easy to assume that the music of Wagner and Liszt reflects progressive tendencies, while that of Brahms remains deeply conservative. Yet all three composers can in different ways be regarded as prophets of modernism. Wagner's influence, of course, was paramount, the restless chromaticism and heightened eroticism of his music-drama *Tristan und Isolde* (1860) exercising a profound impact not only on the early works of Schönberg, but also on the musical language of many French composers, including Debussy. Equally prophetic of Schönberg is the opening theme of Liszt's *Faust Symphony* (1857), in which the twelve notes of the chromatic scale are stated one after the other without any perceptible tonal centre. Although Liszt's music never enjoyed the same widespread currency as that of Wagner, it is worth noting that the relentless experimentation of his late works from the 1880s goes even beyond Wagner in anticipating a number of musical developments that would become central to the early twentieth century.[2]

On the surface, Brahms's music represents the complete antithesis of everything Wagner and Liszt stood for. Rejecting both music-drama and symphonic poem, and steadfastly ignoring such technological advances as the invention of valved brass instruments in the late 1840s, Brahms remained loyal to the classical forms and the orchestra of Beethoven and Schubert's time. Yet it would be misleading to assume that Brahms's *Four Symphonies* (1876–84) are mere throwbacks to an earlier era. Direct comparison between Brahms's Symphonies and the *Three Symphonies* of the arch-conservative composer Max Bruch (1838–1920) illustrates the degree to which Brahms responded to the chromatic musical language of the New German School, and to its principles of motivic transformation, whereas Bruch was merely content to plough the musical furrow of Mendelssohn and Schumann. But perhaps more significant than this is Brahms's radical and somewhat destabilising use of rhythm, and his preoccupation with the structural potentials of small motivic cells, factors which were only proclaimed as innovatory many years after the composer's death in Schönberg's pioneering article, 'Brahms, the Progressive' (1933).

It is difficult to imagine that Brahms's contemporaries would ever have accepted Schönberg's controversial interpretation of the composer's historical position. Neither would they have regarded Brahms's reverence for the musical past as anything other than anachronistic. Yet this too represents another 'progressive' aspect of Brahms's outlook. Aside from his activities as composer, pianist and conductor, Brahms was also involved in ethnomusicological work, publishing a collection of German folk-songs near the end of his life. More significantly, he was a scholar serving as a consultant for a number of significant publishing projects, including the issue of the complete works of Händel, Schumann and Schubert, and editing a number of works from the Baroque and Classical eras. His transcriptions are remarkably free from the expressive baggage of nineteenth-century romantic performance practice, and as such anticipate many of the impeccable principles of editing adopted by German musicologists of the twentieth century.

Reclamation of Germany's musical heritage was but one manifestation of the burgeoning confidence in musical life that followed German unification in 1871. Other examples that deserve to be mentioned in this context are the opening in 1876 of the Bayreuth Festival which became the major forum for the performance of Wagner's stage works, drawing international audiences to the Bavarian town to the present day, and the formation of the Berlin Philharmonic Orchestra as a musical co-operative in 1887. The orchestra was soon to play a leading role in German musical life, and it became one of a number of similarly constituted ensembles in Germany's major cities to concentrate their attention purely on the symphonic repertoire – a practice which had previously been adopted, only intermittently, by numerous opera orchestras.

If concert-giving activities were considerably enhanced by the formation of new orchestras near the end of the century, composers also were to benefit from copyright laws introduced during this period. A further step towards promoting the general welfare of German composers was the establishment of the *Allgemeiner Deutscher Musikverein* (General German Music Association, ADMV) in 1861 under the aegis of Franz Liszt. The organisation, which held annual festivals of new music, was formed in order to 'improve musical conditions through the union of all parties and groups'[3] and it was to occupy a prominent and influential position in German musical life for the next seventy-five years.

Towards the tonal abyss, 1890–1918

Despite the utopian ideals of organisations such as the ADMV, the ideological rifts between the New German School and the devotees of Brahms persisted to the end of the nineteenth century, to the extent that they affected the aesthetic outlooks of the three most significant composers of the period, Richard Strauss (1864–1949), Gustav Mahler (1860–1911) and Max Reger (1873–1916). The case of Strauss is particularly interesting, since he began his career as a precocious imitator of Mendelssohn, Schumann and Brahms. But in the early 1880s Strauss 'went over to the other side', devoting most of the rest of his long career to the composition of orchestral tone-poems and large-scale operas. Mahler, better-known in his day as an outstanding conductor especially at the Vienna Opera from 1899 to 1907, remained loyal to the symphony, but his epic conception of the form, which in certain works (for example the Resurrection Symphony (1894) and the Third Symphony (1896)) required the introduction of solo singers and chorus, appeared closer to Wagnerian ideals. In comparison with Strauss and Mahler, Reger eschewed programme music and epic forms almost entirely, remaining loyal to the abstract forms favoured by Brahms.

Yet regardless of their contrasting aesthetic outlooks, all three composers contributed significantly towards expanding musical language at the turn of the century. Superficially, Strauss appeared the most daring, attaining international prominence much earlier with a sequence of orchestral tone-poems in the 1890s that in their orchestral virtuosity and in their quest for aural realism (for example, the bleating of sheep in *Don Quixote*, the battleground in *Ein Heldenleben* – A Hero's Life – or the intimate love-making in *Sinfonia Domestica*) outstripped all other contemporary programmatic works. By 1900 Strauss was considered the foremost representative of Germany's avant-garde, a position that was to be considerably enhanced by the proto-Expressionist and highly dissonant operas *Salome* (1905) and *Elektra* (1909).

While Strauss made a profound impact through the audacious nature of his harmonies, Mahler's music also strained the bounds of tonal stability at moments of emotional collapse. Yet his music proved controversial for very different reasons. One aspect of his work that aroused particular contention was his frequent recourse to musical irony, sometimes manifested through the disturbing juxtaposition of trivial and profound elements within a matter of bars. Opponents of Mahler often asserted that such features betrayed his Jewish origins – an argument that was frequently rehearsed during the Nazi era.

In comparison with Strauss and Mahler, Reger's aims must have appeared far more modest and his music, though harmonically adventurous, failed to secure the same level of international attention. Yet Reger's seminal position in twentieth-century German music was assured, not least for its neo-baroque orientation which in works such as the Sonatas for unaccompanied violin and the *Concerto in the Olden Style*, anticipate stylistic trends that were to become fashionable during the 1920s.

Because Mahler and Reger died before the great changes that took place in German musical life after the First World War, one can hardly speculate as to how their styles might have evolved through a different cultural environment. Yet it is highly likely that both would have followed Strauss in stepping back from the 'atonal precipice' – a practice reflected in Strauss's retreat into late nineteenth-century Viennese nostalgia in *Der Rosenkavalier* (1911) and irrelevant neo-Wagnerian myth in *Die Frau ohne Schatten* (The Woman Without a Shadow, 1919). In such works Strauss appeared to have alienated himself from the more radical developments in contemporary music. Having enthusiastically promoted the neo-Wagnerian chamber work *Verklärte Nacht* (Transfigured Night, 1899) and the sumptuously orchestrated symphonic poem *Pelléas et Mélisande* (1902) by Arnold Schönberg (1874–1951), Strauss repudiated the Austrian-born composer's subsequent forays into atonality in such compositions as the Expressionist monodrama *Erwartung* (Expectation, 1909), the *Five Orchestral Pieces* (1909), and the song-cycle *Pierrot Lunaire* – a work for voice and chamber ensemble, first performed in Berlin in 1912, which employs the technique of *Sprechstimme* – a gliding mixture of speech-song which replaces precise pitch.[4]

Strauss was equally disenchanted with the music of Ferruccio Busoni (1866–1924) – the Italian-born composer who followed Schönberg in pushing forward the boundaries of tonal experimentation. Resident in Berlin during the first decade of the twentieth century, Busoni occupied a significant position in the capital's musical life as a pedagogue, conductor and virtuoso pianist. Amongst his generation, Busoni was almost unique in relentlessly withstanding the overwhelming influence of Wagner, and his call for a return to classical ideals ('Young Classicism') was to be largely realised in the aftermath of the First World War. His book *Entwurf einer neuen Ästhetik der Tonkunst* (Draft of a New Aesthetics, 1908), which advocated the evolution of a system of 113 heptatonic modes and suggested the possibility of writing music in exotic scales and subchromatic intervals, caused a particular stir in musical circles where conservatives erroneously branded him a 'dangerous futurist'.

In a wider context, it is possible to argue that the extreme positions of Busoni and Schönberg mirrored the restless and unstable situation that gripped Europe in the years immediately preceding the outbreak of the First World War. While it may seem far-fetched to suggest that the music composers wrote at this time actually anticipated subsequent political events, the brutality of Schönberg's 'Vorgefühle' (Pre-Sentiments) from the *Five Orchestral Pieces*, or the relentless martial rhythms that dominate the outer movements of Mahler's Sixth Symphony (1903) and the third of the *Three Orchestral Pieces* (1913) of Alban Berg, seem to point inexorably to the destructive forces that would be unleashed by the forces of war.

When war actually broke out, German musical life did not experience an immediate haemorrhaging of activity. Although certain prestigious events such as the Bayreuth Festival were obliged to close, operatic activity in other centres continued much as before. Despite a growing lack of funds, some theatres were still prepared to promote new operas by less well-established composers. As examples, one can cite the premieres of *Mona Lisa* by Max von Schillings at Stuttgart and *Violanta* by the prodigiously gifted Erich Wolfgang Korngold in Munich. But the situation was less propitious for German composers with international reputations who became victim to enemy proscription and the consequent loss of earnings. The external political situation had wider ramifications, for the enforced removal of contemporary German music from concert programmes abroad was largely responsible for fracturing the predominant role Germany had occupied in European music over the past hundred years.

Isolated from its neighbours, Germany inevitably turned inwards. In some quarters, the desire to conserve national traditions had never seemed more urgent. It was an ideal expounded most eloquently in the musical legend *Palestrina* by Hans Pfitzner (1869–1949) which received its first performance in Munich in 1917. With its high moralistic agenda, the work aroused powerful endorsement from a number of influential figures, most notably the novelist Thomas Mann. The opera, constructed along Wagnerian principles, is based upon the apocryphal story of the famous sixteenth-century Italian composer Palestrina rescuing music from the destructive policies advocated by the Council of Trent. Pfitzner used this material to construct a parable about contemporary struggles between national conservatism and modernism.

Like Wagner, Pfitzner frequently resorted to the written word in order to reinforce his virulently conservative ideological stance. Amongst his numerous polemical writings of this period, 'Futuristengefahr' (Futurist Danger), which vigorously challenged the arguments put forward in Busoni's *Entwurf*, and 'Die Neue Ästhetik der Musikalischen Impotenz', (The New Aesthetics of Musical Impotency) received the widest dissemination. In both articles, Pfitzner deplored the contemporary musical situation in Germany, accusing 'international groups and the Jews' of exerting too great an influence, and even suggesting that the 'atonal chaos' exploited by some composers was synonymous with bolshevism. Such resentment became magnified in the wake of German defeat, the overthrow of the Empire and the Treaty of Versailles. In the Eichendorff Cantata *Von deutscher Seele* (Of German Soul) composed in 1920, Pfitzner gave eloquent expression to his feeling of anguish and bitterness – the score's overriding mood of deep introspection is only momentarily cast aside in the penultimate movement by a fleeting if disturbingly prophetic vision of a time when Germany would once again overcome its humiliation ('Das Land ist frei').

The Weimar Republic

During the Weimar Republic, musical attitudes became more polarised than ever before. Whereas in the pre-war years, composers as stylistically disparate as Strauss and Reger could with some justification be classified as exponents of late-romanticism, a much more fragmented aesthetic outlook prevailed in the 1920s. However, the well-documented reaction against romanticism was a more gradual process than is sometimes claimed, for many composers including Pfitzner and Strauss maintained their faith in the musical language that they had cultivated before the war. Furthermore, younger composers indebted to late-romanticism continued to secure public recognition. In the opera house, for example, the most successful new works of the early 1920s, Franz Schreker's *Der Schatzgräber* (The Golddigger, 1920) and Erich Wolfgang Korngold's *Die tote Stadt* (Dead City, 1921) were both heavily indebted to the pre-war styles of Strauss and Puccini. Five years later, however, fashions had changed, and the latest works from both these composers were deemed reactionary in many quarters.

Inevitably, the marginalisation of late-romanticism during the 1920s only served to provoke even greater resentment amongst conservative musicians. Opponents of modernism were particularly aggrieved that the new republic demonstrated such an apparent openness to new ideas. Much anger was directed against the appointment of Leo Kestenberg to the post of musical adviser in the Prussian Ministry of Culture. Although only a civil servant rather than a minister, Kestenberg exerted considerable influence upon musical life. For example, it was largely as a result of Kestenberg's recommendations that Busoni was invited to return from exile in Switzerland and take a master class in composition at the Prussian Academy of Arts in 1919. After Busoni's death in 1924, Kestenberg appointed Arnold Schönberg as his successor – a move that incurred particular wrath amongst the conservative music establishment which resented the fact that Berlin taxpayers were subsidising the salary of a Jewish composer.

Yet contrary to the narrow-minded views of the conservatives, Kestenberg's enlightened policies, which later in the 1920s were concentrated towards the organisation of the experimental Kroll Opera house, served to restore Berlin to the position where it rivalled Paris as the most important musical centre in post-war Europe. It was significant too that Berlin's example was followed in Frankfurt, Leipzig, Dresden and Wiesbaden with many theatre directors and conductors elsewhere also espousing contemporary works with energy and enthusiasm. As an antidote to the nationalist posturing of the pre-war era, Weimar Germany became far more cosmopolitan in outlook. In trying to mend fences that had been broken by the war, German concert organisations went out of their way to promote the music of influential non-German composers such as Stravinsky and Bartók. The conservative musical press largely deplored these developments, although such views were countered by the open-minded analysis of European contemporary music presented in the pages of the modern music journals *Anbruch* and *Melos*, the latter founded in 1920 by the conductor Hermann Scherchen.

As a further example of cosmopolitanism, one should cite the leading role played by German musicians in supporting the activities of the International Society for Contemporary Music (ISCM), an organisation which was inaugurated in 1922 for the purpose of presenting annual festivals of new music throughout Europe. Even prior to the first meeting of the ISCM, the new music festival organised at Donaueschingen in 1921 made a considerable impact, bringing widespread public attention to the iconoclastic early chamber works of Paul Hindemith. For the next few years, Donaueschingen remained a central platform for avant-garde German music. After 1925 it was superseded by Baden-Baden whose annual new music festivals embraced more ambitious and experimental projects. Indeed, a number of the most important works of the period such as the *Mahagonny Songspiel* by Kurt Weill and Bertolt Brecht, Hindemith's ten-minute opera *Hin und Zurück* (There and Back) and the Cantata *Tempo der Zeit* (Speed of Time) by Hanns Eisler were given their first performances at Baden-Baden.

The Weimar Republic remains one of the richest periods in German musical history. Yet attempting a straightforward summary of the major musical styles that were favoured at the time is problematic. As in the visual arts and literature, a number of bewilderingly different fashions attained currency almost simultaneously. Furthermore, many composers went through quite distinctive shifts of emphasis. Sometimes, a particular genre might dictate the given musical style. Hindemith, for example, secured his reputation as a composer of expressionist operas such as the setting of Kokoschka's play *Mörder, Hoffnung der Frauen* (Murder, Hope of Women, 1919) and August Stramm's *Sancta Susanna* (1921), while his instrumental works of the same period veer towards a neoclassical style. Hindemith's contemporary, Ernst Krenek (1900–91), was even more extreme in this respect. His early work was heavily indebted to Mahler, but within the space of a few years, he had embraced atonality, expressionism, neo-classicism and American popular dance music (in the opera *Jonny spielt auf* (Jonny's Performance) 1927) before simplifying his style under the influence of Schubert.

Krenek's bewildering array of musical preoccupations exemplifies the difficulty of charting unifying stylistic principles during the Weimar Republic. Yet there are areas of common ground. Krenek, Weill and Hindemith, for example, all subscribed to the concepts of *Neue Sachlichkeit* (New Sobriety) and repudiated the excesses of late-romanticism. Rejecting the lush textures favoured by Strauss and Reger, their orchestral works were conceived in sparer instrumental colours, often featuring the drier sounds of woodwind, brass and percussion. No doubt, economic considerations also played a part in this trend; in the harsher financial climate of the Weimar Republic, works for extravagantly large orchestral ensembles were less likely to secure regular performances.

In general, the new music of the 1920s assumed a more functional and abstract role in line with Hindemith's concept of *Gebrauchsmusik* (music for utilitarian use)[5] instead of composers being concerned with posterity. Neither were they concerned to present some kind of extra-musical justification for their ideas. By its very nature, musical modernism had to reflect the present, not hanker after the immediate past – a point emphasised in some of Hindemith's early works such as the *Kammermusik mit Finale* (Chamber Music with Finale, 1921) and the 1922 *Suite for Piano*. The seemingly transitory nature of such repertoire was given an extra dimension when concerns with the present were transferred to the musical stage in the form of the *Zeitoper* (topical opera) – a genre that became extremely fashionable from 1926 to 1930.

For many, the preoccupation with topical issues was synonymous with a conscious imitation of the idioms of American jazz and popular music. The pulsating rhythms and harsh instrumentation of such music proved irresistible, and in the case of Kurt Weill served as the cornerstone of his musical identity during the late 1920s. In view of the pervasive influence of jazz and popular music, it is interesting to note that recent scholarly debate has cast doubt as to the extent to which Weill and others genuinely assimilated its musical characteristics.[6]

As well as imitations of jazz and the rejection of romanticism, modernist composers frequently looked back to earlier musical eras for inspiration. Baroque music provided particularly fertile ground, with many composers modelling their work on musical principles such as linear counterpoint that were prevalent in the works of Bach and Handel. It is significant that imitation of baroque styles should link both Hindemith and Schönberg, even though both composers were writing in very different styles. Thus one can draw clear stylistic parallels between Hindemith's sequence of *Kammermusik* (in effect a set of modern concerti grossi featuring different solo instruments) composed during the mid-1920s, and the neo-baroque musical gestures of Schönberg's Suite op. 25 for piano – the first work composed in the twelve-note system which he claimed would guarantee the supremacy of German music for the next hundred years.

In the restless artistic climate of the 1920s, musicians responded positively to technological developments in film, radio and recording. The enormous growth in popularity of the silent film during the Weimar Republic exercised an especially profound influence. Not only were young composers inspired to write scores specially designed to accompany such films, but more significantly, cinematic techniques affected structural approaches to composition to the extent that notions of musical continuity were frequently abandoned in favour of more abrupt juxtapositions of ideas. The possibility of adapting film techniques to the operatic stage proved irresistible to composers committed to divesting modern German opera of its pre-war associations with Wagner. It is somewhat ironic therefore that the first German opera composer to make a conscious attempt in this direction was the dedicated Wagnerian, Richard Strauss, whose autobiographical opera *Intermezzo* (1923) embraces short open-ended cinematic scenes that are welded together by more extended orchestral interludes.

Later attempts at integrating film techniques with opera can be found in the works of Hindemith, Krenek and Weill. In Hindemith's satirical sketch *Hin und Zurück*, for example, the action is reversed mid-way through the work as if the projectionist had decided to rewind the film. Significantly, Hindemith's score follows suit at the same point, providing a retrograde of all the musical material that had appeared before. Krenek's *Jonny spielt auf* is similarly informed with cinematic influences –

rapidly changing scenes, car chases and episodes of slapstick humour reminiscent of the Keystone Cops. Yet neither composer absorbed the dramaturgical implications of film technique to the same degree of subtlety as Kurt Weill. The first work to reflect the influence of the cinema was *Royal Palace* (1926) where a silent film sequence forms part of the action on stage. But it was Bertolt Brecht who provided the stimulus for a more fruitful exploration of the medium. Thus in the collaborative music-theatre work *Mahagonny Songspiel* (1927), elements of silent film guide the entire dramatic conception. The work contains no dialogue and no real plot, but a sense of narrative flow is achieved through the use of montage techniques, projections, titles announced by the actors which serve an explanatory purpose similar to silent film captions, and production instructions or gestures. The autonomous nature of the musical score, constructed in self-contained numbers, proclaimed the arrival of what Weill and Brecht termed a 'new epic form of opera' which was later to attain exceptional prominence through works like *Die Dreigroschenoper* (The Threepenny Opera, 1928) and *Aufstieg und Fall der Stadt Mahagonny* (The Rise and Fall of Mahagonny, 1930).

Alongside preoccupation with the silent film, composers were stimulated by the new mass media of recording and radio. Although both technologies lacked sophistication at this stage, they shaped musical thinking in a number of interesting ways. The opportunity of recording music in a permanent form attracted those who wanted to relegate the licence of the performer to re-interpret the composer's exact notational instructions. Again such procedures were adopted on the operatic stage in Weill's *Der Zar lässt sich photographieren* (The Tsar is Being Photographed) where the major protagonists dance a tango to pre-recorded music. But another example of the cross-fertilisation between recording and composition can be witnessed in the temporary interest in 'mechanised music' which surfaced in the late 1920s in such works as the *Triadic Ballet* for mechanical organ by Hindemith.

The evolution of a national broadcasting system in Germany during the mid-1920s also had far-reaching consequences on musical life. Apart from the expanded opportunities of employment for performing musicians which followed the creation of regional broadcasting choirs and orchestras, composers also exploited the new medium with some success. Realising that the quality of sound reproduction was primitive, many adapted their music so that it would sound more effective over a loudspeaker.

An outline of some of the ubiquitous features of musical modernism during the Weimar Republic would seem incomplete without discussion of political engagement. As I stressed earlier, the polarisation of aesthetic outlooks took on a political dimension from the very outset of the era. But the temptation to label all modernists as 'dangerous Bolshevists', a procedure frequently encountered in Nazi propaganda, hardly bears serious scrutiny. Admittedly, many of the radical composers who appeared on the scene in the early 1920s reacted to the bitter experience of the First World War by breaking with hallowed musical traditions. But the music they composed was mainly heard at elitist new music festivals, and therefore exercised a limited impact on the widest stratum of society. Later, social conscience caused Hindemith to modify his style and embrace the idea of *Gemeinschaftsmusik*, literally music intended for children, amateurs and instructional use. Politics also played a part in changing a composer's style. Under the influence of Brecht, Kurt Weill's musical idiom became far more direct. But the most politically active composer was Hanns Eisler, a pupil of Schönberg whose early instrumental and chamber works demonstrated a sophisticated application of his master's newly formed twelve-tone technique. Yet Eisler changed track after becoming involved with the Left. Growing indignation over the way musicians were failing to react towards the ever-worsening class conflicts and the menace of fascism caused him to break with his teacher in 1926 and develop an alternative *angewandte* (applied) style of music that was modern in outlook, yet possessed mass appeal. From 1927 onwards Eisler became active in the revolutionary labour movement, providing choral music for workers, incidental music for agit-prop theatre groups and collaborating with Brecht on a series of didactic pieces (*Lehrstücke*) in the early 1930s.

At the time that Eisler's *Lehrstücke* received their first performances, musical life in the Weimar Republic had already reached a turning point. In effect 1930 was the last year in which contemporary music was able to flourish. A number of factors were responsible for this change, perhaps the most important being the Wall Street Crash of 1929 which had severe repercussions on all cultural activities. State-subsidised opera houses and orchestras were forced to curtail their activities and avoid the financial risks associated with performing contemporary music. Unemployment in the music profession was further exacerbated by the advent of the sound cinema which, at a stroke, invalidated the necessity for hiring cinema orchestras again. This was a particular blow since at this time

Germany was regarded as the most buoyant centre for silent film production in the whole of Europe.

Amidst this crisis, right-wing opposition to all manifestations of Weimar Culture had been successfully mobilised by the *Kampfbund für deutsche Kultur* (Fighting League for German Culture) – an organisation founded in 1928 by the Nazi ideologist Alfred Rosenberg. The chief targets of its musical propaganda were Jewish composers and performers who, it was claimed, exercised too powerful a role in the musical fabric of Germany. Much invective was drawn against Krenek's *Jonny spielt auf* and Weill's *Dreigroschenoper*. The *Kampfbund* regarded both works as degenerate for their assimilation of 'un-German' musical elements such as jazz.

By 1930 increasingly strident anti-Semitic attacks in the right-wing press against such composers as Weill and Krenek were not simply confined to the newspapers. Organised protests at performances of modernist operas now became a regular occurrence. For example, rioting broke out after the Frankfurt performance of Weill's *Aufstieg und Fall der Stadt Mahagonny* in 1930 and similar demonstrations were mounted elsewhere. During the same year, the Nazis temporarily held the portfolio of Ministry of Interior in a regional government coalition in Thuringia. One of their first actions was to issue an 'Ordinance against Negro Culture' which not only outlawed jazz, but also banned further performances of any music by Stravinsky and Hindemith in the province.

The climate of fear engendered by such activity, as well as the ever worsening financial situation, inhibited the spirit of creative adventure and enterprise which had been such a strong feature of musical modernism in the 1920s. Hindemith, for example, appears to have undergone something of a reappraisal of his aesthetic outlook. The satirical element in his music, still very much in evidence in his Zeitoper *Neues vom Tage* (News of the Day, 1930), was now suppressed. In its place, Hindemith assumed a new seriousness of purpose which in the monumental oratorio *Das Unaufhörliche* (The Perpetual, 1931, text by the poet Gottfried Benn) recalls nineteenth-century musical traditions.

The Nazi era

When Hitler came to power in 1933, Hindemith's recent conversion to more traditional musical values served to protect him, at least temporarily, from the worst excesses of Nazi proscription. Many of his colleagues, however, were not so fortunate, since the German music profession suffered the most ruthless purge in its entire history during the early months of Nazi rule. At first, the Nazis resorted to bullying tactics and organised demonstrations to remove prominent musicians who had been victim to intensely hostile propaganda. But the Nazi position was considerably strengthened after seizing control of the broadcasting system and the press, for this enabled them to replace all personnel deemed politically and racially unacceptable with supporters of the new regime. Furthermore, any chance of opposing such drastic moves was countered by the abolition of trade unions, which served the purpose of neutralising the effectiveness of Germany's numerous professional music organisations. From April 1933 onwards, the Nazis were able to resort to decrees and specially targeted legislation in order to effect their declared goal of purification of national culture. For example, the Civil Service Laws promulgated on 7 April empowered regional and local authorities to rescind contracts from any politically or racially tainted musician employed in orchestras, choirs or music conservatoires throughout the country.

By June 1933, the musical map in Germany had been transformed out of all recognition. Many prominent musicians, including those of Jewish descent such as Schönberg, Schreker, Eisler, Weill, Klemperer, Toch, Dessau and Schnabel, had emigrated. Moreover, those who were politically opposed to the regime (for example, the conductors Fritz Busch and Hermann Scherchen) had also left. In the coming months, the Nazi musical press would intensify the campaign against musicians regarded as politically or racially unacceptable; later their names would be published in a number of dictionaries.[7]

Yet while foreign propaganda had railed against the brutality of Nazi cultural policy, a significant number of musicians at home broadly approved of Nazi tactics, believing that the new regime would succeed in bringing much wanted stability after years of chaos and financial deprivation. This explains why the policy of coordinating all aspects of the music profession, ultimately realised by Propaganda Minister Goebbels through the creation of a unified Reich Chamber of Music (in essence a Guild of Professional Musicians), enjoyed considerable support. It was additionally helpful to Nazi interests at this time that internationally respected musicians such as Richard Strauss and the conductor Wilhelm Furtwängler were making largely positive overtures to the regime. In this respect, Goebbels' decision to reward them both with the posts of President and Vice-President in the newly constituted

Reich Chamber of Music proved to be an ingenious propaganda coup. Although neither musician was in any way committed to Nazi policies, the presence of such men in a national organisation could only serve to enhance the respectability of Nazi cultural policies.

Given the dramatic changes in musical life that took place during 1933, one might assume that the Nazis had very clear monolithic objectives when it came to matters of musical policy. Yet this was hardly the case. For one thing, the political leaders were themselves bitterly divided over cultural matters, and one can cite several instances where they reacted with unpredictability to different situations. While Hitler always had the last word when it came to policy decisions, he rarely intervened in musical issues, restricting his interests to guaranteeing the financial security of the Wagner Festival at Bayreuth, where he appeared annually to pay homage to the spiritual forefather of Nazism. In most instances, he left the supervision of culture to Joseph Goebbels, although Goebbels had to fend off intense rivalry from both Goering and Alfred Rosenberg. The latter, in particular, proved to be a thorn in Goebbels' flesh, challenging his sometimes pragmatic approach to ideological issues from a position of uncompromising orthodoxy. For example, it was largely due to Rosenberg's agitation that certain musicians, including Hindemith, Furtwängler and Strauss, were drawn into fierce conflict with the regime.

Apart from the conflicting proprietorial interests of the Nazi leadership, musical policy in the Third Reich was also hindered by a contradictory approach to censorship and a lack of general agreement as to what constituted politically acceptable music. The intangible issue of music and race exercised the minds of many musicologists, but a practical application of racial principles was more difficult to sustain. While the Nazis remained steadfast in their anti-Semitism, to the extent that its effects percolated through all aspects of musical life, they were less resolute when it came to Jazz. Although it was officially banned by German radio, Goebbels sanctioned a diluted form of German jazz to be broadcast during the Second World War in order to motivate troops fighting both on the Home Front and abroad. In the case of contemporary serious music, the Nazis always vociferously opposed the work of modernist composers who had attained prominence during the Weimar Republic. Yet in practice their approach to modernism remained ambiguous. Propaganda events like the 1938 *Entartete Musik* (Degenerate Music) Exhibition, modelled on the famous *Entartete Kunst* (Degenerate Art) Exhibition sponsored by Hitler the previous year, proved divisive, and even incurred the outright opposition of the President of the Reich Chamber of Music, Peter Raabe. While critics expended considerable effort on lambasting modernist tendencies, Goebbels' frequently quoted statement that National Socialist art should manifest a 'romanticism of steel' was sufficiently vague to allow composers to preserve a veneer of modernism in their musical armoury. Such evidence is certainly upheld if one examines the work of some of the composers who sprang to prominence during the 1930s. In contrast to the contention that the new music composed in the Nazi era had successfully thrown off all vestiges of Weimar culture, the influence of Stravinsky remained central to the work of such composers as Werner Egk (1901–82) and Carl Orff (1895–1982), and in the highly successful opera *Der Günstling* (The Favourite, 1935) by Rudolf Wagner-Régeny (1903–69), Brechtian principles of epic music-theatre are clearly in evidence. The Nazi appropriation of such 1920s ideas as *Gemeinschaftsmusik* and the festival of contemporary music should also be noted.

Assessing the extent to which new music in the Third Reich diverged from the immediate past may pose fascinating questions about the nature of continuity and change in twentieth-century German musical development. But it cannot disguise the stark failure of Nazi strong-arm tactics to effect their declared goal of resurrecting contemporary German music to a position of world supremacy. Apart from the operas of Richard Strauss, in particular *Daphne* (1938) and *Capriccio* (1942), and the populist *Carmina Burana* (1937) by Carl Orff, the musical legacy of the Nazi era remains pitifully small. Equally depressing is the fact that with the notable exception of Karl Amadeus Hartmann (1905–63), a composer who openly subscribed to a position of 'inner emigration', few musicians seemed prepared to adopt an independent stance with regard to the regime.

Apart from appraising the internal ramifications of Nazi musical policy, one must also address its impact abroad. The colonisation of the occupied territories of Austria, Czechoslovakia and Poland reaped incalculably destructive consequences on musical life, with many prominent musicians ultimately perishing in the concentration camps. At the same time, the enforced emigration to the United States of so many German musicians of international repute, including the composers Schönberg, Eisler, Hindemith and Weill, proved to have a positive impact on the future course of American music, whether in the concert hall, musical theatre or in the cinema. The extent to which exiled German composers

responded to their new geographical surroundings is open to speculation, though it is interesting to note that those who gravitated to Hollywood to write film scores were probably more insular than their
colleagues in unabashedly transporting the late-romantic idioms of
Wagner and Strauss into the cinema.

Germany after 1945

The issue of exile is germane to the rebuilding of musical life in the aftermath of the war. Having suffered the effects of twelve years of musical
censorship and realising the full horrors of the Holocaust, those German
composers who had not been tainted by too close an association with the
Nazi regime were anxious to re-establish the modernist trends that had
persisted during the Weimar Republic. Yet the post-war division of Germany into two separate countries resulted in somewhat contrasting
responses towards modernism.

In the German Democratic Republic, the influence of Stalinism prevailed throughout the 1950s. Hanns Eisler, deported from the United
States for indulging in 'Un-American activities' during the McCarthy
era, chose to settle in the GDR in 1950, but his subsequent career in his
newly adopted country was dogged by controversy. The libretto to a
projected opera *Johann Faustus* (completed in 1952) was subjected to such
a degree of nation-wide criticism for undermining Goethe's view of the
nucleus of the German people as progressive that Eisler lost the desire
to complete the music. Another source of difficulty was Eisler's continued allegiance to composing in the twelve-note system of his teacher
Schönberg. This proved particularly problematic, for Soviet-dominated
propaganda had consistently branded Schönberg's technique as formalist. Nonetheless, Eisler's position was never really compromised. He
remained a productive composer to the very end of his life, although his
last works fail to capture the power and energy of those he wrote in
exile.

After Eisler's death in 1962, Paul Dessau (1894–1979) assumed the
mantle of the leading composer in the GDR. Like his erstwhile colleague,
he had been a victim of Nazi persecution and in exile also collaborated
extensively with Bertolt Brecht, writing incidental music for the plays
Furcht and Elend des Dritten Reiches (Fear and Misery of the Third Reich,
1938) and *Mutter Courage* (Mother Courage, 1946). During the 1950s,
Dessau completed two operas based on Brecht's plays *Die Verurteilung des*

Lukullus (The Sentencing of Lucullus, 1961) and *Puntila* (1959), but both works initially encountered official disfavour for the ideological stance of the libretti and the composer's intermittent use of twelve-tone technique.

In the cultural thaw of the 1960s and 1970s, composers in the GDR became less inhibited by the official demands of the socialist regime. Dessau's argument that a progressive stance in politics should be matched by a similar awareness of radical musical techniques carried some authority. But despite the fact that the composer was lauded with state honours, his work never enjoyed complete approval of the regime – a point exemplified by relatively infrequent performances of his music. Other GDR composers were similarly restricted, and one might argue quite justifiably that severely limited dissemination of their work has thus far precluded any balanced appraisal of their musical achievements.

In contrast, accessibility of material was never a problem in the former Western Germany. From the very outset, the rebuilding of musical life involved a process of internationalism analogous to the period of the Weimar Republic. In the wake of the economic upturn of the 1960s, generous state, municipal and regional subsidies once again ensured that musicians from all over the world were attracted to work in Germany – a practice that persists to the present day if one examines the major personnel at German opera houses. This resurgence also coincided with the increasing power of German record companies (most notably *Deutsche Grammophon Gesellschaft*) in setting the agenda for musical repertoire and dictating which particular artists would occupy a position of pre-eminence in the international market-place.

In composition, the central concern was a renewed commitment to modernism, and in particular to the twelve-tone methods of Schönberg and his pupil Webern – a technique that had been mercilessly attacked by the Nazis. During the 1950s the obligation to write in a style modelled on these masters created a new orthodoxy fostered by the annual summer courses in composition held at Darmstadt. Furthermore, the emergence during this time of the so-called Darmstadt School served to isolate the impact of composers who had resisted Schönberg's influence. It was for this reason that after years of exile in the United States, Hindemith's attempt to re-establish his career in post-war Germany ended in comparative failure. Other contemporaries of Hindemith who had remained in Germany throughout the Nazi era fared somewhat better. Carl Orff continued to be productive, composing music-theatre works in his own neo-primitive musical style without capturing the musical freshness of *Carmina Burana*. Karl Amadeus Hartmann concerned himself with more weighty musical matters, pouring his energies into a sequence of large-scale symphonies that recalled the traditions of Bruckner and Mahler.

While the works of Orff and Hartmann gained national respect, three younger composers, Bernd Alois Zimmermann (1918–70), Hans Werner Henze (1926–) and Karlheinz Stockhausen (1928–) emerged during the 1950s to ensure that German music once again assumed a predominant role in the European mainstream. Each composer had studied at Darmstadt, but offered contrasting perspectives on modernism. Zimmermann drew heavily upon the influences of Schönberg and Webern, but also responded constructively to modern jazz, as witnessed in his Trumpet Concerto 'Nobody knows the trouble I see' (1955). Later he began to evolve a kind of collage technique that juxtaposed quite disparate musical elements covering the whole gamut of the repertoire from medieval plainchant to the Beatles. This stylistic pluralism was realised to spectacular effect in his opera *Die Soldaten* (The Soldiers, 1965) based on Lenz's play. The work calls for multiple acting levels and three projection screens to preserve the simultaneities of the action, but despite its immense musical complexity, it soon came to be regarded as the most significant German opera since Berg's *Lulu*.

Like Zimmermann, Henze enjoyed considerable success as an opera composer. In his first published works dating from the early 1950s, he had enthusiastically embraced the Schönbergian principles learnt at Darmstadt. At the same time, his receptivity to a wider range of musical styles served to estrange him from the more uncompromising members of the European avant-garde. In 1953 Henze voluntarily left Germany to settle permanently in Italy – a move determined by his disillusionment with aspects of post-war German society that had remained intact despite the overthrow of the Nazis. Yet the country of his birth continued to provide him with prestigious commissions and showered his latest works with critical approval. In particular, the operas *Elegy for Young Lovers* (1961) and *The Bassarids* (1966) were both praised for their virtuosic integration of musical and dramatic effects. But the very success of *The Bassarids,* premiered before a bourgeois audience at the Salzburg Festival, caused Henze once again to re-examine both his political beliefs and his compositional style. He soon became involved with the student revolutionary movement of the 1960s, declaring an open commitment to revolutionary socialism. The music he composed during the late 1960s and 1970s reflects this new political allegiance. It is more hard-edged in sound than the earlier works, and Henze also drew upon a wider range of influences including revolutionary Cuban music and the work of Weill and Eisler. In his more recent works, Henze has attempted a synthesis between his former lyrical style and the revolutionary fervour of his left-wing compositions. Significantly, in his highly regarded Seventh Symphony (1983–4), commissioned for the centenary of the Berlin Philharmonic, the composer consciously set out to write a work that was Beethovenian in spirit and in structure.

Undoubtedly the most radical of this triumvirate of post-war German composers was Karlheinz Stockhausen. One of the first composers to apply Schönberg's technique to other parameters of musical composition (rhythm, texture, dynamics), Stockhausen was also a pioneer of electronic music during the 1950s, establishing his own studio in Cologne and composing a whole host of remarkable works for the medium – *Gesang der Jünglinge* (Song of the Young Men, 1956), *Kontakte* (1960), and *Hymnen* (1965) – the latter a mammoth collage of national anthems of the world. The innovatory nature of all these compositions would in themselves have been sufficient to place Stockhausen at the very forefront of the European avant-garde. But the composer's cosmopolitanism encompassed other techniques including indeterminacy, derived from the musical ideas expounded by American composer, John Cage, moment form, and Oriental mysticism. Although Stockhausen's music made extreme technical demands on performers and listeners, he became a cult figure during the 1960s and 1970s drawing admiration not only from avant-garde musicians, but also from experimental rock performers such as Frank Zappa or the band *Kraftwerk*.

It is significant that in the wake of the postmodernist reaction that has affected musical developments over the past decade or so, Stockhausen's seminal position in twentieth-century German music should have been undermined. The composer himself may have been partially responsible for this, having resolved during the 1980s to wield absolute control over the future dissemination of his music whether through performance, publication or recording. In addition, since 1977 his creative energies have been exclusively oriented towards the composition of a cycle of seven sacred operas, each one representing a day in the week. Known under the collective title of *Licht* (Light), this project of Wagnerian proportions, in which music, text, movement and staging are integrated into a kind of *Gesamtkunstwerk*, has at the time of writing not been staged in Germany, and seems too far removed from the mainstream of musical activity to exert a powerful influence.

Whether future generations will react to Stockhausen's recent musical activities in a more open-minded manner is difficult to predict. Yet within a wider historical context, the composer's decision to embrace opera, after years of rejecting traditional musical genres, is noteworthy. Although no German composer born a generation after Henze and Stockhausen, has as yet emerged to claim the world-wide attention that had been devoted to these masters, opera has proved to be the one musical medium to have engaged both the attention and the creative ingenuity of the most promising talents. There are several reasons for this. The combination of a long-standing tradition of operatic performance and state subsidy is vital. But perhaps more important is the capacity of opera, over and above the symphony or string quartet, to embrace a pluralistic range of musical styles and techniques. In a post-modernist age, the operas of Wolfgang Rihm (1953–), which include *Jacob Lenz* after Büchner (1979) and *Die Eroberung von Mexiko* (The conquest of Mexico) after Artaud (1992), and those of Siegfried Matthus (1934–) such as *Die Weise von Liebe und Tod des Cornets Christoph Rilke* (The Lay of Love and Death of Cornet Christopher Rilke, 1985), *Judith* after Hebbel (1985) and *Graf Mirabeau* (Count Mirabeau, 1989) must be singled out for effecting an imaginative rapprochement between intellectual complexity and accessibility of musical idiom – features which recall some of the finest operas of the Weimar Republic. In charting the turbulent history of German music over the past hundred years, the presence of such considerable musical talents in a united Germany augurs well for the future. At the same time, such optimism has to be countered by the ominous resurgence of fascist ideology in the work of some far-right rock groups – a trend which must give cause for some concern.

NOTES

1. Consultation of the article on Periodicals in the most recent edition of *Grove's Dictionary of Music and Musicians* (London: Macmillan, 1981) suggests that 1,109 separate music periodicals were published in Germany and 300 in Austria. Equivalent figures for France are 729, Great Britain 579 and Italy 290.
2. The late works that especially reflect Liszt's modernism are the piano miniatures *Nuages gris, Bagatelle sans tonalité* and *Csardas Macabre*.
3. Alan Walker, *Franz Liszt: The Weimar Years, 1848–1861*, (London: Faber, 1989), p. 511.
4. The technique was first employed by Engelbert Humperdinck in his incidental music to *Königskinder* (1897).
5. The term originated in the mid-1920s to categorise mechanical music and music for

radio and film, though it was later applied, somewhat disparagingly, to contemporary works composed in order to fill a gap in a particular repertoire.

6. See J. Bradford Robinson, 'Jazz reception in Weimar Germany: in search of a shimmy figure' in Bryan Gilliam (ed.), *Music and Performance during the Weimar Republic* (Cambridge: Cambridge University Press, 1994).

7. Amongst the most widely disseminated of these publications were Christa Maria Rock and Hans Brückner's *Musikalische Juden A-B-C* (Munich: Hans Bruckner Verlag, 1935), and Theo Stengel and Herbert Gerigk's *Lexikon der Juden in der Musik* (Berlin: Bernhard Hahnemann Verlag, 1940).

FURTHER READING

Arguably the most stimulating of post-war German musicologists, Carl Dahlhaus is mandatory reading. For the nineteenth century there are his *Between Romanticism and Modernism* (Berkeley: Princeton University Press, 1980), *Realism in Nineteenth-Century Music* (Cambridge: Cambridge University Press, 1985), *Nineteenth Century Music* (Berkeley: Princeton University Press, 1989) and *Richard Wagner's Music Dramas* (Cambridge: Cambridge University Press, 1979) and for the twentieth century *Schönberg and the New Music* (Cambridge: Cambridge University Press, 1987). David B. Dennis, *Beethoven in German Politics 1870–1989* (New Haven: Yale University Press, 1996) traces the reception history of Beethoven's music and sheds considerable light upon changing cultural attitudes in Germany during the twentieth century.

For the Weimar years, Susan Cook, *Opera for a New Republik: The Zeitopern of Krenek, Weill and Hindemith* (Ann Arbor: Michigan University Press, 1988) offers an exhaustive appraisal of operatic development during the latter part of the Republic, and Albrecht Dümling, *Lasst euch nicht verführen: Brecht und die Musik* (Munich: Kindler, 1985) is the definitive study of Brecht's contribution to twentieth-century music with special reference to Weill, Hindemith and Eisler. Bryan Gilliam, *Music and Performance during the Weimar Republic* (Cambridge: Cambridge University Press, 1994) is a collection of essays on the cinematic influence upon Weill, jazz reception, performance practice and musicology during one of the most fruitful periods of German musical history, while Erik Levi, *Music in the Third Reich* (Basingstoke: Macmillan, 1994) takes the story further and explores the ambiguous relationship between ideology and music under the Nazi regime.

To understand post-war developments, a good introduction is Hans Werner Henze's *Music and Politics* (London: Faber, 1982), a collection of articles by one of the leading contemporary German composers, while Klaus Michael Hinze, *New Developments in Contemporary Music* (Basle: Harwood, 1995), offers a technically detailed analysis of the major works by post-war German composers pleading the cause of many figures who remain rather neglected in English-speaking countries.

12

Modern German art

Introductory background

The course of modern art in Germany has followed a path significantly different from that of its neighbouring European cultures. The artistic achievements of its Renaissance period, notably those of Albrecht Dürer, Hans Holbein, Matthias Grünewald and Hans Baldung Grien, were to remain unequalled in the wake of the Lutheran Reformation, the Peasants' War and the Thirty Years War which worked to weaken both the economy and the morale of the country. The political fragmentation of Germany made cultural communication difficult. In the early nineteenth century the lack of a metropolis and a 'grand tradition' led painters and sculptors to look for enrichment through the adaptation of philosophical, religious and poetic issues and sensibilities. Artists such as Phillip Otto Runge and Caspar David Friedrich, the Nazarenes or the Neo-Romantics Feuerbach and Böcklin were deeply influenced by religious and philosophical treatises and tried to create pictorial expression for them. It is here that we can identify the roots of what is becoming increasingly acknowledged as one of the main hallmarks of German modernism, namely, the unique interconnections between ideas, events and artistic representations within this school of painting and sculpture.

The transition from nineteenth- to twentieth-century German art

The modern movement within the arts began with the crystallisation of a coherent style, in the visual arts as well as in literature and drama, known

as 'Naturalism'. This was a fusion of Realism and Impressionism as practised in France and Holland. In Germany it was applied to the social and
cultural issues particular to that country. For the first time in the visual
arts, painting and sculpture began to reflect contemporary realities and
preoccupations rather than timeless models taken from history, mythology or religion. However, the links with intellectual concepts and poetic
impulses were not broken but transformed into a new pictorial language.
Based on the fusion of direct responses to visual stimulation and excitement, it incorporated a profound involvement with the role and mission
of the arts within the newly founded Empire. Consequently, we also find
an increasing concern among philosophers and popular thinkers for the
central role to be played by the artist as an individual and for the moral
and social responsibility he should ideally assume. This concern resulted
in a proliferation of self-portraiture.

Naturalism as a movement, however, was driven by more than just
visual stimulation or the centrality of the artist to culture as a whole. The
creative activities of the 'Naturalists', such as the playwright Gerhart
Hauptmann, the prose authors Arno Holz and Johannes Schlaf or the
painters Max Liebermann, Max Slevogt and Lovis Corinth, amounted to
an entire re-thinking of the style, the content and the audience of art.
They reflected the severe crises and dramatic changes that were an
inevitable part of the industrialisation and urbanisation which was
intensified by the newly founded Empire and in which, for a time, internal tensions replaced the belligerent confrontations with neighbouring
countries. Within this process of belated and energetic modernisation,
regional economic structures were forsaken for an expansion of capitalist
production and trading. Traditional power hierarchies of ruler and
courtly nobility diminished in importance and were partially replaced
with the central authority of Empire. Similarly, as Berlin became the capital city of the new Empire, Germany experienced for the first time the
impact of a large metropolitan centre. Inevitably, these changes reduced
the importance of regional traditions and feudal corporations, but
stimulated the rise of the urban industrial classes and a new powerful
bourgeoisie.

The pleasures of the latter on the lakes and in the parks or in the theatres and opera houses of Berlin are reflected in the thematic catalogue of
modernist paintings. The style in which these works are executed, so
responsive to the excitement of fleeting light and colour and to the way
they alter forms, is also, at another level, a testimony to an age of transition

Fig. 12.1   Lovis Corinth, *Self Portrait with Palette*, 1924. Oil on Canvas 90 × 75 cm.

and a shift away from the classical immobility which had characterised German political and cultural life for hundreds of years. Nature too, with its dramatic moods and potential pleasures, has been appropriated by these new realities. In *Self-Portrait* (1924; fig. 12.1) the painter, Lovis Corinth, shows himself as both a member of this class and its cultural prophet. He portrays himself painting in a three-piece suit, starched collar and cravat, the working clothes of a banker rather than a painter, clearly meaning to inform us about his social status. The style in which the painting is executed – bold, loose and rapid brush strokes which hint at volume, modelling and texture without describing them exactly – is a testimony to the artistic credo which the painter espouses. Most importantly the intensity and concentration conveyed by the mood of the painting are indicators of the position held by both art and artist.

As the twentieth century progressed representations of the evils inherent in modernisation – displacement of people, the inhumanity of modern warfare as experienced in the First World War, political extremism and repression, mass unemployment and rampant inflation during the 1920s – were to replace the dominant optimism of the Naturalists. Several generations and movements of Expressionist painters evolved a pictorial language of sharp social and political criticism and projected the artist as a critical individualist. This stand became increasingly important to avant-garde artists as popular politics spurred on mass prejudices and fears which culminated in the twelve-year dictatorship of the National Socialists. One of the most vigorous and imaginative of the Expressionist painters was Max Beckmann whose *Self-Portrait* (1930) shows him in the costume of a circus acrobat with a saxophone. His image of the artist is far removed from the bourgeois worker previously discussed. Rather, he has depicted himself as an outsider, that traditionally marginalised artiste of the circus or cabaret, one who takes risks in his work and is not protected by the comforts of bourgeois existence. At the same time the artist depicted by Beckmann does not have to conform to middle-class values or codes of behaviour and can regard his viewers with an uninhibited critical freedom and clarity. In this disguise he is also a figure who does not in any way benefit from the spoils of this process of modernisation which he finds so abhorrent. Yet the painting does look as being distinctly of its time, the figure and objects condensed in a shallow, airless space, distorted and simplified at will and with no concession to reproducing an illusion of reality. What Beckmann is striving for is the attempt to find a new visual language for a set of timeless dilemmas, thereby giving them a contemporary relevance for his public.

The unique history of Germany within Europe, both as an external aggressor and in its rapid and extreme internal developments, has made this tension between new and old, or avant-garde and traditional, one of the main features of its artistic output. The further division of the country after the Second World War added another dimension to the analysis of German art in terms of its conservative and progressive strands and their different patronage. The debates between the two orientations of thought and the attempts to find ways of coexisting with an ancient heritage, a recent past and a rigorous conception of modernity are at the core of twentieth-century German art.

Expressionism – *Die Brücke*

Expressionism is a unique German word for a particularly German phenomenon. The word itself implies extroversion, intensity, the evocation of mood and atmosphere, the harnessing of energy and regenerative powers through the experience of art and a belief in the credo of subjectivity. All of these were components in the search for relevant new visual forms which would convey both the social and the elemental aspects of modern man. At the core of the ambitious aims declared by every tenet of Expressionist culture – be it dance, poetry, architecture or painting – were the utopian ideals of challenging the old order and revolutionising the course of German art. The first of these initiatives was the artists' group '*Brücke*' founded in Dresden in 1905.

Brücke's founding members were Ernst Ludwig Kirchner, Fritz Bleyl, Karl Schmidt-Rottluff and Erich Heckel. Over the next few years they were joined by Emil Nolde, Otto Mueller and Max Pechstein. The initial founding members had all been students of architecture at the Dresden Institute of Technology, and of them only Kirchner had had access to modern art teaching when he spent a term in Munich studying under the *Art Nouveau* artist Hermann Obrist. Their experiments were articulated in a manifesto written and carved in wood by Kirchner. It was published in 1906 entitled simply KÜNSTLERGRUPPE BRÜCKE (Artists' Group Bridge) and revealed both the painters' revolutionary energy and a range of totally new concepts which they brought to bear on painting. In this document Kirchner states:

> With faith in the development of a new generation of creators and consumers we call together all youth. As youth, we carry the future and want to create for ourselves freedom of life and movement against the long-established older forces. Everyone who directly and authentically conveys that which drives him to creation, belongs with us.[1]

Even these few lines are a testimony to the wide-ranging aspirations of the group which already contain the key concept of an *avant-garde*, namely the overthrowing of established social, political and cultural structures.

Within this new utopian world order the spectator assumes a greater importance than ever before. The traditional elitist stance of the arts is called into question by welcoming the consumer of art into the process of aesthetic regeneration and by envisaging art as engaging spectators and changing their consciousness. This desire to reach as wide an audience as possible and interest them in the artistic process was one of the reasons why *Brücke* artists set out to revive the print-making tradition in Germany. Works executed in the media of woodcut, etching, or lithograph could be reproduced and more widely disseminated than paintings.

This revival was part of the group's aesthetic programme, as was their interest in primitive art from both European and non-European sources. The graphic tradition had been one of the highest achievements of the German Renaissance as practised by Dürer, Holbein, Schongauer, Cranach and many others. In their search for visual forms which possessed power and vitality and which were not over-refined by centuries of academic art, *Brücke* artists looked both to their own German past and to the primitive cultures of Africa, the South Sea Islands and Oceania, which could be seen in the Dresden ethnographic collection. It was not only the simplicity and brutality of the forms that they were trying to re-create but also what appeared in the perspective of time and distance to be utopian societies free from the constraints of German bourgeois morality. Emil Nolde, briefly a member of the group, intensified his knowledge of primitive art with an extended South Seas journey in 1913.

In the ideal world which they were trying to create and in which they would be nourished by art, the *Brücke* artists were determined to do away with class, possessions and conventional sexual morality in favour of free and uninhibited self-expression. Coming as they did from conventional middle-class backgrounds, they turned their backs on the comforts and cultural limitations of this environment and rented studios in the working-class districts of Dresden and later of Berlin, when they moved there in 1910. This too was a form of primitivism, of assuming a self-conscious naiveté and defying the rarefied atmosphere and content of the traditional art world. Another aspect of utopian primitivism was their communal painting activities and annual trips to the Moritzburg lakes outside Dresden where they painted each other and their models in the landscape. During the years 1905–10, the nude in nature figures in their work more prominently than any other motif and, although each one of the *Brücke* artists renders it somewhat differently, it remains the central image.

They rejected academic illusionism and, in a rare feat of synthesis guided by Kirchner, managed to combine aspects of the work of Munch with Van Gogh's expressive colour, dispensing with traditional perspective and preferring pictorial agitation. They also, and particularly in the work of Schmidt-Rottluff, applied the lessons learnt from Gauguin and from the Fauve painters in France of the emotive and symbolic properties of non-naturalistic colour. Added to these were the rough textures, the simplified and rhythmical lines of both primitive and Gothic art and architecture. This marriage of new content with a totally new synthesis of form gave pictorial expression to Kirchner's declared aim of a modern language for the preoccupations of contemporary human beings.

It was in the years between their move to Berlin and their disbanding as a group in 1913 and in the disruption of the First World War that the *Brücke* artists gained prominence as Germany's avant-garde. Faced with the realities of metropolitan life their art became more historically and socially specific, more of a modern language and less of a utopian dream. In Kirchner's *Street Scene* (1912; fig. 12.2) we can see the characteristic formal elements of elongated Gothic forms and primitive cross-hatching textures combining with contemporary images to create a visual code for city life. The women in the painting are prostitutes, their faces are like anonymous African masks and they are followed by a horde of faceless male clients. Fashionable clothes, a fashionable dog, a motor car and a well-known street corner add to the historical specificity of the scene. The figures are distorted in a way which is rhythmical and exciting and conveys the movement, pace and noise of big city life. Nothing could be further from the earlier innocent nudes romping in the woods than these predatory females in their fashionable costumes. Why did Kirchner choose to paint city life through the image of prostitution? Precisely because it was the opposite extreme of those earlier utopian images and conveyed the newly commercialised norms of modern life in the ultimate modern environment in which even love is but a commodity.

Der Blaue Reiter

The 'Blue Rider' was chronologically the second major group of artists to be defined by the umbrella-style label of 'Expressionism'. It grew out of a series of schools, artists' associations and exhibition forums initiated by Wassily Kandinsky in Munich during the first years of the century. The group numbered among its members, aside from Kandinsky himself, the painters Franz Marc, August Macke, Alexej von Jawlensky, Gabriele Munter and Paul Klee.

Whereas *Brücke* had perceived itself as a movement deeply rooted in German traditions, *Der Blaue Reiter* was far more internationally oriented with active and affiliated members from several countries and languages.

Fig. 12.2   Ernst Ludwig Kirchner, *Street Scene – Friedrichstrasse, Berlin*, 1912. Oil on Canvas 125 × 91 cm.

Its members in Munich kept in close touch with the international *avant-garde*, visiting and exhibiting in Paris at several of the *Salon d'Automne* and *Salon des Independents* exhibitions. In 1912 Kandinsky and Marc edited the famous *Blue Rider Almanac* which included wide-ranging texts by the artists themselves as well as by the Viennese composer Arnold Schönberg, treatises on Russian art, letters and music and theoretical statements by both Marc and Kandinsky. An even more important indication of the directions taken by this group of painters was the illustrations to the *Almanac*, which included medieval manuscripts and etchings, folk art from both Russia and Bavaria, primitive non-European art, pages from musical scores and examples of the most recent work from Paris such as Cubist, Orphist and Fauve paintings. What sort of artistic creed does this vast range of interests and influences and diverse styles suggest? Perhaps the most important and allusive common denominator is their attempt to find pictorial form for concepts such as mysticism, piety, spirituality and religion. This was articulated by August Macke in the *Almanac* when he wrote:

> Intangible ideas are expressed in tangible forms, tangible through our senses as stars, thunder, flowers, as form. To us form is mystery because it is an expression of mysterious powers. Only through form are we able to divine the hidden powers, the 'invisible God'. The senses form the bridge from the intangible to the tangible. To look at the plants and the animals is to experience their secret. To understand the language of forms is: to be, to live nearer the secret. To create form is to live! Are not children creators from the secret of their perception? Are they not more creative than the imitators of Greek forms? Are not the savages artists who have their own form, as strong as the form of thunder? . . . Man too has an inner urge which drives to find words for concepts, order out of chaos, consciousness out of the unconsciousness. His life is creation.[2]

In this one statement we find all the concepts which characterise the work of the artists of the Blue Rider, the desire to distil, through sincerely felt creative impulses, an essence from natural phenomena and to codify it through forms which the audience will be able to perceive directly through the senses, unencumbered by traditional cultural hierarchies.

The artists of the Blue Rider were also involved in a search for the primitive, not in defiance of social conventions like the *Brücke* artists, but to regain the true and sincere creative spirit. It is for this reason that folk art and children's art featured so prominently in the *Almanac* and that they gathered together many examples of medieval art which predate the creation of an illusionist reality that then became the hallmark of tutored excellence. The paintings of Franz Marc which show a vision of nature through animals unaffected by human strictures or those of Paul Klee which depict a child's view of an adult world are manifestations of this search for an aboriginal perspective.

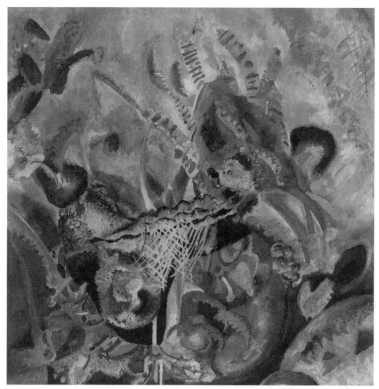

Fig. 12.3   Wassily Kandinsky, *Great Fugue No. 193*, 1914. Oil on Canvas 130 × 130.2 cm.

These pictorial and theoretical factors determined the first exploration of abstraction in the paintings and writings of Wassily Kandinsky.
Between 1909 and 1914 Kandinsky executed a large number of works
which distilled the essence of visual phenomena such as landscape and
figures into an abbreviated language of lines and colours. Paintings such
as *Great Fugue* (1914; fig. 12.3) combine simplified landscape elements in an
attempt to give concrete forms to the idea of the power of nature. These
are fused so as to arrive at the inner truth of things. His repeated use of
musical forms for the titles of his paintings came from his recognition of
music's dependence upon pure form as its main vehicle of expression.
Though Kandinsky's work may appear to eschew all social criticism it is
in fact imbued with utopian idealism. It was his contention that abstraction, the process of tapping the creative impulse and rendering the
essence of all creation, would dispense with the exclusive nature of art.
Since it did not depend on forms learned but on forms perceived, it would

be universally accessible to all peoples regardless of nationality, class or education.

Dada and New Sobriety (*Neue Sachlichkeit*)

The First World War had left Germany defeated, its resources depleted and its culture and politics completely disoriented. The beliefs which had permeated the two pre-war Expressionist movements were now severely qualified by the carnage and destruction of war. While the cataclysmic visions of such artists as Meidner and Grosz had become a dire reality, the utopian anticipation of a universal and emotional basis for a free society seemed irrelevant. The creation of new forms for the arts which were emotionally and politically relevant was an awesome task that found expression in two separate manifestations: Dada and 'Neue Sachlichkeit' (New Sobriety). The former began in Switzerland and then spread to most international art centres, the latter was more particular to Weimar Germany although it had certain counterparts in the French painting of the 1920s. Their modes of expression were diametrically opposed, yet both have to be seen as part of the plurality of responses to the war and to the political and economic traumas which followed it.

Dada was the angry and anarchistic response of a generation deeply disillusioned by the horrors inflicted on Europe in the name of patriotism, loyalty and conventional codes of morality. Its members saw themselves as an 'anti-movement' preoccupied with 'anti-art'. This has a certain logic when seen as the suspicious response to any form of organised activity as well as to an art whose utopian aspirations had so totally failed. The group's first activities took place in Zurich during 1916 when the city became a centre for exiles from the war. Here Hugo Ball, Emmy Hennings, Marcel Janco, Tristan Tzara, Hans Arp and Richard Huelsenbeck founded the 'Cabaret Voltaire' in rebellious pursuit of the ideals of culture and art as a programme for a variety show. It seized its audience with an indefinable intoxication and became a playground for crazy emotion. There were Russian songs, Arp's and Tzara's arbitrary art works, Negro music, sound poems by Ball, Hausmann and Kurt Schwitters and spontaneous outbursts and presentations of radical ideas, all served up with the high theatricality of the cabaret and revue bars. These antics and anarchic impulses were, after 1918, harnessed to a more explicitly political programme by the Berlin Dada group in which Grosz, Heartfield, Hausmann and Hannah Höch were involved. Here too the concept of anti-art was central; conventional tools for the production of pictures were abandoned in favour of newspaper cuttings, glue and debris collected from the rubbish bins of Weimar society. The avant-garde dismantled the pose of the inspired spiritual creator. The artist now operated as a utilitarian maker of works from humble materials which reflected contemporary life and were linked to the mass media. They found Germany's tentative and insecure attempts at democracy stifled by an old guard of civil servants, judges, generals and churchmen. The old ailments were merely dressed up in democratic guises and given modern technological facades. This reality was to be attacked by the Dadaists, be it on the level of Heartfield's biting photomontages (an art-form invented by Dada) in which he connects art and politics or in Hannah Höch's comments on more personal levels of existence. In her collage *DA-Dandy* (1919; fig. 12.4) we see the artist attacking reality with her scissors and giving formal representation to her perception of a fragmented world. The title relates both to the name of the movement and to a male–female conflict in which she applies a name used for male vanities in order to scrutinise a world of female appearances. Clothes, shoes, hats, jewellery and make-up are viewed in a distorted and surreal fashion emphasising how little they have to do with the realities behind them. During the war the women in Germany, as elsewhere, had assumed much of the economic and all of the domestic burden. After the war part of the normalisation process was the promotion of a female image which was preoccupied purely with feminine ornamentation and domestic virtue and it is this form of artificiality and manipulation of women, who were working and earning, that Höch attacks in her collage.

'New Sobriety' counted among its main exponents Otto Dix, Christian Schad, Karl Hubbuch, Rudolph Schlichter, Georg Schrimpf and, in some aspects of their work in the 1920s, Max Beckmann and George Grosz. Here, too, we find a rejection to pre-war utopianism in favour of what seems to be cold and clinical observation of reality. The road towards a wider public is not conceived as a political act, nor is it achieved, as with Dada, through the use of mass media objects and the rejection of traditional painting practices. On the contrary, *Neue Sachlichkeit* artists believed in portraying reality in the minutest and most telling detail, and in a style reminiscent of the great Renaissance tradition of German art. At a time when public events were not easily comprehensible and codes of behaviour were changing rapidly, art bore a responsibility to be directly readable. The reality the painters selected to describe and the attitudes

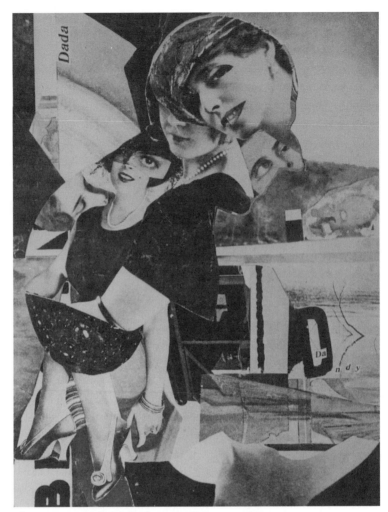

Fig. 12.4   Hanna Höch, *DA-Dandy*, 1919. Collage 30 × 23 cm.

which their clinical and meticulous images seem to convey were often shocking and certainly far from traditional. The dichotomy between claims of objectivity, both in painting and writing, were exposed by Kurt Tucholsky who insisted that however objective or detached from his (her) subject the artist may be, his (her) individuality shone through the painting just as the style of a reportage betrayed its author. So, for example, we find Dix's accounts of prostitutes and cripples used as moral comments on the post-war conditions of unemployment and inflation. The artist

Fig. 12.5   Christian Schad, *Sonja – Max Herrmann-Neisse in the Background*, 1928.
Oil on Canvas 90 × 60 cm.

uses the images of the human body as a symbol of nature corrupted and
degenerated and of himself as fearful of being sucked into the abyss.
Works such as Schad's *Sonja* (1928; fig. 12.5) possess a greater ambivalence
since they describe the painter's own world of café society and the fringes
of bohemian life. The grave Sonja, meticulously drawn, is posed in a café
or nightclub with men in evening dress and a champagne bottle on the

table. Behind her on the left is the poet Max Herrmann-Neisse, but he, the man of substantial intellectual gifts, has been deliberately pushed aside; in this twilight world of entertainment and diversion he is of little consequence. It is Sonja with her ambiguous sexuality and total concentration on whoever is coming in that provides us with a succinct image of the extreme artificiality of the time. While the hard-edged clarity of the image is obviously inspired by the film and still photography pioneered during the 1920s, the *selection* of the subject is the subjective act of the artist himself.

The Bauhaus

The *Staatliches Bauhaus*, a combination of the local Academy of Art and the School of Arts and Crafts, was founded in 1919 in the city of Weimar under the directorship of the architect Walter Gropius. Its foundation and programme must be seen against the background of two concurrent but differing developments. The initial inspirations were located in a post-war socialist revolution which included such initiatives as the 'Workers Councils for Art and Art Education' and the '*Novembergruppe*'. Art and the people, it was thought, must be brought into unity, with art being the life and joy of the masses. The goal was the unification of the arts under the aegis of architecture and design. It is precisely this goal that the Bauhaus programmatically set out to achieve. But this unique teaching institution was not only a manifestation of post-war and post-revolutionary turbulence. It was also the culmination of the Arts and Crafts movements of Europe which had started with William Morris's teachings and had subsequently developed a dialogue with the aesthetics of the factory and the machine age. As a school the Bauhaus aimed at social unity as well as beauty; the destruction of boundaries between pure and applied art and the eradication of the superiority of 'fine' art; the replacement of bureaucratic organs to administer the arts with supervision by the artists themselves; instruction in each workshop by a 'Master of Form' and a 'Master of Craft' to ensure balance between beauty and practicality; a reunion of all the disciplines of productive art in a New Architecture. The ultimate aim was a type of building, in which there would be no distinction between structural and decorative art. A foundation course for all students was taught under the guidance of Johannes Itten. Later courses in Form, Materials and Design were conducted by, amongst others, Paul Klee, Wassily Kandinsky, Lionel

Feininger, Joseph Albers, Laszlo Moholy-Nagy, Marcel Breuer and Walter Gropius.

In architecture in particular great strides were made towards simplification of building forms which would allow housing and industrial structures to be erected on a large but economic scale. The architect, Mies van der Rohe, encapsulated its design philosophy in his maxim 'less is more'. Aside from revolutionary innovations in architecture and also in furniture design there was a great flowering in other areas of Bauhaus activity such as metalwork, weaving and fashion design. Each benefited from the school's belief that teachers should work in media other than their own. This meant that craft designers were exposed to Klee's theories of knowledge and intuition or to Kandinsky's theories of the correspondence between basic colours, forms and psychological states. These concepts of interaction, the universality of the artistic pursuit, the predominance of design and the submission of the individual ego to the typifying vision of the artist are notably to be found in the work of Oskar Schlemmer, particularly in paintings such as *Quiet Room* (1925) or *Concentric Group* (1925) or *Entry into the Stadium* (1930–6), all now housed in Stuttgart galleries. Schlemmer was one of the masters of the Bauhaus who worked in design and experimented with stage-sets and dance as well as painting. During the 1920s he withdrew like many other artists from easel painting with its elitist connotations and worked almost exclusively on design projects. In his painting *Concentric Group* we see members of the Bauhaus – there is no differentiation between staff and students – who have been simplified to a basic form reminiscent of wooden marionettes. Above them is a real wooden model. The figures are superimposed on a background which is divided geometrically in a balanced and harmonious way and gives the impression of being an architectonic space. In one succinct image we have the ideal of a universal unity through the endeavours of art and design.

Art under fascism

One of the Nazi regime's first major campaigns was the formulation of a policy for the arts which discredited all the major national and international avant-garde movements. Modernist artists were isolated and dismissed from public positions. Deprived of teaching jobs, public outlets for exhibition and critical coverage in newspapers, and faced with terrorisation, many artists decided to leave Germany. Grosz, Kandinsky,

Klee, Schwitters, Gropius, and many others, were in the first wave of emigration. During the next four years an increasingly stringent and comprehensive arts policy was formulated under the ideological guidance of Paul Schultze-Naumburg and Alfred Rosenberg and executed by Goebbels' Ministry of Propaganda. Artists who had rejected naturalism in favour of an anti-naturalist or abstract visual vocabulary were declared to be 'decadent' and their art labelled 'degenerate'. Such policies, which aimed to destroy modernism in Germany, culminated in 1937 in the infamous 'Degenerate Art' exhibition held in Munich.

This exhibition represented the climax of an organised and thorough programme of the Ministry of Propaganda and the Reich Chamber of Art. The painter, Alfred Ziegler, who served as president of the Chamber, was empowered to requisition 'decadent' works of art created after 1910. A total of 15,997 paintings, drawings and sculptures were taken from over one hundred museums. The works were removed because they were deemed to offend against 'German' sentiment or distort natural form or were thought to lack adequate craftsmanship. Of these, 730 works were selected for the exhibition and displayed under such group titles as 'Mockery of German Womanhood', 'Destruction of the Last Vestige of Race Consciousness' and so on. The installation of the exhibit itself, with the works hung claustrophobically close together or propped against the wall without frames and surrounded by vilifying slogans, was designed to increase the fears and insecurities of the visitors and provide them with a cultural scapegoat.

Nazism objected to the international character of the modern movement, with its integration of influences from 'dangerously foreign' cultures. These were associated with Jewish economic interests of which the Nazis had a paranoid fear. Modern art was condemned for its obscurity, subjectivity and distance from *völkisch* tradition. The 'Degenerate Art' exhibition was seen by record crowds of over two million visitors in Munich alone. They were then sold by the State in 1939 at public auction in Lucerne, Switzerland, to discerning international buyers. The state substituted for these avant-garde paintings and sculptures a distorted form of Neo-Classicism in which the proportions which were indicative of calm and nobility were brutalised to great dramatic effect. While the paintings and sculptures of the period by such artists as Arno Breker and Georg Kolbe have disappeared into basements and are now very rarely seen, many of the buildings erected by the state still stand.

The process of coming to terms with a legacy of barbarism, racial prejudice, murderous inhumanity and military aggression has been a long and painful one for the German nation. In the arts it was much hampered not only by a general disinclination to deal with the subject but also by the fact that so many of the artists had been forced to leave Germany, creating a vacuum in both teaching and practice. It was only in the 1960s, when a rebuilt economy provided a semblance of security and a burgeoning students' movement began to question the roots of this security, that the legacy of fascistic art was confronted. Young painters, writers and filmmakers began to explore these images as part of the reception of fascism and its effect on contemporary lives. In Hödicke's painting *The Ministry of War* (1977; fig. 12.6) we see the huge, desolate building outlined in black and greys which accentuate the exaggerated classical elements. While it is obviously hollow of any content, the building is a shell of foreboding, its brutal and aggressive qualities unsubdued by time. What is clear from the painting is that this building looming darkly over the street cannot be ignored and like the recent past must be reckoned with. The very detachment and impersonality of the image confront the viewer with the artist as an individual trying to come to terms with this legacy.

Post-war art and the Zero Group

There are three main questions to be considered in trying to understand the development of German art in the decades following the Second

Fig. 12.6   K. H. Hödicke, *Ministry of War*, 1977. Acrylic on Canvas 185 × 270 cm.

World War. The first is to enquire whether German art was completely isolated from artistic developments elsewhere due to emigration and 'inner emigration' (clandestine artistic activity). The second question is whether post-war art rejected the forms and practices of the artists working in Germany before the Third Reich, or whether, in fact, it continued to be preoccupied with the same issues. Thirdly, we must try and assess to what extent the split between East and West German art reflected the hardening of political and ideological attitudes in both countries.

Stylistically, the general trend of post-war art seems to have been towards abstraction, although some of the older generation of artists such as Karl Hubbuch and Karl Hofer had lived in Germany throughout the war and continued to practise a form of critical realism. The prominence of abstraction proved that the Germans had overcome the aberration in taste under National Socialism and were again in a position to practise and accept modern art. At the same time uncomfortable questions remained largely repressed, such as how art should react to the catastrophic situation after 1945, how the new art should be linked to Germany's tradition and history and whether post-war German art wanted to achieve anything beyond simply adopting the latest ideas from abroad.

Public, financial and moral support also favoured abstraction, which was seen to have both universal and decorative properties capable of providing some much-needed healing of the spirit. Aside from commissions for public buildings and the establishment of an extensive series of art competitions and prizes by local and regional authorities during the 1950s, some private patronage also took place. One was the establishment of the Kassel *Documenta* which today is one of the most interesting of the great international forums for contemporary art. Founded by a group of local citizens and civil servants the initiative was a two-fold attempt at continuity – on the one hand that of the *Sonderbund* (Special League) and similar non-aligned exhibitions of pre-war Germany and on the other of the tradition of regional patronage of the arts.

Another significant factor in these post-war developments was the amount of public funds spent to acquire abstract works by foreign artists, particularly those of the New York School of Abstract Expressionists. These are to be seen in the great modern art collections throughout Germany and were not only part of the evolution of a particular style but also an attempt at incorporating Germany into the new, post-war international community. This enthusiasm for foreign abstract art also brought with it a neglect by the art world and its official sponsors of indigenous abstract artists such as Nay, Heldt and Hofer. It was against this background that a group of artists gathered together in Düsseldorf in 1957 for a series of one-evening exhibitions in the studio of Otto Piene. They had all seen Yves Klein's work and were greatly influenced by his concept of the artist as a generator of limitless ideas rather than a reproducer of realities. A series of exhibitions, both national and international, and of publications under the name of ZERO brought Piene, Mack, Uecker and several others together to formulate a common programme. Their most succinct aim was to obliterate reality. This could be achieved through movement similar to that in Op Art. Reality could be erased further only if physical matter were to be transformed into a weightless field of energy. Piene's *Venus of Willendorf* (1963), with its barely distinguishable internal contours, is an example of this attempt at creating an immaterial work of art.

Joseph Beuys and the Regenerative Revolution

Of all the artists who began to work after 1945, it is clear that Joseph Beuys alone made it his life's work to come to terms with the experience of the war and its consequences and to find a new visual language which would combine past, present and future. Beuys' position as the most prominent artist in West Germany was a result of his ability to combine critical issues, exceptionally innovative artistic procedures and an engagement with national politics. It is his unique ability to combine tactile and suggestive sensations, engaging the viewer on a personal and physical level, with complex concepts and ideas, capturing the viewer's intellect, to create succinct and striking images. Although the language pioneered by Beuys is radical, experimental and exploratory, its roots lie in the familiar concepts of crisis which have typified much of twentieth-century German art. Thus, for example, we find in his works and teachings an insistence upon freedom from middle-class social and economic beliefs, on the central role of art in any fundamental and regenerative social change and on the investigation of the future in terms of the past. He considered every human being to be an artist capable of a contribution to the total work of art, i.e. the social order of the future. Despite its commitment to the future, Beuys' work contains an exploration of the past which is conveyed through subliminal subjects in which autobiographical experience and national myth are subtly linked. Beuys substitutes symbolic language for the more familiar formal language of politics.

In a speech at the opening of an exhibition of his drawings in 1974 Beuys pointed out that he had tried to arrange those with backward-looking subjects as shamanistic concepts to awaken interest in the consciousness of the spectator. He hoped that they would be of interest in respect to a total vision of the human being in time, not only for the present, not only looking backward and viewing history anthropologically, but also offering solutions for the future by opening up new problems. His programme seems to consist of an interconnection of eternal time, historical time and personal time. He could thus make reference to the fat and the felt in which he was wrapped to prevent frostbite when shot down over Siberia as a Luftwaffe pilot in the Second World War, and to the need to relate this personal experience to common cultural myths.

Beuys set his art within the sphere of a specific crisis which he discussed in terms remarkably similar to those used by social and political critics. In a text written for *Documenta 7* in 1982, entitled 'An Appeal for an Alternative' and aimed at all who belonged to European culture and civilisation, he listed four main aspects of the crisis: (i) the relationship between East and West, e.g. that between communism and capitalism; (ii) the relationship between North and South, glut and famine; (iii) the threat of increased nuclear armament; (iv) the ecological crises threatening to destroy nature.

Beuys suggests that the first three aspects must be re-examined in terms of coexistence and cooperation and the fourth demands an investigation of how the social organism which we maintain interacts with the natural order. He suspected that the contemporary social order had made humanity sick, inflicted wounds on it, brought disaster upon it and was today putting its very survival in jeopardy. Here again we find that characteristic feature of art which the National Socialists tried to eradicate and discredit, namely a personal artistic vision put at the disposal of a critical programme.

Beuys favoured a comprehensive cultural revolution of direct action which included the formation of the German Students Party and the take-over of the Düsseldorf Academy in 1967. As a bid against authoritarianism and in favour of creativity this take-over consolidated Düsseldorf's position as the new capital city of German post-war art. Not since the early days of Dada had art so totally reflected every facet of the contemporary cultural and economic debate. Like other critical intellectuals Beuys later became involved with the creation of a radical ecological platform by the Green Party, which gained representation in the West German Federal Parliament in 1983.

Although condemned as anarchic, Beuys remained at the centre of several successive generations of the cultural intelligentsia engaging with politics. This unique position was informed by a disdain for traditional modernism, a turning of political rhetoric to his own personal ends, and an integration of historically unpalatable subjects into a new vital visual language. Images made up of fat, blood, bodily excretions and everyday objects are personal reflections of the experience of birth, death, fear and destruction as well as an exploration of experiences within the recent German past. So, for example, the predominance of such images as wounds in his work provides a subconscious response in which personal experience merges with the corporate experience of political upheaval. *Tram Stop* (1976; fig. 12.7) is described as that singular artefact: a monument to the future. All made of iron it relates to the three elements of air, earth and water. Originally the monument rose vertically out of the ground. Round the upright barrel of a field cannon are clustered four primitive seventeenth-century mortar bombs. Emerging from the cannon is the head of a man with a pained, elusive, expression. His identity,

Fig. 12.7   Joseph Beuys, *Tram Stop*, 1976. Rail (iron 860 × 15 × 10.5 cm) cylinders (iron) 61 × 47 cm, 59 × 38 cm, 51 × 44 cm, 73 × 51 cm, barrel with mouth and head 376 × 45 × 29 cm, 22 stanchions (iron), longest: 107 cm, shortest: 55.5 cm, 1 crank (iron), 103 × 101 × 104 cm.

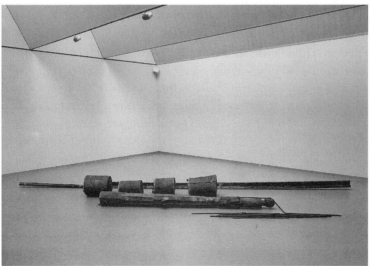

too, is elusive, part Celt, part martial Roman, part ordinary worker, simultaneously heroic, archaic and anonymous. Past the monument runs the tramline, a horizontal element along the earth's surface and a link to the landscape of Beuys' youth in Cleves. The image evoked by the work includes autobiography and history and brings together experience of the past, pain of the present and aspirations towards a balanced future.

Expressive tendencies and the 'New Vehemence' paintings

In the 1980s a new school of German painting made a major impression on the international art world. Its vitality caught both the public imagination and the art market; its forms, images and ideas had an impact on art schools and museums. Although this tendency became consolidated into a 'movement' through a series of major international exhibitions such as *Zeitgeist* (Berlin, 1982), *Documenta 7* (Kassel, 1982), *Westkunst* (Art in the West, Düsseldorf, 1983) and *From Here Onwards* (Düsseldorf, 1984), the artists who were judged to be its exponents belonged to three separate generations. Moreover, the most innovative and stimulating aspects of the works by these artists arose from their relationship with earlier traditions of painting. Not only was there a proliferation of narrative, figurative and emblematic painting in the Europe of the 1980s, but art itself engaged in a great internal dialogue on its relation both to the past and to a specific tradition of painting. Interestingly, this created a concern to re-evaluate the lineage of modern art. Traditionally seen as a succession of interrelated avant-garde styles whose ultimate goal was abstraction, art in Germany since the 1980s has suggested the existence of a parallel tradition within modern art which has been preoccupied with updating the imagery of the past and giving it contemporary relevance. Thus, for example, Max Beckmann, for whom critics had never found a convenient niche and who was labelled an 'independent expressionist', has finally been recognised as one of the most remarkable and influential of this century's artists. On the centenary of Beckmann's birth eleven separate exhibitions of his work were held at major museums throughout the world and attracted a record number of visitors. Judging by the critical reaction to these exhibitions it seemed as if the new school of figurative painting had located and celebrated its founding father in much the same way as Picasso is celebrated as the founder of modernism's school of abstraction.

The three generations which make up the dominant school of contemporary art in Germany begin with Joseph Beuys who was the first to be aware of the convergence of the modern and the traditional and create a totally original language for the dialogue between the unchanging and the new. Beuys' activities as a creative artist did much to reconcile these polarities. As a teacher he profoundly influenced the work of several of his students such as Jörg Immendorf and Anselm Kiefer and his political activities created a platform, however utopian, for an entire generation of young Germans.

The second generation of contemporary artists such as Lüpertz, Baselitz and Penck has taken up this dialogue, extending it to a dismissal of the traditional divisions between high culture and low art. They use political and cultural myths as bits of historical ephemera. It is clear in their work that the new German painting attempts to deal simultaneously with conflicts within Germany as well as those within modern art. While Baselitz translated the monumental clarity of German medieval painting into a contemporary idiom by literally turning it upside-down, Lüpertz used the emblems of aggressive nationalism such as steel helmets and armour to represent a form of historical bric-à-brac, an ephemeral image of junk objects which is more strongly condemnatory than any serious treatise.

Penck's work, too, takes up a traditional dialogue between the primitive influence within modernism and the supposedly holy status of high art. In *Bobo Dschu's Mistake Opens Pandora's Box* (1975; fig. 12.8) we can see a scene executed in a style combining cave painting and graffiti. Looking closely the sexual interplay between the protagonists becomes discernible. Thus a supposedly simple and primitive pictorial language is used for an exploration of contemporary urban and sexual experiences. The subject also oscillates wildly between extremes: it is mythological; it refers to a famous German play and to a film of the 1920s (by Wedekind and by Pabst respectively) and, perhaps most importantly, it assumes that painting has opened the Pandora's Box of German history. This energy and vitality originate in a marriage between two rejected traditions: the act of painting, which had been greatly devalued by Minimalism and Conceptualism, and German culture, which in the wake of the fascist atrocities found itself tainted by its past.

The reaction of the younger generation of painters such as Fetting, Salomé, Middendorf, Bach and Dokupil has been to dismiss all high-minded, exclusive culture. They combine a lurid and joyous portrayal of Rock culture at its most frenzied with the depiction of grave and

Fig. 12.8   A. R. Penck, *Bobo Dschu's Mistake Opens Pandora's Box*, 1975. Oil on Canvas 285 × 285 cm.

important issues. Looking, for example, at Immendorf's great series of *Café Deutschland* paintings executed throughout the 1970s, we see that the entire gamut of recent political history has been set in the contemporary and often hallucinatory spaces of discotheques, cabarets and the flight deck of aeroplanes. Painting has become raucously informal; the symbols of the German spirit and German nationalism are treated with an irony compounded of a sense of absurd incomprehension and anarchic abandon. Even the scale of the picture, the application of the paint, the size and speed of the creative act have a bravura about them that engages simultaneously our intellect and our senses.

NOTES

1. Quoted in Peter Selz, *German Expressionist Painting* (Berkeley/ London: University of California Press, 1957, paperback 1974), p. 95.
2. August Macke, 'Die Masken', in Wassily Kandinsky and Franz Marc, *Der Blaue Reiter* (Munich: R. Piper & Co., 1912), p. 22

FURTHER READING

A good introduction to the development of modern art can be found in the collection of essays entitled *Concepts of Modern Art* and edited by Nikos Stangos (London: Thames and Hudson, 1981) and in Irit Rogoff, *The Divided Heritage: Themes and Problems in German Modernism* (Cambridge: Cambridge University Press, 1991) which focuses specifically on Germany and the place of German art in modern culture.

One of the best books on artistic movements in twentieth-century Germany is Jill Lloyd's *German Expressionism: Primitivism and Modernity* (New Haven: Yale University Press, 1991) although Peter Selz, *German Expressionist Painting*, (Berkeley: University of California Press, 1957) has remained a classic source on individual painters and their work. Hans Richter, *Dada. Art and Anti-Art* (London: Thames and Hudson, 1966) presents an evocative account of this movement on the threshold of the 1920s. Arguably the most original and influential artistic venture of the Weimar years was the Bauhaus which involved a great number of leading artists in its creative agenda. The most authoritative study remains Frank Whitford, *Bauhaus* (London: Conran Octopus, 1992) while Bertholt Hinz, *Die Malerei im Deutschen Faschismus* (Munich: Hanser, 1974) offers compelling insights into Nazi concepts of art and its utilisation for the purposes of ideology and the state. In the post-war period, German art regained independence from state interference and also reflected international artistic agendas. Edward Lucie-Smith, *Movements in Art since 1945* (London: Thames and Hudson, 3rd. edn. 1995) is a good introduction to these developments.

Of lasting interest as the founding document of modern art in Germany is Wassily Kandinsky and Franz Marc (eds.), *Der Blaue Reiter Almanach* (Munich: R. Piper & Co., 1912), translated into English in 1974 (London: Thames and Hudson). Richard Verdi, *Klee and Nature* (London: Zwenner, 1984) and Maude Lavin, *Cut with the kitchen knife: the Weimar photomontages of Hannah Höch* (New Haven and London: Yale University Press, 1993) concentrate on two of the most original creative artists of the first half of the century, while the monograph by Götz Adriani, *Joseph Beuys. Life and Works* (Cologne: DuMont, 1994) illuminates the contribution to modern art of one of contemporary Germany's most innovative and challenging artists.

13

Modern German architecture

The stylistic debate, 1830–1900

In the first half of the nineteenth century German architects and theorists were engaged in a vigorous debate over which architectural style was most appropriate to the age and the location. Initially only two models were admitted, the Classical style of Greece and the Gothic style of Northern Europe. While the structural premises of these two styles – based, respectively, on the beam and the vault – were quite different, there was a strong belief in the possibility of fusing them in a new style that would combine the best attributes of both. Karl Friedrich Schinkel succeeded in doing exactly this in his design for the *Bauakademie* in Berlin (1831–6) in which the structural principles of the Gothic vault were combined with the formal and decorative elements of Neo-Classicism. An alternative to Schinkel's brilliant reconciliation of the Greek and the Gothic was the invention of a third, alternative style, and this was achieved with Friedrich von Gärtner's Staatsbibliothek in Munich (1831–42), in the Neo-Romanesque '*Rundbogenstil*'. Between 1830 and 1840 the respective virtues of the three styles now on offer were the subject of lively discussion, as was the most likely means of resolving the conflict. The most promising development came from the realm of materials, with the emergence of iron as a building material.

Paxton's Crystal Palace in London (1850–1) found an immediate echo in August Voit's glass palace for the First German Industry Exhibition in Munich (1853–4), but the shortcomings of iron as a building material soon became apparent, and the new iron age foundered almost at birth. Structurally, iron proved too brittle and too prone to fire. Aesthetically, the lattice-like constructions demanded by the new material were criticised for their lack of substance and corporeality. Cladding the iron frame suggested itself as a solution to both problems, and this disengagement of frame and cladding stimulated a phase of unprecedented stylistic pluralism in German architecture. After 1850 the whole spectrum of European architecture from the fifteenth to the eighteenth century was pillaged for stylistic inspiration, under the general rubric of '*Renaissanceismus*'. As a manner of building in which the decorative scheme and the structure enjoyed substantially independent existences, the Renaissance style was particularly appropriate to the historical moment. This technical attraction was reinforced by an infatuation with the Italian Renaissance that burgeoned among the educated classes, fostered by Jacob Christoph Burckhardt's pioneering studies *Der Cicerone* (1855) and *Die Kultur der Renaissance in Italien* (1860).

The Orangerie at Sanssouci, redesigned for Friedrich Wilhelm IV by Friedrich August Stüler and Ludwig Ferdinand Hesse between 1851 and 1860, typifies the mood of the moment in its references to the Villa Medici in Rome and to the courtyard front of the Uffizi Palace in Florence. With such eminent endorsement, the Neo-Renaissance became the obligatory style for university and public buildings, for banks and financial institutions, and for the urban villas built by the new elites of the modern, industrial society. Academic institutions in the Neo-Renaissance style include the Polytechnikum in Munich (Gottfried Neureuther, 1866), the Polytechnikum in Dresden (Rudolf Heyn, 1872–5), and the Technische Hochschule in Charlottenburg (Richard Lucae and Friedrich Hitzig, 1878). At both the Gewandhaus in Leipzig (Gropius, Schmieden, Weltzien and Speer, 1882–4) and the rebuilt Hoftheater in Dresden (Gottfried Semper, 1871–8), the full decorative potential of the Neo-Renaissance style was put to brilliant use in creating a dazzling context not only for musical and theatrical performance, but also for the self-representation of the educated classes. The generators of the new wealth not only worked in Neo-Renaissance palazzi – for example the Reichsbank in Berlin (Friedrich Hitzig, 1869) or the Dresden Stock Exchange (Zumpe and Ehrig, 1873–5) – but also went home to them in the evening. Among the grandest examples of the Neo-Renaissance villas of this period are the Villa Meyer, Dresden (Hermann Nicolai, 1867), the Palais Borsig, Berlin (Richard Lucae, 1875), and Villa Meißner, Leipzig (Ende and Böckmann, 1874–6). At the more public level, the Italian High Renaissance provided the model for innumerable courthouses, post offices, and station booking halls throughout Germany.

While the Neo-Renaissance was by far the most influential style in the 1860s and 70s, its dominance was not unchallenged. In ecclesiastical architecture, variations on the Gothic Revival style reigned supreme. Work on Cologne Cathedral was recommenced in 1842 on the initiative of August Reichensperger, a tireless campaigner for the Gothic cause. In 1844 the English architect Gilbert Scott won the competition for the Nikolaikirche in Hamburg with a Neo-Gothic design, and other notable Gothic churches from the mid-century are the Mauritiuskirche in Cologne (Vincenz Satz, 1857–64), and the Petrikirche in Berlin (1846–52). For profane buildings Gothic models found far less favour than their Renaissance counterparts. Notable exceptions, however, are the Town Hall in Munich (Georg Hauberisser, 1867–74, 1888–93, 1899–1908) and a series of houses and public buildings constructed in the Hanover area under the influence of Conrad Wilhelm Hase.

Following German unification in 1871, the issue of a national style of architecture gained a sharpened focus. As a reprise of earlier attempts at stylistic reconciliation, a specifically German Neo-Renaissance style flourished in the 1870s and 1880s, drawing on indigenous models from the sixteenth century. Representative examples include the Villa Knoop in Bremen (J. G. Poppe, 1873–6), the Klinger-Haus in Leipzig (Arwed Roßbach, 1887–8), and the Deutsches Buchhändlerhaus, also in Leipzig (Kayser and Großheim, 1886–8). Particularly favoured for town halls due to its associations with medieval guild halls, the German Renaissance style was chosen for the vast new Town Hall in Hamburg (Grotjan, Haller, Hanssen, Hauers, Lamprecht, Meerwein, Robertson, Stammann and Zinnow, 1886–97), and for its more modest counterpart in Leipzig (Hugo Licht, 1899–1905).

The urban context, 1870–1910

Urban expansion and its control was the dominant theme in the German architectural debate around the turn of the century, when the accelerating industrialisation of the German economy led to a massive flow of population into the major cities. Against this background, the discussions over urban planning and the relationship between architecture and the urban context gained a new urgency.

The brash self-confidence of the new German state was marked, inevitably, by lavish displays of public architecture. Over the last two decades of the nineteenth century governmental, religious and judicial buildings were conceived on a vast scale, with an extravagant neo-Baroque favoured as the official architectural language of the new German Reich. Outstanding examples are the Reichstag (Parliament) building in Berlin (Paul Wallot, 1884–94), Berlin Cathedral (Julius Raschdorff, 1894–1904), and the principal courthouses in Leipzig (Reichsgericht, Ludwig Hoffmann, 1887–95), Dresden (Königliches Amtsgericht, Arwed Roßbach, 1888–91), and Munich (Justizpalast, Friedrich von Thiersch, 1891–8). While some of these projects displayed greater competence in monumental composition than others, the overriding impression was of a graphically conceived manner of design, in which figurative elements that looked well on the drawing board took on a grotesque quality when enlarged and built in stone and stucco. Wallot's Reichstag was the most hapless case of this tendency to inflate graphic caprices into architectural details and was likened by a contemporary critic to a 'first class hearse'. In the wake of such powerful statements of regal and governmental taste, the commercial sector followed with smaller Neo-Baroque extravagances, such as the Theater unter den Linden in Berlin (Fellner and Helmer, 1891–2), or the Bayerische Hypotheken und Wechselbank in Munich (Emil Schmidt, 1895–6).

In response to the burgeoning populations, the speculative apartment house dominated domestic architecture in the large cities, ranging from the palatial and opulent on the fashionable arteries to the mean, dark, and insanitary '*Mietskaserne*' (rental barracks) that marched in rows across the working-class areas of the city. Courtyard plans were favoured, with apartments lit and accessed from a series of internal courts that ran axially off the principal entrance on the street front. In the poorest housing these courtyards barely functioned as light-wells. In Berlin, for example, yards as small as 5.1 square metres were allowed before the building regulations were revised in 1887, and disease and contagion flourished, exacerbated by minimal sanitary provision. Within the local limits set for street lines and cornice heights, the individual house blocks were free to adopt for their facades whichever decorative scheme appealed to the speculator or builder, with results not dissimilar to those achieved by Wallot on the Reichstag. While this visual free-for-all denied any possibility of creating a coherent architectural scheme on the larger scale, it gave a brash vitality to the city streets that exactly matched the rapacious and self-confident individualism of the '*Gründerzeit*' (period of entrepreneurial foundations).

The misery and depravation engendered by the speculative housing in the large cities towards the close of the century appeared to confirm the pessimistic theories of urban degeneration that had dominated the mid-century debate on the city. By the turn of the century, however, a more positive reading was emerging, with the city accepted as the essential focus of cultural activity. This was the theme of Georg Simmel's celebrated essay 'Die Großstädte und das Geistesleben' (The Metropolis and Intellectual Life) penned in 1903 at the very centre of Berlin, in Simmel's apartment on the corner of Leipzigerstraße and Friedrichstraße. For Simmel and his contemporaries the city was no longer damned as a threat to health, morality and civilisation, where the revolutionary masses gathered in pestilent alleys, but regarded as the product of technical and cultural forces that were accessible to rational and artistic control. The city itself could be reformed and redesigned to make it healthier, better functioning, and more beautiful.

Exactly how this was to be done was the subject of passionate debate in the 1890s and 1900s, which originated in the German-speaking context with the publication in Vienna in 1889 of Camillo Sitte's *Der Städtebau nach seinen künstlerischen Grundsätzen* (City Planning According to Artistic Principles). Sitte called for an 'artistic' approach to urban design modelled on historical precedents, and in particular on the picturesque configurations of the medieval city. This retrospective utopia was challenged by Otto Wagner's General Regulation Plan for Vienna, produced in 1892–3, which insisted that modern traffic and a realistic approach to city design demanded the wide boulevard and the straight line. In Germany the same debate flared up in the early 1890s in the columns of the *Deutsche Bauzeitung*, with Karl Henrici advocating picturesque planning and Joseph Stübben proclaiming the primacy of traffic planning and efficient circulation. A third reform strategy, led by Rudolf Eberstadt and Theodor Goecke, placed emphasis on housing reform as a means of calming proletarian unrest, thus guaranteeing the political stability of the city.

With the emergence of the city planning discussion in the 1890s, architecture in Germany became self-consciously politicised. By stressing the primacy of visual imperatives and historical authenticity, the aesthetic faction of Sitte and Henrici ignored the pressing issues of housing speculation and land ownership in favour of conservative appeals to national history, and local characteristics. While small towns like Ludwigshafen and Altona had already redrawn their development plans along Sittesque lines by 1891, the first major city to be remodelled was Munich, where Theodor Fischer, an outstanding architect and city plan-

ner, was employed as director of the City Development Office. Although a
follower of Sitte, Fischer's aesthetic interventions were invariably guided
by a concern for practical and economic realities, and this combination of
the visually sensitive and the pragmatic made him one of the most
influential teachers of the early twentieth century and the essential link
between nineteenth century aestheticism and twentieth century functionalism. Many of the future leaders of the profession could be counted
among his pupils and assistants, including Bruno Taut, Erich Mendelsohn, Hugo Häring, Ernst May, Martin Elsaesser and Dominikus Böhm.

The Reform Movement, 1900–1914

In his essay 'The Philosophy of Money', published in 1900, Georg Simmel
condemned the capitalist society of the '*Gründerzeit*', with its excessive
stress on money values and the division of labour, for promoting abstraction and calculation at the expense of feeling and imagination. Yet he also
detected a backlash, and a profound longing in German society to bestow
a new meaningfulness and a deeper significance on the processes of daily
life. In the architectural context, hopes for reform were focused around
hand-craftsmanship and the example of the applied arts. Several factors
influenced this perception. At the theoretical level it reflected the linger-
ing influence of Gottfried Semper, who had proposed in his influential
book *Der Stil* (On Style, 1860–3) that the primeval origins of architecture
lay in weaving and in the applied arts. By removing the distinction
between *Kunst* and *Kunstgewerbe* – high art and applied art – Semper had
prepared the ground for the practices of the *Jugendstil* era around the turn
of the century, which saw architects like August Endell engaged in the
whole spectrum of design, from large apartment houses down to
embroidery patterns. The belief that design products of every type and
scale were ultimately susceptible to the same controlling spirit and could
work together as elements of a visual *Gesamtkunstwerk* (comprehensive
work of art) took on the character of a catechism in the early years of the
century, with graphic artists like Peter Behrens evolving into architects,
and architects like Bruno Paul employed in the design of everything from
cartoons, posters and furniture, to steamship interiors and patrician villas.

The British Arts and Crafts movement offered important models: the
writings of John Ruskin and William Morris, and the domestic architecture of Shaw, Voysey, Ashbee, and Mackintosh. A vital conduit between

Britain and Germany was the architect Hermann Muthesius, whose German-government sponsored study of the British Arts and Crafts movement *Das englische Haus* was published in three volumes in 1904 and 1905. Muthesius introduced the German readership to contemporary domestic architecture in Britain, which proclaimed the virtues of honesty to materials, dedication to craft skills and vernacular traditions, and the elevation of comfort and pragmatism in house planning above academicism or the merely decorative caprice. Not content with simply writing about the British domestic revivial, Muthesius also built a series of grand villas in the British manner in the western suburbs of Berlin (Freudenberg House, Berlin-Nikolassee, 1907–8, Cramer House, Berlin-Dahlem, 1911–12).

The British example was strongly reinforced by parallel appeals to the architectural calm and tranquillity that had been lost, according to the mythology, with the advent of German industrialisation. The most important source here was a collection of images of buildings and furniture drawn from the Empire and Biedermeier periods, and published in 1908 by the Berlin architect Paul Mebes under the title *Um 1800* (Around 1800). Among the illustrations was Goethe's garden house at Weimar, characterised by the poet in 1827 as 'unpretentious in appearance, a high roof and a lowly house'. As a fusion of high German culture and the virtues of innocence, simplicity, and bourgeois austerity, Goethe's house offered a highly sympathetic model to those architects who were seeking to reform German housing practice at the start of the century. Heinrich Tessenow, for example, sketched it in 1904 and developed the theme of hipped roof and cubic block in the houses that he designed for the model estate at Hellerau near Dresden, Germany's first garden city, on which building began in June 1909. Hellerau housed the workers of the Deutsche Werkstätten, a furniture producer that sought to reconcile the conflicting claims of hand-craftsmanship on one side and machine production on the other.

Early modernism, 1907–1914

Similar ambitions, but on a national scale, lay behind the foundation of the *Deutscher Werkbund* in 1907, an alliance of designers and industrialists dedicated to improving the standard of German industrial design and production, which in the late nineteenth century had become synonymous with low quality and imitative form. In a series of lectures given in 1901 and reworked in 1903 as a book entitled *Stilarchitektur und Baukunst* (Style-architecture and Building-art), Hermann Muthesius condemned the stylistic eclecticism that had dominated German design in the late nineteenth century, and proposed it its place abstention from all superficial decoration and a renewed concentration on a rigorous objectivity. The style of the age, he insisted, was to be found in the creations of the engineers, in the architecture of the railway stations and exhibition pavilions, in bridges, railway locomotives, and bicycles. This conviction informed the aesthetic programme of the *Werkbund* and was given visual expression in the celebrated and highly influential yearbooks, in which essays on the design issues of the day were accompanied by images of desirable contemporary design: industrial buildings and modern commercial interiors in the 1913 edition; cars, planes and ocean liners the following year. Among the buildings featured prominently in the 1913 yearbook were Alfred Messel's Wertheim Store in Berlin (first phase opened 1897), a chemical factory at Luban by Hans Poelzig (1911–12), and the celebrated series of assembly halls and factory buildings designed by Peter Behrens for AEG, following his appointment to the firm in 1907 as artistic adviser. In this role, Behrens was responsible for every aspect of the firm's visual existence, from brochures, posters and product designs, to the great turbine factory in Berlin-Moabit (1909), one of the canonical buildings of architectural modernism. The relationship between AEG and Behrens – as creator of the first corporate identity for a major manufacturing company – exemplified the goals of the *Werkbund*. Behrens also taught, and his studio at Neu-Babelsburg outside Berlin became the epicentre of the early modern movement, as the brightest young talents flocked to work with the prophet of the new architecture. Between 1908 and 1913 Behrens' assistants included Walter Gropius, Adolf Meyer, Ludwig Mies van der Rohe, and Charles-Edouard Jeanneret, who was later to restyle himself as Le Corbusier.

Writing in the catalogue to an exhibition on industrial buildings held in Hagen in 1911, Walter Gropius insisted that new forms could not be invented arbitrarily, but would emerge spontaneously from the spirit and technology of the age. In the same year he designed the Fagus shoe-last factory at Alfeld an der Leine, in collaboration with Adolf Meyer. This essay in steel and glass construction achieves its polemical climax in the glazed corner stairwells, above which the roof appears to float totally unsupported. Moving away from the historical references that give such authority to Behrens' AEG buildings, the Fagus factory provided a definitive model for the functionalist architecture of the twentieth century.

Yet even within the *Werkbund* itself the respective claims of artistic freedom and the technological imperative remained a contentious issue. It dominated an acrimonious discussion at the annual *Werkbund* meeting of 1914, at which Hermann Muthesius' proposal that the standard or typical solution was the most desirable was vigorously attacked by a radical faction that included Hermann Obrist, Henry van de Velde, Walter Gropius, and Bruno Taut. Among the early proponents of modernism in Germany, the merely mechanistic solution was not considered adequate.

Expressionism, 1914–1923

Bruno Taut's 'Glashaus' at the 1914 *Werkbund* Exhibition in Cologne made this point perfectly. This little glass temple, set on a concrete plinth, had fourteen glazed sides – each with a motto from the poet Paul Scheerbart inscribed into the lintel – and was topped by a prismatic dome of double-skin glass. Hailed as the first Expressionist building, it also had the melancholy distinction of being the last, as the outbreak of war in August 1914 and the political and economic turmoil that followed for the next decade condemned the Expressionist vision to paper. The archetypical Expressionist work was Bruno Taut's folio of drawings entitled *Alpine Architektur*, published in 1919. These images of glass cathedrals set high in the Alps and of cosmic constructions of coloured glass speeding through the eternal night were conceived both as a protest against the insanity of World War I and as a pointer to a better society, which would devote its energies to peace and understanding rather than self-destruction.

The few actual buildings to which the term Expressionist is generally attached include the observatory built by Erich Mendelsohn for Albert Einstein outside Potsdam (1917–21), Hans Poelzig's conversion of the Zirkus Schumann in Berlin into the Großes Schauspielhaus for the productions of Max Reinhardt (1918–19), Bernhard Hoetger's Böttcherstraße in Bremen (1923–31), and the office building designed for IG Farben at Höchst by Peter Behrens (1920–4). Although patently unbuildable, the visionary schemes of Taut and his Crystal Chain group – which included Hans Scharoun, Max Taut, the brothers Hans and Wassili Luckhardt, and Walter Gropius as a sleeping partner – did define a series of propositions that were to influence German architecture long after the first impulse had expired in the early 1920s. These included the primacy of architecture among the visual arts, the singular role of the architect as messiah, leader, or social engineer, the importance of craft training, and the reforming potential of new materials and constructional techniques.

Walter Gropius, a close associate of Taut in the immediate post-war months, founded the Bauhaus at Weimar according to these precepts in April 1919, with a manifesto illustrated by Lyonel Feininger's woodcut of a crystalline cathedral. The early architectural production of Gropius and his Bauhaus associates was strongly affected by Expressionism. The Sommerfeld House in Berlin-Steglitz (1920–1), for example, was built of wood with stained glass and furnishings designed by Bauhaus masters and students. This almost mystical belief in the totality of the arts was reinforced within the school by an interest among the student body in cults like Zoroastrianism and Theosophy, stimulated by teachers like Johannes Itten and Wassily Kandinsky.

'Neues Bauen' – the New Architecture, 1923–1933

With gathering pace over the early years of the 1920s, the utopian faith in a redemptive architecture that would, simply by its own grandeur and beauty, stimulate social harmony and political reform, was replaced by a new, and in many instances equally mystical belief in the power of the engineer, the machine, and the new technology. Rationalisation of materials and techniques, industrial production, standardised and normalised solutions, and an insistence on 'objective' clarity were the principal themes of the architectural avant-garde in the mid-1920s, and dominated the pages of the new magazines such as G: Zeitschrift für elementare Gestaltung (G: Journal for Elementary Designing), edited by Werner Gräff, Frederick Kiesler, Ludwig Mies van der Rohe, and Hans Richter. Echoing the 1914 Werkbund debate, the typical solution was pursued in preference to the unique.

The inspirations for these new preferences were not exclusively German, however, and the cult of the engineer and of the machine developed simultaneously in the 1920s in many locations: in Soviet Constructivism, in the geometric abstractions of the De Stijl movement in Holland, and in the infatuation with consumable technology that prompted Le Corbusier to illustrate his essays in the French magazine L'Esprit Nouveau with images of sports cars and ocean liners. Equally important was the example of North America. In the 1890s the Deutsche Bauzeitung had carried many articles on architecture in the USA, and this interest gathered pace in the new century. In 1911 Frank Lloyd Wright's early works were published in Berlin as *Frank Lloyd Wright: Ausgeführte Bauten* (Frank Lloyd Wright: Executed Buildings), a book which immediately became the office bible for Walter Gropius, and still exerted great influence after the war in schemes like the Kallenbach House, Berlin (1921–2). In the early 1920s American mass culture was greeted in Germany as a radical and apparently democratic alternative to the high culture of pre-war Germany. Charlie Chaplin and Buster Keaton, black jazz and Josphine Baker, boxing and the Wild West were seen in the German cities as modern, progressive and appropriate to the ambitions and needs of the urban masses. Architects like Erich Mendelsohn and his former assistant Richard Neutra went to North America and reported on vibrant commercial cities that appeared to offer a more realistic model for the future than the mystical 'city crown' of the Expressionist period, topped by a crystal cathedral. Mendelsohn's *Amerika: Bilderbuch eines Architekten* (America: An Architect's Picture Book) was published in 1926, Neutra's *Wie baut Amerika?* (How Does America Build?) in 1927.

In the context of a 1921–2 competition for an office tower on Friedrichstraße in Berlin, the German architects and city planners took their first, halting steps towards the American skyscraper. Nothing was finally built, but Mies van der Rohe's glazed prismatic tower pointed most clearly to the office building to come, as did a subsequent unbuilt proposal for a six-storey office block with a reinforced concrete frame, praised by fellow architect Ludwig Hilberseimer in the magazine G for the consummate way in which the form of the building expresses its function. But the development of the skyscraper was greatly inhibited by building regulations in Germany in the 1920s, and little progress was made in the skyward direction.

It was in the realm of the two and three storey housing block that the greatest modernist achievements are to be found. Here too, however, American 'know-how' was employed, initially by the housing association DEWOG (Deutsche Wohnungsfürsorge AG), with a group of designers that included Martin Wagner, the city architect of Berlin, Ernst May, Bruno Taut, and Walter Gropius. Between them, these architects were responsible for the most important housing schemes of the Weimar period. At Dessau-Törten (1926–8), Gropius employed serial production methods indebted to the precepts of Taylorism and of Henry Ford, whose autobiography appeared in German translation in 1923 and sold 200,000 copies by 1930. In the interiors too, efficient household management became a central concern. A pioneering text was Bruno Taut's *Die Neue Wohnung: Die Frau als Schöpferin* (The New Apartment: Woman as Creatress), published in 1924, which introduced the American notion of household engineering into the German context. More practically, Greta Schütte-Lihotsky produced a kitchen design for the public housing schemes in Frankfurt, in which all the necessary equipment was shoehorned into a tiny area 3.44 m long and 1.90 m wide.

Ernst May was the chief city architect in Frankfurt and was responsible for some of the most impressive housing schemes built in Europe between the wars, creating some 30,000 dwellings on ten major sites between 1925 and 1930. Estates comparable in size and quality were built in Berlin to the design of Martin Wagner and Bruno Taut for the GEHAG housing association, and for the Siemens industrial concern, also in Berlin, by a group of architects that included Walter Gropius, Otto Bartning, Hugo Häring, and Hans Scharoun. Within the common dedication to workers' housing, however, there was great diversity, exemplified in Siemensstadt by the contrast between the austere blocks of Gropius, based on repetitive, cellular principles, and the more playful and organicist designs of Häring and Scharoun, who were inclined to define functionalism differently, as the provision of spaces that promote individual identity and decision-making.

A similar diversity within the modernist canon also marked the showpiece development of the decade, the Weissenhof Estate in Stuttgart, promoted and built by the *Deutscher Werkbund* in 1927 as a collection of exemplary modern homes. Under the overall direction of Mies van der Rohe, fourteen leading European modernists were invited to design dwellings that ranged from two room apartments to modest detached homes. The siting of this estate in Stuttgart, however, was seen as provocative by many local architects and by the school of architecture at the Technische Hochschule in Stuttgart, which was one of the leading centres of traditional architectural education. As a protest against the Weissenhof scheme, the traditionalists built the Kochenhof Estate on a nearby site, a 'research estate' conceived by the Stuttgart architect Paul Schmitthenner, and comprising twenty-four houses built by conventional constructional techniques. This confrontation on a hill above Stuttgart between the white concrete walls and flat roofs at the Weissenhof and the wood-frame walls and saddleback roofs at the Kochenhof confirmed that the battle between the modernists and traditionalists in

Germany was by no means settled in favour of the radical modernists. The struggle was accompanied by polemical tracts: Siegfried Giedion's *Bauen in Frankreich: Bauen in Eisen: Bauen in Eisenbeton* (1928: Building in France: Building in Iron: Building in Ferroconcrete) was exemplary for the modernist camp; Paul Schultze-Naumburg's *Flaches oder geneigtes Dach?* (1927: Flat or Pitched Roof?) for the conservatives.

Giedion was Secretary of CIAM (Congrès Internationaux d'Architecture Moderne), the international mouthpiece of the modernists that first met in 1928. Under the tight control of Le Corbusier and Giedion a strongly reductivist programme was adopted, which reduced housing design to five main points, and urban design to six. At the same time, dissenting voices such as that of Hugo Häring were effectively silenced. The result was a weakening of the modernist position, which was further accelerated by the abandonment of the mass housing programmes in the cities – the backbone of the modernist architectural programme – by the Brüning government of 1930–1 in the wake of the world economic crisis. In architecture as in every other aspect of German social and political life, the apparent certainties of the mid-1920s had ceased to be certainties, and the modernist perspectives were already narrowing.

The Third Reich, 1933–1945

In the early months following the Nazi accession to power in January 1933 the new regime gave out ambiguous messages, which encouraged leading modernists like Walter Gropius and Ludwig Mies van der Rohe to submit projects for the 1934 Reichsbank competition, alongside such traditionalist colleagues as Heinrich Tessenow and Wilhelm Kreis. This was the last competition for a major public building in Berlin between 1933 and 1945. Thereafter, major commissions were awarded exclusively to members of the National Socialist inner circle. The end of open architectural competitions coincided with the rise of the Reich Culture Chamber, the Party organisation responsible for all the arts. The '*Architektengesetz*' (Architects' Law) of October 1934 specified that the title 'architect' could only be used by members of the Reich Chamber for the Visual Arts, responsible for architecture and the visual arts. Both the public nature of the profession and the experience of several years of unemployment during the recession of the early 1930s made the architects particularly vulnerable to this political pressure, and by 1935 the 15,000 architects represented the single largest group in the Reichskulturkammer. With absolute power over the architectural profession focused at the centre, conditions were favourable for the emergence of a coherent design. That this did not happen reflected both the personality of Hitler himself and structure of the National Socialist state.

Some of the leading figures in the party such as Robert Ley, Fritz Todt, and Albert Speer were essentially modernist in their thinking, while others, such as Heinrich Himmler, Walther Darré or Alfred Rosenberg had a mystical attachment to the German soil and to the whole apparatus of '*Blut und Boden*'. The technocrats had visions of a modernist National Socialist state, almost American in its commitment to technology and industrial rationalisation, while the anti-modernists dreamed of rebuilding German greatness through the labours and ethics of the German peasant. In his necessarily ambiguous position at the centre, Hitler espoused both causes but identified solely with neither.

As in every other area of state policy, this nurtured ambivalence can be found in the modernist/traditionalist debate as it affected architecture. On the one hand, Hitler's government warned in 1936 against hostility towards technology and Gerdy Troost's *Das Bauen im Dritten Reich* (Building in the Third Reich), a quasi-official propaganda text on the new state architecture, hymned the beauty of industrial architecture, of exposed concrete, steel and glass. In direct contrast, however, Hitler delivered a speech on architecture at the Party Rally in 1937, in which he affirmed his intention to construct the greatest buildings ever seen in German history using granite and marble. The Nazi government commissioned projects in a wide range of styles, depending on their purpose, location, and rank in the Party hierarchy. At the most prosaic level Hitler Villages were built in the local vernacular style, as were rural party buildings and Hitler-Youth hostels: Alpine for the Town Hall in Garmisch-Patenkirchen (Oswald Eduard Bieber, 1935), high-pitched and half-timbered in Bavaria, thatched for the weather stations built for the Luftwaffe along the North Sea coast. Modernist, high-technology architecture was permitted, and indeed encouraged in the industrial context. A former colleague of Walter Gropius, Herbert Rimpl, led a team that designed the ultra-modern Heinkel aircraft factory in Oranienburg to the north of Berlin, employing former assistants of Ernst May, the city architect of Frankfurt in the 1920s. Symptomatically, Rimpl's office also designed traditional housing, with rustic shutters and high-pitched roofs for the Heinkel factory workers. At a comparable level in the hierarchy of styles, Egon Eiermann designed a factory block for the Total-Werke at

Apolda, Thuringia (1938–9), using the rhetoric of pure 1920s Corbusian modernism.

One of the most lasting architectural contributions of National Socialism in the urban context was the simple, pared-down functionalist style that had been evolved for public buildings at the end of the Weimar Republic, and survived in the Nazi era as the favoured manner for low-ranking party, military and public buildings. Ernst Sagebiel's Tempelhof Airport in Berlin (1937–8) is a very typical example of this 'Rohbau' (carcass) functionalism, in which the most modern structural frames were covered with smooth, rather bland facades that were neither classicist nor modernist, but which nodded in both directions. The plans for the vast *Reichsparteigelände* (Party parade ground) in Nuremberg (Albert Speer, begun 1934, uncompleted), were dominated by the main grandstand on the Zeppelin Field, formed in the manner of a Greek stoa, the German Stadium, modelled on the Roman hippodrome, and a Congress Hall with a fully glazed roof that completely defied the technological means of the period.

A similar confusion of eclecticism and modernity, of low and high technology, prevails in Albert Speer's plans for the North–South axis in Berlin, the most spectacular of the many comparable urban renewal proposals produced by the National Socialist planners for the major German and Austrian cities. Working on the basis of guidelines and formal motifs devised by Hitler himself – the giant axis, the 220-metre-high domed hall, and the triumphal arch – Speer's vision for Berlin was both megalomanic in its scale, yet very simple in its basic strategy. Two axes were to be established, running north–south and east–west. These would cross just to the south of a giant new square flanked by the existing Reichstag, a vast domed hall, the Führer's Palace, and the Armed Forces High Command. At their extremities, the axes were planned to link with the outer Autobahn ring, with a further four inner ring roads providing concentric circulation. The central area of the North–South axis was conceived as a vast parade ground, designed to house the principal public buildings, ministries, and commercial offices of the new Reich on a boulevard 5 kilometres long and 120 metres wide. Although large-scale demolition and site clearance was undertaken, little was actually built, and the North–South axis remains a paper monument to the megalomania of Hitler's Reich. The 1936 Olympic Stadium (Werner March) survives in the western suburbs of Berlin as the only major element on either of the two axes to be completed.

Post-war reconstruction, 1945–1960

When the guns fell silent in 1945 the German architects and city planners were not only faced with the challenge of housing hundreds of thousands of homeless and displaced people, but also had to create for these disorientated masses new symbols of order, of place, and of the possibility of beginning a new life in a new state. The two alternatives of continuity and rupture dominated the immediate post-war debate on the rebuilding of the German cities: should the historical structures and the pre-war street patterns be restored, or should the architects and planners seize the unique opportunity offered by the war-time destruction to build entirely new cities, untrammelled by the baggage of history? The opposing factions lined up according to a complex range of interests: architectural, political, confessional, and regional. In the bitter power struggle between the advocates of reconstruction (*Wiederaufbau*) and of new construction (*Aufbau*), the modernist planners were victorious in Düsseldorf, Hamburg, Cologne, and Frankfurt/Main, while the traditionalists held sway in Munich, Freiburg, Würzburg, and Münster. In planning and design terms, however, the end of the war did not mark a total rupture, and many of the schemes implemented after 1945 were based directly on the reconstruction plans drawn up by Albert Speer's *Arbeitsstab Wiederaufbauplanung bombenzerstörter Städte* (Working Staff for the Reconstruction Planning of Bombed Cities).

Housing presented the most pressing problem in the post-war German cities with the shortfall in the Federal Republic alone measured at 6.5 million units in 1948. The solutions offered in the 1950s generally reflect urgency and haste rather than design quality and favoured low-rise schemes of two and three storeys, such as Neue Vahr, Bremen, 1957–62. Notable exceptions to the prevailing dullness of the period were the eleven storey block designed by Hans and Wassili Luckhardt at Kottbusser Tor, Berlin (1952–5) and Alvar Aalto's Neue Vahr high-rise apartment block in Bremen (1958–62). Current international fashions found expression at the 1957 *Interbau* exhibition, sited in the Hansaviertel in West Berlin, for which leading German and foreign architects were invited to design model housing schemes, many of them high-rise, which were set in a park landscape in complete denial of the block pattern of pre-war Berlin. At the same time in East Berlin (German Democratic Republic), the planning collective led by Hermann Henselmann was designing the Stalinallee (later Karl-Marx-Allee) in a heroic Neoclassical manner that was indebted both to 1930s Soviet precedent and to the Prussian classicism of the late eighteenth century. Although quite different in their solutions, both the Hansaviertel in the West and the Stalin-allee in the East addressed the issue of urban living from an historically committed standpoint. In the 1960s and 1970s, however, the characterless tower block estate, stripped of all but the most essential social infra-structure, dominated the housing programmes in both German states. Berlin, again, provided paradigmatic examples: the Märkisches Viertel in the West (1963–74), with 17,000 apartments and a population of 60,000, was mirrored in the East by the second phase of Karl-Marx-Allee (1959–65) and ultimately by the Marzahn development (1984–90), designed to house 150,000 residents.

In contrast to the blandness of much of the domestic architecture, post-war church design flourished in the Federal Republic under a gener-ous fiscal system. Bravura performances abound, in which innovative spatial planning is matched by adventurous structural design in modern materials. Otto Bartning led the way in 1946 with a design for an emer-gency prefabricated church made of timber, and he was followed by such outstanding designs as St Josef, Cologne-Braunsfeld (Rudolf Schwarz with Josef Bernard, 1954), St Maria Königin at Cologne-Marienburg (Dominikus Böhm, 1954), and the Protestant Church at Lietzensee, Berlin (Paul Baumgarten, 1956–9).

With the need to restore shattered communities a paramount concern in the immediate post-war decades was the construction of theatres, con-cert halls, and similar communal buildings. A wide diversity of architec-tural styles were favoured for these buildings, which often assumed polemical positions in the architectural debate. Among the more extrav-agant gestures in the Federal Republic were the high-technology Stadthalle in Bremen (1957, 1961–4) in which the structural technology of a sports stadium was combined with a suspended roof; the neo-Expressionist Town Hall at Bensburg (Gottfried Böhm, 1962–7); and the Municipal Theatre at Ingolstadt (Hardt-Walther Hämer, Marie-Brigitte Hämer, 1960, 1962–6), a monolithic concrete structure in the New Brutal-ist manner. In West Berlin, Hans Scharoun's Philharmonie (1956, 1960–3), with its tent-like exterior, polygonal plan and cascades of terraced seat-ing surrounding the stage on all sides, marked a rethinking of the rela-tionship between audience and performer. In marked contrast, Ludwig Mies van der Rohe's neighbouring glass and steel structure for the Neue Nationalgalerie was based on the strict stereometric ordering of space, and located the permanent collection underground. Across the Wall in East Berlin, the Palast der Republik (Kollektive Heinz Graffunder, Karl-Ernst Swora, Manfred Prasser, Heinz Aust, 1973–6) offered more conventional interiors in which to enjoy the political and cultural offerings of the GDR leadership.

Economic miracle and beyond, 1960 to the present

The contrast in Berlin between Miesian control and the freedom pursued by Hans Scharoun and his followers was a dominant feature of the German architectural discussion in the later 1950s and 1960s. Large-scale commercial and office architecture in the Federal Republic was dominated by transatlantic models, which themselves derived in part from the work of German emigré architects. Thus the rectilinear discipline and purity of Ludwig Mies van der Rohe's high-rise American blocks (South Shore Drive Apartments, Chicago, 1949; Seagram Building, New York City, 1957–8) played godfather to many similar towers in the West German cities, among the best of which is the Phoenix-Rheinrohr skyscraper in Düsseldorf (Helmut Hentrich and Herbert Petschnigg, 1957–60). Among the home-bred modernists, Egon Eiermann combined the austere control of Miesian design method with delicate detailing and elegant massing in a set of buildings that captured the progressive spirit of the Federal Republic (German Pavilion at the Brussels World Fair, with Sep Ruf, 1958; Chancellory of the German Embassy, Washington, 1959, 1962–4).

An alternative modernism, more concerned with functional disposition than formalist purity, flourished in the 1960s around the beacon of Hans Scharoun, whose twin apartment blocks at Stuttgart Zuffenhausen, dubbed Romeo and Juliet (1954–9), deny the primacy of the right-angle in their plans. A similar reluctance to force human activity into box-like compartments characterises the major public commissions of Scharoun's late career (State Library, Berlin, 1966–78; German Maritime Museum, Bremen, with Helmut Bohnsack, 1969–75). Scharoun's challenge to the tyranny of the set square and the portal frame was taken further in the 1970s and 80s by Günter Behnisch. In the late 1960s Behnisch was one of a team of designers that also included Fritz Auer and Frei Otto, who were responsible for the Olympic Games Complex in Munich (1965–72), celebrated for the soaring tent roof that linked the Stadium, Olympic Hall, and Olympic Pool. Subsequent works by Behnisch that brought together high-technology structures with organic form include the University Library at Eichstätt and the Solar Research Institute at Stuttgart University (both completed 1987). A comparably radical focus on the function and occupants of the building rather than on predetermined formal solutions marks the work of Otto Steidle, whose designs have a spontaneous and even improvised quality, with great attention paid to the circulation spaces – stairs, walkways, and balconies – which are designed to stimulate visual interest and social intercourse (International Meeting Centre, Rüdesheimer Platz, Berlin, 1982; Offices for Gruner & Jahr, Hamburg, 1984).

The flagship architectural project in Germany in the 1980s was the International Building Exhibition (IBA) in Berlin, an initiative launched in 1979 under the motto 'the inner city as a residential area'. While the '*Altbau*' (old building) section under the leadership of Hardt Walther Hämer was devoted to the rehabilitation of some 4,000 dilapidated dwellings in the Kreuzberg area of the city, the '*Neubau*' (new building) section under Josef Paul Kleihues sought to repair holes in the urban fabric left by the war and by post-war planning. Focused on the Südliche Friedrichstadt, a baroque extension to the city centre, IBA sought not to place objects in space, as the 1957 *Interbau* exhibition had done, but to restructure the city on the historical pattern, favouring perimeter blocks designed by a galaxy of German and international stars.

In subsequent histories the 1980s in German architecture will be marked as the decade of the museum, with a large number of distinguished contributions located throughout the Federal Republic. Frankfurt am Main was the epicentre of this activity, with a row of museums set along the Schaumainkai that included the German Architecture Museum (Fritz Geldmacher, 1912–13 and Oswald Mathias Ungers, 1979–84), the Museum of Arts and Crafts (Richard Meier, 1979–85), and the German Post Museum (Günter Behnisch, 1987–8). Across the river the Museum of Modern Art in Frankfurt was designed by the Viennese architect Hans Hollein (1985, 1987–91), who was also responsible for the very successful Municipal Museum at Mönchengladbach (1972–82), the site of a vigorous dialogue between the built form and the surrounding landscape. Perhaps the most contentious new museum of the decade was the extension to the Staatsgalerie in Stuttgart by James Stirling and Michael Wilford (1977–82), with a plan that echoes Schinkel's Altes Museum in Berlin (1826) and postmodernist citations from the historical canon at every turn.

With the collapse of the German Democratic Republic in 1989 and the subsequent unification of the two German states, the architectural landscape in Germany changed radically. The successful larger practices such as Von Gerkan, Marg & Partner, which was responsible for some of the more interesting design in the closing years of the old Federal Republic (IBA housing, Berlin, 1983–4; Stuttgart Airport, 1989, History Museum, Hamburg, 1989; Passenger Terminal, Hamburg Airport, 1986, 1990–3), are now active in the rebuilding of the new federal states in the east (Neue Messe, Leipzig, 1993–5). Initially the prime focus of the rebuilding programme was central Berlin, formerly in the GDR. Faced with radical proposals for the rebuilding of the city centre on one hand, and more conservative pleas for the restoration of the historical city grid with tight block forms and 22 metre cornice heights, the city authorities chose the latter option. Early results of this decision are the three blocks built in the Friedrichstadt by Pei, Cob and Freed, Oswald Mathias Ungers, and Jean Nouvel (all 1991–5), the last-named a striking department store for Galéries Lafayette, ranged around a glazed internal funnel. Major redevelopment projects for the Spreebogen as a ministerial quarter and for Potsdamer Platz and Alexander Platz as a commercial and business centre are planned for completion in the new century.

FURTHER READING

Mitchell Schwarzer, *German Architectural Theory and the Search for Modern Identity* (Cambridge: Cambridge University Press, 1995) provides a good introduction to nineteenth-century theories in response to German industrial society while Wolfgang Hermann, *Deutsche Baukunst des 19. und 20. Jahrhunderts* (Basel: Birkhäuser 1977) offers a well-informed survey of all aspects of architectural development. Germany's role as the crucible of architectural modernity in the century between 1830 and 1930 is explored in depth in Francesco Dal Co, *Figures of Architecture and Thought: German Architectural Culture, 1880–1930* (New York: Rizzoli, 1990).

For the twentieth century, two books stand out as introductions. Winfried Nerdinger and Cornelius Tafel, *Architectural Guide to Germany: 20th Century* (Basel: Birkhäuser, 1996) is a well-written general gazetteer for the whole period and Gerhard G. Feldmeyer, *The New Architecture* (New (New York: Rizzoli, 1993) surveys in particular recent developments in Germany since re-unification.

MARTIN BRADY *and*
HELEN HUGHES

14

German cinema

The birth of film in Germany

On 1 November 1895, nearly two months before the famous Lumière screening in Paris, the brothers Max and Emil Skladanowsky showed a fifteen-minute film programme at the Berlin Wintergarten using their Bioscop, and by June of the following year the inventor and entrepreneur Oskar Messter had sold his first flicker-free projector incorporating the Maltese cross mechanism. Soon after the turn of the century Messter was experimenting with the synchronisation of film footage and gramophone records and establishing his reputation as Germany's first major film producer. Germany thus had its share of pioneers at the start of film history. However, large-scale production of narrative film was slow to develop, allowing French, Danish, Italian and American films to dominate until the First World War.

In the wake of increasingly vociferous attacks on cinema for its low moral standards and corrupting influence the term *Autorenfilm* (writer's film) was coined in 1913. This tag was intended to enhance the reputation of the medium through the script of a recognised author, as exemplified by Max Mack's *Der Andere* (The Other, 1913), a variation on the Jekyll-and-Hyde motif, written by the playwright Paul Lindau. It was during this period that leading theatre directors, including Max Reinhardt, began to work in cinema, and filmmakers, drawing creatively on the German Romantic tradition, devised special effects to stage fantastic narratives: Stellan Rye's *Der Student von Prag* (The Student of Prague, 1913) introduced the motif of the *Doppelgänger*, and Paul Wegener and Henrik Galeen's *Der Golem* (The Golem, 1914) drew on the cabbalistic legend of the clay man. It was these developments which marked the first tentative steps towards a distinctive national film culture.

This was also the era in which the Danish actress Asta Nielsen provided German cinema with a popular star of international calibre. Much admired for her dramatic range, she was equally convincing as an immature, vivacious young aristocrat in Urban Gad's *Die Verräterin* (The Treacherous Woman, 1911) and as the scheming owner of a copper mine in Edmund Edel's *Die Börsenkönigin* (The Queen of the Stock Exchange, 1919).

Film in the Weimar Republic

During the First World War most foreign films were banned in Germany. As a result the domestic film industry emerged in a strong position in 1918, with no less than 130 production companies. The formation of Ufa (Universum-Film AG) on 18 December 1917 initiated a series of mergers, and from 1918 to 1933 the German film industry ranked second only to Hollywood, encouraged by government support, protectionism, and favourable exchange rates. The aspirations of the immediate post-war period found expression in a series of spectacular costume dramas such as *Madame Dubarry* (1919) by Ernst Lubitsch.

Scale, however, was not the only way in which early Weimar cinema celebrated a new sense of liberation. Sexual freedom, encouraged by the temporary relaxation of censorship, spawned a plethora of so-called *Aufklärungsfilme* ('educational films'), including Richard Oswald's *Anders als die andern* (Different from the Others, 1919), a plea for the reform of laws on homosexuality influenced by the sexologist Magnus Hirschfeld.

Expressionism

Internationally, early Weimar cinema has become synonymous with the Expressionist style epitomised by Robert Wiene's *Das Cabinet des Dr. Caligari* (The Cabinet of Dr Caligari, 1920) with its distorted, angular sets and impassioned, theatrical performances. Cinema had been slow to pick up on Expressionism, and both painting and literature functioned as prototypes, with sets and costumes often resembling *Brücke* paintings, and stories, dialogues and performances which owe a debt to Expressionist drama.

The importance of Expressionist cinema lies in its extension of psychology and dramatic tension to all aspects of a film's *mise en scène* and camerawork. A predilection for grotesque and macabre subject matter went hand-in-hand with the style – examples include F. W. Murnau's *Nosferatu*, the first vampire film. However, Expressionist films were by no means all remote from reality, as demonstrated by Lang's highly topical *Dr. Mabuse der Spieler* (Dr Mabuse, the Gambler, 1922), a study of gambling and extortion set in contemporary Berlin. Lang's *Metropolis* (1926), the story of oppression in an infernal city of the future, roughly coincides with the end of Expressionist cinema. The spectacular futuristic sets, which swelled the budget to an unprecedented 5.3 million Reichsmark, made *Metropolis* one of the most internationally influential films of the Weimar Republic. As late as 1931 Lang was still using Expressionist lighting and camerawork to excellent effect in his thriller *M* to create a claustrophobic atmosphere which was to make it a prototype for the Hollywood *film noir*.

New Sobriety

Weimar was also the era of *Neue Sachlichkeit* (New Sobriety), which initially manifested itself as a sober counter-reaction to Expressionism in the form of the *Kammerspielfilm* (chamber film), a modest brand of cinematic realism with a keen eye for detail, focusing on character rather than spectacle. The majority of these chamber films are set in a working-class milieu, reflecting the concerns of scriptwriter Carl Mayer, the main force behind the *Kammerspielfilm*. Outstanding examples include Lupu Pick's *Scherben* (Shattered, 1921), Leopold Jessner's *Die Hintertreppe* (Backstairs, 1921) and Murnau's *Der letzte Mann* (The Last Laugh, 1924). The ever-versatile Murnau can be seen as bridging the gap between Expressionism and the *Kammerspielfilm*, combining dramatic visual effects with a sure eye for psychological nuance in his Molière adaptation *Tartüff* (1926).

Both thematically and stylistically, the films of G. W. Pabst epitomise the spirit of *Neue Sachlichkeit*. With *Die Büchse der Pandora* (Pandora's Box, 1929), based on Wedekind's Lulu plays and starring the American actress Louise Brooks, he achieved a synthesis of hard-edged realism and sensuality. His first sound film, *Westfront 1918* (1930), is an uncompromising portrayal of the futility of war.

Pabst was deeply impressed by Eisenstein's *Battleship Potemkin* (1925), first screened in Berlin to great acclaim in 1926. Encouraged by its success, a number of directors turned to overtly political themes, resulting in a series of socially critical 'proletarian films'. The most famous of these is Piel Jutzi's *Mutter Krausens Fahrt ins Glück* (Mother Krause's Journey to

Happiness, 1929), a powerful story of unemployment and suicide set in Berlin's Wedding District. Based on the memoirs of Heinrich Zille, it influenced Bertolt Brecht and Slatan Dudow's Marxist 'Berlin film' *Kuhle Wampe oder Wem gehört die Welt?* (Kuhle Wampe, 1932).

The cosmopolitan quality of *Neue Sachlichkeit* cinema is reflected in one of its most productive genres, the *Straßenfilm* (street film). Generally focusing on fear and misery in the metropolis these include Karl Grune's *Die Straße* (The Street, 1923), Pabst's *Die freudlose Gasse* (The Joyless Street, 1925), and Joe May's crime thriller *Asphalt* (1929). A variation on the *Straßenfilm* theme, *Menschen am Sonntag* (People on Sunday, 1930) paints a very different picture of Berlin city life. Set in the milieu of the white-collar worker, and improvised by amateur actors, this lively and atmospheric film follows five young people on a Sunday outing to the Wannsee. It is remarkable, not least, for being a collaborative venture involving four future Hollywood directors: Robert Siodmak, Edgar G. Ulmer, Billy Wilder and Fred Zinnemann.

Despite the dominance of Berlin, the spirit of the modern city did not entirely dominate *Neue Sachlichkeit*. The 'mountain films' of Arnold Fanck, Luis Trenker, and Leni Riefenstahl offered a beguiling antidote to the claustrophobia and hardship of city life with images of untrammelled nature.

Experimental film

The twenties saw the first golden age of abstract painting, and a number of directors, most notably Viking Eggeling, Hans Richter, Oskar Fischinger and Walter Ruttmann, set about translating paintings into 'moving pictures'. There is no agreement as to who produced the first abstract film in Germany, but candidates include Ruttmann's *Lichtspiel Opus 1* (Film Opus 1, 1921), Richter's *Rhythmus* series (Rhythm, c.1921–5) and Eggeling's *Diagonalsymphonie* (Diagonal Symphony, c.1920–5). Whilst these films are geometric – influenced by Russian Constructivism, De Stijl, and the Bauhaus – their titles betray the role of music in the orchestration of lines and shapes.

Whereas the erstwhile Dadaist Richter expanded his palette by incorporating documentary footage and staged scenes into his films of the late twenties (*Inflation* (1927); *Vormittagsspuk* (Ghosts Before Breakfast) of 1928), Fischinger pioneered a range of new techniques, including three-dimensional animation and colour processes. Following a delightful series of *Studien* (Studies, 1929–34), his experiments culminated in a popular advertisement for the Muratti tobacco company featuring rows of marching cigarettes in bright colours, *Muratti greift ein* (Here Comes Muratti, 1934), and the complex abstract study *Komposition in Blau* (Composition in Blue, 1935).

Having contributed an animated sequence to the first part of Lang's *Nibelungen* (1924), and worked with the pioneering animator of shadow puppets Lotte Reiniger on *Die Abenteuer des Prinzen Achmed* (The Adventures of Prince Achmed, 1926), Ruttmann turned to documentary and, under the influence of Eisenstein and Dziga Vertov, produced the most famous 'city film' of the twenties, *Berlin. Die Sinfonie der Großstadt* (Berlin: Symphony of a City, 1927). A celebration of modernity, movement and the metropolis, it documents a day in the life of Berlin. Ruttmann continued making films during the Third Reich in which he employed the documentary realism of *Neue Sachlichkeit* and the structural rigour of abstract film for propaganda purposes (*Deutsche Panzer* (German Tanks), 1940).

During the twenties technical inventiveness and daring camerawork were by no means restricted to avant-garde films. Before noise became a problem with the advent of sound in 1929, swings, cranes and turntables 'unleashed' the camera and audiences experienced new sensations of restlessness and perpetual motion. One of the most famous examples in mainstream cinema is the swinging camera in the trapeze shots of E. A. Dupont's *Varieté* (1925).

Weimar sound film

With the introduction of sound Ufa swiftly established, in a profusion of musicals, comedies and star vehicles, the lively popular style which was to form the basis of its challenge to Hollywood throughout the thirties. Celebrated early examples include Wilhelm Thiele's musical comedy *Die Drei von der Tankstelle* (The Three from the Filling Station, 1930) and Eric Charell's spectacular *Der Kongress tanzt* (Congress Dances, 1931). Major ingredients in the success of German sound film include the production of multi-language versions for export and the introduction of a fresh generation of stars including Lilian Harvey and Marika Rökk. Josef von Sternberg's *Der blaue Engel* (The Blue Angel, 1930), an adaptation of Heinrich Mann's *Professor Unrat*, is notable for having achieved both critical and popular success thanks to its literary source material and stars Marlene Dietrich and Emil Jannings. By the end of the Weimar Republic German cinema had thus established an international reputation for sophistication and technical ingenuity. Whilst the styles and genres pioneered by 1933 survived in Germany throughout the Third Reich, many of its early practitioners, including Dietrich, Thiele and Charell, were soon to follow Lubitsch and Murnau to Hollywood in what, after 1933, with the exodus of around a third of film personnel in Germany, amounted to a wholesale drain of talent.

Film in the Third Reich

Propaganda Minister Joseph Goebbels assumed overall charge of the German film industry in March 1933, and in July the *Reichsfilmkammer* (Reich Film Chamber) was formed. Membership of this organisation was compulsory for all those working in the film industry, and Jews and those unable to prove political loyalty were excluded.

Goebbels was keenly aware of the potential of cinema for the dissemination of ideology. He believed in particular in the power of light entertainment to create affirmative role models and in consequence a mere 14 per cent of around 1,100 feature films produced between 1933 and 1945 fit readily into the category of explicit propaganda. Such works were reserved for important occasions. The first of these was the seizure of power in 1933, which was marked by a small number of films immortalising heroes of the movement and celebrating the process of conversion to National Socialism. Typical of these is Hans Steinhoff's *Hitlerjunge Quex* (Hitler Youth Quex, 1933) which tells the story of Heini Völker, son of a committed Communist, who is won over to the Nazi cause only to die as a martyr. Stylistically it bears a striking resemblance to Weimar proletarian cinema. This wave of films was short-lived for, as Goebbels noted, 'We National Socialists place little value on having the SA march about on stage or screen. They belong on the street.'[1]

The most significant propaganda films of the pre-war period, aside from the newsreels which accompanied every screening, were the documentaries of Riefenstahl: *Triumph des Willens* (Triumph of the Will), a record of the 1934 Party Rally in Nuremberg, and *Olympia*, a two-part celebration of the 1936 Olympic Games in Berlin. These spectacularly grand and expensive films have remained some of the most controversial of the period, by a director personally selected by Hitler. Whilst some commentators see them as remarkable experiments in *cinéma vérité*, others have interpreted them as blatant propaganda for the party and its ideology.

With the outbreak of war there was a resurgence of overtly propagandist filmmaking: German victories were celebrated in numerous documentaries, and Karl Ritter produced a series of films in praise of the Luftwaffe. It was, however, two anti-Semitic films justifying the 'Final Solution' that were to become the most notorious examples of National Socialist cinema: Fritz Hippler's pseudo-documentary *Der ewige Jude* (The Eternal Jew, 1940) and Veit Harlan's savage drama *Jud Süß* (1940). Harlan's film was seen by an audience of twenty million, around a third of the population of the Reich. It was Harlan who was also entrusted with Goebbels's last major project, *Kolberg* (1945), a quasi-mythical story set in the Napoleonic wars, intended as an appeal to the Germans to resist the Allies to the last. This bombastic, visually spectacular film evokes a resurrection from the ashes of defeat.

Popular genres

The bulk of National Socialist feature filmmaking comprised light entertainment in the popular genres pioneered during the late Weimar Republic: comedies such as Wolfgang Liebeneiner's *Der Mustergatte* (The Ideal Husband, 1937), a popular hit starring Heinz Rühmann, melodramas including Detlef Sierck's *La Habanera* (1937) with Zarah Leander, and literary adaptations such as Gustaf Gründgens's Fontane adaptation *Der Schritt vom Wege* (Effi Briest, 1939) and Harlan's *Immensee* (1943). Musicals were particularly in demand throughout the Third Reich and included one of the biggest box-office successes of the period, Rolf Hansen's *Die große Liebe* (The Great Love, 1942), rivalled in popularity only by Harlan's melodrama *Die goldene Stadt* (The Golden City, 1942), an early colour film seen by thirty-one million spectators.

During the war, escapist fantasies such as Josef von Baky's *Münchhausen* (1943), historical costume dramas and so-called 'genius films' (including Pabst's *Paracelsus* of 1943) served a new function, distracting audiences from the horrors of the present – in particular the bombing raids – with images of a glorious German past or of life without fear and destruction. Peter Pewas's *Der verzauberte Tag* (The Enchanted Day, 1944), an intensely lyrical and visually arresting tale of two women who long to break out of their humdrum existence, deserves special mention in this respect. Anni invents an imaginary lover, whilst her friend Christine meets the man of her dreams. The Nazis banned the film for its mocking depiction of the German petty-bourgeois, and it remains a rare example of 'aesthetic opposition' in the cinema of the Third Reich.[2]

The Cinema of Ruins, 1945–9

The title of Roberto Rossellini's Berlin 'rubble' film *Germania anno zero* (1947) notwithstanding, it is impossible to speak of 1945 as a zero hour in German cinema. The immediate post-war years are characterised by a manifest continuity of personnel and style despite the fact that German films during this period had to pass Allied censors, who attempted to ban former Nazis from filmmaking.

The first film made in Germany after the war, Wolfgang Staudte's *Die Mörder sind unter uns* (The Murderers are Among Us, 1946), is a courageous attempt to confront the legacy of National Socialism, following a traumatised doctor trying to build a new life and bring his former commanding officer to justice. In its blend of gritty realism and Expressionist *angst* Staudte's film consciously evokes the 'innocence' of pre-Nazi cinema. Subsequent films, and in particular their titles, often betray confusion and a lack of direction: *Zwischen gestern und morgen* (Between Yesterday and Tomorrow, 1947) by Harald Braun concludes that 'Life must go on, there's nothing for it', whilst in *Film ohne Titel* (Film Without a Title, 1947) Rudolf Jugert confronts the crisis of confidence in German filmmaking under the guise of a light-hearted love story. Jugert's film was scripted by Helmut Käutner, one of the most distinguished directors of this unsettled period. Having produced a number of highly individual, predominently melancholic films during the war, his first post-war feature, *In jenen Tagen* (In Former Days, 1947), is an attempt at collective reconciliation.

Film in the German Democratic Republic

In the Soviet-occupied zone film production had begun quickly, encouraged by the authorities as a means of re-education. By the time the Deutsche Film-Aktiengesellschaft (DEFA) was licensed on 17 May 1946, around ten issues of the newly founded East German newsreel *Der Augenzeuge* (The Eyewitness) had been completed. The newsreel appeared under the democratic, anti-fascist slogan, 'See for yourself – Hear for yourself – Judge for yourself!', but the liberal spirit of the immediate post-war years was gradually replaced during the late forties by the more doctrinal business of promoting the image and plans of the SED.

Filmmaking in East Germany was directly controlled by the Party politically, economically and aesthetically, with DEFA maintaining an

almost complete monopoly over production and distribution. Thematically GDR films reflect directly or indirectly the political concerns of the
SED at different historical moments: the Party's proclaimed roots in
anti-fascism, as well as its attitudes towards the capitalist West, find
immediate expression in the new genre of the 'anti-fascist film'; the need
for increased productivity and political vigilence at home are reflected in
the *Gegenwartsfilm* (topical film); the concern to entertain and educate
the young is demonstrated by the generous funding of films for children. Documentary film also received consistent support, both as a vehicle for propaganda and as a means of recording and rallying local
communities.

The anti-fascist film

Following DEFA's move to Potsdam-Babelsberg in 1948 the former Ufa
studios, which until 1945 had been the headquarters of National Socialist
film production, became the home of the anti-fascist film. This genre was
to remain a staple of GDR filmmaking for the next forty years, with the
most celebrated DEFA filmmaker, Konrad Wolf, making no less than four
major contributions to the genre: *Lissy* (1957), an adaptation of a novel by
F. C. Weiskopf about a young woman's struggle against fascism within
her own family, *Sterne* (Stars, 1959), in which a soldier falls in love with a
Jewish woman due to be deported to Auschwitz, *Professor Mamlock* (1961),
about a Jewish doctor in the early thirties, and *Ich war neunzehn* (I Was
Nineteen, 1967), based on the director's own experiences as a Red Army
soldier at the end of the war.

The *Gegenwartsfilm*

Important as the anti-fascist films were in confronting National Socialism, this preoccupation with the past could also amount to ignoring the
present. The GDR appeared to offer an ideal opportunity to pick up
where the 'proletarian film' of the Weimar Republic had left off. However, many GDR filmmakers initially found it difficult to represent the
issues of their own time. Staudte's celebrated historical film *Der Untertan*
(The Underdog, 1951), for example, was a literary adaptation set at the
turn of the century. One notable exception was Dudow's *Unser täglich Brot*
(Our Daily Bread, 1949), the first socialist feature film about life in a
divided Germany.

The year 1952 marked a low-point in GDR film production with only
six completed feature films. The Politbüro demanded the 'development

of forward-looking German cinema', and in response a number of directors turned to heroes of socialism for their subject matter. Most famous and expensive amongst these films is Kurt Maetzig's two-part dramatisation of the life of Ernst Thälmann (1954–5).

In the mid-1950s Gerhard Klein's frank portraits of Berlin youth (including *Berlin – Ecke Schönhauser...* (Berlin – Down Schönhauser Way...) of 1957) marked a new departure for the *Gegenwartsfilm*. Maetzig's two-part *Schlösser und Katen* (Castles and Cottages, 1956), a meticulous study of the upheavels and land reforms in a rural community between 1945 and the uprising of 17 June 1953, chronicled the austerities of village life with comparable veracity. This development was short-lived, however, as stricter censorship was imposed in the wake of the 1956 uprising in Hungary. It was not until the relaxation of censorship following the closing of the border in 1961 that filmmakers were permitted once again to tackle topical issues openly. Wolf's *Der geteilte Himmel* (The Divided Heaven, 1964), based on the novel by Christa Wolf, addressed the division of Germany and was followed by a series of films by younger directors exploring other controversial themes including education, conflict between the generations and corruption in the judiciary. These debates were silenced by the Eleventh Plenum of the Central Committee of the SED in 1965, following which half a year's production was shelved, whilst other films were only released with major cuts. These *Verbotsfilme* (forbidden films) were by no means all subversive, but represented the restlessness of a new generation critical of the old. They included Maetzig's *Das Kaninchen bin ich* (I Am the Rabbit, 1965) and Hermann Zschoche's *Karla* (1965). Frank Beyer's powerful study of the conflict between a party representative and a local family of builders, *Spur der Steine* (Trail of Stones, 1966), made it to the cinema, but was withdrawn almost immediately.

A new spirit of openness followed Erich Honecker's famous speech in 1971 condemning taboos in the arts. Heiner Carow's hit film *Die Legende von Paul und Paula* (The Legend of Paul and Paula, 1972), based on a novel by Ulrich Plenzdorf, controversially portrayed the search for individual rather than collective happiness; it also became famous for its frank treatment of sexuality. Konrad Wolf's immensely popular *Solo Sunny* (1979), depicting a woman's failed attempt to become a professional singer, confirmed the trend.

Carow's Plenzdorf adaptation coincides with a productive period of DEFA literary adaptations in which directors turned both to the classics (Siegfried Kühn's *Die Wahlverwandtschaften* (Elective Affinities, 1974) and

Egon Günther's *Lotte in Weimar* of 1975) and to contemporary writers for material. Beyer's *Jakob der Lügner* (Jakob the Liar, 1974), based on the novel by Jurek Becker, was indeed the first and only DEFA film to be nominated for an 'Oscar'.

A notable beneficiary of state funding in the GDR was the children's film. A charming early example of the genre, Francesco Stefani's *Das singende klingende Bäumchen* (The Singing Ringing Tree, 1957), is now regarded as a classic. There are also many fine examples from the eighties, including Helmut Dziuba's *Sabine Kleist, 7 Jahre* (Sabine Kleist, Aged Seven, 1982) in which a little girl runs away from a children's home and wanders the streets of East Berlin. Dziuba's film presents a remarkably honest and down-to-earth picture of the GDR.

Shortly before the *Wende*, censorship was relaxed once again and it became possible to touch on taboo subjects. Carow had fought for eight years to make a film about homosexuality, and the result, *Coming Out*, was finally premiered on 9 November 1989.

Documentary film

The GDR's greatest contribution to the history of film was in the field of documentary. Andrew and Annelie Thorndike, the leading documentarists of the first generation, worked with archive material, which they edited into epic chronicles of the progress of humankind towards a socialist utopia (*Du und mancher Kamrad* (The German Story) of 1956 and *Das russische Wunder* (The Russian Miracle) of 1963).

Beginning with *Brüder und Schwestern* (Brothers and Sisters) in 1962 – a biting and visually inventive attack on the patronising attitude of the West Germans to their 'brothers and sisters behind the Iron Curtain' – Walter Heynowski and Gerhard Scheumann developed the agitational propaganda film to new levels of sophistication, addressing such themes as the activities of West German mercenaries in the Congo, the US military, and the Vietnam war.

Whilst the historical narratives of the Thorndikes and the agitational films of Heynowski and Scheumann drew on Marxist ideology, a new generation of filmmakers was to turn to everyday life in the GDR for its subject matter. Painter and filmmaker Jürgen Böttcher, the GDR's foremost documentarist, pioneered an East German version of *cinéma vérité*. His mature films of the late seventies and eighties, including *Martha* (1978), *Rangierer* (Shunters, 1984) and *Die Küche* (The Kitchen, 1986), can be read as subversive, not least in their lack of authorial comment. *Rangierer*, a mesmerising study of shunters at work in Dresden, has become one of the most celebrated DEFA documentaries.

The 1980s was a decade in which documentary film reaped the benefits of a tightly knit, technically assured group of filmmakers and their cameramen. With *Lebensläufe* (Biographies, 1981) Winfried Junge continued a project begun in 1961 to record life in the village of Golzow. This fascinating document outlived the state itself, receiving continued funding in 1995. Volker Koepp also observed a single group for several years, beginning his 'Wittstock series' in 1975 with *Mädchen in Wittstock* (Girls in Wittstock). Focusing on textile workers, Koepp discovered that women were more open and willing to be critical about their situation than men. A film that touched many through its sympathetic and sometimes harrowing portrayal of the lives of women in the GDR was Helke Misselwitz's *Winter adé* (1988), in which she interviewed a diverse cross-section of women right across the GDR.

Film in the Federal Republic

Initial signs of rejuvenation in the *Trümmerfilm* (Cinema of Ruins) were not to be sustained. Not even returning emigrants such as Peter Lorre (*Der Verlorene* (The Lost One), 1951) were able to make a significant impact. A tidal wave of dubbed films from America, together with a lack of government subsidy and the fragmentation of the industry, discouraged homegrown talent. The few outstanding films of the decade are the exception, rather than the rule: Robert Siodmak's Gerhard Hauptmann adaptation *Die Ratten* (The Rats, 1955), Herbert Vesely's existentialist, avant-garde feature film *Nicht mehr fliehen* (No Escape, 1955), Georg Tressler's *Die Halbstarken* (The Hooligans, 1956), which introduced a new realist tone into West German cinema, Kurt Hoffmann's comedy *Wir Wunderkinder* (Aren't We Wonderful, 1958), about an industrialist of the Economic Miracle with a Nazi past, Rolf Thiele's *Das Mädchen Rosemarie* (A Girl Called Rosemarie, 1958), on the Frankfurt high-society prostitute Rosemarie Nitribitt, and Bernhard Wicki's powerful anti-war film *Die Brücke* (The Bridge, 1959). A film focusing directly on the contradictions and anxieties of the fifties is Ottomar Domnick's *Jonas* (1957), scripted by Hans Magnus Enzensberger, a stark psychoanalytical study of a beleaguered victim of the Economic Miracle unable to lay his guilty past to rest.

In general, however, this period of rebuilding and growing material success was the heyday of escapist optimism, of *Heimatfilme* – rustic romances such as Hans Deppe's *Grün ist die Heide* (Green is the Heath, 1951) – and of the 'Sissi' films with Romy Schneider, set in Imperial Austria. This trend was to continue well into the sixties with a series of Edgar Wallace thrillers starring Klaus Kinski, and Karl May Westerns, beginning in 1963 with Harald Reinl's *Winnetou I*. The fifties were boom years at the box-office – 128 films were released in 1955, and in 1956 there were 817 million cinema visits, or 16 per head. The decade also marked an aesthetic nadir, what John Sandford has succinctly termed a 'general paralysis of inspiration and talent', from which German film was only to rise slowly and hesitantly during the sixties.[3]

Young German Cinema

At the Berlin Film Festival in 1961 the Federal Film Prize was not awarded. No film was considered worthy of it. However, a young generation of *Autorenfilmer*, writer-directors inspired by Italian Neo-Realism and the French New Wave, had already begun around 1960 to make short films in new styles and with contemporary subject matter. Alexander Kluge and Peter Schamoni's *Brutalität in Stein* (Brutality in Stone, 1960), for example, tackled the theme of Nazi ideology by focusing on its architecture through a disjointed montage of texts, documents, archive footage, commentary and music, juxtaposed with tracking shots of the surviving ruins. Here in miniature was a prototype of the topical, political cinema that was to become the New German Cinema.

In 1962, at the Oberhausen Short Film Festival, a group of twenty-six young directors, including Kluge, Schamoni and Edgar Reitz, signed the founding document of the New German Cinema, the Oberhausen Manifesto, proclaiming their goal to be 'the creation of the new German feature film'.

However, a lack of funding and a suitable distribution infrastructure, coupled with the disenchantment of audiences and critics alike with German cinema, made the first steps arduous. Milestones of this period of 'Young German Cinema' include much work by filmmakers from abroad: the Czech Ferdinand Khittl shot his epic philosophical essay-film *Die Parallelstraße* (The Parallel Street, 1961) during two trips round the globe, Vlado Kristl fled to Germany from Tito's Yugoslavia to make a series of anarchic, poetic shorts and feature-length films (including *Der Damm* (The Dam), 1964), and Jean-Marie Straub and Danièle Huillet arrived from France to shoot two of the first post-Oberhausen films to address the Nazi past and its legacy, *Machorka-Muff* (1962) and *Nicht versöhnt oder Es hilft nur Gewalt, wo Gewalt herrscht* (Not Reconciled, 1965), both adaptations of works by Heinrich Böll. These films were largely rejected in Germany but celebrated at festivals abroad.

In 1965 a body was set up to help subsidise new films by young directors, the *Kuratorium junger deutscher Film*, and in 1966 Kluge's debut feature, the programmatically titled *Abschied von gestern* (Goodbye to Yesterday/Yesterday Girl), received international recognition including a Silver Lion in Venice.

The sixties also saw the debuts of a number of directors destined to be the big names of German cinema after 1970, Volker Schlöndorff's Musil adaptation *Der junge Törless* (Young Törless, 1966), Reitz's neo-realist study of a fiercely independent young woman who drives her husband to suicide, *Mahlzeiten* (Meal Times, 1967), Rudolf Thome's gangster movie *Detektive* (Detectives, 1968) and Hans Jürgen Syberberg's idiosyncratic Tolstoy adaptation, *Scarabea* (1968).

Experimental film

The Oberhausen Manifesto proclaimed short films to be a 'training ground and laboratory for the feature film', but did not ascribe any value to experiment in its own right. Since 1933 there had been little or no avant-garde cinema in Germany, and when a new generation of artists and photographers in the sixties wanted to explore the possibilities of 'film as film', the material potential of celluloid, light and projection, they had to look abroad to Austrian structural film and the American underground for inspiration. Birgit and Wilhelm Hein (*Rohfilm* (Raw Film), 1968), Werner Nekes (*Kelek*, 1968), and Dore O. (*Alaska*, 1968) became the main representatives of experimental filmmaking in Germany in the sixties and early seventies, focusing on structure, rhythm and gaze. During the 1970s certain experimental filmmakers, including Klaus Wyborny (*Die Geburt der Nation* (The Birth of a Nation, 1973), a homage to D. W. Griffith) and Heinz Emigholz (*Dämon* (Demon, 1977), based on a poem by Mallarmé) enriched structural filmmaking by introducing narrative and text.

During the late seventies and eighties experimental film was sustained by new themes and styles: Nekes included slapstick and Greek mythology in his epic compendium of experimental techniques *Uliisses* (1982), and Emigholz's *The Basis of Make-Up* (1974–83), a headlong dash through dozens of volumes of his diary, became the starting-point for a tetralogy of experimental feature films.

The New German Cinema

Supported by new funding organisations, including self-help in the form of the *Filmverlag der Autoren*, founded in 1971, and television money (the majority from ZDF and WDR), German cinema experienced a renaissance in the 1970s. The year 1968 had seen the first feature-length film of Werner Herzog, *Lebenszeichen* (Signs of Life), in which a soldier, forced to conform, escapes into madness and attempts to wage war against the sun with home-made fireworks. Herzog's film, like much of his later work, is inhabited by bizarre loners and outcasts and shot through with absurd humour. In 1969 Rainer Werner Fassbinder made the first in a trilogy of gangster movies distorting American film clichés into an ascetic study of loneliness and isolation, *Liebe ist kälter als der Tod* (Love is Colder than Death) featuring Hanna Schygulla, whilst Werner Schroeter's debut, *Eika Katappa*, fused American underground cinema, gay and religious iconography, melodrama, Verdi and German Romanticism into a heady and camp mixture. The year 1970 saw the debut feature of Wim Wenders, the minimalist road movie *Summer in the City*, and by 1971 the major directors had begun to assert their mature style in works which were to establish the international reputation of New German Cinema: Fassbinder's *Händler der vier Jahreszeiten* (The Merchant of Four Seasons), a melodrama about the decline and fall of a small-time Munich trader, and Wenders's second collaboration with the Austrian writer Peter Handke, *Die Angst des Tormanns beim Elfmeter* (The Goalie's Fear of the Penalty), a study in social and linguistic alienation.

Although the New German Cinema is often labelled 'political cinema', this is misleading. Certainly Fassbinder, Kluge, Straub/Huillet and, to a lesser extent, Margarethe von Trotta, Schlöndorff and Reinhard Hauff were what Thomas Elsaesser terms 'contentist' filmmakers, addressing such themes as National Socialism (Schlöndorff's *Die Blechtrommel* (The Tin Drum, 1978) based on Grass's novel), immigrant workers (Fassbinder's *Angst essen Seele auf* (Fear Eats the Soul), 1974), the press (Schlöndorff and von Trotta's Böll adaptation *Die verlorene Ehre der Katharina Blum* (The Lost Honour of Katharina Blum), 1975) and terrorism (the collective film *Deutschland im Herbst* (Germany in Autumn) and Hauff's *Messer im Kopf* (Knife in the Head), both of 1978; Fassbinder's *Die dritte Generation* (The Third Generation) of 1979).[4] They were not in general, however, quick to respond to political events. There are few films before the mid-1970s on National Socialism, and German division is largely ignored. Furthermore the New German Cinema was extremely heterogeneous.

Unlike their more political colleagues, Wenders and Herzog are 'sensibilist' filmmakers, focusing on states of mind and favouring images and music over words (Herzog's *Aguirre, der Zorn Gottes* (Aguirre, Wrath of God, 1972), Wenders's *Alice in den Städten* (Alice in the Cities) of 1973). The landscape imagery in their films owes a considerable debt to German Romanticism, and Herzog in particular has been keen to bridge the gap with both pre-war cinema and the German literary heritage, programmatically in his remake of Murnau's *Nosferatu* (1978), and Büchner adaptation *Woyzeck* (1978). Syberberg is a special case, producing a remarkable trilogy of films in the seventies under the motto 'Brecht + Wagner', spectacular investigations into the German psyche and 'fascinating fascism', concluding with the four-part *Hitler, ein Film aus Deutschland* (Hitler, a Film from Germany, 1977).

Whilst the artistic achievements of the New German Cinema were celebrated both at home and abroad, the films themselves were unable to make any significant impression at the box-office in Germany. Only a handful broke even, and of these the majority were literary adaptations (Fassbinder's *Fontane Effi Briest* (1974), *Katharina Blum* and *Die Blechtrommel* foremost amongst them). 'On the arts pages we are strong, in the film industry we are marginal figures' as Hauff neatly put it.[5] In 1978, the *annus mirabilis* of the New German Cinema, the share of the home market captured by German films sank to a mere 8 per cent. Without what Herzog termed the 'artificial respiration' of government subsidy and prizes, and without television co-production, he and his colleagues would have been unable to survive.[6]

As long as the government felt it could benefit from the positive image of German cinema abroad and the willingness of its filmmakers to take on the nation's *Trauerarbeit* (work of mourning) it was keen to service the life support machine, but in the new political climate of the early eighties, following Kohl's victory in 1982, the Minister of the Interior Friedrich Zimmermann decided that the time had come to stop funding dissent with government money. The filmmakers' equivocal stance on terrorism and the controversy in Bavaria surrounding Herbert Achternbusch's film *Das Gespenst* (The Ghost, 1982), which was denounced as blasphemous, were used to justify the change in policy.

This crisis was exacerbated by the death of Fassbinder in 1982, by which time Wenders, Schlöndorff and Herzog were all working abroad. For most commentators this marked the end of the second great flowering of German film, although Straub/Huillet (*Klassenverhältnisse* (Class

Relations), 1983) and Syberberg (*Nacht* (Night), 1985) remained as productive and provocative as ever. Other outstanding achievements by established *Autorenfilmer* during this period include Reitz's *Heimat* (1984), an eleven-part chronicle of life in the fictional Hunsrück village of Schabbach, which was shown to great acclaim on television both at home and abroad, and Wenders's *Der Himmel über Berlin* (Wings of Desire, 1987), a lyrical homage to the city in which German cinema was born. Moreover, documentarists such as Klaus Wildenhahn, Harun Farocki and Hartmut Bitomsky, who had begun working in the sixties, remained largely unaffected by the problems confronting feature filmmakers. Indeed Farocki and Bitomsky produced some of their most acclaimed work during the 1980s (Farocki's *Bilder der Welt und Inschrift des Krieges* (Images of the World and the Inscription of War) and Bitomsky's *VW-Komplex*, both of 1988).

Many women directors came to prominence during the eighties, and by the end of the decade Germany had proportionally more women filmmakers than any other country. The majority emerged from the women's movement, and their work demonstrates different attempts to define a feminine/feminist aesthetic. Whilst Helma Sanders-Brahms retold the history of the war and its aftermath from a woman's perspective (*Deutschland, bleiche Mutter* (Germany Pale Mother), 1980), von Trotta concentrated on inter-personal relationships in different socio-political contexts (including *Die bleierne Zeit* (The German Sisters) of 1981), and Helke Sander focused on the history of emancipation (*Der subjektive Faktor* (The Subjective Factor), 1981), Ulrike Ottinger developed a quasi-anthropological, postmodern aesthetic to assess the role of women both at home (*Bildnis einer Trinkerin* (Ticket of No Return, 1979) about Berlin) and abroad (*Johanna d'Arc of Mongolia*, 1989). In 1985 Doris Dörrie scored a major box-office hit with her comedy *Männer* (Men).

The New German cinema's heterogeneity also encouraged maverick, in some cases regionally coloured filmmaking, including the work of the Bavarian author and director Achternbusch, who by 1989 had made nineteen visionary, anarchic features on a shoestring budget. In West Berlin the lively gay scene gave rise to a colourful genre of erotic, cosmopolitan features (Rosa von Praunheim's *Nicht der Homosexuelle ist pervers, sondern die Situation in der er lebt* (Not the Homosexual is Perverse, but the Situation in which He Finds Himself, 1970), Frank Ripploh's *Taxi zum Klo* (1981) and Lothar Lambert's *Fräulein Berlin* of 1983) and challenging documentaries (Praunheim's *AIDS-Trilogie* of 1989–90).

Film after unification

With the fall of the Wall, hopes were expressed that a rejuvenation of filmmaking could emerge out of the union of two distinct cinematic traditions. Certainly documentary film in Germany experienced an unprecedented flowering during and after the events of November 1989. A number of GDR filmmakers, including Andreas Voigt (*Letztes Jahr Titanic* (Last Year Titanic), 1990), captured events as they unfolded. Others, from both East and West, examined individual aspects of the unification process and its pre-history: Sibylle Schönemann, for example, researched the truth behind her own imprisonment as a GDR filmmaker in *Verriegelte Zeit* (Locked Up Time, 1990), and in *Der schwarze Kasten* (The Black Box, 1992) Johann Feindt and Tamara Trampe explored the mechanisms of state control in an extended interview with a former Stasi training officer.

In the aftermath of unification, documentary filmmaking remained both topical and controversial, confronting head-on the problems facing the New Germany. Thomas Heise's *STAU – Jetzt geht's los* (Jammed, Let's Get Moving, 1992), for example, addressed the rise of the New Right, and a number of documentaries examined the status of the former German territories in the East, including Koepp's *Kalte Heimat* (Cold Homeland, 1995), a poetic portrait of contemporary East Prussia, and Pavel Schnabel's *Der böhmische Knoten* (The Bohemian Knot, 1995), a montage of vivid reminiscences and contrasting viewpoints on the tangled history of German–Czech relations.

Amongst post-unification feature films, comedies were particularly successful at the box-office, with Helmut Dietl's *Schtonk!* (1992), a satire on the Hitler Diaries fiasco, Katja von Garnier's *Abgeschminkt!* (Making Up, 1992) and Sönke Wortmann's *Der bewegte Mann* (The Most Desirable Man, 1994) all vying with Hollywood for a share of the domestic market. Moreover, the most striking new genre of the early nineties was the re-unification comedy, typified by Vadim Glowna's *Der Brocken* (The Brocken, 1991), a satire set on the Baltic coast in which corporate culture colonises a rural East German community. A more caustic brand of satire was celebrated in Christoph Schlingensief's *Das deutsche Kettensägenmassaker* (The German Chainsaw Massacre, 1990), a trash horror movie parodying the supremacy of consumerist culture, in which a manic West German family, equipped with axes and chainsaws, hunts down *Ossis* and turns them into sausages.

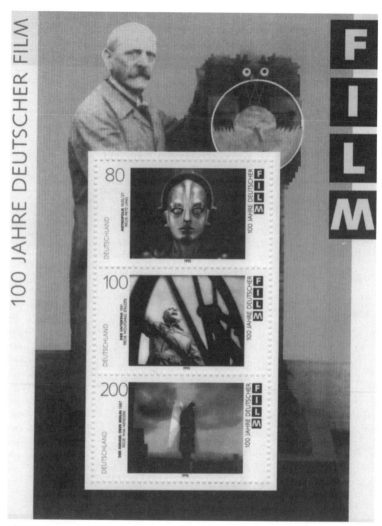

Fig. 14.1 One Hundred Years of German Cinema.

When it came to the hundredth anniversary of film in 1995, the Deutsche Bundespost chose three images for a series of stamps to celebrate the achievements of German cinema (fig. 14.1): the metallic face of the futuristic robot Maria from Lang's *Metropolis*, Werner Peters as the subject caught up in the wheels of history in Staudte's *Der Untertan* and Damiel, one of the angels of memory in Wenders's *Der Himmel über Berlin*, looking down at the divided city from the Gedächtniskirche. These stills, set into a photograph of Max Skladanowsky operating his Bioscop, not only represent three important chapters in the history of German cinema – Ufa, DEFA and the New German Cinema – but also, in juxtaposing iconic images of modernity, demagogy and commemoration, testify to the unique part German films have played in the documentation of an age of extremes.

NOTES

1. Quoted in Wolfgang Jacobsen, Anton Kaes and Hans Helmut Prinzler (eds.), *Geschichte des deutschen Films* (Stuttgart, Weimar: Metzler, 1993), p. 122.
2. *Ibid.*, p.165.
3. John Sandford, *The New German Cinema* (London: Oswald Wolff, 1980), p. 12.
4. Thomas Elsaesser, *New German Cinema: A History* (Houndmills, London: BFI Macmillan, 1989), pp. 56–63.
5. Barbara Bronnen and Corinna Brocher, *Die Filmemacher: Der neue deutsche Film nach Oberhausen mit einem Beitrag von Alexander Kluge* (Munich, Gütersloh, Vienna: Bertelsmann, 1973), p. 193.
6. *Ibid.*, p. 21.

FURTHER READING

For a comprehensive history of German cinema see Wolfgang Jacobsen, Anton Kaes and Hans Helmut Prinzler (eds.), *Geschichte des deutschen Films* (Stuttgart, Weimar: Metzler, 1993), which has an extensive bibliography arranged by period and genre. The principal reference work on German filmmakers is Hans-Michael Bock (ed.), *CineGraph: Lexikon zum deutschsprachigen Film* (Munich: edition text + kritik, 1984–). Two classic studies have dominated debate on film in the Weimar Republic: Siegfried Kracauer, *From Caligari to Hitler: A Psychological History of the German Film* (Princeton: Princeton University Press, 1947) and Lotte H. Eisner, *The Haunted Screen* (London: Secker & Warburg, 1973). For cinema in the Third Reich see Eric Rentschler, *The Ministry of Illusion: Nazi Cinema and its Afterlife* (Cambridge, Mass.: Harvard University Press, 1996). An exhaustive source of information on the DEFA feature film is Ralf Schenk (ed.), *Das zweite Leben der Filmstadt Babelsberg: DEFA-Spielfilme 1946–1992* (Berlin: Henschel, 1994). Günter Jordan and Ralf Schenk (eds.), *Schwarzweiß und Farbe: DEFA-Dokumentarfilme 1946–92* (Berlin: Jovis, 1996), is a similarly comprehensive study of DEFA documentaries. Standard works on the New German Cinema are John Sandford, *The New German Cinema* (London: Oswald Wolff, 1980) and Thomas Elsaesser, *The New German Cinema: A History* (Houndmills, London: BFI Macmillan, 1989). Julia Knight, *Women and the New German Cinema* (London: Verso, 1992) examines women's filmmaking in the FRG. An important handbook on contemporary cinema in Germany, including information on institutions and filmographies of individual filmmakers, is Hans Günther Pflaum and Hans Helmut Prinzler, *Cinema in the Federal Republic of Germany* (Bonn: Inter Nationes, 1993).

15

The media of mass communication: the press, radio and television

322   In a modern-day society, the means by which its members communicate with each other are a constitutive element of its make-up. The central place of communication and mass communication applies to the world of work but has also become an integral part of leisure activities. In contemporary Germany, leisure and the media of mass communication have become inseparable facets of everyday culture: 'according to recent leisure research . . . reading books . . . occupies only the tenth place of the most frequent leisure activities, after watching television (80 per cent), reading newspapers or magazines (62 per cent), listening to the radio (59 per cent), talking on the telephone (44 per cent), having a cup of coffee or a glass of beer (42 per cent), socialising with friends (37 per cent), gardening (36 per cent), sleeping late (36 per cent) and listening to records or audio cassettes (33 per cent).'[1] Thus, much of the leisure time of Germans is taken up by interacting with and through media. Media of mass communication such as newspapers, the telephone, television and radio rank highly in contemporary society and culture.

Societies are constructs of the media and at the same time their creators. Within the media national borders play an ever-decreasing role. By definition, media are concerned with communicating information, providing interfaces and expressing social concerns. Communication does not stop at national borders; Germany, like other countries, has become porous as foreign media enter and excite its national communicative domain. On the one hand, media have become more diverse and encompass many channels of communication; on the other hand, they have grown together and become concentrated in the hands of a few conglomerates. The globalisation of media culture has already taken place.

Today, much of media history is quasi-universal due to the use of universal technology, means of distribution and patterns of reception. Yet important cultural differences remain. These can be pinpointed by asking for whose benefit media function in a given culture and how they affect the lives of people in cultural, social or political terms. Do media contribute to people's quality of life, and if so, how is this visible? This chapter follows the emergence, diversity and impact of media in Germany and their place in German culture. It will look specifically at the printed message distributed via books, newspapers, magazines and the like, at the electronic message via radio, television and telephone, and concludes with a brief account of the media of communication in Germany since unification.

The printed message

From the invention of the printing press in the second half of the fifteenth century by Johannes Gutenberg in Mainz, printed texts have had a decisive influence on the development of German culture. The Reformation cannot be imagined without the arrival of ever greater numbers of printed texts. Martin Luther's translation of the Bible into German established the German language as it is known today and by extension changed German society and culture. With the Bible translation the standardisation of written German had arrived. But it was to take another three centuries before the printed message became a true mass medium. Noteworthy in this respect was the founding in 1867 of Reclam Universal-Bibliothek, affordable pocket-style books for the mass market of the period. In the twentieth century, this development found its logical progression in the production of paperback books while hard-back books become increasingly expensive. Today, many books are published in a paperback edition from the start in a bid to secure quantity sales.

In terms of influence, the book gave way to newsprint as society turned into mass society. At first, newspapers only published official announcements from tax inspectors, military news and market times, but it was not long before editorials began to appear, prompting almost immediate censorship from officials. Yet newspapers became a formidable voice in shaping and reflecting opinions. The press has even been dubbed the fourth power in the state alongside the legislature, the police and the justice system. Jürgen Habermas linked the rise of newspapers and their power to the emergence of the bourgeoisie as a new social class and its attempt to create and control its own public sphere. While proclaiming itself to be committed to providing information and enlightenment, the press is said to generate a pseudo public sphere which misleads and obfuscates.[2] Habermas applies this pessimistic assessment to the past as well as to the present.

In Germany, the freedom of the press was granted explicitly by Bismarck in 1871. However, this only involved the abolition of state pre-publication censorship; what was not abolished was post-publication censorship. Furthermore, with the passing of the anti-socialist legislation of 1878, the dissemination of any text deemed 'socialist' was forbidden. Stark measures against the freedom of the press were also taken during World War I and by the National Socialists after 1933. The Basic Law of 1949 finally guaranteed in its Article 5 the freedom of the press. However, post-publication censorship can still be imposed on the printed message and also, as we shall see later, on electronic media.

By 1866, about 3,000 newspapers were published in Germany; at the turn of the century their number had risen to 3,500. In 1910, 36 per cent of the German population were newspaper readers. The Weimar Republic was the high-time of media conglomerates. The most important one was controlled by Alfred Hugenberg. Having founded an advertising company in 1914, he later acquired film companies such as 'Deutsche Lichtbild Gesellschaft' (German Picture Company) and Ufa in addition to controlling a great number of provincial newspapers which ensured mass circulation for his anti-democratic, conservative views. As chairman of the right-wing German National People's Party Hugenberg supported Hitler in his rise to power and was rewarded with the post of Minister for the Economy and Food Supply in the first Nazi government. Yet, he soon fell out of favour and saw his media empire dominated and centralised further by the Nazi Minister of Propaganda, Joseph Goebbels. After 1933 newspapers were banned outright or forced to endorse National Socialist ideology while the *Völkische Beobachter* (People's Observer) emerged as the official daily paper of the Nazi state.

Immediately after the Second World War, the Allies granted only a small number of publication licences. The French and British zones of occupation saw the establishment of several newspapers along party political lines while the American occupying powers chose to license only newspapers which adopted an objective and politically neutral approach. The Soviet zone took a completely different route as the press was placed under state control and centralised from the outset. In 1949, licensing powers were returned to the newly founded German states who retained the pattern that had been laid down after the war. The following decades saw an increasing market for print media in West Germany as a multitude of newspapers aimed at meeting the social demands of an affluent and diversified consumer society. In East Germany, state control of the press and print media generally remained in place.

In present-day Germany, there are only a few major players in newspaper publishing. The largest of these is Springer whose papers include *Bild* (Picture), *Die Welt* (The World), *Berliner Morgenpost* (Berlin Morning Post) and others, together comprising a market share of 24 per cent in 1991.[3] Other large newspaper publishers include the recently merged Bertelsmann/Gruner & Jahr as well as Burda and Bauer whose media interests also include television and radio. Germany also boasts a large national – or, rather, supra-regional – press, i.e. newspapers which have gained significance and a readership beyond the region in which they are published: *Frankfurter Allgemeine Zeitung* (Frankfurt General Newspaper), *Frankfurter Rundschau* (Frankfurt Review) and *Süddeutsche Zeitung* (South German Paper) are the most important. Since most Germans read a local or regional paper, the regional media may have a more substantial impact in shaping views and culture than their more visible national cousins.

Magazines

As with newspapers, magazines emerged as mass media in the second half of the nineteenth century. In Germany, this happened some time after England or the United States. A particularly important magazine of the period was the *Gartenlaube* (Garden Pergola), the first entertainment periodical in Germany whose subjects ranged from family matters or fashion to discussions of political issues and social events of the day, making it the most popular reading matter of the emerging middle class. Magazine readership received a boost when photography became an integral feature in the closing years of the nineteenth century, turning each magazine into something of an *Illustrierte*, a 'Picture Post'.

Magazines continued to be popular leisure reading into the twentieth century and were also turned into propaganda tools by the National Socialists. After the Second World War, a great number of new magazines sprang up as people tried to find a voice in the new beginning and as readers were eager to hear new voices. The currency reform of 1948 put an end to this early blossoming of post-war magazines as prices rose and economic pressures curtailed idealistic and aesthetic ventures. Thus, only a handful of larger journals survived into the 1950s. Commercially by far the most successful of these post-war magazines was *HörZu* (Listen, 1946), a radio and later also television guide interspersed with feature articles and human interest stories. *Der Spiegel* (The Mirror) was founded in 1947 and modelled on the American *Time Magazine*. Today it remains the most influential and most feared of a varied and competitive clutch including *Die Zeit* (Time), which was founded in 1946 and appears as a weekly newspaper, and *Stern* (Star), founded in 1947 in the 'Picture Post' format. All have cultivated a brand of critical, investigative journalism, although *Der Spiegel* also built up the reputation of having the best archive in the German media world and the best sources of information in the corridors of power. The journal had its finest hour in 1962. After running a report on manoeuvres by the West German army it was accused of espionage and had its offices raided on the orders of the then Defence Minister Franz Josef Strauss. In the fall-out of the '*Spiegel* affair', Strauss was forced to resign while the journal was able to consolidate its reputation for accurate reporting and refine its own brand of aggressive and ironic journalism.

The so-called *Alternative Presse* (Alternative Press) constitutes a special facet of German media culture. It emerged in the 1970s in the wake of the German student movement which had voiced sharp criticism against the established press and inspired a counter culture of political action and communication. Thus, small presses emerged to infuse diversity into the communicative culture. The journal *Pflasterstrand* (Cobble Beach) is a notable example of this counter culture. Founded by Daniel Cohn-Bendit, one of the erstwhile heroes of the student protests, the name *Pflasterstrand* signalled that there was a 'beach' – symbolising hope, beauty and change – within and beyond the concrete world of urban living. In 1980, the *tageszeitung* (daily paper), commonly known as *taz*, emerged as the preferred daily newspaper of German counter culture. One problem common to all these ventures was underfunding. While their style and their reporting were somewhat eclectic and breathless, the media of the counter culture succeeded in establishing themselves as effective bearers of news items which were often missed or intentionally overlooked by mainstream media channels. Thus, the media of the counter culture played an important part in highlighting environmental issues and contributed to the 'greening' of Germany. It could even be argued that the publishing ventures of the counter culture in Germany are forerunners of publications on the Internet in their attempt at revealing a hidden reality and breaking the monopoly of established communications.

Finally, the 1980s saw the appearance of glossy and irreverent urban magazines. Building on and extending the mass market of specialist leisure journals, these newcomers were associated with a 'yuppie' culture of linking cutting-edge text and graphic design. Inspired by products such as the British magazine *The Face*, the alternative message of these glossies had none of the political punch of the German counter culture. Thus, *Tempo* and *Wiener* (Viennese) won a large market share among 20- to 35-year-olds but folded in the 1990s. The magazine market of the present thrives on diversity although magazines focusing on computer development and other technological advances in communication constitute an ever-increasing segment.

The electronic message

With industrialisation transforming the face of Germany in the nineteenth century, technological advances also impacted heavily on the media and their distribution. Books were published in larger numbers, newspapers achieved wider circulation, bigger and better printing machines and processes extended the role of media and their potential influence. Technological innovation did not stop at enhancing the influence of existing media; rather, it led to inventions – notably the telephone and radio – that revolutionised the public sphere even more profoundly than newspapers and other media had done, although the latter had been instrumental in creating it in the first place.

In Germany, radio technology received a major boost during World War I, the first war in which information technology played a decisive role. In 1917, Hans Bredow, who is generally considered the father of German radio, experimented on the German western front with transmitting music and lectures. Immediately after the war, revolutionaries in Germany availed themselves of this technology, thus foreshadowing the interest in radio for purposes of political mobilisation. In the 1920s, this interest was particularly strong among the left in Germany. As early as 1919, the German authorities introduced a code of law to regulate broadcasting. Indeed, until the 1980s, successive German governments kept a tight reign on broadcasting, thereby acknowledging the potential political influence of the medium.

It took Hans Bredow several years to be granted a licence to broadcast programmes with 'entertaining and fortifying contents'. The first broadcast consisted of classical music and was transmitted on 29 October 1923 from Berlin. In these early days, subscribers had to pay two Reichsmark per month for their radio licence. Ever since, Germans have paid a licensing fee for radio which today incorporates television as well. German broadcasting was organised in the *Reichsrundfunkgesellschaft* (Reich Broadcasting Company). Fifty-one per cent of it was owned by the Post Office which held a broadcasting monopoly. This distribution monopoly made it all the easier for the National Socialists to control broadcasting in Germany after 1933. They dismissed the still powerful Hans Bredow and set out to make listening to the radio and in particular to Hitler's speeches the duty of every German. From late 1933 onwards, Germans could purchase their own radio set, the so-called *Volksempfänger* (People's Receiver), very cheaply. During the war, the battle of the airwaves ensued as the BBC and Radio Moscow transmitted into Germany. In 1939, the Nazis made listening to non-German stations a criminal offence. This was by no means an empty threat: people were imprisoned and even executed for tuning into a foreign station. In this state-controlled communication system, entertainment became a government-controlled distraction while information, the key function of the media, deteriorated to in-formation, a kind of getting people into line by showering them only with official versions of events doused in Nazi ideology.

After 1945, the licensing of radio stations was, like that of print media, in the hands of the occupying powers and their military governments. In 1948, the BBC model of public broadcasting was adopted in the three western zones. This meant that radio – and later television – was regulated by committees consisting of various factions of society: the clergy, representatives of the main political parties, educators, public service officials and others to reflect a cross-section of interests. Unlike the print media, broadcasting was linked to Germany's federal structure and administered by the Ministry of Culture in the region where it was located. Thus, federal legislation defined and regulated the broadcasting system while regional legislation pertained to its operation. As in the Weimar years, the Post Office functioned as sole provider of the service although regional committees decided on the actual programmes that were to be broadcast. The federal structure of German broadcasting ensured diversity since every Land maintained at least one station. In addition, three trans-regional stations were created to provide a more authoritative 'national' voice: the *Deutsche Welle* (German Wavelength) modelled on the BBC World Service, the *Deutschlandfunk* (German Broadcasting Service) serving audiences inside and outside Germany and *RIAS Berlin* which had emerged from the American Sector Broadcasting Service in divided Berlin and until German unification had a special function as voice of the West at the frontier with the East.

In addition, Allied forces stationed in Germany set up their own radio stations which broadcast in the relevant foreign language inside Germany. The American Forces Network (AFN) achieved cult status among young Germans in the 1950s, 1960s and 1970s for its unstuffy broadcasts of rock music and country and western. Even members of the German alternative scene, which echoed American civil disobedience culture, listened to AFN.

In the mid-1980s, the broadcasting laws were liberalised to encourage diversification and allow private broadcasting. Many of the new commercial stations offered restyled programmes which appealed to young audiences and attracted listeners away from the more sedate public broadcasting stations. The winning formula was based on American broadcasting formats, forcing public sector radio to respond to serious competition for the first time. Since then, some ninety different private radio stations have gone on the air, leading to an increase in customer choice but also to a proliferation of advertising on air to provide revenue for the private, commercially funded ventures. While it is difficult to assess whether programming quality has improved, diversity and choice certainly have.

Television and the public sector tradition

With the arrival of television, mass media changed once again. Now a new, seductive and compelling visual medium threatened to capture the information and entertainment functions from radio and other media. Television became the most popular and time-intensive leisure activity in Germany.

There are several reasons for this fascination with this new medium of mass communication which soon overshadowed earlier contenders. First, like radio, television can be described as an accompanying medium, i.e. an appliance that runs in the background while people continue doing other things at the same time. This is often overlooked when pollsters compute the amount of time spent watching television. Secondly, television has taken over the function of the book as a cultural leading or defining medium. Finally, there is television's ubiquity. Since the 1980s, 24-hour television has become the norm, and some 99 per cent of German households own at least one television set.

German television began with a first public screening at the University of Leipzig in 1923. It remained an experiment without, as yet, a public impact. In 1936, one of the highlights of the Berlin Olympic Games and of early television was a television record of the games shown to about 150,000 people in public assembly halls all over Germany. It had been orchestrated by the Nazi propaganda machine. The experiment with television in Germany was halted by the war.

After the war, television development was located in the regional broadcasting stations mentioned earlier whose structure and organisation was modelled on the BBC. North-West German Broadcasting (NWDR) devised the formula which was to remain in place for a decade or so: a programming structure combining cinema programmes of a main film preceded by a news review and a cultural feature with radio broadcasts such as variety shows, advice columns and cultural performances or comment. But it was the broadcast of the 1954 World Cup final between Germany and Hungary in Berne, from which Germany emerged victorious, that proved to be the pivotal event of early post-war German television. It can be argued that this televisually mediated victory gave Germans, for the first time after the end of the war, a sense of national unity and identity. The year 1954 also saw the creation of ARD, an Association of German Radio Stations to facilitate coordinating regional television schedules and exchanging programmes between participating stations. ARD began broadcasting on 1 November 1954, adding a supra-regional dimension to Germany's regionally based television sector.

From its inception, public television in Germany had been in the political cross-fire. Owing to the shifting alliances in the various states and the tradition of regional diversity, the federal government in Bonn deemed its views and policies under-represented in this increasingly important medium and sought a more government-friendly approach to reporting. The campaign for a second public service channel commenced in the Adenauer era and came to fruition at its end. On 1 April 1963 the *Zweites Deutsches Fernsehen* (Second German Television Channel) began broadcasting. The new channel, which was allowed a limited amount of advertising was to provide a conservative counter-balance to the less predictable and altogether more liberal ARD. Today, ZDF is the largest television station in Europe. Yet the public's appetite for more television was not satisfied by a second channel and, again emulating British practices, German regional stations introduced a 'third channel' in 1964 featuring quality cultural programmes.

German post-war acceptance of the new medium was staggering. In 1957, a watershed of one million viewers was reached. Yet television's acclaim was by no means universal. Leading intellectuals took a critical view of the medium and warned of its negative impact. Thus T. W. Adorno, the eminent professor of sociology and director of the Institute for Social Research at the University of Frankfurt, spoke out against television in no uncertain terms. He had been forced to flee Germany during the Nazi years and spent his exile in the United States. It was here that he formulated this theory of the culture industry: masquerading as culture, the popular culture of mass communication, he argued, produced a society of crass consumerism placated by false choices. After his return to Germany he and other left-wing intellectuals fought the 'Americanisation' of German culture. One of its worst manifestations seemed the blatantly entertainment- and advertisement-driven type of television imported from the USA.

Other German intellectuals developed their own critique of television. The philosophers Günther Anders and Jürgen Habermas and the writer Hans-Magnus Enzensberger portrayed the impact of television as a retrogressive step in the cultural development of Germany and mankind generally and an enslavement to technology. These feelings ran deep with many educated Germans, forcing proponents of television to highlight the cultural potential and achievements of the medium. Hence, just as the first radio transmissions consisted of classical music, the first official regional television programme on 2 March 1951 consisted of the Prologue to Goethe's *Faust*, symbolising the commitment of television to German national culture and its affinity to the theatre as an accepted stronghold of this culture.

Nevertheless, the victory march of television continued, especially as television sets became affordable for the majority of Germans. A mass leisure activity, television soon created its own culture and cults. The 1960s became the period of the *Straßenfeger* (Street Cleaners), a series of crime stories which were so popular as to empty public places and have the whole nation watching 'the box'. Similar hits were the German adaptations of mystery novels by Francis Durbridge and Edgar Wallace. It was events like these, including the broadcast of major sporting competitions, that constituted a large, unified audience, a television that was watched by practically everyone and thus informed everyone. After the 1960s, the arrival of more and more stations fractured audiences. The truly national tele-events of the early years came to an end, making room for new, global audiences.

The arrival and impact of private television

Prompted by fears of the German electronics industry that it might no longer be able to compete in the world market, a commission was set up in 1974 to investigate the new media and in particular cable and satellite television. The commission recommended that the telephone network be modernised and digitalised but it did not foresee much demand for cable television. While the Post Office, the advertising lobby and the electronics industry were all in favour, the German Chancellor at the time, Helmut Schmidt, stated that 'cable was more dangerous than nuclear power'.[4] Clearly, old fears of television as a low-brow culture and seducer of the young still reverberated in German society of the 1970s. Yet the federal structure of the communication system in Germany enabled pilot projects to go ahead, first in Ludwigshafen and Munich (1984), then in Berlin (1985). By that time, several satellite channels had begun to broadcast, including SAT–1 and RTL, whose programmes were fed into the cable system. Slowly but surely, these new stations attracted more viewers. They were not interested in the culture war surrounding the introduction of private broadcasting but simply demanded more choice from the medium.

One of the problems private stations faced concerned the huge subsidies in the form of licensing fees available to public stations. Another problem was the legal restriction in Germany on the amount of advertising that can be shown. It became clear that a new Communications Act had to be drafted. In 1986, the Federal Constitutional Court in Karlsruhe recommended a 'dual broadcasting system'. Public broadcasting should continue to fulfil its role of 'providing basic broadcasting services for the whole population'[5] while the private sector should be deregulated. The court also acknowledged that as a result of new technological advances, each of the German Länder would have little control over what was being beamed in; therefore, broadcasting legislation for the whole of Germany needed to be formulated. This ruling resulted in a new federal law on telecommunications in 1987. It attempted to clarify several issues, and in particular issues regarding advertising. While public stations are limited to only twenty minutes of advertising per day which have to be screened between six o'clock and eight o'clock in the evening and 'third' channels carry no advertising at all, private stations could now carry advertising for up to 20 per cent of their overall broadcasting time. This concession on advertising time addressed the issue of revenue. Hitherto, public stations received a considerable part of their revenue through licensing fees – in the mid-1980s, ARD derived 20 per cent of their income, ZDF 37 per cent from this source – in addition to advertising revenue, while private stations were excluded from public funding and restricted in their advertising activity. In the wake of the new telecommunications law, many new television and radio stations sprang up, allowing satellite viewers to receive some thirty channels operating in Germany in addition to those beamed from outside.

With so many channels to choose from, video recorders met an enthusiastic reception by the German public as a means to record and watch favourite programmes independently of television scheduling. The camcorder took this development even further. Now people could shoot their own footage and replay it at leisure on their home equipment. The video recorder's continued success is demonstrated by the popular series *Bitte Lächeln* (Smile Please) on RTL-2 which depends on videos filmed by the audience and sent in to be screened during the show. The boundary between the personal and the public which seemed defined and immutable in the past, has become ever more permeable.

In 1992, 57 per cent of households in the west and 48 per cent in the east of Germany owned a video recorder. They were served by 7,000 video rental outlets and a much broader sales network as distribution included petrol stations and supermarkets. It is interesting to note that among foreigners and in particular among Germany's Turkish minority, the number of households owning a video recorder is much higher than among Germans. This also applies to ownership of satellite dishes. In the past, the former guest workers had only been allotted one or two hours per week of programming in their mother tongue. Now they could tune into programmes from their countries of origin. While much media criticism rightly stresses the negative effects of television, here at least is one instance where television relieves the isolation of individuals or cultural groups and even fosters the creation of a new site-independent tele-community within German culture and society.

German unification and the mediascape

German unification had an immense impact on the media landscape. On the one hand, East German publications, publishing houses and media providers were quickly snapped up by West German media conglomerates. On the other hand, this perceived sell-out of East German culture provoked other East German media to treasure their clientele, precisely because these media were now viewed as a bastion of resistance to western dominance. If German unification had a great impact on newspapers and journals, it had an even greater impact on radio and television production and their reception. After unification, the first visible changes in the East occurred on the rooftops. The old aerials – all of them trained in a westerly direction – vanished. Even before many houses received a new coat of paint or the Trabis and Wartburgs had been exchanged for a western-made car, a satellite dish would appear. East Germans, it seems, had fewer problems with accepting the new media than their western compatriots. Of course, East Germans may have reacted against years of state control which left them televisually undernourished. When the Berlin Wall had fallen, they were not confined to West Germany's historically matured and politically balanced public television networks but could jump straight into the new and appealing consumer-oriented view of the world that privately owned television stations had to offer.

Moreover, East Germans had clearly been influenced by what they saw on television. As had been the practice since World War II, opposing sides had attempted to broadcast programmes into each other's territories. In post-war Germany, this cross-border broadcasting may have resulted at least as much from the proximity of the two countries as from any explicit intentions of winning political converts.

In the GDR, West German programmes could be received – and were watched – everywhere except in a small area around Dresden which was dubbed the *Tal der Ahnungslosen* (Valley of the Clueless). Given the fact that much of West German television is saturated and even driven by advertisements, it can be argued that West German television contributed in part to shaping the wish of East Germans to join the West German consumer society. Invariably, some of the hopes and expectations kindled in this way remained disappointed. Similar to the western take-over of many print media, almost all the electronic media were taken over as well. Generally speaking, the people in the eastern part of Germany seem to have fewer ideological problems with accepting privatised television and its messages. Media have mattered to them in a different way and they were, of course, not part of the Federal Republic of Germany when the public debate on this new form of broadcasting spelt out alternatives and shaped opinions.

The media future

The media of communication are changing rapidly in Germany and elsewhere in the contemporary world. While it took about 500 years to move from printed to electronically disseminated information, new media appear with ever increasing frequency. New electronic and computer based media, above all the Internet, have underlined and intensified a process of globalisation which reduces the cultural distinctiveness of media communication in one country and links it with broader developments. Today, major impulses and media mechanisms tend to originate in the United States of America. Germany has to come to terms with these developments. The advent of European integration will further denationalise and diversify the mediascape and confront German media culture with new challenges.

Despite these global trends, the local acceptance of media and their usage continue to differ between countries and cultures. In Germany, many intellectuals continue to dislike newer media, especially private radio and television stations and also computers. This dislike is not a general, vague technological Luddism but harks back to the disastrous effects of manipulation by media during the Hitler era. Furthermore, German society continues to differentiate between high and low culture. In this duality, high culture is disseminated by traditional channels and as written text while low culture relies on new, electronic media.

But the ever-increasing abundance of different modes of communicating in print, by public or private radio, television or even on the Internet shows that producers as well as audiences are more heterogeneous and more vocal than in the past. The recent influx of labour migrants and other social groups from foreign countries as well as unification have boosted the acceptance of electronic media in contemporary Germany.

Not everything, however, has changed with the advent of new media. A battle in 1995 between the Bavarian regional governments and the Internet provider CompuServe over the dissemination of information deemed pornographic echoed previous struggles to win and retain the freedom of information. A similar conflict surfaced in 1996 over the

Internet version of the journal *Radikal,* a mouthpiece of the left-wing terrorist group 'Red Army Faction', and at the other end of the political spectrum over the dissemination of neo-Nazi materials. These conflicts over the balance between freedom of information and censorship in Germany are the latest in a long line reaching back to the emergence of modern media in the seventeenth and eighteenth centuries, the onset of media concentration and mass communication in the nineteenth and the diversification of the mediascape in the twentieth century. The balance between freedom and restriction concerns and defines the role of individuals and the nature of society. Given the power of the media to recast opinion and cast cultures, these issues must remain contentious and contestable. Germany's insistence on linking the diversification of media with their commitment to democracy holds the promise – albeit not a guarantee – that media will serve society by informing citizens and enhancing their cultural environment and not, as had happened in Germany's past, curtail freedom by serving the purposes of an unjust state.

NOTES

1. Werner Faulstich, *Grundwissen Medien*, Munich: Fink, 1994, p. 140.
2. Jürgen Habermas, *Strukturwandel der Öffentlichkeit*, Neuwied: Luchterhand, 1962.
3. Peter Humphreys, *Media and Media Policy in Germany*, 2nd rev. edn., Oxford: Berg, 1994, p. 333.
4. *Ibid.*, p. 213.
5. *Ibid.*, p. 255.

FURTHER READING

Hans Bausch (ed.), *Rundfunk in Deutschland*, 5 vols. (Munich: dtv, 1980) provides a comprehensive overview of all aspects of broadcasting development in Germany until 1980, while the Hans Bredow Institute's *Internationales Handbuch für Rundfunk und Fernsehen* (Baden-Baden: Nomos) is updated annually and constitutes the most comprehensive publication on radio and television in Germany. In English, by far the best book is Peter Humphreys, *Media and Media Policy in Germany* (Oxford: Berg, 1994) which surveys the changes in the mediascape before and after unification and also includes an excellent discussion of the legal and political wrangling over privatisation.

Joan Kristin Bleicher, *Chronik zur Programmgeschichte des Deutschen Fernsehens* (Berlin: edition Sigma, 1993) tells the story since World War II in chronological order, while Werner Faulstich (ed.), *Grundwissen Medien* (Munich: Fink, 1994) has the quality of a comprehensive handbook covering the whole range of mass media in Germany, including print and electronic media.

Helmut Kreuzer and Christian W. Thomson (eds.), *Geschichte des Fernsehens in der Bundesrepublik*, 5 vols. (Munich: Fink, 1993–4) is an impressive guide to television and its practices with contributions on the political, technical and aesthetic agendas that have influenced television in Germany. The shift from a book-based society and print-based media to new media and a non-linear, computer-based society is the theme of the evocative study by Norbert Bolz, *Am Ende der Gutenberg Galaxis* (Munich: Funk, 1993).

Of the many publications which take a critical view of mass media and their impact on culture, the two most important are T. W. Adorno, *The Culture Industry. Selected Essays on Mass Culture*, ed. J. M. Bernstein (London: Routledge, 1991) and Jürgen Habermas, *Strukturwandel der Öffentlichkeit* (Neuwied: Luchterhand, 1962) where he develops his theory of mass communication and the public sphere in modern Germany.

For readers interested in media research and its debate on the emergence and functions of mass communication, a good introductory book is Dieter Prokop (ed.), *Medienforschung*, 3 vols. (Frankfurt/Main: Fischer, 1985).

Index